A SECOND
MISCELLANY-AT-LAW

A Second Miscellany-at-Law

*A Further Diversion
for Lawyers and Others*

BY

THE HON. SIR ROBERT MEGARRY

LONDON
STEVENS & SONS LIMITED
1973

AUSTRALIA

The Law Book Company Ltd.
Sydney : Melbourne : Brisbane

CANADA AND U.S.A.

The Carswell Company
Agincourt, Ontario

INDIA

N. M. Tripathi Private Ltd.
Bombay

ISRAEL

Steimatzky's Agency Ltd.
Jerusalem : Tel Aviv : Haifa

MALAYSIA : SINGAPORE : BRUNEI

Malayan Law Journal (Pte.) Ltd.
Singapore

NEW ZEALAND

Sweet & Maxwell (N.Z.) Ltd.
Wellington

PAKISTAN

Pakistan Law House
Karachi

SBN   420   44390   8

Published by Stevens & Sons
Limited of 11 New Fetter Lane
London E.C.4—Law Publishers
and printed in Great Britain
by The Eastern Press Limited
of London and Reading

TO

OLD FATHER ANTICK, THE LAW,

AND ALL WHO REVERE HIM

Contents

I

THE PATH OF THE LAW

II

SEMANTICITY

III

VILE BODIES

vii

IV
CORPUS JURIS

CHAPTERS

I: PROCESS

II: WORDS

III: MAN

IV: LAW

Preface

Miscellany-at-Law was first published in 1955. It sought to include not only wise and witty sayings of the judges but also curiosities of lawyers and the law. For me, it was a book not of obligation but of delight. The Preface included a frank confession of my ignorance of much that ought to have been included, particularly from overseas jurisdictions; and I uttered a gentle prayer that those who knew better would lighten my darkness. The bounteous response was as surprising as it was pleasant. With this rich harvest, coupled with material for which I had found no convenient home in the book and the fruits of further researches and accidental discoveries of my own, there was enough matter not only for this further volume but also for a *Miscellany III* and, perhaps, a *Miscellany IV*. This *embarras de richesse* presented serious problems of selection, organisation and presentation which I cannot pretend wholly to have solved. Serjeant Arabin, indeed, insisted on carrying off his outrages of utterance into a separate volume, *Arabinesque-at-Law*.[1] This solved little, for the volume was slim; but there must be an end to all things, and so here at last, *de bene esse*,[2] is *Miscellany II*.

Over the last decade there have been many inquiries whether and when a new edition of *Miscellany I* would appear. I should accordingly make it explicit that this is no new edition of *Miscellany I*, but an entirely new book; only on rare occasions and for good cause does it repeat anything contained in *Miscellany I*. The two books are, however, intended to be uniform, and most of what is said in the Preface to *Miscellany I* applies equally to this book. The only conscious change arises from representations that a functional table of chapters would help those who seek to find a collection of materials upon a particular topic and do not readily recollect the import of the

---

[1] London: Wildy & Sons Ltd., 1969.
[2] See 1 Misc. 36.

ix

titles of each chapter. Somewhat reluctantly I have yielded, and so the table of contents proper is followed, in apologetically smaller type, by a list of chapters pragmatic. I have also recognised the accelerating disappearance of the classics as staples of education by inserting in the footnotes translations of those Latin phrases which are not sufficiently well known or explained by the context; but as a European I have assumed a knowledge of modern French which will suffice for even the more extreme barbarities of Law French. As before, despite the printers' commendable zeal for uniformity, I have tried to reproduce quotations verbatim, with all their diverse styles of spelling, punctuation and the like. At times, however, I have abated the passion of past ages for italics and capitals where these have seemed tiresome. In the interests of intelligibility some contractions have been expanded; and in places the paragraphing has been altered, especially by dividing some over-long paragraphs.

Like *Miscellany I, Miscellany II* is a book to be dipped into rather than read as a whole. Both in origin and in content it seems, if anything, rather more miscellaneous than *Miscellany I*, with perhaps something of a shift towards the oddities of life in the law. Once more, the sole test for inclusion has been whether the candidate pleased me; and again I expressly negative all conditions and warranties, whether statutory, express, implied or otherwise howsoever, that the book will please anyone else. *Ex abundanti cautela*, no doubt, " fundamental terms " should now be added to that list. I grieved but was not astonished when I learned that a proposal to make *Miscellany I* required reading for the jurisprudence examination in an antipodean university had been narrowly defeated in a faculty vote; this leaves the way clear for the trail to be blazed elsewhere with *Miscellany II*. In any case, I am confident that I am not alone in my refusal to believe that the law is tedious or that the English really like all their law dull. There are some passages in the book that possibly would have been expressed a trifle differently had they been written after I had gone on the Bench; but with material collected over a period of some forty years I have thought it permissible to refrain from any general re-writing. After all, a miscellany may properly be miscellaneous in style and approach as well as in substance.

I must express my very real sense of indebtedness to all those who have taken the time and the trouble to proffer suggestions. I fear that the list of acknowledgments that I have compiled may be woefully incomplete. This is sometimes due to the informality of the occasion upon which the contribution was made, and sometimes to my failure to collect and collate every fugitive piece of paper. At times, too, the connection between the suggestion and the suggester has been lost, so that all that I can do is to print the list as it is, and state (as is the fact) that what has failed to appear in this volume may well be waiting poised for publication in a later volume. To those whose names are wrongly omitted from the list I can only tender my profound apologies, and ask that I should be given the opportunity of making amends in the next *Miscellany*. With some diffidence I add that the list of candidates for later *Miscellanies* remains open, and that I shall gratefully receive any further suggestions.

I give warm thanks to all those mentioned in the other list of acknowledgments for their generosity in giving me permission to quote from their publications. If I have failed to obtain any requisite permission, I am in mercy, and to my contrition I must add a supplication for pardon. I can only say that I have tried to give the best possible reference to the source and authorship of every quotation, and to seek any necessary authority. I am also indebted to all those who, consciously or unconsciously, have helped me to trace or verify quotations. As before, Mr. C. W. Ringrose, the Librarian of Lincoln's Inn for most of the period while the book was being compiled, pursued many strange requests with learning and tenacity; and in respect of some material not readily available elsewhere I am again indebted to the Treasurer and Benchers of the Middle Temple for their hospitality and to their library staff for their assistance.

Last, and far from least, I have received much help with the text from many quarters. Mr. Paul Baker, of the Inner Bar, read the proofs; Mr. Nicholas Merriman, of the Common Law

Preface

Bar, read the typescript; and Miss Lindsay Megarry, of the
Chancery Bar, not only read both the typescript and the proofs
but also made an index which combines utility with enjoyment,
with entries designed to lead and mislead in about equal proportions. My wife, of Lincoln's Inn, also read both the typescript
and the proofs, and contributed many imponderables. For their
invaluable aid, with many helpful criticisms and suggestions, I
am deeply grateful. For all that has escaped these percipient
eyes, *mea culpa maxima.*

Lincoln's Inn
Gettysburg Day, 1973.   R. E. M.

Acknowledgments

I AM grateful to the following for readily giving me permission to reproduce extracts from the publications indicated here in general terms, and more specifically by the footnotes to the text. Butterworths in respect of *Hayesiana*; the Cambridge University Press in respect of C. T. Carr's *Delegated Legislation*; the Clarendon Press, Oxford, in respect of the *Oxford Book of Light Verse*; Columbia University in respect of Cardozo's *The Growth of the Law* and *Law and Literature*; the Columbia University Press in respect of Hughes' *The Supreme Court of the United States*; Eyre & Spottiswoode Ltd. in respect of Haynes' *A Lawyer's Notebook*; the Harvard University Press in respect of the *Holmes-Laski Letters,* the *Holmes-Pollock Letters, The Occasional Speeches of Justice Oliver Wendell Holmes,* and Jackson's *The Supreme Court in the American System of Government*; Michael Joseph Ltd. in respect of Healy's *The Old Munster Circuit*; John Murray (Publishers) Ltd. in respect of Atlay's *The Victorian Chancellors,* Sir Edward Parry's *What the Judge Saw,* Sir Frederick Pollock's *For My Grandson,* and Twiss's *Eldon*; James Nisbet & Co. Ltd. in respect of H. Fletcher Moulton's *Life of Lord Moulton*; Yale University Press Ltd. in respect of Cardozo's *The Growth of the Law*; and the Editor of *The Shingle* (Philadelphia Bar Association) and James M. Marsh in respect of *Mr. Dooley Discovers a Unanimous Dissent*.

I am also most grateful for the many helpful suggestions that have been made to me by those whose names are set out below, some of whom are no longer with us.

H. G. Alderman Q.C. (New South Wales); C. V. Baker; P. V. Baker Q.C.; Sir William Ball; G. P. Barton (Wellington, New Zealand); F. H. Bell; T. A. Blanco White Q.C.; L. J. Blom-Cooper Q.C.; Professor E. K. Braybrooke (Western Australia); Richard H. Brown (Valley Stream, New York); John Burke; Rt. Hon. Lord Justice Cairns; J. F. Caldwell C.B. (Belfast); Professor A. H. Campbell; Sir Cecil Carr Q.C.; His Honour Judge Carr; Professor James H. Chadbourn (California); Bryan Clauson; Master Colin Clayton; Rt. Hon. Lord Clyde; Professor Alfred H. Conard (Michigan); Hon. Mr. Justice Cooper (Nova Scotia); Professor Bradley Crawford (Toronto); Patrick Crotty; Joseph Dach (New York); His Honour Judge Daly Lewis; Rt. Hon. Sir Harold Danckwerts; Professor A. G. Davis (Auckland); Dean Miguel de Capriles (New York); Dr. V. T. H.

Acknowledgments

Delany; Rt. Hon. Lord Denning; George I. Devor (Los Angeles); Charles E. Early (Florida); J. T. Edgerley; Dr. T. Ellis Lewis; Rev. K. J. T. Elphinstone; Hon. Mr. Justice Else-Mitchell (New South Wales); Michael Essayan; Rt. Hon. Lord Evershed; C. F. Fairleigh (Brisbane); W. A. Fearnley Whittingstall Q.C.; His Honour Judge A. H. Forbes; Dr. Harold G. Fox Q.C. (Toronto); Hon. Mr. Justice Frankfurter; Chief Justice Hon. Stanley H. Fuld (New York); Professor L. C. B. Gower; Professor R. H. Graveson Q.C.; Professor L. C. Green (Saskatchewan); Professor E. J. Griew; Professor A. D. Hargreaves; Professor Cameron Harvey (Manitoba); Hon. Mr. Justice Haslam (New Zealand); W. L. Hayhurst Q.C. (Toronto); Professor R. F. V. Heuston; Andrew Hiller (New South Wales); Professor H. A. Hollond; T. G. Holt (Birmingham, Alabama); Professor Mark DeWolfe Howe (Harvard); John H. Howling; Harold F. Jackson Q.C. (Nova Scotia); Rt. Hon. Lord Jenkins; Sir Raymond Jennings Q.C.; Edward L. Johnson; Miss Elaine Jones; Professor Ellison Kahn (Johannesburg); Professor Alfred Kamin (Chicago); Chief Justice Hon. Frank R. Kenison (New Hampshire); Valentine E. Kirwan (Dublin); Professor Horace Krevor (Ontario); Professor P. S. A. Lamek (Toronto); E. W. Lawn (Melbourne); Professor W. Barton Leach (Harvard); Professor R. A. Leflar (Arkansas); T. Legg; Oliver Lodge; His Honour Judge McIntyre Q.C.; James M. Marsh (Philadelphia); E. C. Micks S.C. (Dublin); Professor Elmer Million (New York); Professor S. F. C. Milsom; Professor J. D. B. Mitchell; Professor F. H. Newark C.B.E. (Belfast); Professor G. V. V. Nicholls Q.C. (Nova Scotia); Professor F. J. Odgers; Dr. W. J. Patterson (Glasgow); Cyril Pearl; Andrew Phelan; Hon. Mr. Justice Plowman; R. S. W. Pollard; A. F. N. Poole (Toronto); Professor James C. Rehberg (Georgia); J. Scott Henderson Q.C.; Professor J. M. Sharp (Manitoba); Hon. Mr. Justice Sholl (Victoria, Australia); Rt. Hon. Lord Simon of Glaisdale; Dean C. E. Smalley-Baker Q.C. (Toronto); A. C. Sparrow Q.C.; Rt. Hon. Lord Justice Stamp; J. Gordon Stanier; Hon. Sir Bernard Sugerman (New South Wales); H. F. J. Teague; T. C. Tobias (Dublin); J. L. B. Todhunter; Judge Hon. B. Fain Tucker (Chicago); Francis Walker; Frank Whitworth Q.C.; Rt. Hon. Lord Widgery; Frederick Bernays Wiener; Professor Glanville Williams Q.C.; John Wright.

R. E. M.

Glossary

[This glossary makes no attempt to be exhaustive or exact. It essays no more than to give the layman enough of an explanation of technical terms to prevent them from standing between him and an appreciation of the text.]

A.-G. (or Att.-Gen.). Attorney-General: the chief advocate for the Crown.

Attachment. Arrest and imprisonment for not complying with an order of the court to do some act; regarded as a lesser penalty than committal; now obsolete.

B. Baron (a judge of the former Court of Exchequer).

Bill of Exceptions. A litigant's statement of the alleged errors made by a judge in directing a jury or ruling on the admissibility of evidence.

C.B. Chief Baron (head of the former Court of Exchequer).

C.J. Chief Justice (plural, C.JJ.).

C.J.C.P. Chief Justice of the former Court of Common Pleas.

C.J.K.B. Chief Justice of the former Court of King's Bench.

Committal. Committal to prison for contempt of court.

Common Bench. An alternative name for the former Court of Common Pleas.

Covenant to stand seised. An agreement by deed to hold land for the benefit of another.

Criminal conversation. A former term for adultery, and for the husband's action for damages against the adulterer.

Curtesy. A widower's former life estate in his deceased wife's land.

Demurrer. A plea that even if the facts alleged are true they give no right to relief.

Deodand. The weapon or other chattel which had directly caused the death of a human and so was formerly forfeit to the Crown.

Dom.proc. "*domus procerum*": House of Lords.

Dower. A widow's former life estate in one-third of her deceased husband's land.

Ejectment. An action to recover possession of land, and damages.

Glossary

Equity. A supplementary system of justice which grew up under the Chancellors towards the end of the Middle Ages to deal with gaps left in a system of law that had become over-rigid and would not, *e.g.*, enforce trusts. Later it became rigid itself, but initially it was wide and flexible, being based upon what seemed fair, equitable and in good conscience.

Exchequer Chamber. The former Court of Appeal from the courts of common law.

Exigent. A judicial writ formerly used in making a person an outlaw.

Fine. (1) A monetary penalty or payment. (2) A collusive compromise (*finalis concordia*: an agreement in final settlement), formerly used to transfer land.

Fleet. The Fleet Prison (abolished 1842), near Fleet Street, London.

Interdict. The Scottish equivalent of an injunction.

J. Mr. Justice (plural, JJ.).

J.O. Judge Ordinary: the judge of the Divorce Court before 1876.

L.C. Lord Chancellor (plural, L.CC.).

L.C.J. Lord Chief Justice.

L.J. Lord Justice (plural, L.JJ.).

L.K. Lord Keeper (of the Great Seal); the Lord Chancellor in all save name and rank. The last was Lord Henley, in 1760.

Lie in grant. Can be conveyed by a deed of grant.

Lie in livery. Can be conveyed only by delivery of seisin (possession).

M.R. Master of the Rolls. Formerly the head of the Court of Chancery under the Lord Chancellor; latterly the virtual head of the Court of Appeal.

Master. A judicial officer of the court, below the rank of the judges.

Motion. An oral application in open court for an order such as a temporary injunction.

Nisi prius. "Unless previously": a civil trial at Assizes.

P. President (in England, head of the Probate, Divorce and Admiralty Division, now the Family Division).

P.J. Presiding Judge.

Praemunire. A former crime involving forfeiture of all property.

Prescription. The acquisition of rights (*e.g.* a right of way) by long enjoyment.

Puisne judge, puisne. A High Court judge other than a Chief Justice etc.

Quaere. Query; it is a question; it is doubtful.

Quare clausum fregit. "Why he broke the close": the old action for trespass to land.

Quo warranto. "By what authority": a writ for inquiring by what authority a person holds office.

Register. A former name for Registrar, an official who sits in court and prepares the formal orders of the court.

Rule. A former name for an order or direction of the court of certain types.

Rule absolute. An operative rule.

Rule *nisi*. A rule that will become a rule absolute unless successfully objected to (*nisi*: unless).

S.-G. Solicitor-General: the deputy chief advocate for the Crown (always a barrister).

Sign manual. The Sovereign's own signature.

Stare decisis. "To stand by the decisions": the doctrine that decisions of the courts establish binding precedents.

Statute of Frauds. An Act making many contracts unenforceable unless evidenced in writing.

Supersedeas. A writ putting an end to proceedings.

Taxation of costs. The process whereby a Taxing Master examines a solicitor's bill of costs and disallows unnecessary or excessive charges.

Uses. The early form of trusts.

V.-C. Vice-Chancellor: one of the judges of the old Court of Chancery; the present administrative head of the Chancery Division.

Waiver. Forgoing some right.

Year books. Early law reports, from the thirteenth century to the sixteenth.

Abbreviations

Atlay: *The Victorian Chancellors*, by J. B. Atlay (1906–8: in two volumes).

Boswell's *Hebrides*: *A Journal of a Tour to the Hebrides*, by James Boswell; ed. P. Fitzgerald, 2nd ed. 1888 (vol. 3 of Boswell's *Johnson*).

Boswell's *Johnson*: *The Life of Samuel Johnson, LL.D.*, by James Boswell; ed. P. Fitzgerald (2nd ed. 1888: in three volumes, including Boswell's *Hebrides*).

Camp. C.JJ.: *The Lives of the Chief Justices of England*, by John, Lord Campbell (2nd ed. 1858: in three volumes).

Camp. L.CC.: *Lives of the Lord Chancellors and Keepers of the Great Seal of England*, by John, Lord Campbell (5th ed. 1868: in ten volumes).

D.N.B.: Dictionary of National Biography.

Foss's *Judges*: *The Judges of England*, by E. Foss (1848–64: in nine volumes. The single volume version of 1870 is cited in full).

Holmes-Laski Letters: *Holmes-Laski Letters*, ed. M. DeW. Howe (1953: in two volumes).

Holmes-Pollock Letters: *Holmes-Pollock Letters*, ed. M. DeW. Howe (1941: in two volumes). (The English edition is entitled *Pollock-Holmes Letters*.)

Lds.Jnl.: Journals of the House of Lords, 1509– .

Manson: *Builders of Our Law during the Reign of Queen Victoria*, by E. Manson (2nd ed. 1904).

1 Misc.: *Miscellany-at-Law*, by R. E. Megarry (1955).

Pull.: *The Order of the Coif*, by Serjeant Alexander Pulling (1884).

Rob.: *Bench and Bar*, by Mr. Serjeant Robinson (B. Coulson Robinson) (2nd ed. 1889).

S.S.: Selden Society.

Selden, *Table Talk*: *Table Talk of John Selden*, ed. Sir Frederick Pollock (1927).

Twiss, *Eldon*: *The Public and Private Life of Lord Chancellor Eldon*, by H. Twiss Q.C. (3rd ed. 1846: in two volumes).

I

The Path of the Law

Somewhat of the Cunctative

THE Bench claims pride of place; and what the Bench claims, the Bench often receives. Out of the years 1801 to 1827, Lord Eldon spent some twenty-five on the Woolsack. His path to this eminence had begun little more than twenty years earlier. In 1779 there was the first reported case [1] in which he had appeared while at the Bar as plain John Scott. Barely a year later came the appeal in *Ackroyd* v. *Smithson*.[2] Before Sewell M.R. in 1778, John Scott had been given a guinea brief to consent to judgment against his client, the heir-at-law. However, he came to the conclusion that his client was nevertheless entitled to a share of the estate, and, after informing his instructing solicitor, he argued the point, and lost. There was an appeal to Lord Thurlow L.C. by another party, and this was heard in 1780. Again John Scott had a guinea brief to consent, and again, with the acquiescence of his instructing solicitor, he argued the point. This time he won, with an argument which occupies over nine pages of the report; and his name was made.[3] " Mr. Scott argued the case of his clients so ably, that Lord Thurlow said, I thought at first that Mr. Scott was clearly wrong, but now I see he is right." [4] To this case, *Dering* v. *Earl of Winchelsea* [5] perhaps provides something of a complement. In 1787 the future Lord Eldon argued the case and lost. Thirty-three years later the case was cited to Lord Eldon as he presided in the Court of Chancery. He said that he remembered the case, " and very angry I was with the decision; but I lived long enough to find out that one may be very angry and very wrong." [6]

---

[1] *Green* v. *Howard* (1779) 1 Bro.C.C. 31; W. H. Bennet, *Select Biographical Sketches* (1867) pp. 64, 65. The case is evidently the same as that referred to in W. C. Townsend, *Lives of Twelve Eminent Judges* (1846) vol. 2, p. 381.
[2] (1780) 1 Bro.C.C. 503.
[3] See Twiss, *Eldon*, vol. 1, p. 84 *et seq.*
[4] *Noel* v. *Lord Henley* (1819) Dan.Ex. 211 at 228, *per* Richards C.B.
[5] 1 Cox Eq. 318; 2 B. & P. 270.
[6] *Ex p. Hunter* (1820) Buck 552 at 556.

On the Woolsack, Lord Eldon's doubts and delays became proverbial. The most ample version of the verses describing the course of argument before him seems to be the following [7]:

> Mr. Leach made a speech,
>   Angry, neat, but wrong;
> Mr. Hart, on the other part,
>   Was prosy, dull, and long.

> Mr. Bell spoke very well,
>   Though nobody knew about what;
> Mr. Trower talk'd for an hour,
>   Sat down, fatigued, and hot.

> Mr. Parker made the case darker,
>   Which was dark enough without;
> Mr. Cooke quoted his book,
>   And the Chancellor said, I doubt.

It was to Lord Eldon that one of the most remarkable letters ever to have been sent by a solicitor to a Lord Chancellor was written. It was dated July 15, 1820, and ran as follows:

" Ware v. Horwood—My Lord; my clients have great reason to complain of the great injury suffered by them in consequence of these causes not keeping their situation at the head of your lordship's paper, agreeably to your lordship's order repeatedly given in my hearing. It is now nearly seven years since they have been waiting for your lordship's judgment; and upwards of two years and a half ago, they had arrived at the top of the paper; at which I humbly entreat they may, until you can decide upon them, remain. There is a fund in Court of £10,000 and upwards, locked up until your lordship decides on these causes; and it is therefore matter of great importance to my unfortunate clients that your lordship's decision may not be delayed by the circumstances to which I have above alluded. It is painful to me to state to your lordship, that I have learnt from authority, which I have no reason to doubt, that the infant, for whose benefit these suits were instituted twenty years ago, *died of*

---

[7] *Anon.*, *Oxford Book of Light Verse* (1938) p. 272. Many versions omit the second verse: see, *e.g.*, 10 Camp.L.CC. 239 and Twiss, *Eldon*, vol. 2, p. 400, which attribute the verses to Sir George Rose, while at the Bar.

a broken heart, on account of being kept out of his property; and that I have to contend against the bitter feelings of his relations. Under this distressing circumstance, knowing that your lordship will pardon the liberty I have taken in thus addressing you, and which nothing but the imperious necessity of the case could have induced me to have done, I have the honour, &c." [8] This remarkable letter was matched by one of the items in the solicitor's remarkable bill of costs: " Attending the lord chancellor in his private room, when his lordship begged for further indulgence till tomorrow, 13s. 4d." [9]

The letter, indeed, seems to have been a little overdrawn; the infant's interest in the £10,000 seems to have been a mere £134, and the cause of death appears to have been unconnected with any Chancery suit.[10] Nevertheless, there can be no doubt that Lord Eldon was guilty of unjustifiable delays, both in this and in other causes. Another example is *Collis* v. *Nott*, which was argued in 1817. When in 1823 Lord Eldon was pressed for a decision in the case, it was found that " he had entirely forgotten it," and it had to be re-argued.[11] Such cases cannot be justified under the guise of " considering his judgments," nor are they fair instances of what Mr. Asquith was to say, more than once, " Wait and see." [12] The views of Holmes J. on reserving judgment are characteristic: " If a man keeps a case six months it is supposed to be decided on ' great consideration.' It seems to me that intensity is the only thing. A day's impact is better than a month of dead pull." [13]

Lord Eldon was, of course, well aware that he was accused of being slow in reaching his decisions; but he put it a little differently. " With Lord Bacon [14] ' I confess I have somewhat

---

[8] Hansard (N.S.), vol. 9, col. 717 (1823).
[9] *Ibid.*, col. 719.
[10] *Ibid.*, col. 717n. And see generally Twiss, *Eldon*, vol. 2, p. 403 *et seq.* The case may have been *Ware* v. *Horwood* (1807) 14 Ves. 28 at a later stage; for that was a rehearing of *Underhill* v. *Horwood* (1804) 10 Ves. 209, and so is consistent with " suits " which, in 1820, had been " instituted twenty years ago."
[11] Hansard (N.S.), vol. 9, col. 745 (1823).
[12] Hansard H.C. (5th ser.), vol. 14, col. 972 (1910); *ibid.*, vol. 16, col. 25.
[13] *Holmes-Pollock Letters* (1941), vol. 1, p. 154.
[14] Consider Bacon's *Essays*, Nos. 21, 25.

of the Cunctative' and, with him, I thought that 'Whosoever is not wiser upon Advice than upon the sudden, the same Man is no wiser at Fifty than he was at Thirty.' " [15] In one appeal to the House of Lords he was critical of the failure of the printed cases to set out the relevant parts of the deeds, and said " It will be consolation to me during my remaining life, knowing that it has been said that I have been dilatory in decision, that I have, by looking at the original instruments, saved to the right owner many a landed estate which would otherwise, probably, have been given to his adversary." [16]

Subsequently Eldon gave further and better particulars. He wrote that " I never could be confident that Counsel had fully informed me of the facts, or of the Law of many of the Cases. And there may be found not a few Instances, in which most satisfactory Judgements were pronounced, which were founded upon facts or Instruments, with which none of the Counsel, who argued the cases, were acquainted, tho' such facts and Instruments formed part of the evidence in the Cause. . . .

" One remarkable case was a case of   and Legard— This had been heard at the Rolls, and an elaborate Judgement given upon it—a Case was sent to the Court of King's Bench for the opinion of the Judges, and they certified their opinion after an elaborate Argument. The Cause then came on, upon further directions, before another Branch of the Court of Chancery, and Judgement was given. This produced an appeal to me as Chancellor. The Matter was long and ably argued, but, before the Attorney General, afterwards Lord Gifford, replied, I took the papers to my house, and afterwards, going into Court, I stated that the Cause might stand over for a week and then mentioning certain Circumstances, which I had discovered from the papers, and which had never been mentioned in the Course of any of the hearings, I put it to the Attorney General to tell me, at the End of the week, whether, instead of there having been such a Judgement as was appealed from, there ought not to have been,

15 *Lord Eldon's Anecdote Book* (1960) p. 131; and see 10 Camp.L.CC. 204. See also *ibid.*, at pp. 226, 230; Campbell, *Lives of Lord Lyndhurst and Lord Brougham* (1869) p. 38.
16 *Ruscombe* v. *Hare* (1818) 6 Dow 1 at 16.

upon the very first hearing, a dismissal of the Bill. When the matter was again mentioned in Court, it was admitted by all parties that such ought to have been and must be the end of the Suit. In the last Session, 1827, there was an appeal from the Judgement of the Vice Chancellor in a cause to set aside a Lease, as having been improperly obtained from a Landlord by his Steward and Attorney—The bill treating the Lease as good at Law, but that, being so obtained, it should be declared in Equity to be void—After all the Arguments in the Court below, and at the Bar of the House of Lords, I called for the Lease. It was then found not to be a good Lease at Law, and that Equity had nothing to do with it." [17]

Of the two cases to which Eldon refers, the first seems to have been *Johnson* v. *Legard*.[18] Not only does the defendant's name fit, but the case was also first " heard at the Rolls " [19] and a case [20] was sent to the Court of King's Bench.[1] When that court had certified its opinion,[2] the case went before " another Branch of the Court of Chancery," namely, Leach V.-C.[3] Further, Gifford A.-G. was of counsel before Lord Eldon, who dismissed the bill and thus reversed Leach V.-C. and the Court of King's Bench.[4] What seems to have been overlooked and never mentioned in the case sent to the King's Bench was a private Act of Parliament.[5] However, according to the report that Act was relied upon by counsel in argument before Lord Eldon L.C.,[6] and there is nothing there to indicate that the discovery was Lord Eldon's.

The second case appears to have been *Lord Selsey* v. *Rhoades*.[7] The date is right; it was a bill in equity to set aside a lease obtained from a landlord by his steward and solicitor;

[17] *Lord Eldon's Anecdote Book* (1960) p. 131.
[18] (1822) T. & R. 281.
[19] By Grant M.R.
[20] Set out verbatim in *Johnson* v. *Legard* (1818) 3 Madd. 283.
[1] (1822) T. & R. 281 at 287.
[2] *Johnson* v. *Legard* (1817) 6 M. & S. 60.
[3] *Johnson* v. *Legard* (1818) 3 Madd. 283.
[4] *Johnson* v. *Legard* (1822) T. & R. 281.
[5] *Ibid.*, at p. 295.
[6] *Ibid.*, at pp. 291, 292; and see the reference to Lord Eldon's intervention at p. 293.
[7] (1827) 1 Bli.N.S. 1.

and Lord Eldon L.C. was sitting in the House of Lords on an
appeal from the Vice-Chancellor. Leach V.-C. had dismissed
the bill,[8] and the House of Lords affirmed his decision. Lord
Eldon's was the only reported speech, and it may be contrasted
with the account that has been quoted above. He said " I have
looked into this case, with a desire to affect the lease; for the
situation of the parties was such as to induce a Court of Equity
to look at the transaction with great suspicion. If the suit had
been instituted recently after the contract, and there had been
no acts of confirmation, probably the lease might not have stood;
but James Lord Selsey and John Lord Selsey acquiesced so long,
being well acquainted with the facts, that it is difficult to say
that they could have impeached the lease, and the Appellant
H. J. Lord Selsey cannot do that which they could not have
done. We cannot set aside the lease, upon the grounds stated
in the pleadings. There is a ground upon which the lease
might have been set aside; but the parties have not gone upon
that ground, and we cannot set aside the lease upon grounds on
which they did not proceed." [9]

Lord Eldon also once said " It has occurred to me to send the
same case successively to the Courts of King's Bench and
Common Pleas, and not to adopt the opinion (though highly to
be respected) of either of these courts." [10] Lord Campbell gives
more detail of what doubtless was the same episode. Lord
Eldon, he said, " took a particular delight in relating how, to
ascertain what estate passed to trustees under a settlement, he
sent a case to the Court of King's Bench, who told him they
took an estate in fee; and how he then sent the same case to the
Court of Common Pleas, who certified that the trustees took no
estate at all. ' Now, I was impertinent enough to think,' he
used to proceed, ' that they were both wrong; I held that the
trustees took a chattel interest; and, what is more, my decision
satisfied all parties.' " [11]

Lord Campbell gives the references to ten reports in support;

8 *Lord Selsey* v. *Rhoades* (1824) 2 Sim. & St. 41.
9 *Lord Selsey* v. *Rhoades* (1827) 1 Bli.N.S. 1 at 8.
10 *Marchioness of Lansdowne* v. *Marquis of Lansdowne* (1820) 2 Bli. 60 at 86.
11 10 Camp.L.CC. 250.

but these are a mixed lot.[12]   One possible candidate is *Trent v. Hanning*, though the details do not coincide with Lord Campbell's account.   In that case, a case was sent from Chancery for the opinion of the Court of Common Pleas as to the estate taken by trustees under a will.   The court certified that the trustees took no estate[13]; but this did not satisfy Lord Eldon, who then sent a case on the same point to the Court of King's Bench to see whether the judges of that court agreed with those of the Common Pleas.[14]   Only Lawrence J. did; the others certified that the trustees took a fee simple,[15] and both Lord Eldon[16] and, on appeal, the House of Lords[17] accepted this latter view.   *Prebble* v. *Boghurst*[18] is an even less likely candidate, for there Lord Eldon, and Richards C.B. and Abbott J., who sat with him, merely disagreed with the certificate of the Court of Common Pleas as to the effect of a bond.

Wykham v. *Wykham* is a better fit, however.   In that case the Court of King's Bench certified that the trustees took a fee simple,[19] whereas the Court of Common Pleas, when Lord Eldon later sent the case to that court,[20] certified that the trustees took no estate.[1]   This time Lord Eldon managed to decide what were the equitable rights of the parties concerned without resolving which court was right as to the position at law,[2] and there seems to have been no appeal from his decision. If indeed this is the case, it is to be feared that the tale has grown in the telling.   For various sources[3] repeat the story that

---

12 Apart from the references given below, " 1 Swanst. 32 " is a slip for " 1 Swanst. 320 "; " 18 Ves. 325 " is a slip for " 18 Ves. 395 "; and " 1 Wils.Ch.Cas. 45 " merely refers to a dictum that the Chancery was not bound by the views of the Court of King's Bench. " 1 N.R. 116 " in fact refers not to " 1 N.R. 116 " but to " 1 B. & P.(N.R.) 116."
13 *Trent* v. *Hanning* (1804) 1 B. & P.(N.R.) 116.
14 See *Trent* v. *Hanning* (1805) 10 Ves. 495 at 500.
15 *Trent* v. *Hanning* (1806) 7 East 97.
16 See 1 Dow 105.
17 *Trent* v. *Trent* (1813) 1 Dow 102.
18 (1818) 1 Swans. 309.
19 *Wykham* v. *Wykham* (1809) 11 East 458.
20 See 18 Ves. 402.
1 *Wykham* v. *Wykham* (1810) 3 Taunt. 316.
2 *Wykham* v. *Wykham* (1811) 18 Ves. 395.
3 *e.g.*, J. Willock, *Legal Facetiae* (1887) p. 120; A. H. Engelbach, *More Anecdotes of Bench and Bar* (1915) p. 269; J. Larwood, *Forensic Anecdotes* (1882) p. 4, ascribing this account to Lord Brougham in the House of Lords.

Lord Eldon once referred a case to " three chief Courts below, to decide what a particular document was. The Court of King's Bench decided it was a lease in fee; the Common Pleas, that it was a lease in tail; the Exchequer, that it was a lease for years. Whereupon Lord Eldon, when it came back to him, decided for himself that it was no lease at all."

Nothing so neatly diverse as this seems in fact to have occurred, though Lord Eldon's technique was at least to try a different court if he did not find the first decision welcome. Lord Thurlow L.C., on the other hand, had on occasion returned a case for reconsideration by the same court. Thus in *Utterson* v. *Vernon* the Court of King's Bench (Ashurst J. dissenting) first found for the plaintiff.[4] Lord Thurlow entertained doubts about the decision, and returned the case to the same court for reconsideration. The case was then twice argued again, and this time the court, its composition unchanged, unanimously found for the defendant.[5] It is a matter for speculation what would have happened if the court had adhered to its original decision, for as Lord Eldon later said in a rather different context, " I should think it disrespectful to the Court of King's Bench to send it a third time." [6]

While Lord Eldon was in his eighty-fifth year, his qualities were well described by Lord Abinger C.B. in a reserved judgment. " I think I may safely appeal to the gentlemen whom I now have the honour of addressing whether any judge ever sat in any Court whose mind was more full of principles, however narrow the lines of his decisions might sometimes be, who yet took a more enlarged and discursive view of the whole of the case than my Lord Eldon. Lord Eldon was not a case lawyer only. He was deeply imbued with the principles both of common law and of equity; and any judgment of his, whatever effect it might have as a precedent, perhaps somewhat narrowed by his great anxiety to individualise cases, yet is a very instructive judgment to those who wish to learn. I well remember when that noble and learned Lord first sat as a judge at common law,

4 *Utterson* v. *Vernon* (1790) 3 T.R. 539.
5 *Utterson* v. *Vernon* (1792) 4 T.R. 570.
6 *Bromley* v. *Holland* (1802) 7 Ves. 3 at 15.

that the impression which he made upon my mind when he summed up a case to the jury was, that if in some cases he made distinctions too numerous and too refined, which might perhaps perplex a jury not accustomed to legal discrimination, he was a most admirable judge, in all cases, for illustrating every point and giving due effect to every argument suggested by the counsel or by the case before him, on the one side and on the other." [7]

In speed of decision, Leach V.-C. was in marked contrast to Lord Eldon.[8] Sir Samuel Romilly once said " I begin to think that the tardy justice of the Chancellor is better than the swift injustice of his deputy." [9] When Leach V.-C. had finished all his cases while there were still three or four days of term left, someone inquired how the judge was to fill up the time. " Why," said Sir George Rose, " he could have his causes set down again, and hear the other side." [10]

It is hardly surprising that the valedictory oration which Lord Brougham L.C. made when about to surrender the Great Seal dwelt with some complacency on the absence of any arrears in the Court of Chancery [11]; and certainly there had been none of the delays usually associated with Lord Eldon. But despatch may be purchased at too great a price, as is shown by an examination of the way in which Lord Brougham got through some of his work. One instance was *Townley* v. *Bedwell*, an old friend of the court.[12] A fund in the case had been found to be more than was required for the purposes for which it had been set aside, and two rival petitions had been presented by parties concerned, each claiming the surplus: each was an original petition, and not a petition of appeal. The claims were argued before Lord Brougham L.C. in the spring of 1834, and judgment was reserved. In November, on the day before

---

[7] *Glyn* v. *Soares* (1836) 1 Y. & C.Ex. 644 at 683, reversed *sub nom. Queen of Portugal* v. *Glyn* (1840) 7 Cl. & F. 466 (where the delivery of the speeches of the law lords at times resembled a debate more than the giving of judgment).

[8] See 1 Misc. 245.

[9] Twiss, *Eldon*, vol. 2, p. 488.

[10] *Ibid.*; and see Lord Kingsdown, *Recollections* (1868) p. 28.

[11] See *Kennedy* v. *Green* (1834) 3 My. & K. 699 at 723.

[12] See, *e.g.*, *Townley* v. *Bedwell* (1801) 6 Ves. 194; *Townley* v. *Bedwell* (1808) 14 Ves. 596; and see *Townley* v. *Bedwell* (1851) 15 Beav. 78.

he gave up the Great Seal,[13] he " sent his judgment in writing to the registrar, in the following words : ' Petition dismissed; orders affirmed with costs.' " [14] In fact, of course, there were two competing petitions, not one, and there were no orders that could be affirmed, with or without costs.

Poor Brougham! "Samuel Rogers the poet remarked of him, ' There go Solon, Lycurgus, Demosthenes, Archimedes, Sir Isaac Newton, Lord Chesterfield, and a great many more in one post-chaise.' " [15] Even better known is "the sarcasm attributed to Baron Alderson upon Brougham. ' What a wonderful versatile mind has Brougham! he knows politics, Greek, history, science; if only he knew a little of law, he would know a little of everything.' " [16] To paternity of this last phrase, O'Connell [17] and Sugden [18] are also claimants; but it seems to be an adaptation of a French import. " You may find the original of this gibe in Grimm, who says that Louis XVI, going out of chapel after hearing a sermon from the Abbé Maury, said, ' Si l'Abbé nous avait parlé un peu de religion, il nous aurait parlé de tout.' " [19]

There can be no doubt which Lord Chancellor has most frequently appeared in *Punch*. Quite apart from ordinary cartoons, in which Brougham's prominent nose was the joy of the caricaturists over much of his long life, the traditional cover used for over a century brought Brougham to the reader each week. " For some forgotten cause Brougham had given bitter umbrage to the designer, who vowed to ' drag his face through the mire.' A glance will show that, amid the troop of imps and elves who dance round the border of the frontispiece, one trails by a string a mask with upturned face from which is visible and distinct the proboscis which once adorned the countenance of Lord Brougham." [20]

---

[13] He gave it up on November 21, 1834 : see 3 My. & K. 714, 724.
[14] (1835) 13 *Law Magazine* 279; for another instance, see *ibid.*, p. 280.
[15] *The Greville Diary*, ed. P. W. Wilson (1927) vol. 1, p. 125; 2 *Atlay* 280.
[16] R. W. Emerson, *Letters and Social Aims* (vol. 8 of *Complete Works*, 1883 ed.) p. 176.
[17] *The Greville Diary*, loc. cit.
[18] 2 *Atlay* 20.
[19] R. W. Emerson, *loc. cit.* (" If the Abbé had spoken to us a little about religion, he would have spoken to us about everything "). [20] 1 *Atlay* 377.

Brougham's troubles were widespread. In 1831, an attorney was committed for contempt by Lord Brougham L.C., sitting in bankruptcy. The attorney then sued Lord Brougham in the Court of Exchequer for assault and false imprisonment, alleging, *inter alia*, that in bankruptcy there was no jurisdiction to commit for contempt. The result of the case was that Lord Lyndhurst C.B. directed a verdict for the defendant, on the ground that even if there were some irregularity, the Lord Chancellor could not be made liable for acts done by him in his judicial capacity.[1] The case was remarkable in that the attorney subpoenaed Lord Eldon, then in his eighty-third year, to give evidence on the practice of the Court of Chancery in cases of committal for contempt, and it fell to Sir John Campbell S.-G. to cross-examine him. The attendance sheet in terms of Lord Chancellors thus showed a score of four: one present (Brougham), one past (Eldon), one future (Campbell), and one both past and future (Lyndhurst).[2]

Another Lord Chancellor who was less than fortunate was Lord Cottenham. Indeed, *Dimes* v. *Proprietors of the Grand Junction Canal*[3] is the case that is said to have killed him.[4] The substantive issue was whether Dimes, a " crazy attorney "[5] who was lord of the manor, was entitled, by reason of certain technicalities of conveyancing and copyhold law, to claim that a portion of the Grand Junction Canal was his, so that he could lawfully obstruct it. He brought an action for ejectment against the canal company, but in 1836 he was non-suited by Lord Abinger C.B. Two years later, however, the Court of Queen's Bench made absolute a rule nisi to set aside the non-suit.[6]

Dimes then obtained possession of the land under a writ of possession, placed a bar across the canal, and threw a large quantity of bricks into it. The company thereupon filed a bill in Chancery claiming, *inter alia*, an injunction to restrain Dimes

1 *Dicas* v. *Lord Brougham and Vaux* (1833) 6 C. & P. 249.
2 See Twiss, *Eldon*, vol. 2, p. 322. For judges giving evidence, see *post*, p. 93.
3 (1852) 3 H.L.C. 759.
4 1 *Atlay* 415.
5 *Ibid.*   6 See 3 H.L.C. 761.

from interfering with the navigation. This was granted *ex parte* by Shadwell V.-C., who, on motion a few days later, continued the injunction until further order; and Lord Cottenham L.C. duly affirmed this.[7]   After certain proceedings at law in the Queen's Bench and Exchequer Chamber,[8] in 1846 Shadwell V.-C. decided the action in favour of the company, and made the injunction perpetual[9]; and in 1848 Lord Cottenham L.C. affirmed this decision.[10]

Soon afterwards Dimes discovered that Lord Cottenham had for over ten years held ninety-two shares in the company, seventeen beneficially and seventy-five in a representative capacity, though with also a beneficial interest in some of these.[11] He accordingly gave notice of motion to discharge Lord Cottenham's order on the ground that the judge had had a personal interest in the proceedings; and Lord Cottenham requested Lord Langdale M.R. to hear the motion. Lord Langdale, after considering at some length the difficulties which arose from the Lord Chancellor being technically the sole judge in the Court of Chancery, held that the motion failed.[12] Dimes then commenced fifteen actions for trespass, and the company retaliated by a motion to commit Dimes for breach of the injunction in bringing these actions, and for a further injunction restraining Dimes from prosecuting the fifteen actions for trespass, or bringing any others. Shadwell V.-C. refused to commit Dimes, but granted the injunction.[13]

Dimes' next move was to place a chain across the canal and dig a trench across the tow-path. Ten days later, on the motion of the company, Shadwell V.-C. ordered Dimes to be committed to prison for his contempt in disobeying the injunction granted ten years earlier; and on a warrant signed by Lord Cottenham L.C. shortly afterwards, Dimes was cast into gaol.[14]   Within a

[7] See 3 H.L.C. 761, 762.
[8] See *Dimes v. The Company of Proprietors of the Grand Junction Canal* (1846) 9 Q.B. 469.
[9] *Grand Junction Canal Co.* v. *Dimes* (1846) 15 Sim. 402.
[10] *Grand Junction Canal Co.* v. *Dimes* (1848) 17 L.J.Ch. 206.
[11] 2 Mac. & G. 286n.
[12] *Grand Junction Canal Co.* v. *Dimes* (1849) 12 Beav. 63.
[13] *Grand Junction Canal Co.* v. *Dimes* (1849) 17 Sim. 38; and see 3 H.L.C. 765.
[14] 3 H.L.C. 766.

month, an application by Dimes to discharge Shadwell V.-C.'s order of committal was heard by Lord Cottenham L.C., assisted by Lord Langdale M.R.; but acting on the advice of the Master of the Rolls, Lord Cottenham dismissed the application.[15]

Some six months later, ill-health forced Lord Cottenham to resign, and after the Great Seal had been in commission for rather less than two months, Sir Thomas Wilde C.J.C.P. became Lord Chancellor as Lord Truro.[16] One of his first judicial acts was to grant Dimes a writ of habeas corpus[17]; but on the return of the writ three days later he held the committal to be regular. However, he suggested that Dimes should be released on giving an undertaking not further to infringe the injunction, and, this being done and the company consenting, Dimes was set free.[18] He used his liberty in appealing to the House of Lords against the decisions of Shadwell V.-C. and Lord Cottenham L.C. in favour of the company on the substantive point, and against eight other orders of the Court of Chancery on the other proceedings relating to the injunction.

In June 1852, rather over a year after Lord Cottenham's death,[19] the case came on for hearing by Lord St. Leonards L.C., Lord Brougham and Lord Campbell. On the substantive point they unanimously held the decision of Shadwell V.-C. to be right; indeed, they did not call upon counsel for the company for any argument.[20] But the real issue was that of the effect of Lord Cottenham's undisclosed shareholding upon his decree. As was pointed out in argument, Dimes was in a singular position: he was contending that Lord Cottenham's interest made all the proceedings in Chancery void, for the Vice-Chancellor was merely the deputy of the Lord Chancellor: yet the appeal to the House of Lords was of necessity founded upon a decision which the appellant contended was void.[1] As Lord

---

[15] *Grand Junction Canal Co.* v. *Dimes* (1850) 2 Mac. & G. 285; 2 H. & Tw. 92.
[16] See 1 *Atlay* 416, 448.
[17] Lord Truro was appointed on July 15, 1850, and granted the writ eight days later: see *Re Dimes* (1850) 3 Mac. & G. 4.
[18] *Re Dimes*, *supra*.
[19] On April 29, 1851: see 1 *Atlay* 416.
[20] *Dimes* v. *Proprietors of the Grand Junction Canal* (1852) 3 H.L.C. 794 (see at p. 801).
[1] See *ibid.*, at pp. 767, 768.

Macmillan was to observe over eighty years later, "Where a judge has assumed jurisdiction which he did not possess, and on appeal it is held that he had no jurisdiction, is his judgment treated as a nullity, if so, how can you appeal against it? You get a most curious logical dilemma." [2] However, Parke B., speaking for all the judges, advised the House that the Lord Chancellor's decree was not void but voidable, and that the Vice-Chancellor was not merely the Lord Chancellor's deputy, but had an independent jurisdiction. [3] The law lords agreed with this view, and so set aside Lord Cottenham's decree. [4]

That, however, left the Vice-Chancellor's decision to the same effect still in existence; and, treating the appeal as an appeal from the Vice-Chancellor direct, the House unanimously affirmed it. [5] Lord Campbell, indeed, moralised a little. "No one can suppose that Lord Cottenham could be, in the remotest degree, influenced by the interest that he had in this concern; but, my Lords, it is of the last importance that the maxim that no man is to be a judge in his own cause should be held sacred. And that is not to be confined to a cause in which he is a party, but applies to a cause in which he has an interest. Since I have had the honour to be Chief Justice of the Court of Queen's Bench, we have again and again set aside proceedings in inferior tribunals because an individual, who had an interest in a cause, took a part in the decision. And it will have a most salutary influence on these tribunals when it is known that this high Court of last resort, in a case in which the Lord Chancellor of England [6] had an interest, considered that his decree was on that account a decree not according to law, and was set aside. This will be a lesson to all inferior tribunals to take care not only that in their decrees they are not influenced by their personal interest, but to avoid the appearance of labouring under such an influence." [7]

Some thirty-five years later there was a distant echo of *Dimes'*

---

[2] *McPherson* v. *McPherson* [1936] A.C. 177 at 189; and see *post*, p. 55.
[3] *Dimes* v. *Proprietors of the Grand Junction Canal, supra*, at pp. 784–788.
[4] *Ibid.*, at pp. 790–794.
[5] *Ibid.*, at pp. 794–811.
[6] *Sic* : he is Lord Chancellor of Great Britain.
[7] *Dimes* v. *Proprietors of the Grand Junction Canal, supra*, at p. 793.

case in a somewhat less exalted sphere.[8]   An assault had been committed at Taunton, and one of the two victims sent for his doctor, who not only attended to the injuries but also endeavoured to dissuade him from taking proceedings in respect of the assault.   However, summonses for assault and (later) for unlawful wounding were taken out against the assailant, who then subpoenaed the doctor to give evidence at the trial.   The doctor was in fact the Mayor of Taunton and a magistrate, and when it appeared that he proposed to sit when the court was to hear the charges, the accused not surprisingly applied for a rule nisi for a writ of prohibition to restrain the doctor from sitting; and Kekewich J. granted it (no doubt he was sitting in the Vacation Court).

The doctor then moved to set aside the prohibition, and Stephen and Charles JJ. somewhat surprisingly granted the motion and issued a writ of supersedeas.   They could find no bias in the doctor, and as to the subpoena, " it might cause great mischief if we were to hold as a matter of law that, because a magistrate or judge is likely to be called as a witness, he is bound not to sit.   Such a doctrine might cause great inconvenience, as, for instance, if a judge of assize were subpoenaed just before the trial, the effect might be to necessitate a postponement to the next assizes, and it would be in the power of either party, by serving a subpoena, to prevent any particular judge or magistrate from sitting.   It would be a serious thing to lay down a rule which might have such an application." [9]

In fact, however, if there were such a rule it would not lie in the power of any party to disqualify a judge simply by serving a subpoena upon him; for if the judge could give no material evidence, the court would simply set the subpoena aside.[10]   The real *ratio decidendi* of the case seems to be that the prospect of a judge giving evidence in the course of a case which he is trying (and no doubt ruling judicially on the admissibility of his own evidence) appears to have been thought an inconsiderable objection when compared with the " great mischief " of

---

[8] *R.* v. *Farrant* (1887) 20 Q.B.D. 58; contrast *R.* v. *Meyer* (1875) 1 Q.B.D. 173.
[9] *R.* v. *Farrant, supra,* at p. 62, *per* Stephen J.
[10] See *R.* v. *Baines* [1909] 1 K.B. 258; 1 Misc. 185.

the " great inconvenience " which would be caused by post-
poning the trial to the next assizes. *Fiat opportunitas ruat
coelum*: let what is convenient be done, though the heavens fall.

Several centuries earlier an enterprising landowner, on being
sued at common law for tithes, obtained from the Court of
Chancery an injunction restraining the action at law on the
ground that the tithe owner should have sued for the tithes in
the appropriate ecclesiastical court. It then appeared that the
landowner was Chancellor of the consistory court of the diocese
in question, so that the tithe owner would be forced to proceed
before a judge who would also be the defendant. Not surprisingly Bacon L.C. dissolved the injunction.[11] Nor did such
devices fare better at common law. Holt C.J. once referred to
a Mayor of Hertford [12] (or Hereford [13]) and the occasion " where
a court was held before him only, and he, pretending right to a
house, made himself lessor of the plaintiff, and gave judgment
for his own lessee; and for this he was brought up by attachment, and laid by the heels; though he got off the easier, for
that he had been an old cavalier; this he said was in my Lord
Hyde's time," [14] *i.e.*, probably between 1663 and 1665, when
Robert Hyde was C.J.K.B.[15]

Holt C.J., indeed, was prepared to carry this doctrine to the
ultimate. " If an Act of Parliament should ordain that the
same person should be party and Judge, or, which is the same
thing, Judge in his own cause, it would be a void Act of
Parliament; for it is impossible that one should be Judge and
party, for the Judge is to determine between party and party,
or between the Government and the party; and an Act of
Parliament can do no wrong, though it may do several things
that look pretty odd." [16] In this, he followed earlier authority.

11 *Lambe* v. *Barnaby* (1618) J. Ritchie, *Bacon's Cases* (1932) p. 85.
12 *Wright* v. *Crump* (1702) 7 Mod. 1.
13 *Wright* v. *Crump* (1702) 2 Ld.Raym. 766; *Anon.* (1702) 1 Salk. 201; *Anon.*
(1698) 1 Salk. 396.
14 *Wright* v. *Crump* (1702) 7 Mod. 1.
15 The reference to " old cavalier " rules out Nicholas Hyde, C.J.K.B. 1627–
1631; and " when Hyde was Chief Justice " (2 Ld.Raym. 766) excludes Sir
Edward Hyde, Lord Hyde, Earl of Clarendon L.C.
16 *City of London* v. *Wood* (1701) 12 Mod. 669 at 687 (the last part of this
sentence was quoted at 1 Misc. 346).

"Even an Act of Parliament, made against natural equity, as to make a man Judge in his own case, is void in it self."[17]

This view, however, did not command universal assent. In one case in 1693, a matter in dispute had been submitted by the parties to the decision of one of the parties himself and another; and it was contended that it was "against right and law, that the plaintiff should be judge in his own cause."[18] But the award was held good. Dolben J. referred to the case of Serjeant Hards, where the serjeant had taken "a horse from my Lord of Canterbury's bailiff for a deodand, and the archbishop brought his action; and it coming to a trial at the assizes in Kent, the serjeant, by rule of Court, referred it to the archbishop to set the price of the horse, which was done accordingly; and the serjeant afterwards moved the Court to set aside the award for the reason now offered; but it was denied by Lord Hale and *per totam Curiam*."[19] As Lord Mansfield C.J. said, "A man may judge impartially even in his own cause."[20]

Difficulties have also arisen where a person has been involved in a case in more litigious capacities than one. Thus it seems that the sheriff of a county could not suffer a common recovery of land in that county, because he could not summon himself.[1] Again, a man may wish in his own right to sue himself in his capacity of trustee. The obstacle is that "there is no principle by which a man can be at the same time Plaintiff and Defendant."[2] Farwell J. seems to have overlooked this rule when in 1931 he not only allowed the Public Trustee to appear, separately represented, as both plaintiff and defendant, but also allowed him his costs in both capacities.[3] However, within a year Maugham J. had refused to allow this venture to be repeated, and in a similar case struck out the Public Trustee as a defendant.[4] The position is not improved if, instead of seeking

[17] *Day* v. *Savadge* (1614) Hob. 85 at 87, *per cur.*
[18] *Matthew* v. *Ollerton* (1693) Comb. 218.
[19] *Matthew* v. *Ollerton* (1693) 4 Mod. 226.
[20] *R.* v. *Cowle* (1759) 2 Burr. 834 at 863. See also *post*, p. 90.
[1] See *Sir Ralph Rowlet's Case* (1560) 2 Dy. 188a.
[2] *Neale* v. *Turton* (1827) 4 Bing. 149 at 151, *per* Best C.J.
[3] *Re Abercrombie's Will Trusts* [1931] W.N. 109; and see *Woolley* v. *Colman* [1886] W.N. 36.
[4] *Re Phillips* (1931) 101 L.J.Ch. 338.

to put a litigant on both sides of a case, it is attempted to put him on one side or the other twice over, in different capacities. " It is incorrect to make any individual a defendant twice over because he happens to fill two capacities or has two different interests." [5]

These difficulties in constituting an action have not been allowed to extend into the sphere of effecting service of documents once an action has been duly constituted. Thus one plaintiff sued a deputy sheriff in Natal for damages for wrongful attachment. " When the plaintiff's attorneys forwarded the summons to the deputy sheriff for service, he raised the question whether it would be regular for him to serve it on himself, and their reply was that this course would not be irregular, and indeed that if the summons were not served without further delay, the plaintiff would regard this as an irregularity! Thereupon the deputy sheriff served the summons on himself. He does not say how he accomplished this dextrous feat, save to aver modestly that he ' went through the motions '—thereby no doubt letting his left hand know what his right hand was doing. For this nimble service he charged the plaintiff a fee of 10s. 7d., which included cost-of-living allowance—an ambidextrous sheriff must live. The return of service indicates that he explained to himself the ' nature and exigency of the summons.' Doubtless this involved a little auto-suggestion. Thereafter he was prudent enough to enter appearance to defend. But the arrival of the declaration apparently caused him to have some misgivings, and he now applies, as defendant, for the service to be set aside as irregular. His right hand however has not lost its cunning, for he seeks to turn the irregularity to his advantage with a tactical prayer that the plaintiff be ordered to pay the costs of this application before re-serving the summons, upon the ground that the plaintiff is a man of straw— a prayer which, if granted, might have the effect of preventing him from bringing his case before the Court.

---

[5] *Hardie & Lane Ltd.* v. *Chiltern* [1928] 1 K.B. 663 at 699, *per* Sargant L.J. Cp. the world of company law: *Lee* v. *Lee's Air Farming Ltd.* [1961] A.C. 12.

" Well now, what is the Court to do about this drollery? " [6] The answer was that although the service was irregular, the court had a discretion in the matter, and in the circumstances of the case " plain justice between man and man requires that the irregularity be condoned and the application dismissed," [7] though without costs.

[6] *Dreyer* v. *Naidoo*, 1958 (2) S.A. 628, *per* Holmes J.
[7] *Ibid.*, at p. 629, *per* Holmes J.

Advocat Non Larron

TODAY, the race of serjeants-at-law is defunct. To many, both within the law and without, it is far from clear exactly what their position was, and in particular how they compared with Q.C.s. Broadly, serjeants were " an intermediate grade between Her Majesty's Counsel and the rest of the Bar." [1] In some ways, a serjeanty was a position of greater honour. A serjeant was created by writ under the Great Seal, whereas a Q.C. is created merely by patent. Q.C.s also have no recognised position or precedence outside the profession, whereas serjeants took rank in society immediately after judges of county courts and before masters in lunacy. As between themselves, the question arose in 1700 as to the seniority of those who were called to be serjeants at the same time. Were they to take seniority according to the dates on their writs calling them to be serjeants, or according to their seniority in call to the Bar? Wright L.K. held that the latter was the case, though the reporter observed that when Wright had been a serjeant he had taken seniority according to the former rule. [2]

In the courts, serjeants ranked after Q.C.s, however senior the serjeant and however junior the Q.C. This, however, did not apply to serjeants who held a patent of precedence; they ranked among themselves and among Q.C.s according to the dates and order of their patents. [3] Such patents, which seem to have originated with the future Lord Mansfield, were at first confined to Members of Parliament who, if appointed Q.C., would have vacated their seats as holding an office of profit under the Crown. Patents lacked this disadvantage, [4] although

---

[1] Mr. Serjeant Robinson, *Bench and Bar* (2nd ed. 1889) p. 295 (cited as " Rob."). See generally the discussion of serjeants and their Inns in my *Inns Ancient and Modern* (1972) pp. 14–23.

[2] 1 Ld.Raym. 604 at 605.

[3] See Rob. 294, 295. There were variants: when Strange S.-G. resigned in 1742 he was given a patent conferring on him precedence for life next to the Attorney-General: 2 Str. 1176.

[4] A. Pulling, *Order of the Coif* (1884) pp. 200, 268 (cited as " Pull.").

patents expired on the demise of the Crown and, not being an
" office," were not preserved by statute.[5] Thus under a patent
of precedence Mr. Casberd took his seat within the Bar in
January 1819. But when George III died during the Hilary
term a year later, " Mr. Casberd, during the remainder of the
term, sat without the Bar." [6] Traditionally, a serjeanty was
the highest degree in the common law, whereas a doctorate was
the highest degree in the civil law; but it was said that a doctor
of law was superior to a serjeant-at-law, on the curious ground
that the former was magisterial and the latter only ministerial.[7]

At common law, serjeants had an exclusive right of audience
in the Court of Common Pleas during term time, while sitting
in banc [8]; no other member of the Bar was entitled to be heard
there. In other courts, serjeants had a right of audience as
members of the Bar; but in the other two common law courts
(though not in the Court of Chancery) they could not sit in
the front row until in 1864 Cockburn C.J. announced that the
judges had agreed to serjeants having the privilege of sitting
in the front row in all courts.[9] This was where Q.C.s had
always sat, probably since 1596 when Francis Bacon became the
first Q.C., and certainly since 1668 when North and Miller were
made " de Councel del Roy & veigne deins les barrs." [10]

Like Q.C.s, serjeants were appointed by the Crown on the
advice of the Lord Chancellor; but in the case of serjeants this
advice was never given save on the recommendation of the Chief
Justice of the Common Pleas.[11] As for gowns, the serjeants
had a variety of them for different occasions: black cloth in
term time, but purple cloth on saints' days; black silk out of
term at *nisi prius*, but scarlet at the judges' service at St. Paul's
in Trinity term, and at the Guildhall Banquet.[12] Soon after
1865, however, these distinctions fell into disuse, and serjeants
wore their black silk gowns on all occasions.[13]

[5] 57 Geo. 3, c. 45, 1817.   [6] 2 B. & Ald. 242; 3 B. & Ald. 484.
[7] See Spelman, *Glossary* (1687) p. 512.
[8] See *Re Serjeants at Law* (1840) 6 Bing.N.C. 235; 1 *Atlay* 433.
[9] See 33 L.J.Ch. vi; Rob. 294; Pull. 205.
[10] 1 Sid. 365.
[11] Rob. 300; Pull. 227.   [12] Rob. 295.
[13] Rob. 295; Pull. 226. Hawkins J. suggested that only serjeants with a patent
of precedence had the privilege of wearing a silk gown and a Q.C.'s wig:

Serjeants also wore their coif. In latter days this was represented by a white crimped border, less than an inch wide, surrounding a small round smooth black silk patch, some two inches in diameter, attached to the central depression on the top of their full-bottomed wigs.[14] Originally the coif was a close-fitting cap of fine white linen or silk, covering the whole head of hair and the ears, and fastening under the chin. On top of this, a smaller black skull cap was usually worn.[15] When wigs came into fashion with Charles II, they had to be designed so as not wholly to conceal the coif, and so at first this was left to peep out at the back of the wig. In time, this was replaced by the space on top of the wig for the display of a miniature coif and black skull cap.[16]

Serjeants had the privilege of being immune from being sued in any court save the Common Pleas. However, not long before the unpopular Serjeant Scroggs became C.J.K.B.,[17] the court denied him his plea of serjeanty when he was sued jointly with another in the King's Bench for a battery.[18] Some seven years later, " Sir William Scroggs " was again defendant in an action for battery, though it does not appear whether this was the former Chief Justice after his impeachment and removal from office, or whether it was his son of the same name. However, after an instructive little argument on venue, the plaintiff, a barrister, " forgave it, and desisted; on a treat given by Sir William, &c." [19] Perhaps this resolves the doubt, in favour of Scroggs the son; the father might have given a " treat," but hardly an " &c." as well.

In the nineteenth century the serjeants rarely exceeded 40 or 45 in number,[20] and often there were fewer. The Law Lists of the day show the numbers of non-judicial serjeants as

Reminiscences of Sir Henry Hawkins (Baron Brampton), ed. Richard Harris K.C., (1904) vol. 1, p. 120.
[14] Rob. 292, 303; and see the illustration in Pull. 12.
[15] Lord Campbell seems to have had an *idée fixe* that it was the black cap that was the coif: see, *e.g.*, 1 Camp.C.JJ. 72, 482, 585.
[16] Pull. 13, 225, 226.
[17] On May 31, 1678.
[18] *Deakins* v. *Scroggs* (1675) 2 Lev. 129; *sub nom. Hamilton* v. *Scrogs* (1674) 3 Keb. 424.
[19] *Thompson* v. *Scroggs* (1682) 2 Show.K.B. 176 at 177.
[20] Pull. 258.

fluctuating between 17 and 28. These numbers were much greater than those in the fifteenth and sixteenth centuries, when the number of non-judicial serjeants often fell below double figures, and replenishments came only at long intervals, in batches averaging something like ten every decade.[1] In 1778 there were 14 serjeants and 165 juniors at the Bar.[2] A serjeant might be appointed a Q.C., in which case he was called a Queen's Serjeant[3]; and there were even higher ranks of serjeanty, such as the Queen's Premier Serjeant and the Queen's Ancient Serjeant, to which appointments were occasionally made.

From early in the fourteenth century the judges of the Courts of King's Bench and Common Pleas were appointed only from among the serjeants. Apart from the Chief Baron, this practice was not applied to the Court of Exchequer until 1579, when Serjeant Shute became Shute B.[4] Thereafter the rule operated in all the superior courts of common law, though it was never extended to any other courts. In more modern times, however, comparatively few serjeants were of judicial calibre, and so when any appointment to the common law Bench was made from outside their ranks, conformity with the ancient rule was preserved by appointing the candidate a serjeant immediately before making him a judge. Long before the nineteenth century a rule that only a serjeant could be made a judge had become a rule that if a new judge was not already a serjeant, he must be made one first. The first instance of this seems to have been as long ago as the appointment of Monson J. in 1572.[5]

As soon as a barrister received the writ calling upon him to take the degree of serjeant-at-law, his Inn made him a bencher.[6] However, he normally continued a bencher only for the short period that remained before the ceremony of his call to the coif was completed; for thereupon he almost invariably became a

---

1 See E. W. Ives (1959) 75 L.Q.R. 354, 360, 361.
2 Pull. 193.
3 Pull. 37; and see, *e.g.*, 2 B. & Ald. 242.
4 Pull. 267; E. Foss, *The Judges of England* (1870) p. viii.
5 E. Foss, *supra*, pp. viii, 448; E. Foss, *Tabulae Curiales* (1865) p. 54.
6 Pull. 168, 229.

member of Serjeants' Inn, and ceremonially departed from his Inn of call, being "rung out" to the tolling of a bell, as for one dead.[7] In the nineteenth century the entrance fee to Serjeants' Inn was £350 for a practising serjeant, and £500 for a judicial serjeant.[8] Membership was not, however, obligatory. Thus Sir Robert Collier, who in 1871 was to be appointed a salaried member of the Judicial Committee of the Privy Council, had to be appointed a judge first in order to qualify him for the appointment. He was accordingly made a serjeant and appointed a judge, and fifteen days later,[9] after an industrious period in the Court of Common Pleas in which he delivered seven brief judgments that attained the Law Reports,[10] he was translated to the Judicial Committee, without ever joining Serjeants' Inn.[11] The serjeants unanimously agreed to inform him that he was not expected to join the Inn when he had held an office for which serjeanty was obligatory for so short a time.[12] As all the common law judges were serjeants, they addressed serjeants at the Bar as "Brother," though the serjeants never returned the familiarity, and in the usual way addressed judges as "My lord" in court and "judge" in private.[13]

The exclusive right of audience enjoyed by the serjeants in the Court of Common Pleas was assailed by a Royal Mandate under the sign manual dated April 24, 1834, procured by Sir

---

[7] For a brief description of the ringing out of Honyman J. from the Middle Temple, see (1873) 8 L.J.News. 103.

[8] Rob. 304.

[9] See [1872] 18 H.L.Sess.Pap. 144 (Letters Patent for Common Pleas, November 7, 1871; Royal Warrant for Judicial Committee, November 22. He was sworn in for the Common Pleas on November 11: see *ibid.*, 140). The "two or three days" that is usually stated (see, *e.g.*, Rob. 313; 2 *Atlay* 369 ("two days")) exaggerates the brevity. So does the statement in 12 App.Cas. xv that he was appointed on November 7 and resigned on November 9. If true, this would mean that he had a unique distinction; for on this footing it was not until after he had resigned that he was sworn in and delivered all his reported judgments in the Common Pleas (see next footnote).

[10] See (1871) L.R. 7 C.P.: p. 9, *Bateson* v. *Gosling* (Nov. 14); p. 143, *Townshend* v. *Overseers of St. Marylebone*, and p. 163, *Bendle* v. *Watson* (Nov. 17); p. 150, *Ford* v. *Boon*, p. 172, *Firth* v. *Overseers of Widdicombe-in-the-Moor*, and p. 178, *Chorlton* v. *Overseers of Tonge* (Nov. 18); p. 18, *Tyson* v. *Mayor of London* (Nov. 20). See also *Calver* v. *Roberts* (1871) 25 L.T. 751 (Nov. 17).

[11] Rob. 303, 312, 313; and see *ibid.*, 311, for a practising serjeant who never joined the Inn.

[12] Rob. 313.   [13] Rob. 303. See, *e.g.*, *post*, pp. 219, 220.

John Campbell A.-G. and addressed to Lord Brougham L.C.[14]
This purported to open the court to all other members of the
Bar, whether silks or juniors. By way of consolation, the
Mandate also gave fifteen serjeants-at-law who were then in
actual practice precedence at the Bar, according to their seniority
among themselves, next after John Balguy K.C., thus ending
for them the serjeants' old grievance that every new K.C. took
precedence over them. Thereupon, after the Mandate had
been read in open court, " the several serjeants at law above
named took their seats within the Bar in the Court of King's
Bench." [15] Among the fifteen was William St. Julian Arabin,
whose linguistic glory or inglory lives on today.[16] This batch
of precedencies seems to have caused the old grievance to be
felt the more keenly by those subsequently created serjeant, for
whom it did nothing.[17]

During the remainder of the reign of William IV the
Mandate was obeyed. In 1837, however, five of the serjeants
presented a memorial to the newly ascended Queen Victoria,
praying her to take advice as to the legality of the Mandate; and
in 1839 Lord Cottenham L.C. presided over a strongly constituted Judicial Committee of the Privy Council to which the
Queen had referred the memorial for advice under the Judicial
Committee Act, 1833.[18] The argument lasted three days,[19] and
during this it appeared that the law officers of the Crown felt
unable to support the legality of the Mandate. No formal
decision was ever given, though there seemed to be virtual
unanimity among the judges that the Mandate was invalid.
Having thus discharged their duty of respect to the Crown, the
five serjeants, speaking through Serjeant Wilde, then submitted
the matter to the Court of Common Pleas; and in 1840, after

---

[14] See 1 A. & E. 122; 10 Bing. 571; 3 Nev. & Man. 535; Pull. 100, 271; but see
    1 *Atlay* 434.
[15] 1 A. & E. 123.　　　　　　　　　[16] See my *Arabinesque-at-Law* (1969).
[17] See Pull. 203. Serjeant Pulling, made serjeant in 1864, seems to have had no
    patent of precedence: see Rob. 299.
[18] s. 4. The argument is fully reported in *Re a Petition by Serjeants at Law*
    (1839), J. Manning, *Serviens ad Legem* (1840) 1 at 14–168. On the second
    day, the Marquess of Lansdowne, who had been absent on the first day,
    presided, as Lord President of the Council: p. 85.
[19] According to Serjeant Wilde as reported at 6 Bing.N.C. 190; but J. Manning,
    supra, at pp. 14, 85, indicates only two days.

full argument, the court held the Mandate ineffective to deprive the serjeants of their exclusive right of audience in the court during term time.[20] According to Peregrine Bingham, the law reporter, during the delivery of judgment by Tindal C.J., " a furious tempest of wind prevailed, which seemed to shake the fabric of Westminster Hall, and nearly burst open the windows and doors of the Court of Common Pleas " [1]; but Bingham was not a serjeant. This contribution of nature may have had a decisive effect on the position of the Attorney-General. In 1831 it had been held that if he was not a serjeant he could not be heard in the Common Pleas during term time, even on behalf of the Crown,[2] but less than six months after the wind, the court held exactly the reverse, without mention of the earlier decision.[3]

The triumph of the serjeants was short-lived, however; for in 1846 statute opened the Common Pleas to all barristers, on equal terms with the serjeants.[4] That, of course, presaged the end of the serjeants. Four years later Parliament provided that any Q.C., or any barrister with a patent of precedence, could be named and act as a judge or commissioner of assize, even though not a serjeant.[5] After 1868, none save judges-elect were made serjeants,[6] and by 1881 most of the six remaining non-judicial serjeants had ceased to practise.[7] When in 1875 statute [8] abolished the requirement that only a serjeant could be appointed a judge, there was no need for any more serjeants to be created; and Lindley J., on his elevation to the Common Bench in May 1875, was the last English serjeant to be appointed.[9] With his

---

[20] *Re Serjeants-at-Law* (1839) 6 Bing.N.C. 187; (1840) 6 Bing.N.C. 232, 235; *Privileges of the Serjeants-at-Law* (1840) 9 L.J.C.P. 339; J. Manning, *supra*, pp. 316–334; 1 *Atlay* 434–436.

[1] 6 Bing.N.C. 239n.

[2] *Marchant* v. *Flight* (1831) 9 L.J.C.P.(O.S.) 226. Both Campbell A.-G. and Tindal C.J. (*inter alia*) seem to have been unaware of this decision during the argument of *Re a Petition of Serjeants at Law* (1839) J. Manning, *supra*, 1 (see at pp. 115, 116), and in *Paddock* v. *Forrester*, *infra*.

[3] *Paddock* v. *Forrester* (1840) 1 Man. & G. 583; 9 L.J.C.P. 342.

[4] 9 & 10 Vict. c. 54, 1846.

[5] 13 & 14 Vict. c. 25, 1850.

[6] Earl Jowitt, *Dictionary of English Law* (1959) p. 1615.

[7] Rob. 298, 299.

[8] Judicature Act, 1873, s. 8.

[9] *Pace* Sir Cecil Carr, *Pension Book of Clement's Inn* (1960: S.S. vol. 78)

death in 1921,[10] the race of English serjeants became extinct, although the dignity has never been formally abolished.[11] Indeed, to this day the County Palatine of Lancaster has an Attorney-General whose full title is " Attorney-General and Attorney and Serjeant within the County Palatine of Lancaster." [12] In Ireland, there were never any serjeants of the Common Pleas; but King's Serjeants were appointed under the Great Seal of Ireland until the constitutional changes of 1922.[13] The last survivor there was Serjeant A. M. Sullivan Q.C., who was appointed in 1920 and died in 1959.[14]

With the end of any prospect of new creations of serjeants to replenish the funds, the death of Serjeants' Inn was in sight; and in 1877 the serjeants sold it to one of their number, Serjeant Cox, for £57,100, the surviving serjeants dividing the proceeds of sale.[15] The serjeants thereupon became homeless. One Inn of Court, the Middle Temple, invited all its former members to return as members without any further payment, the judicial serjeants as Benchers and the others as barristers, with the same precedence as if they had never left the Inn,[16] whereas Gray's Inn, it seems, merely reinstated their judicial serjeants as Benchers.[17] What the other Inns did does not appear, though some writers assert that there was a general reinstatement.[18]

p. lxii, which in effect states that Huddleston B. was the last serjeant; and for " 1873 " read " November 1, 1875 " as the date when statute ended the system of serjeanty as a stepping stone to judicial office.
[10] D.N.B. 1912–21, p. 336; 3 *Halsbury's Laws of England* (3rd ed. 1953) p. 3.
[11] Jowitt, *supra*, at p. 1615. Assertions such as " The Order of Serjeants was abolished in 1877 " (W. N. Hargreaves-Mawdsley, *A History of Legal Dress in Europe* (1963) p. 70; and see p. 82) are without foundation.
[12] Until late in the 19th century the County Palatine still had its own Q.C.s: see (1971) 87 L.Q.R. 477.
[13] A. M. Sullivan, *Old Ireland* (1927) p. 106.
[14] (1959) 227 L.T.News. 42. The last Q.C. of Ireland living was F. FitzGibbon, who died in 1970: (1970) 104 Ir.L.T. & S.J. 304.
[15] See, *e.g.*, Sir Cecil Carr, *supra*, p. lxii.
[16] See *Middle Temple Bench Book* (1912), ed. A. R. Ingpen, pp. 48, 49, Orders of May 24 and 30, 1878. In Rob. 303, Serjeant Robinson, who had been called by Middle Temple, asserted that all that was offered was " the right of dining in hall, as well as the use of the library "; yet the Order is explicit as to returning " as members."
[17] See the Order of Pension of November 20, 1878, noted in Lincoln's Inn *Black Book* (mss.: vol. 34, p. 414, November 25, 1878).
[18] See F. Watt, *The Law's Lumber Room* (2nd ser. 1898) p. 199; T. Mathew, *For Lawyers and Others* (1937) p. 197 (which asserts that they returned " as

The decline of the serjeants was matched by the rise of the K.C.s. The average rate of creation of K.C.s changed greatly with William IV. Until then, there had rarely been more than one or two new silks a year; the 140 years from 1660 to 1800 yielded no more than some 165 new silks, including holders of patents of precedence.[19] Before William IV, the average yearly figures were, broadly: Charles II, 0·75; James II, 2·5; William and Mary, 1; Anne, 1; George I, 1; George II, 1; George III, 1·5; and George IV, 2·5.[20] In 1816, there were only 28 K.C.s in all,[1] though this was double the number of 1778.[2] But in the seven years of William IV, 65 new silks were created,[3] giving an average of a little over nine a year; and this trend continued with Victoria, with an average of about seven a year during the first half of her reign.[4]

By the end of the nineteenth century, new silks were emerging at an annual rate of about 11 or 12. The 63 silks of 1840 had by 1890 become some 200, although it was said that less than a third of these were in actual practice.[5] In the decade 1886–95, 115 were created, with the two of 1889 as the "low" (numerically, of course) and the 23 of 1895 as the "high."[6] In this century, 1919 was exceptional. There had been no general appointment of silks since 1914, and so Lord Birkenhead L.C. created 39 new silks at a blow.[7] One of them, Serjeant Sullivan, recounts that they were promptly dubbed the Thirty-Nine Articles; one application, it is said, was refused in order to

---

Benchers to the Inns which had rung them out." *Quaere* as to the "as Benchers" for non-judicial serjeants).

[19] See J. Haydn, *Book of Dignities* (1890) pp. 414, 415.
[20] J. C. Jeaffreson, *A Book About Lawyers* (2nd ed. 1867), vol. 1, p. 305; and see J. Haydn, *supra*, p. 414.
[1] Serjeant Ballantine's *Experiences* (8th ed. 1883) p. 372.
[2] Pull. 193.
[3] But Pull. 258 puts the number at 50.
[4] J. C. Jeaffreson, *loc. cit.* See also *Encyclopaedia of the Laws of England*, vol. 7 (2nd ed. 1907) p. 609 (where, however, the figure given for 1850 seems suspect).
[5] Rob. 30, 296; Pull. 197. The "300" Q.C.s stated in Rob. 296 is wrong, and the "third" stated in Pull. 197 as being in practice should, I suspect, be a half.
[6] See the annual volumes of L.J.Ch. reports.
[7] See (1919) 63 S.J. 309, 420. The 39 were quickly followed by two more: *ibid.*, 437.

prevent the batch from being known as the Forty Thieves.[8]
The 11 silks of 1956[9] and the 45 of 1972[10] seem to mark the
ebb and flow of today, with the mean in recent years a good
deal nearer the latter figure than the former. By 1972 there
were some 500 Q.C.s living, although some 200 of these were
no longer in practice.[11] In Scotland, the institution of silk is
of relatively recent origin; not until 1897 was the Scottish roll of
Q.C.s founded. Before that, a Scottish advocate who intended
to confine himself to senior practice used to intimate that he
intended to " give up writing." [12]

Today, there are a number of peers in practice at the Bar,
some as silks and others as juniors. It was not always so. In
1840 it was possible for it to be laid down as a general rule that
" by the etiquette of the profession, no peer can practise at the
bar—and for a very obvious reason. Every peer is a member
of the court of supreme judicature, and might, therefore, be
called upon to decide the very case in which he had previously
acted as an advocate." [13] That, however, was four years before
O'Connell v. *The Queen* [14] in effect established the convention
that peers who had never held high judicial office should not
take part in the hearing of appeals. Yet it was not until 1905
that the point was put beyond doubt. In *Re Lord Kinross* [15]
the Committee for Privileges of the House of Lords gave the
death-blow to an already moribund rule. The Committee laid
it down that a peer was entitled to appear as counsel before the
House of Lords in its appellate capacity. It seems that the
second Lord Coleridge was the first peer to practise as counsel
in the ordinary courts of law.[16] He succeeded to the peerage in

---

[8] A. M. Sullivan, *The Last Serjeant* (1952) p. 274. But see the shameful
blunder of a Q.C. who, in writing about Q.C.s, used the sub-title " La Gazza
Ladra " in place of " La Scala di Seta " : (1963) 79 L.Q.R. 48.
[9] A vintage year, good (especially) to the last drop.
[10] 1965, with 40, was the previous " high." It is hardly surprising that Lord
Gardiner L.C. in 1965 should have differed from Lord Birkenhead L.C. in
1919. Lord Hailsham of St. Marylebone L.C. has now surpassed 1972 with
the 46 of 1973.
[11] See *The Law List*, 1972, pp. xx, 723–726.
[12] Lord Macmillan, *A Man of Law's Tale* (1952) p. 27.
[13] *Law and Lawyers* (1840) vol. 1, p. 142.
[14] (1844) 11 Cl. & F. 155; see 1 Misc. 11.
[15] [1905] A.C. 468.   [16] *Ibid.*, at p. 470.

1894, two years after taking silk, and continued his practice at the Bar until appointed to the Bench in 1907.

A not dissimilar point arose in relation to the Judicial Committee of the Privy Council. Certain counsel who were Privy Councillors, including Sir John Karslake and Sir Henry James, refused to practise before the Committee because they were members of the Council.[17] Sir John had become a Privy Councillor in 1876, soon after ceasing to be Attorney-General, and Sir Henry (afterwards Lord James of Hereford, and a member of the Committee for Privileges in *Re Lord Kinross*) had become a Privy Councillor in 1885, the year in which he lost office as Attorney-General. It is far from clear whether or not there was ever anything that could be called a settled rule on the subject, but if there was, H. H. Asquith Q.C. (later Prime Minister and Earl of Oxford and Asquith) put an end to it. He was made a Privy Councillor when he became Home Secretary in 1892, and on the change of government in 1895 he returned to practice at the Bar until he again took office in 1905. During those ten years he often appeared before the Judicial Committee [18]; and not even Lord James of Hereford, who in *Re Kinross* opposed the motion that peers should be permitted to practise before the House of Lords, felt able to criticise him for it.[19]

In the Chancery Division, too, times are not what they were. Where today is there a case that will bring forth anything to match the aggregate of talent that in 1924 confronted Russell J. in *Re Northcliffe* [20]? There were Jenkins K.C., G. B. Hurst K.C., and W. P. Spens; W. A. Greene K.C. and Whinney; Maugham K.C. and A. L. Ellis; Preston K.C. and Bryan Farrer; Bennett K.C. and Lionel Cohen; Luxmoore K.C. and Gavin Simonds; W. J. Whittaker; Clauson K.C. and Wilfrid Hunt; Sir James Greig K.C. and Cecil Turner; Courthorpe Wilson K.C. and W. E. Vernon; Sir Malcolm Macnaghten K.C. and J. E. Harman; T. E. Haydon K.C. and H. Jacobs; John

[17] *Ibid.*, at p. 472.   [18] *Ibid.*, at pp. 470, 472; and see at p. 475.
[19] *Ibid.*, at p. 472.
[20] [1924] *The Times*, April 4; and see *London & Globe Finance Corporation Ltd*. v. *Montgomery* (1902) 18 T.L.R. 661.

Beaumont; and Sir Patrick Hastings K.C., A.-G. and Dighton Pollock. In terms of the then present, there were thirteen silks and fourteen juniors; in terms of the then future, there were two L.CC. (Maugham and Simonds), two L.JJ. (Luxmoore and Clauson), two JJ. (Bennett and Macnaghten), one law lord (Cohen), one M.R. and law lord (Greene), and much else also, as, for example, India would testify (Spens and Beaumont). One wonders how room for them all was found. In a heavily documented case in 1971,[1] in which a mere seven silks were engaged, the front row could accommodate only two on each side,[2] and the other three had to sit in junior counsel's row.[3]

Even *Re Northcliffe*[4] fell a little short of the opulence of *London Financial Association* v. *Kelk*,[5] decided forty years earlier. The issue was merely whether the purchase of Alexandra Palace, near London, by a company could be successfully attacked as being *ultra vires*. To resolve this, there appeared before Bacon V.-C. fifteen silks and thirteen juniors, namely, Davey Q.C., Everitt Q.C., Stirling and H. Burton Buckley; Charles Russell Q.C., Crossley Q.C., Edward Beaumont and G. S. Barnes; Sir H. Giffard Q.C., Marten Q.C. and Speed; Rigby Q.C. and Ingle Joyce; Macnaghten Q.C., Davenport and Cunliffe; Sir Farrer Herschell Q.C., S.-G., Romer Q.C. and Northmore Lawrence; Robinson Q.C. and Maidlow; Robson; Millar Q.C., Warmington Q.C. and P. F. S. Stokes; and Edward Clarke Q.C., H. A. Giffard Q.C. and W. B. Heath. In terms of the future, there were two L.CC. (Herschell and Halsbury), one L.C.J. (Russell), four law lords (Davey, Wrenbury,[6] Macnaghten and Robson), three L.JJ. (Stirling, Rigby and Romer) and one J. (Joyce).

Much has been spoken and written about the duty of counsel in a doubtful case. It was Charles I who, before he came to

---

[1] *Carl Zeiss Stiftung* v. *Rayner & Keeler Ltd.* (*No.* 4) [1971] *The Times* April 27, *cor.* Megarry J.
[2] Arnold (now Arnold J.) and Falconer; and Kerr (now Kerr J.) and MacCrindle.
[3] Slade, Harman and Lauterpacht.
[4] *Supra.*   [5] (1884) 26 Ch.D. 107.
[6] Not a Lord of Appeal in Ordinary, but a retired L.J. who had been ennobled, and so was a " Lord of Appeal " within the Appellate Jurisdiction Act, 1876, s. 5; and he sat judicially *in dom. proc.* often enough to have become a law lord by prescription, as it were.

the throne, said that if he had to take a profession, he would not have become a lawyer, because " I cannot," said he, " defend a bad, nor yield in a good cause." Dr. Johnson's comment on this was brief and pointed. " Sir, this is false reasoning; because every cause has a bad side: and a lawyer is not over-come, though the cause which he has endeavoured to support be determined against him." [7]

This comment is in line with Dr. Johnson's well-known views on the ethics of legal practice. Boswell asked him " whether, as a moralist, he did not think that the practice of the law, in some degree, hurt the nice feeling of honesty. JOHNSON: ' Why no, Sir, if you act properly. You are not to deceive your clients with false representations of your opinion; you are not to tell lies to a judge.' BOSWELL: ' But what do you think of supporting a cause which you know to be bad?' JOHNSON: ' Sir, you do not know it to be good or bad till the Judge determines it. I have said that you are to state facts fairly; so that your thinking, or what you call knowing a cause to be bad, must be from reasoning, must be from your suppos-ing your arguments to be weak and inconclusive. But, Sir, that is not enough. An argument which does not convince yourself, may convince the Judge to whom you urge it: and if it does convince him, why then, Sir, you are wrong, and he is right. It is his business to judge; and you are not to be confident in your own opinion that a cause is bad, but to say all you can for your client, and then hear the Judge's opinion.' BOSWELL: ' But, Sir, does not affecting a warmth when you have no warmth, and appearing to be clearly of one opinion when you are in reality of another opinion, does not such dissimulation impair one's honesty? Is there not some danger that a lawyer may put on the same mask in common life, in the intercourse with his friends?' JOHNSON: ' Why no, Sir. Every body knows you are paid for affecting warmth for your client; and it is, there-fore, properly no dissimulation: the moment you come from the bar you resume your usual behaviour. Sir, a man will no more carry the artifice of the bar into the common intercourse of

[7] Boswell's *Johnson*, vol. i, p. 455.

society, than a man who is paid for tumbling upon his hands will continue to tumble upon his hands when he should walk on his feet.' " [8]

Five years later Dr. Johnson expressed himself more fully. It had been suggested that an honest lawyer should never undertake a cause which he was satisfied was not a just one. " Sir," said Dr. Johnson, " a lawyer has no business with the justice or injustice of the cause which he undertakes, unless his client asks his opinion, and then he is bound to give it honestly. The justice or injustice of the cause is to be decided by the judge. Consider, Sir, what is the purpose of courts of justice? It is, that every man may have his cause fairly tried, by men appointed to try causes. A lawyer is not to tell what he knows to be a lie: he is not to produce what he knows to be a false deed; but he is not to usurp the province of the jury and of the judge, and determine what shall be the effect of evidence— what shall be the result of legal argument. As it rarely happens that a man is fit to plead his own cause, lawyers are a class of the community, who, by study and experience, have acquired the art and power of arranging evidence, and of applying to the points at issue what the law has settled. A lawyer is to do for his client all that his client might fairly do for himself, if he could.[9] If, by a superiority of attention, of knowledge, of skill, and a better method of communication, he has the advantage of his adversary, it is an advantage to which he is entitled. There must always be some advantage, on one side or other; and it is better that advantage should be had by talents, than by chance. If lawyers were to undertake no causes till they were sure they were just, a man might be precluded altogether from a trial of his claim, though, were it judicially examined, it might be found a very just claim." [10] As Bramwell B. once succinctly pointed out, " A man's rights are to be determined by the Court, not by his attorney or counsel. It is for want of remembering this that foolish people object to lawyers that they

---

[8] *Ibid.*, at p. 341.
[9] See *Myers* v. *Elman* [1940] A.C. 282 at 316; Megarry, *Lawyer and Litigant in England* (1962) pp. 52, 53.
[10] Boswell's *Hebrides*, p. 212.

will advocate a case against their own opinions. A client is entitled to say to his counsel, I want your advocacy, not your judgment; I prefer that of the Court." [11]

Views have differed on the paramountcy of the client's interests. At a dinner in the Middle Temple Hall on November 8, 1864, given by the Bar of England to the eminent French advocate M. Berryer, Lord Brougham, then aged eighty-six, made a speech. In it he said that the first great quality of an advocate was " to reckon everything subordinate to the interests of his client." Cockburn C.J. also spoke; and he put things right. " The arms which an Advocate wields, he ought to use as a warrior, not as an assassin. He ought to uphold the interests of his clients *per fas*, but not *per nefas*. He ought to know how to reconcile the interests of his client with the eternal interests of truth and justice." [12]

Nearly thirty years later, in 1893, Lord Halsbury referred to Lord Brougham's thesis that an advocate must sacrifice everything to the interests of his client, and then sought to prevent the pendulum swinging too far in the opposite direction. " A thesis has been propounded on the other side more extravagant, and certainly more impossible of fulfilment; that is, that an advocate is bound to convince himself, by something like an original investigation, that his client is in the right before he undertakes the duty of acting for him. I think such a contention ridiculous, impossible of performance, and calculated to lead to great injustice. If an advocate were to reject a story because it seemed improbable to him, he would be usurping the office of the judge, by which I mean the judicial function, whether that function is performed by a single man, or by the composite arrangement of judge and jury which finds favour with us. Very little experience of courts of justice would convince any one that improbable stories are very often true notwithstanding their improbability." [13]

---

[11] *Johnson* v. *Emerson* (1871) L.R. 6 Ex. 329 at 367 (in a judgment which, the court being equally divided (see *post*, p. 145), Bramwell B. subsequently withdrew so as to avoid any difficulty as to an appeal: L.R. 6 Ex. 403n.).

[12] Earl of Selborne, *Memorials, Part I : Family and Personal* (1896), vol. 2, p. 473.

[13] (1899) 15 L.Q.R. 265; and see *post*, p. 98.

Others have expressed similar views. " A counsel's position
is one of the utmost difficulty. He is not to speak of that
which he knows; he is not called upon to consider, whether the
facts with which he is dealing are true or false. What he has
to do, is to argue as best he can, without degrading himself, in
order to maintain the proposition which will carry with it either
the protection or the remedy which he desires for his client. If
amidst the difficulties of his position he were to be called upon
during the heat of his argument to consider whether what he
says is true or false, whether what he says is relevant or
irrelevant, he would have his mind so embarrassed that he could
not do the duty which he is called upon to perform. For,
more than a judge, infinitely more than a witness, he wants
protection on the ground of benefit to the public." [14]

In one case in Pennsylvania counsel was employed by a
private prosecutor to prosecute for forgery. At the hearing, on
the evidence of an unbiased witness, he came to believe the
innocence of the accused, and, against the wishes of his client,
he consented to withdraw the charge. He recovered his fees
from his client, who then called him a thief, robber and cheat;
whereupon counsel sued the client for damages for slander.
The action succeeded and an appeal failed. In the words of
Gibson C.J., " It is a popular, but gross mistake, to suppose that
a lawyer owes no fidelity to any one except his client; and that
the latter is the keeper of his professional conscience. He is
expressly bound by his official oath to behave himself in his
office of attorney with all due fidelity to the court as well as the
client; and he violates it when he consciously presses for an
unjust judgment: much more so when he presses for the
conviction of an innocent man. But the prosecution was
depending before an alderman, to whom, it may be said, the
plaintiff was bound to no such fidelity. Still he was bound by
those obligations which, without oaths, rest upon all men. The
high and honourable office of a counsel would be degraded to
that of a mercenary, were he compelled to do the biddings of
his client against the dictates of his conscience. The origin of

[14] *Munster* v. *Lamb* (1883) 11 Q.B.D. 588 at 603, *per* Brett M.R.

the name proves the client to be subordinate to his counsel as his patron." [15] As was once said by Pollock C.B., " When I was at the bar . . . I always said, I will be my client's advocate, not his agent. To hire himself to any particular course, is a position in which no member of the profession ought to place himself." [16]

The views of Lord Langdale M.R. were similar. " With respect to the task, which I may be considered to have imposed upon counsel, I wish to observe that it arises from the confidence which long experience induces me to repose in them, and from a sense which I entertain of the truly honourable and important services which they constantly perform as ministers of justice, acting in aid of the judge before whom they practise. No counsel supposes himself to be the mere advocate or agent of his client, to gain a victory, if he can, on a particular occasion. The zeal and arguments of every counsel, knowing what is due to himself and his honourable profession, are qualified not only by considerations affecting his own character as a man of honour, experience, and learning, but also by considerations affecting the general interests of justice. It is to these considerations that I apply myself; and I am far from thinking that any counsel who attends here will knowingly violate, or silently permit to be violated, any established rule of the Court to promote the purposes of any client, or refuse to afford me the assistance which I ask in these cases." [17]

An additional burden lies on prosecuting counsel. Thus an attorney appearing for the United States " is the representative not of an ordinary party to a controversy, but of a sovereignty whose obligation to govern impartially is as compelling as its obligation to govern at all; and whose interest, therefore, in a criminal prosecution is not that it shall win a case, but that justice shall be done. As such, he is in a peculiar and very definite sense the servant of the law, the twofold aim of which is that guilt shall not escape or innocence suffer. He may prosecute with earnestness and vigor—indeed, he should do so.

[15] *Rush* v. *Cavenaugh*, 2 Pa. 187 at 189 (1845).
[16] *Swinfen* v. *Lord Chelmsford* (1860) 2 L.T. 406 at 411.
[17] *Hutchinson* v. *Stephens* (1837) 1 Keen 659 at 668.

But, while he may strike hard blows, he is not at liberty to strike foul ones. It is as much his duty to refrain from improper methods calculated to produce a wrongful conviction as it is to use every legitimate means to bring about a just one." [18]   The attorney in question had been " guilty of misstating the facts in his cross-examination of witnesses; of putting into the mouths of such witnesses things which they had not said; of suggesting by his questions that statements had been made to him personally out of court, in respect of which no proof was offered; of pretending to understand that a witness had said something which he had not said and persistently cross-examining the witness upon that basis; of assuming prejudicial facts not in evidence; of bullying and arguing with witnesses; and in general, of conducting himself in a thoroughly indecorous and improper manner." [19]   Not surprisingly, a new trial was ordered.

It was Erskine who laid down, once for all time, the duty of counsel towards those who seek his aid. In his memorable speech for the defence at the trial of Thomas Paine, he said " I will for ever, at all hazards, assert the dignity, independence, and integrity of the English bar; without which, impartial justice, the most valuable part of the English constitution, can have no existence.—From the moment that any advocate can be permitted to say, that he *will* or will *not* stand between the Crown and the subject arraigned in the court where he daily sits to practise, from that moment the liberties of England are at an end.—If the advocate refuses to defend, from what *he may think* of the charge or of the defence, he assumes the character of the judge; nay, he assumes it before the hour of judgment; and in proportion to his rank and reputation, puts the heavy influence of perhaps a mistaken opinion into the scale against the accused, in whose favour the benevolent principle of English law makes all presumptions, and which commands the very judge to be his counsel." [20]

Some courts have carried the duties of counsel to considerable lengths. The Supreme Court of Tennessee once indicated that

[18] *Berger* v. *United States*, 295 U.S. 78 at 88 (1935), *per* Sutherland J.
[19] *Ibid.*, at p. 84, *per* Sutherland J.
[20] *R.* v. *Paine* (1792) 22 St.Tr. 357 at 412.

39

there were cases in which it might be the duty of counsel, as
part of his forensic display, to weep in court. The action was
one for seduction under promise of marriage, and the plaintiff
succeeded. The defendant then appealed, alleging many
grounds of error in the conduct of the trial. On some of these
the defendant succeeded in obtaining a new trial; but others
failed. Thus "It is further assigned as error that plaintiff's
counsel, in his closing argument, called defendant hard names,
such as ' villain,' ' scoundrel,' ' fiend,' ' hell hound,' etc., which,
it is alleged, was calculated to prejudice defendant before the
jury. It must be admitted these are rather harsh terms, and
other language could have been used, no doubt, equally as
descriptive, and not so vituperative; but it does not appear that
defendant asked the court to interpose, and we cannot put the
trial judge in error under these circumstances." [1]

The most important point, however, was that of counsel's
tears. "It is next assigned as error that counsel for plaintiff,
in his closing argument, in the midst of a very eloquent and
impassioned appeal to the jury, shed tears, and unduly excited
the sympathies of the jury in favor of the plaintiff, and greatly
prejudiced them against defendant. Bearing upon this assignment of error we have been cited to [2] no authority, and after
diligent search we have been able to find none ourselves. The
conduct of counsel in presenting their cases to juries is a matter
which must be left largely to the ethics of the profession and
the discretion of the trial judge. Perhaps no two counsel observe
the same rules in presenting their cases to the jury. Some deal
wholly in logic,—argument without embellishments of any
kind. Others use rhetoric, and occasional flights of fancy and
imagination. Others employ only noise and gesticulation, relying upon their earnestness and vehemence instead of logic and
rhetoric. Others appeal to the sympathies—it may be the
passions and peculiarities—of the jurors. Others combine all
these with variations and accompaniments of different kinds.

" No cast-iron rule can or should be laid down. Tears have

[1] *Ferguson* v. *Moore*, 39 S.W. 341 at 342 (1897), *per* Wilkes J.
[2] *Sic*.

always been considered legitimate arguments before a jury, and, while the question has never arisen out of any such behavior in this court, we know of no rule or jurisdiction in the court below to check them. It would appear to be one of the natural rights of counsel which no court or constitution could take away. It is certainly, if no more, a matter of the highest personal privilege. Indeed, if counsel has them at command, it may be seriously questioned whether it is not his professional duty to shed them whenever proper occasion arises, and the trial judge would not feel constrained to interfere unless they were indulged in to such excess as to impede or delay the business of the court. This must be left largely to the discretion of the trial judge, who has all the counsel and parties before him, and can see their demeanor as well as the demeanor of the jury. In this case the trial judge was not asked to check the tears, and it was, we think, an eminently proper occasion for their use, and we cannot reverse for this." [3]

The traditional account of the way in which lawyers acquired their patron saint was given nearly three centuries ago by William Carr. He recounted " a story I mett with when I lived in *Rome*, goeing with a Romane to see some *Antiquityes*, he shewed me a Chapell dedicated to one St. *Evona* a Lawyer of *Brittanie* who he said came to *Rome* to Entreat the *Pope* to give the *Lawyers* of *Brittanie* a *Patron*, to which the Pope replyed that he knew of no *Saint* but what was disposed of to other Professions, at which *Evona* was very sad and earnestly begd of the *Pope* to think of one for them: At the last the *Pope* proposed to St. *Evona* that he should goe round the Church of St. *John* de *Latera* blind fould, and after he had said so many Ave *Marias*, that the first *Saint* he layd hold of, should be his *Patron*, which the good old *Lawyer* willingly undertook, and at the end of his Ave Maryes, he stopt at St. *Michels* Altar, where he layd hold of the *Divell*, under St. Michels feet, and cryd out, this is our Saint, let him be our *Patron*, so beeing unblindfolded and seeing what a *Patron* he had chosen, he went

[3] *Ferguson* v. *Moore*, *supra*, at p. 343, *per* Wilkes J. I have subdivided the text.

to his Lodgings so dejected, that in a few moneths after he die'd and coming to *heavens Gates* knockt hard, whereupon St. *Peoter* asked who it was that knockt so bouldly, he replyed, that he was St. *Evona* the *Advocate*, Away, away said St. *Peter* here is but one *Advocate* in *heaven*, here is no roome for you *Lawyers*, O but said St. *Evona*, I am that honest lawyer who never tooke fees on both sides, or ever pleaded in a bad Cause, nor did I ever set my Naibours together by the Eares, or lived by the sins of the people; well then said St. *Peter*, come in; This newes comeing downe to *Rome* a witty Poet writ upon St. *Evonas* Tomb these words: St. *Evona* un *Briton, Advocat non Larron, Haleluiah.*" [4]

4 William Carr, *Remarks of the Government of Several Parts of Germanie, Denmark, Sweedland, Hamburg, Lubeck, and Hansiatique Townes, but more particularly of the United Provinces, with some few directions how to Travell in the States Dominions* (1688) p. 80.

An Exuberance of Sympathy

HISTORY does not always exemplify the justly high repute in which the solicitors' branch of the legal profession stands today. Times have indeed changed. In 1455 Parliament laid down that thenceforward there should be no more than six common attorneys in Norfolk, six in Suffolk, and two in Norwich, to be "elected and admitted by the Two Chief Justices of our Lord the King for the Time being, of the most sufficient and best instructed, by their Discretions."[1] The reason for this enactment appears in the preamble. "Whereas of Time not long past within the City of Norwich, and the Counties of Norfolk and Suffolk, there were no more but six or eight Attornies at the most, coming to the King's Courts, in which Time great Tranquillity reigned in the said City and Counties, and little Trouble or Vexation was made by untrue or foreign Suits; And now so it is, that in the said City and Counties there be Fourscore Attornies, or more, the more Part of them having no other Thing to live upon, but only his Gain by the Practice of Attorneyship, and also the more part of them not being of sufficient Knowledge to be an Attorney, which come to every Fair, Market, and other Places, where is any Assembly of People, exhorting, procuring, moving, and inciting the People to attempt untrue and foreign Suits, for small Trespasses, little Offences, and small Sums of Debt, whose Actions be triable and determinable in Court Barons; whereby proceed many Suits, more of evil Will and Malice, than of the Truth of the Thing, to manifold Vexation and no little Damage of the Inhabitants of the said City and Counties, and also to the perpetual Diminution of all the Court Barons in the said Counties, unless convenient Remedy be provided in this Behalf."[2]

Of this Act, Barrington bitingly observed that the ignorance

[1] 33 Hen. 6, c. 7, 1455.
[2] Ibid.

43

of the Parliament that passed the Act " far exceeded that of the attornies complained against." ³ The Act prescribed a penalty of £20 for each conviction of any person presuming to act as an attorney in courts of record in Norfolk, Suffolk or Norwich, divisible equally between the Crown and any common informer. According to the *Law Lists*, in Norwich alone there were thirty-three attorneys in 1789 and sixty-seven in 1842,⁴ so that when at last in 1843 the Act was repealed ⁵ the lawless lawyers of East Anglia were delivered from a peril that, despite the fall in the value of money over nearly four centuries, might well have greatly enriched a common informer.

Early in the seventeenth century, William Hudson, in writing of the Star Chamber, referred to Egerton L.K., and proceeded " In our age there are stepped up a new sort of people called solicitors, unknown to the records of the law, who, like the grasshoppers of Egypt, devour the whole land; and these I dare say (being authorised by the opinion of the most reverend and learned lord chancellor that ever was before him) were express maintainers, and could not justify their maintenance upon any action brought: I mean not where a lord or a gentleman employed his servant to solicit his cause, for he may justify his doing thereof; but I mean those which are common solicitors of causes, and set up a new profession, not being allowed in any court, or at least not in this court, where they follow causes; and these are the retainers of causes, and devourers of men's estates by contention, and prolonging suits to make them without end." ⁶

Abbreviations in a solicitor's bill of costs have sometimes caused much trouble. An Act of 1729 required the bill to be " written in a common legible Hand, and in the English Tongue (except Law Terms and Names of Writs) and in Words at

---

³ Daines Barrington, *Observations on the More Ancient Statutes* (5th ed. 1796) p. 414.
⁴ See *Law List*, 1789, p. 99; *Law List*, 1842, p. 311.
⁵ By the Solicitors Act, 1843, s. 1, Sched. I, Pt. I.
⁶ W. Hudson, *A Treatise of the Court of Star Chamber*, 2 *Collectanea Juridica* (1792) 1 at 94. Hudson's son gave a manuscript copy of the book to Finch L.K. in 1635: see *ibid.*, p. 1, cited by Lord Mansfield C.J. in *R. v. Wilkes* (1770) 4 Burr. 2527 at 2554.

length (except Times and Sums) " [7]; but an amending Act of 1739 permitted the use of " such Abbreviations as are now commonly used in the English Language." [8] In 1811 this puzzled the Court of Common Pleas. The bill in question used abbreviations such as " fo.," " &," " &c.," " Lres &c.," " Pd.," " Serjt." and " Atty.," and Mansfield C.J. observed that " many of the words in the bill are not common in the English language: they never occur but in attornies' bill, and in books of practice. I really do not know what the act means." [9] But the other members of the court considered the abbreviations to be very common, and intelligible to any professional man, and in the upshot the objections to the bill failed.

It was a retired solicitor in Chancery,[10] one Edwards, who achieved a deserved immortality by saying to Dr. Johnson, " You are a philosopher, Dr. Johnson. I have tried too in my time to be a philosopher; but, I don't know how, cheerfulness was always breaking in." [11] Johnson was not unappreciative. " You are a lawyer, Mr. Edwards. Lawyers know life practically. A bookish man should always have them to converse with. They have what he wants." [12] However, all was not sweetness. Upon inquiry being made as to a man who had just left, Dr. Johnson once observed, " I do not care to speak ill of any man behind his back, but I believe the gentleman is an attorney." [13]

In Ireland there was a recognised practice whereby the motion list before a judge was called twice. On the first calling a solicitor whose counsel was not available could rise in his place and say " Second calling, if your Lordship pleases "; and the case would then automatically be heard on the second calling. This practice came a little obliquely into a case concerning the liability of certain members of a local authority under a surcharge made upon them by the district auditor.

---

[7] 2 Geo. 2, c. 23, 1729, s. 23.
[8] 12 Geo. 2, c. 13, 1739, s. 5.
[9] *Reynolds, Gent., one, &c.,* v. *Caswell* (1811) 4 Taunt. 193 at 194.
[10] Boswell's *Johnson*, vol. 2, p. 305.
[11] *Ibid.*, p. 307.
[12] *Ibid.*
[13] *Ibid.*, vol. 1, p. 396 (with the *oratio obliqua* transposed into *oratio recta*).

The surcharge was made for authorising the payment of certain
annuities charged upon property which, but for the gross delay
of the local authority's solicitor, would long before have been
transferred to another local authority. It was held that the
auditor (for whom Healy K.C. was counsel) was not justified
in making the surcharge. In so deciding, Dodd J. observed
that " the Council was in a position of almost as great embarrassment as the auditor. The situation was not of their making.
They got over this burden from a previous Board. They also
got over the solicitor who had taken the initial proceedings.
Mr. Healy says there has been delay from 1886. Short of
actually dismissing the solicitor, the Council did everything they
could to get the duty of having these cottages transferred to the
Urban District Council carried out. The auditor exhausted
remonstrance with the Council. The Council exhausted remonstrance with their solicitor. The work was not a work that
could be done save through a solicitor. The embarrassment has
been caused to auditor and Council alike by the deplorable
inactivity of the solicitor, with reference to which I shall not
say another word, as he is not formally before the Court.

"I may, however, perhaps, be pardoned if I preserve here
what may give a value and interest to my judgment which of
itself it would lack. I refer to Mr. Healy's answer to the
question of the Lord Chief Justice:—' What kind of a man
would you say, Mr. Healy, this solicitor was? ' The reply was
as prompt as it was bright—' The kind of man, my Lord, that
when the last trumpet sounds would wake up and mutter,
" Second calling." ' " [14]

As is well known, solicitors exercise to a considerable degree
their right of audience in chambers in the High Court, both
before masters and judges. But not everyone could at once
explain the circumstances in which a solicitor could exercise a
personal right of audience in open court in the High Court or

[14] *R. (Butler)* v. *Browne* [1909] 2 I.R. 333 at 351. M. Healy, *The Old Munster
Circuit* (1939) p. 255, attributes the case to a court composed of Palles C.B.,
Dodd J. and an unnamed third judge; in fact, the court consisted of Lord
O'Brien C.J., and Madden, Wright and Dodd JJ. The language, too, is
different; but the spirit is the same.

at Assizes, or address the House of Lords. For the High Court, the answer is " In bankruptcy," and this is so even if the court is a Divisional Court hearing an appeal from the county court [15]; for statute has conferred and preserved this right of audience,[16] though it does not extend to the Court of Appeal, which is no part of the High Court.[17] For Assizes, the answer was " By leave of the judge, in the absence of counsel " [18]; and perhaps the same applies to ordinary cases in the High Court.[19] If any counsel objected to a solicitor being heard in such cases, it has been suggested that the objection would be unanswerable, for only Parliament can take away the Bar's exclusive right of audience.[20] For the House of Lords, the answer is " Before the Appeal Committee." [1]

Affidavits live in a world of their own. It is now well settled that in various interlocutory and procedural matters, an affidavit may be used even if it is sworn by a person who deposes not from his own knowledge, but from information received by him which he believes to be true, so that on the strict rules of evidence it is mere hearsay, and thus inadmissible. Gainsford Bruce Q.C. once launched a frontal attack on the operation of this rule in the sphere of garnishee proceedings. He attempted to persuade the House of Lords that the rule led to much inconvenience, and was apt to introduce a dangerous practice. In illustration, he said " Knight Bruce L.J.[2] is reported to have said that every well-managed firm [of solicitors] in Lincoln's Inn had two clerks; an informing clerk and a believing clerk; it was the duty of the informing clerk to be

---

[15] *Ex p. Reynolds* (1885) 15 Q.B.D. 169.

[16] Bankruptcy Act, 1883, s. 151; Bankruptcy Act, 1914, s. 152; and see *Re A Debtor* [1934] Ch. 280 at 286; *Re Eichholz* [1959] *The Times* Feb. 17.

[17] *Re Elderton* (1887) 4 Mor. 36.

[18] *Doxford & Sons Ltd.* v. *Sea Shipping Co. Ltd.* (1897) 14 T.L.R. 111 (Bruce J.).

[19] See *Butterworth* v. *Butterworth* (1913) 57 S.J. 266 (Evans P.: solicitor but not solicitor's unadmitted clerk); (1883) 18 L.J.News. 617 (Smith J.); and contrast (1885) 78 L.T.News. 286 (Stephen J.). It does not appear whether these cases were on Assizes or in the High Court.

[20] See (1883) 18 L.J.News. 617.

[1] See *House of Lords Directions as to Procedure, 1971*, 1 (iii), 30 (i); and see. *e.g.*, *Leather* v. *Kirby* [1965] 1 W.L.R. 1489 (settlement).

[2] Unrelated to Bruce Q.C. (afterwards Bruce J.).

informed of whatever might be to the advantage of the firm's clients, and of the believing clerk to believe it." [3]   But even this did not impress their Lordships, and the rule stood affirmed.[4]

A solicitor's close identification with the interests of his client has long been traditional.   In 1773 it was even argued that " The connection between attorney and client is considered in law, as nearer than that between baron and feme; the former being considered only as one single person; the latter, as two souls in one flesh." [5]   Ninety years later this contention struck a responsive judicial chord across the Atlantic.   " Although it is not necessary to adopt this argument literally, it is, however, a very forcible illustration, and conveys a not unapt idea of the identity of attorney and client." [6]

The extent to which a client may rely upon his solicitor is illustrated by a transaction which took place shortly before the war of 1939.   A wealthy Austrian who had some bearer bonds of the Bank of England wished to put them out of the reach of the Germans.   He dared not risk sending them out of the country, and so he arranged for two English solicitors of high repute in the City of London to meet him in a room in a hotel in Vienna.   There he produced the bonds to them, and bade them take careful note of the values and contents of all the bonds.   As soon as they had done this, he told them to watch him carefully. He then rose from his chair, and one by one put all the bonds on the fire.   When the bonds had all been consumed, he asked the astonished solicitors to return to London and inform the Bank of England of what they had seen.   All, he said, had been arranged; as soon as the solicitors had made a statutory declaration that the bonds had been destroyed, the Bank would issue a new set to replace them, and these would never come to Austria.[7]

Nevertheless, there are limits to the duties of a solicitor

---

[3] *Vinall* v. *De Pass* [1892] A.C. 90 at 92.
[4] *Vinall* v. *De Pass* [1892] A.C. 90.
[5] *Barker* v. *Braham* (1773) 3 Wils.K.B. 368 at 374, *per* Serjeant Sayer.   For the unity of man and wife, see *post*, p. 220.
[6] *Sweetnam* v. *Lemon* (1863) 13 U.C.C.P. 534 at 547, *per* Adam Wilson J.
[7] See Sir William Ball, *Lincoln's Inn* (1947) p. 195.

towards his client. As Hannen J.O. once said in the Divorce
Court, " It would be in the highest degree prejudicial to the
interests of the women who are litigants in this Court to cast
upon the attorneys whom they consult the dangerous responsibility of coming to a conclusion in doubtful cases as to what
is likely to be the finding of the Court upon the facts submitted
to them." [8] Some years later, as President of the Probate
Divorce and Admiralty Division, he said " It would be impossible to ascertain in what cases the solicitor has become aware
that his client was guilty; or at what stage of the proceedings
he may have acquired that knowledge. Nor do I think that a
solicitor, as soon as he discovers that the wife cannot deny the
charge made against her, is bound to abandon her. If he did
so, it would cause her to seek the assistance of some less
scrupulous adviser. There is an honourable way of defending
the worst of cases." [9]

There have, of course, been things which ought not to have
been. In 1673 it was established that one Simon Mason, an
attorney, " had been an *ambidexter, viz.* after he was retained
by one side he was retained on the other side; and for this he
was committed to the Fleet, and turned out of the roll." [10]
Again, when judgment has been given against a litigant who is
over forty years old, it is obviously imprudent for his attorney
to conduct proceedings on a writ of error founded on the
allegation that the litigant is an infant.[11] So also " If an
attorney in the country, of standing, experience, and influence,
will set such an example to the younger members of his profession, and exhibit such a spectacle to the world, as that of
buying property which he is employed to sell; of so dealing,
especially in the case of a client, who is a youth in the position
of a small farmer—to say nothing of putting up an infant's
landed estate for sale by auction, and that without apprising the
public of the fact of the minority—such an attorney must not
be overpowered with surprise, or expect to meet an exuberance

[8] *Flower* v. *Flower* (1873) L.R. 3 P. & D. 132 at 134.
[9] *Smith* v. *Smith* (1882) 7 P.D. 84 at 89.
[10] *Simon Mason's Case* (1673) 1 Free.K.B. 74.
[11] See *Pierce* v. *Blake* (1696) 2 Salk. 515 at 516, *per* Holt C.J.

of sympathy, if he shall find his motives and conduct harshly construed and described roughly." [12]

Once where a firm of solicitors was held personally liable for the increased costs resulting from their improper conduct of a case, it was sought to defend them by the argument that they had relied upon the views of the appropriate Area Committee under the Legal Aid Scheme. Sachs J. gave this contention short shrift. "For a number of generations solicitors have been given special and indeed generous cover when they obtain the advice of properly instructed counsel. It is in my view neither necessary from the professional angle nor permissible in principle to provide a proliferation of further umbrellas." [13]

Espinasse, the reporter,[14] records that an *ex parte* complaint was once made to Lord Kenyon C.J. against Mr. Lawless, an honourable attorney, for some alleged misconduct. Lord Kenyon not only said " Take a rule to show cause," which was entirely proper and would give the attorney an opportunity of answering the allegations, but also added " And let Mr. Lawless be suspended from practising until the rule is disposed of." Mr. Lawless "happened to be present in court when this unexampled judgment was pronounced, and heard the sentence which led to his ruin; he rose in a state of most bitter agitation: ' My lord, I entreat you to recall that judgment—the charge is wholly unfounded—suspension will lead to my ruin—I have eighty causes now in my office.' What was Lord Kenyon's reply to this supplicatory appeal to him? ' So much the worse for your clients, who have employed such a man! You shall remain suspended until the court decides on the rule.' " When the rule was heard, " the charges against him were found to be wholly without foundation, and the rule against him was accordingly discharged. Mr. Lawless was in consequence restored to his profession "; but he " sunk under the unmerited

---

[12] *Salmon* v. *Cutts* (1850) 4 De G. & Sm. 125 at 128, *per* Knight Bruce V.-C.

[13] *Edwards* v. *Edwards* [1958] P. 235 at 238.

[14] The articles in *Fraser's Magazine* are anonymous (" a Retired Barrister "). But internal evidence indicates Espinasse (see vol. 6, pp. 315, 317; vol. 7, pp. 48, 52); and W. C. Townsend, *Lives of Twelve Eminent Judges* (1846) vol. 1, p. 3, names him as the author.

disgrace, and died of a broken heart." [15]   This story appears to justify the comment that " it may be fairly suspected that there is a great exaggeration in this narrative " [16]; yet one of Lord Kenyon's successors in office, Lord Campbell, uncritically repeats it as if it were undoubted fact.[17]

The dissolution of partnership is a misfortune that afflicts firms of solicitors in common with other professional or business partnerships.   Those who feel that such events are accomplished without sufficient pomp and circumstance may be comforted by an unauthorised but felicitous liturgical pleasantry composed for the dissolution in 1922 of the firm of Messieurs Hunter & Haynes.

" *Order of Service Authorized to be said on the* DISSOLUTION *of Messrs. Hunter & Haynes.*

On the appointed day the Minister, wearing a clean linen surplice, and accompanied by Mrs. Pennington-Bickford,[18] *shall call at 9 New Square, Lincoln's Inn, and shall say in an audible voice the words here following* : —

COLLECT :

O Lord, for as much as it pleased Thee in times past to join together these thy servants, Robert Lewin Hunter & Edmund Sidney Pollock Haynes, in a remarkable manner, let it now please Thee to put them lawfully and irremediably asunder, that forsaking one another they may simultaneously and severally work for their own advancement, and as their union has been singularly fruitless grant that their disconnexion may be rich with increase, and let them avoid all recrimination, neither turning to other (except in certified sickness) so long as they both shall live, according to the promises distinctly conveyed to our forefathers Abraham and Lot in the Holy Scriptures.

AMEN.

---

[15] " My Contemporaries : From the Note-Book of a Retired Barrister " (1832) 6 *Fraser's Magazine* 422.
[16] Townsend, *supra*, at p. 65.
[17] 3 Camp.C.JJ. 84.
[18] Mr. Pennington-Bickford was the Rector of St. Clement Danes.

HYMN

(*by Louie Pennington-Bickford; music by the Reverend W. Pennington-Bickford*)

<blockquote>
mf Children of Saint Clement Danes

ff Pray for Hunter *dim* pray for Haynes.

cr Doubt of what may be in store

mf Makes us pray for Haynes the more.

      And as nothing else will rhyme

f Pray for Hunter *ff* all the time.

Haynes and Hunter in the past

Made a pact that could not last;

In the ordinary course

p Hunter claims a quick divorce;

      All's arranged behind the scenes.

f No King's Proctor *ff* intervenes.

Orange sweet and lemon sour

Lay before them in this hour,

Wherein symbolised we see

f Incompatibility.

      Lest this prove a time of loss

p Grant them, Master, thy divorce.   Amen.
</blockquote>

At this point oranges and/or lemons will be distributed among the clerks of the dissolving partners. Hunter & Haynes will then be taken to the Old Roman Bath in Strand Lane and partially immersed.

A Collection will then be made.

Hunter & Haynes will be dried and conducted to their several offices where they will proceed to DISSOLVE." [19]

---

[19] *A Lawyer's Notebook* (1932) p. 162. The author of the book, though anonymous, is believed to have been E. S. P. Haynes; he attributes the parody printed above to Charles Scott-Moncrieff (*ibid.*, p. 161).

A Unanimous Dissent

LIKE all human endeavour, the judicial process is subject always to the paramount claims of death. Thus Fraser J. died in the night while he was engaged in a jury action at Assizes, and Acton J. was sent down to complete the hearing. At the request of the parties, he read the shorthand notes of the hearing before Fraser J., and continued the trial with the same jury, without recalling the witnesses who had given their evidence. Subsequently there was an appeal on a point of law, and this succeeded. On the issue of Acton J. continuing the trial, Scrutton L.J. observed that although it was unnecessary to take objection to what had occurred, " I think it is a precedent which should not be followed in future. I doubt whether a judge has any jurisdiction to continue the hearing of a case in which witnesses have been called in Court in the course of the trial before the jury and another judge. . . ." [1]

Where there is no jury, the case might be thought to be *a fortiori*; for a decision made by a judge who has not seen or heard some of the witnesses might well seem more vulnerable than one made by a jury which has seen and heard them all. Yet the view taken by Scrutton L.J. is often inconvenient, and both litigants and courts have contrived to escape it. Thus, sitting in the Railway and Canal Commission after the death of Salter J., MacKinnon J. declined to apply the dictum to a non-jury case in which, although some witnesses had been heard, no conflict of evidence had arisen.[2] And a similar course, accompanied by a similar warning, was taken in a matrimonial case which had been begun before one metropolitan magistrate and, after his death, concluded before another, despite a direct conflict of evidence, on the ground that the case was " so clear." [3] So also in Admiralty when

[1] *Coleshill* v. *Manchester Corporation* [1928] 1 K.B. 776 at 786.
[2] *Re Application of British Reinforced Concrete Engineering Co. Ltd.* (1929) 45 T.L.R. 186 at 187.
[3] *Bolton* v. *Bolton* [1949] 2 All E.R. 908 at 911.

Langton J. died. In two cases the litigants had to begin afresh, but they agreed that the evidence which had been given before Langton J. should be treated as evidence in the new trial.[4] In one case they also agreed that the trial judge should have the benefit of any comments about the witnesses which Langton J. might have made in his notebook; and there was one such comment (" A very good witness, clear and alert, also very fair ").[5] Indeed, although the words of Scrutton L.J. have at least twice been applied by a Divisional Court of the Probate, Divorce and Admiralty Division in relation to magistrates' courts,[6] it is perhaps not unfair to say that they have been distinguished with more zest than they have been followed.[7]

In Scotland, Lord Murray died after reserving judgment in a divorce case. He had left a draft judgment, but it was impossible to tell whether this expressed his final view of the case.[8] In the end it was held that the proper course to take was for another judge to hear argument on the evidence that had been given, and to decide the case himself, with power to refer to Lord Murray's notes and his draft judgment, though only for the limited purpose of ascertaining the judge's view of the credibility of the witnesses.[9]

The difficulty of ascertaining whether a written judgment represents the judge's final views will not normally apply where the judge has not died but has merely resigned; and in one such case, after the retirement of Hill J., his reserved judgment was, by consent, read by Lord Merrivale P.[10] During an illness of Collingwood J., too, Sir Jocelyn Simon P. followed a similar

---

[4] *The Hopemount* (1943) 75 Ll.L.R. 94 at 96; *H.M.S. Vanity* (1946) 79 Ll.L.R. 594 at 597.   [5] *The Hopemount, supra*, at p. 96.
[6] *Fulker* v. *Fulker* [1936] 3 All E.R. 636; *Whittle* v. *Whittle* [1939] 1 All E.R. 374.
[7] See *The Forest Lake* [1968] P. 270, in which the two cases in the last footnote do not seem to have been cited.
[8] For this reason, at least one judge of the Chancery Division has given his clerk written instructions that any draft judgment of his represents his final view if it is initialled and dated by him, but not otherwise.
[9] *Ferguson* v. *Ferguson*, 1936 S.C. 808.
[10] *Hallam* v. *Hallam* (1930) 47 T.L.R. 207; and see *Re Leslie* (1883) 23 Ch.D. 552 at 559, where Pearson J. adopted as his own the judgment of Fry J., who had become L.J. In Ontario, the Judicature Act (c. 228), s. 11 allows eight weeks for giving judgment to a judge who has resigned or ceased to hold office from age or has been appointed to another court.

course [11]; and when Lord Westbury L.C. resigned after hearing argument but before giving judgment, a " written judgment... was afterwards given by his Lordship to the parties." [12] In Ireland, the Court of Appeal once reserved judgment for over a year, and during that period O'Brien L.C., who had presided at the hearing, resigned and became Lord Shandon. He then sent a letter giving his reasons for allowing the appeal, and the parties agreed to accept this as his judgment. However, it became a mere dissent, for Ronan L.J. and Molony L.J. (who had become Molony L.C.J.) concurred in affirming the judgment below. [13]

A somewhat surprising latitude has been held to exist in criminal cases. One man was convicted at quarter sessions before a Recorder who postponed sentence and then died. The accused appealed against the conviction, and the question was raised whether there was any jurisdiction to pass sentence. The Court of Criminal Appeal adjourned the appeal for a rehearing before five judges, [14] and on the rehearing held that the Recorder's successor was entitled to pass sentence at the next quarter sessions, after a shorthand note of the trial had been supplied to him and he had given the accused an opportunity of being heard. [15]

Similar questions have arisen on cases stated. What, for example, if an income tax appeal is heard and decided by two special commissioners (a quorum being two), but then one of them dies before a case can be stated; is it competent for the survivor alone to state a case? Macnaghten J. found no difficulty in answering " Yes " to this question, [16] and the Court of Appeal made it plain that at least an appellant who had founded an appeal on such a case stated was in no position to question its validity. [17] The death of one of three justices of the

---

[11] *Allen* v. *Allen* [1962] *The Times* April 19; 106 S.J. 374.

[12] *Goold* v. *Great Western Deep Coal Co.* (1865) 2 De G.J. & S. 600.

[13] *Frost* v. *R.* [1919] 1 I.R. 81.

[14] *R.* v. *Pepper* (1921) 16 Cr.App.R. 10.

[15] *R.* v. *Pepper* [1921] 3 K.B. 167; 16 Cr.App.R. 12.

[16] *Norman* v. *Golder* [1944] 1 All E.R. 632; 26 T.C. 293 at 297.

[17] *Norman* v. *Golder* [1945] 1 All E.R. 352; 26 T.C. 293 at 299.   See also *ante*, p. 16; *post*, p. 109.

The Path of the Law

peace after deciding a case has likewise been held to be no objection to the validity of a case stated by the two survivors.[18] As Shearman J. said, "Justices come and go, but justice itself should endure. I see no reason to uphold an objection which would result in justice coming to an end owing to the death of a magistrate because s. 2 of the Summary Jurisdiction Act, 1857, is worded as it is. This sort of objection ought to be as extinct as the thumbscrew." [19] This approach may be contrasted with a nineteenth-century decision that if a judge died before he had sealed a bill of exceptions, none of his brethren could seal it for him, and the right to proceed on the bill died with the judge.[20]

Appellate tribunals, too, have been assailed by problems of this sort. Sometimes the quorum has been impaired. Thus one case in the House of Lords was argued before the Earl of Halsbury L.C., Lord Macnaghten and Lord Ludlow (better known as Lopes L.J.), who provided the necessary quorum of three; and Lord Ludlow died without leaving a written opinion. This difficulty was met by having the case reargued, this time before the two survivors and Lords Morris, Shand, Davey and James of Hereford [1]; double the number, and there must be ample reserves against possible disaster.

A few years later the Court of Appeal (where again the quorum is normally three) was more fortunate, for Kennedy L.J. had left a written judgment; Lord Cozens-Hardy M.R. and Warrington J., the other members of the court, agreed that this should be taken as the judgment of the court, and so it was. However, "to regularize this procedure, we propose that the judgment should be dated January 16, the day before Kennedy L.J.'s death." [2] Oddly enough, when Kennedy L.J. had been a judge of first instance, and had once reserved judgment over the Long Vacation, the parties had prudently concurred in insuring his life for a sum sufficient to cover the costs that

18 *Marsland* v. *Taggart* [1928] 2 K.B. 447.
19 *Ibid.*, at p. 450.
20 *Newton* v. *Boodle* (1847) 3 C.B. 795 (where, however, a rule nisi for a new trial was granted).
1 *Wyman* v. *Paterson* [1900] A.C. 271.
2 *Polurrian Steamship Co. Ltd.* v. *Young* [1915] 1 K.B. 922 at 927, *per* Lord Cozens-Hardy M.R.

would be thrown away if he died without delivering his judgment.[3]

Such expedients, however, are unnecessary where death has not deprived the court of its quorum. In the old Court of Appeal in Chancery, Lord Cairns L.J. was able to give judgment in a case which he and Turner L.J. had heard, even though Turner L.J. had died in the interval: for the relevant statute[4] made this possible.[5] In the House of Lords, the former practice was for one of the law lords simply to read any judgment which had been left by one of his brethren who had died between hearing and judgment. This was done in 1861 by Lord Brougham for Lord Campbell L.C.[6] and in 1899 by Lord Shand for Lord Herschell.[7] In more recent years, the practice seems to have been somewhat less forthright. Thus in 1954 Lord Normand adopted " as my own " a draft speech or judgment left by the late Viscount Simon[8]; and in 1962 Lord Hodson added to his own speech the speech of Lord Merriman,[9] who had died that morning.[10] More recently, the deceased law lord's speech has simply been published after a few prefatory words by the presiding law lord, such as that " the late Lord Donovan's opinion is now in print." [11] On Lord Upjohn's death in 1971 the situation in one case was potentially more precarious; his four brethren were equally divided, so that had he lived his would have been the casting vote. However, the speech that he had prepared was in favour of dismissing the appeal, and so, under the rule that in the case of an equal division the appeal fails, the vote of two against two produced the same result as if there had been a majority of three to two.

---

3 See (1944) 197 L.T.News. 199. Though exceptional then, the process is not uncommon now. In *Carl Zeiss Stiftung* v. *Rayner & Keeler Ltd.* (*No.* 4) [1971] *The Times* April 27, I believe that I was insured for £250,000.

4 30 & 31 Vict. c. 64, 1867, s. 1.

5 *Baxendale* v. *McMurray* (1867) 2 Ch.App. 790.

6 *Galloway* v. *Craig* (1861) 4 Macq. 267 at 272.

7 *Lord Advocate* v. *Wemyss* [1900] A.C. 48 at 59.

8 *Inland Revenue Commissioners* v. *Wilsons (Dunblane) Ltd.* [1954] 1 W.L.R. 282 at 288.

9 *Ross Smith* v. *Ross Smith* [1963] A.C. 280 at 332.

10 *Ibid.*, at p. 291.

11 *Ealing London Borough Council* v. *Race Relations Board* [1972] A.C. 342 at 352, *per* Viscount Dilhorne.

In accordance with practice, Lord Reid read Lord Upjohn's speech and adopted it as his own.[12]

As in death, so in life. Thus Lord Oaksey once delivered as his own a speech prepared by Lord Reid which Lord Reid, not having taken the oath in the House of Lords by reason of his absence abroad, was unable to deliver himself [13]; and Lord Simonds did the same when Lord Reid was ill.[14] Life and death may mingle, too, so that only half of those who hear an appeal may decide it. Thus in one case [15] Lord Watson died, and Lord Halsbury L.C. and Lord Shand "took no part in the judgment." Fortunately, the others (Lord Macnaghten, Lord Morris and Lord Davey) were unanimous.

There is, of course, a majestic ring in the words " a decision of the House of Lords "; the voices of infallibility (as they once were [16]) have spoken. Yet what is one to say of a decision of the House made in the absence of any law lord by the Master of the Rolls or Chief Baron of the Exchequer, each a mere commoner, and founded upon reasons which appear in no speech in the House but were communicated privately to the parties in a side-room? In 1827 there were many of such far from majestic performances. Lord Eldon L.C. had resigned and Lord Lyndhurst was Lord Chancellor. By two commissions under the Great Seal dated May 5, 1827, Sir John Leach M.R. and Sir William Alexander C.B. were in effect made Deputy Speakers of the House of Lords. By each commission the Crown did " constitute, name and authorise " the judge " from Time to Time, during Our Pleasure, to use, occupy and enjoy the Room and Place of a Lord Chancellor or Lord Keeper of

12 *Kennedy* v. *Spratt* [1972] A.C. 83 at 89; and see the note at p. 99. (Despite the modern practice of the law lords not reading their speeches in the House (see *Practice Direction* [1963] 1 W.L.R. 1382), Lord Reid at p. 89 used the word " read.") Contrast *Inland Revenue Commissioners* v. *Richards' Executors* [1971] 1 W.L.R. 571, where Lord Upjohn, had he lived, would merely have converted a score of 3–1 into 3–2.
13 *Tool Metal Manufacturing Co. Ltd.* v. *Tungsten Electric Co. Ltd.* [1955] 1 W.L.R. 761 at 771.
14 *Whitworth Park Coal Co. Ltd.* v. *Inland Revenue Commissioners* [1961] A.C. 31 at 51.
15 *Somersetshire Drainage Commissioners* v. *Corporation of Bridgwater* (1899) 81 L.T. 729.
16 Before the *Practice Statement* [1966] 1 W.L.R. 1234.

Our Great Seal of Our United Kingdom of Great Britain and Ireland, in the Upper House of Parliament, amongst the Lords Spiritual and Temporal there assembled, and then and there to do and execute all such Things as the said Lord Chancellor or Lord Keeper of Our Great Seal should or might in that behalf do if he were then personally present, using and supplying the said Room." [17]

A major problem of these appointments was that although such a commission entitled the recipient to preside in the House of Lords when the Lord Chancellor was absent, sitting on the Woolsack which is technically outside the House, it did not make him a member of the House. He therefore could not make a speech or move that judgment be given for one party or the other. Instead, he had to put his judgment " into the hands of a peer to move that it be received by their Lordships." [18] Alternatively, the case would be decided without any overt expression of the grounds for the decision, but afterwards the Master of the Rolls or Chief Baron would communicate them to the parties in a side-room.[19] Reporters were thus reduced to obtaining notes of these private expressions of opinion to the parties, or inferring the grounds of a decision from the course of argument [20]; for despite speechlessness in the House at judgment, the Deputy Speaker seems on occasion to have engaged vigorously in discussion with counsel during the argument.[1] For some decisions, however, no reasons appear.[2]

---

[17] (1827) 59 Lds.Jnl. 278. And see Lord Campbell's *Lives of Lord Lyndhurst and Lord Brougham* (1869) p. 43, suggesting that in the previous year Lord Eldon had procured a similar appointment for Leach (then V.-C.) and Alexander.

[18] (1827) Hansard (2nd ser.) vol. 17, col. 573 (and see at col. 575), *per* Earl of Lauderdale.

[19] As in *Crawfurd* v. *M'Cormick* (1827) 2 Wils. & Shaw 569 at 575n.; *Lawsons* v. *Stewarts* (1827) 2 Wils. & Shaw 625 at 636n.

[20] See 2 Wils. & Shaw 558n.

[1] See, *e.g.*, *Low* v. *Bell* (1827) 2 Wils. & Shaw 579 at 582; *M'Donell* v. *Cameron* (1827) 2 Wils. & Shaw 592 at 594; *Auld* v. *Magistrates of Ayr* (1827) 2 Wils. & Shaw 600 at 606, 607; *sub nom. Auld* v. *Hamilton* (1827) 1 Dow & Cl. 43 at 52–54; *Crawford* v. *Bennet* (1827) 2 Wils. & Shaw 608 at 612, 613.

[2] See, *e.g.*, *Wyllie* v. *Ross* (1827) 2 Wils. & Shaw 576 at 579; *Low* v. *Duncan* (1827) 2 Wils. & Shaw 583 at 588; *Budge* v. *Magistrates of Edinburgh* (1827) 2 Wils. & Shaw 588 at 591.

One of these cases [3] was subsequently cited by Lord Campbell L.C.,[4] who quoted some words as being those of Leach M.R. " sitting as Speaker of the House of Lords." At this, the puzzled reporter was forced to surmise that Sir John had given " an explanation privately, and that some note has been preserved of what he said." [5]

The reason for the curious arrangement [6] was that when Lord Eldon L.C. lost office and Lord Lyndhurst was appointed, there were some seventy Scottish appeals awaiting hearing. Lord Eldon seems at first to have been unwilling to sit to hear these, and Lord Lyndhurst had, of course, all the English and Irish appeals to hear, as well as the work of the Court of Chancery. It does not appear why Lord Redesdale did not come to the rescue. The device of Deputy Speakers was accordingly adopted as a temporary expedient, despite criticism in the House of Lords to which Lord Lyndhurst replied in his maiden speech in that House.[7] And it was not long before Lord Eldon and Lord Redesdale,[8] and Lord Lyndhurst L.C. himself,[9] made the expedient no longer necessary. All that remains is a collection of decisions which, however sound in substance, can hardly in their manner be a subject for pride *in dom. proc.*

Even under more orthodox conditions, accidents have sometimes happened. If at judgment a law lord was unable to be present, the usual arrangement (until the oral delivery of speeches was abandoned in 1963 [10]) was for some other law lord to read the absentee's speech. If this went awry, it would seem to be too late, in strict constitutional theory, for the absent peer's voice to be heard in the matter; for the debate is over and the vote taken. But what in fact has been done is that the next day

---

[3] *Lang* v. *Struthers* (1827) 2 Wils. & Shaw 563.
[4] *Robertson* v. *Fleming* (1861) 4 Macq. 166 at 179.
[5] 4 Macq. 180 n.
[6] See Lord Campbell's derisory footnote: *Lives of Lord Lyndhurst & Lord Brougham* (1869) p. 43n.
[7] (1827) Hansard (2nd ser.) vol. 17, cols. 573–576.
[8] See, *e.g.*, *Earl of Stair* v. *Earl of Stair's Trustees* (1827) 2 Wils. & Shaw 614.
[9] See, *e.g.*, *Gordon* v. *Anderson* (1828) 3 Wils. & Shaw 1.
[10] See *Practice Direction* [1963] 1 W.L.R. 1382, which took effect from November 21, 1963.

the Lord Chancellor has moved (and the House has apparently agreed) that the opinion should be handed in and form part of the record.[11]

It was in 1899 that what seems to have been the numerically most ample House of Lords of modern times sat judicially. The House was hearing an appeal from the full Court of Appeal,[12] in which Rigby L.J. had dissented from Lord Esher M.R., and Lindley, Lopes, A. L. Smith and Chitty L.JJ.[13] The House comprised the Earl of Halsbury L.C., Lord Watson, Lord Herschell, Lord Hobhouse, Lord Ashbourne, Lord Macnaghten, Lord Morris, Lord Shand, Lord Davey and Lord James of Hereford; and by eight voices to two the House affirmed the decision below and held that an enclosure on a racecourse to which bookmakers and the public resorted was not a " place " for the purposes of the Betting Act, 1853.[14] In the famous *Vagliano* case, too, a full Court of Appeal had sat, with Cotton, Lindley, Bowen, Fry and Lopes L.JJ. against Lord Esher M.R.[15] affirming the decision of Charles J.[16] Eight peers sat in the House of Lords, but although Lord Bramwell and Lord Field were for affirming the decision, they were outvoted by Lord Halsbury L.C., the Earl of Selborne, Lord Watson, Lord Herschell, Lord Macnaghten and Lord Morris.[17] Though the judges thus divided by eight to seven, the power lay with the seven.

On the other hand, *Allen* v. *Flood*[18] had to be satisfied with a Court of Appeal comprising the usual three members; but

---

11 See *Lloyd* v. *Powell Duffryn Steam Coal Co. Ltd.* [1914] A.C. 733 at 749n.; *Earl Fitzwilliam* v. *Inland Revenue Commissioners* [1914] A.C. 753 at 762n.; *Lightfoot* v. *Maybery* [1914] A.C. 782 at 803n. In all three cases the silenced absentee was Lord Moulton.
12 In L. Blom-Cooper and G. Drewry, *Final Appeal* (1972) p. 525 there is a comment on the infrequency of a full Court of Appeal sitting in civil cases in modern times; but their tally of a mere three cases during 1951–66 is incomplete: see, *e.g.*, *Berkeley* v. *Papadoyannis* [1954] 2 Q.B. 149.
13 *Powell* v. *Kempton Park Racecourse Co.* [1897] 2 Q.B. 242.
14 *Powell* v. *Kempton Park Racecourse Co. Ltd.* [1899] A.C. 143.
15 *Vagliano Brothers* v. *The Bank of England* (1889) 23 Q.B.D. 243.
16 *Vagliano Brothers* v. *Governor and Company of the Bank of England* (1888) 22 Q.B.D. 103.
17 *Governor and Company of the Bank of England* v. *Vagliano Brothers* [1891] A.C. 107.
18 [1898] A.C. 1.

61

the House of Lords made amends. After being argued for four days before seven law lords (Lord Halsbury L.C., Lord Watson, Lord Herschell, Lord Macnaghten, Lord Morris, Lord Shand and Lord Davey), it was re-argued for six days before nine law lords (Lord Ashbourne and Lord James of Hereford having joined the seven) and eight of the judges, including one Chancery judge,[19] North J.; and although the advice to the House given by six of the eight was that the decision of the Court of Appeal should be affirmed, the law lords voted by six voices to three to reverse that decision, setting out their reasons in some 115 pages of the Law Reports. The summoning of the judges seems to have been the unilateral act of Lord Halsbury, who was one of the dissentient law lords, as part of an unsuccessful attempt to obtain a majority for his view. Certainly the letters which he received from Lord Herschell, who was of the majority, indicate that Lord Halsbury had ridden roughshod over the feelings of at least some of his brethren.[20]

Sometimes an equal division of voices has persisted until the last leap. In *Mollett* v. *Robinson* the plaintiff succeeded at the trial before Bovill C.J., and on a motion for a non-suit before the Court of Common Pleas, Bovill C.J. and Smith J. held the decision to be right. Willes and Keating JJ., however, held it to be wrong, though as the court was equally divided, the verdict stood.[1] In days when courts of four judges sat, the trial judge had only to find one of his brethren to agree with him for the decision to stand. In the Exchequer Chamber, the first three judgments, delivered by Cleasby B., Hannen J. and Mellor J., were all in favour of allowing the appeal: but as Blackburn J., Channell B. and Kelly C.B. were all of the contrary view, equal division once again resulted in the original decision being affirmed.[2]

This made a sortie to the House of Lords almost inevitable;

---

[19] Not merely the common law judges, as is suggested by L. Blom-Cooper and G. Drewry, *Final Appeal* (1972) p. 524.
[20] See R. F. V. Heuston, *Lives of the Lord Chancellors 1885–1940* (1964) pp. 120–122.
[1] *Mollett* v. *Robinson* (1870) L.R. 5 C.P. 646.
[2] *Mollett* v. *Robinson* (1872) L.R. 7 C.P. 84.

and the House duly summoned certain of the judges to assist
them. Three were new to the case (Brett and Grove JJ. and
Amphlett B.), two had already given judgments in favour of
allowing the appeal (Mellor J. and Cleasby B.) and one, Blackburn J., had given judgment dismissing the appeal. Blackburn
J. adhered to his view that the initial decision was right, and
recruited Amphlett B. to this view: but as Mellor J. and
Cleasby B. not only remained steadfast in their views but also
each obtained a new adherent (in the shape of Brett and Grove
JJ.), the advice of the judges was 4–2 in favour of allowing the
appeal. Lord Cairns L.C., Lord Chelmsford, Lord Hatherley
and Lord O'Hagen unanimously accepted this majority advice,[3]
and so at the last (and most important) hurdle the defendant
triumphed.

In other cases, the last word, though decisive, has been less
convincing. *Harris* v. *Earl of Chesterfield*[4] was argued in the
House of Lords from March 27 to 31, 1911. On July 14, Earl
Loreburn L.C., Lord Ashbourne and Lord Shaw spoke in
favour of allowing the appeal, whereas the Earl of Halsbury,
Lord Macnaghten and Lord Gorrell were in favour of dismissing it. The remaining law lord who had heard the
argument, Lord Kinnear,[5] was not present, and so "Judgment
was reserved until July 17th."[6] On that day, Lord Kinnear
was still absent; but Lord Loreburn said "My Lords, Lord
Kinnear is not able to be present today, but he considers that
the order appealed from ought to be affirmed."[7] On any
view, in an important case establishing that a right of fishing in
a river for commercial purposes cannot be established by prescription, the decisive voice, even if present only by proxy, spoke
with sad brevity.[8] The case, indeed, had other peculiarities.
In the words of Lord Loreburn, "It is manifestly deplorable

[3] *Robinson* v. *Mollett* (1875) L.R. 7 H.L. 802.
[4] [1911] A.C. 623.
[5] Lord Kinnear was not a Lord of Appeal in Ordinary, but a Scottish judge who had been ennobled.
[6] [1911] A.C. at p. 640.
[7] *Ibid.*
[8] Though the result would have been the same had the voice not spoken at all; for on an equal division, the appeal fails.

63

that a case should be decided here upon a ground which any
of the judges thought to be abandoned in the Court below." [9]
However, the case at least contributed some seventeen pages of
reasoned though conflicting discussion to the Law Reports,
which is more than can be said of another case decided some
two years earlier. There, " Lord Loreburn L.C., without giving
any reasons, moved that the appeal be dismissed. The Earl of
Halsbury and Lords Ashbourne, Macnaghten and James of
Hereford silently concurred." [10]

It has, indeed, not been unknown for the House of Lords to
find itself equally divided at the conclusion of the argument,
and then to call in another peer (even though merely a judge of
first instance) to hear the case re-argued. Thus in *Johnstone* v.
Beattie [11] one issue was whether Scottish testamentary tutors of
an infant were entitled to be appointed her guardians in
England: Shadwell V.-C. held that they were, but Lord
Cottenham L.C. reversed this decision. In the House of Lords,
Lord Cottenham adhered to his opinion, and Lord Lyndhurst,
who had then become Lord Chancellor, agreed with him; but
Lord Brougham and Lord Campbell took the opposite view.
Lord Langdale M.R. was then called in to hear a second
argument. [12] He spoke last (save for a short second speech by
the irrepressible Lord Brougham), and voted with the former
and then Lord Chancellor to affirm Lord Cottenham's decision.
His attendance thus did no more than add to the costs: for had
the House remained equally divided, the decision below would
have stood and so the result would have been the same.

Where the equal division was between two law lords instead
of four, the case for calling in a third law lord for a re-argument
seems *a fortiori*; for the quorum in the House of Lords is three,
and as the lay peer or peers who were called in to make up
numbers could hardly be expected to give a sapient casting vote,
it would not have been unreasonable to look for at least a
quorum of voting lawyers. However, when Lord Cranworth

[9] *Harris* v. *Earl of Chesterfield* [1911] A.C. 623 at 630.
[10] *Refuge Assurance Co. Ltd.* v. *Kettlewell* [1909] A.C. 243 at 245.
[11] (1843) 10 Cl. & F. 42.
[12] See *ibid.*, p. 83.

L.C. and Lord St. Leonards once differed in this way, the appeal was dismissed.[13] At the conclusion of the two speeches, Sir Richard Bethell S.-G., who had appeared for the appellant, asked that the House should follow the course adopted in *Johnstone* v. *Beattie*.[14] When this request was rejected, he boldly said " My Lords, this amounts to a complete denial of justice " [15]; but even this struck no answering sparks. On the same day another decision was affirmed by the same equal division of two voices.[16]

A change of status often brought with it no change of opinion. In one case, a decision by Page Wood V.-C. was reversed on appeal by Lord Chelmsford L.C., and was then carried to the House of Lords. On the appeal, both judges sat, Page Wood V.-C. having in the meantime become Lord Hatherley L.C. Each judge adhered to his former view, but as Lord Westbury and Lord Colonsay concurred in the views of Lord Chelmsford, the Lord Chancellor remained in isolation.[17]

Sometimes matters were more complex. In *Grey* v. *Friar*, the Court of Exchequer found for the defendant, Rolfe B. delivering the judgment of the court.[18] The Court of Exchequer Chamber reversed that decision.[19] In the House of Lords [20] the appeal was argued before Lord Cranworth L.C. (as Rolfe B. had by then become) and Lord Brougham. When it came to judgment, Lord Brougham was absent, and Lord Cranworth, adhering to his old views, was in favour of allowing the appeal and restoring the judgment that he had delivered at first instance. But of the judges summoned to advise the House, only three supported this opinion, whereas eight were against it. Further, Lord Brougham had told Lord Cranworth that he had reached the conclusion that the appeal should be dismissed, though he apparently gave no reasons for this, and had prepared

[13] *Finnie* v. *Glasgow & South-Western Railway Co.* (1855) 2 Macq. 177.
[14] *Supra.*
[15] *Finnie* v. *Glasgow & South-Western Railway Co.*, *supra*, at p. 204.
[16] *Norton* v. *Stirling* (1855) 2 Macq. 205.
[17] *Knox* v. *Gye* (1872) L.R. 5 H.L. 656.
[18] *Friar* v. *Grey* (1850) 5 Exch. 584.
[19] *Friar* v. *Grey* (1851) 5 Exch. 597.
[20] *Grey* v. *Friar* (1853) 4 H.L.C. 565; the report misdates the case 1854 (see (1853) 85 Lds.Jnl. 577; 18 Jur. 1036).

no speech. Accordingly, Lord Cranworth felt obliged to advise the House to dismiss the appeal; and on his motion this was done. The case thus stands in the books as an instance of the only law lord present at judgment speaking in one sense and voting in the other, and also as an example of the decisive voice being that of a law lord who not only was absent, but also gave no reasons.

It has even been known for a Lord Chancellor to propose to the House of Lords that a decision should be affirmed, and at the same time announce that he will vote against that motion. In a Scottish case in 1801, Lord Eldon L.C. seems to have been the only law lord present.[1] He was confronted with a line of authorities on entails which he found uncongenial. " What reason induced the Court to go so far as they have done in those decided cases, I am at a loss to know. . . . The judgments . . . appear to me to shock every principle of common sense." Yet the authorities had stood for many years, and so, he said, " when I move your Lordships to affirm the interlocutors complained of, I shall give my vote as *not content*, protesting that, as a judge, I never could have concurred in the former decisions originally when they were pronounced." [2] And so, it seems, on the motion of Lord Eldon L.C. the House dismissed the appeal, Lord Eldon L.C. dissenting.

As might be expected, the United States has gone one better. One decision of the Supreme Court in 1957[3] at first sight appears to be no more than a majority decision of no especial importance. But that is a superficial view, as is made plain by a delightful pastiche of the late Finley Peter Dunne's incomparable Mr. Dooley,[4] intituled " Mr. Dooley Discovers A Unanimous Dissent."

---

[1] See (1801) 43 Lds.Jnl. 226, 231, 239, 292.
[2] *Bruce* v. *Bruce* (1801) 4 Pat. 231 at 236, 237; and see the doubts expressed by Lord Loughborough L.C. in *Smith* v. *Newlands* (1798) 4 Pat. 43 at 54 (" I own I have not courage to venture upon a reversal ").
[3] *Rogers* v. *Missouri Pacific Railroad Co.*, 352 U.S. 500 (1957).
[4] By James M. Marsh (1957) 20 *The Shingle* 143 (published by the Philadelphia Bar Association), and reprinted at (1968) 31 *The Shingle* 191. The article is here reproduced (with minor revisions) by kind permission of the author and the editor. Some 500 Dooleys, on a wide range of subjects, appeared between 1892 and 1914. In *Mr. Dooley on the Choice of Law* (1963) Edward J. Bander reproduces some 39 on law and politics which he considered the

" 'Every one of them dissented,' said Mr. Dooley. ' It was unanimous. They's nine jedges on that coort, and every one of them dissented—includin' me brother Brennan, who wrote the opinion they're all dissentin' from.'

'That don't make sinse,' said Mr. Hennessy, ' You can't have all the jedges dissentin'—it's impossible.'

'Well, it may be impossible, but it happened anyhow,' said Mr. Dooley, ' And it's printed right here in the Coort's own Joornal of its Proceedings for February 25th. Read it for yourself.'

'No. 28. *James C. Rogers, petitioner* v. *Missouri Pacific Railroad Company, a Corporation.* On writ of certiorari to the Supreme Court of Missouri.

Judgment reversed with costs and case remanded to the Supreme Court of Missouri for proceedings not inconsistent with the opinion of this Court.

Opinion by Mr. Justice Brennan.

Mr. Justice Burton concurs in the result.

Mr. Justice Reed would affirm the judgment of the Supreme Court of Missouri.

Mr. Justice Harlan, dissenting in Nos. 28, 42, and 59 and concurring in No. 46, filed a separate opinion.

Mr. Justice Burton concurred in Part I of Mr. Justice Harlan's opinion.

Mr. Chief Justice Warren, Mr. Justice Black, Mr. Justice Douglas, Mr. Justice Clark, and Mr. Justice Brennan concurred in Part I of Mr. Justice Harlan's opinion except insofar as it disapproves the grant of the writ of certiorari.

Mr. Justice Frankfurter filed a separate dissenting opinion for Nos. 28, 42, 46, and 50.'

'See what I mean,' said Mr. Dooley. ' Each and ivery one of them dissented in this No. 28, called Rogers varsus the Missouri Pacific. Even Brennan, J., who wrote the opinion for the Coort. He signed Harlan's dissent. Me old friend Holmes

best and most enduring; yet none attains the standard of this pastiche. For Serjeant Sullivan's account of the original of Mr. Dooley, see A. M. Sullivan, *The Last Serjeant* (1952) p. 217.

would've sooner been caught with a split writ than to show up on both sides of a case like that.'

'But Brennan only signed Part I, and he says "except insofar as,"' said Mr. Hennessy, 'don't that mean anything?'

'Sure it does,' said Mr. Dooley. 'It means Brennan dissents from Harlan, too. I guess he figgers one good dissent deserves another.'

'Where was me friend Burton?' asked Mr. Hennessy.

'He's all over the place,' said Mr. Dooley. 'As they say, he concurs in the result—which means he likes the answer but he can't stand Brennan's opinion. Thin he concurs in wan part of Harlan, J., but he can't stand the rest of him either.'

'How could they git in such a mess?' asked Mr. Hennessy.

'That's what Felix says—in twinty thousand words,' said Mr. Dooley.

'Felix who?' asked Mr. Hennessy.

'Frankfurter,' said Mr. Dooley. 'He's a Havvard, and a perfesser at that; he gave the rest of them a free lecture in this case—and that ain't like most of them Havvards; they come pretty dear.'

'Well, what happened to this fellow Rogers anyhow?' asked Mr. Hennessy, 'and the Missouri Pacific?'

'Plenty,' said Mr. Dooley. 'Rogers gits his money, wich the Supreme Coort of Missouri said he couldn't have; and the Missouri Pacific gits to pay it, wich they would probably just as soon not do.'

'How's come?' asked Mr. Hennessy.

'Well, pinitratin' all the joodicial gobbley-dook, it's like this: Rogers was workin' on the tracks of the Missouri Pacific and he fell off a culvert; the jury gave him damages but the Supreme Coort of Missouri took them away. Then the Supreme Coort of the United States listened to the loiyers' argyments and gave Rogers his money back again. Me brother Brennan is supposed to tell the reasons why—at three hunderd fifty two U.S. five hunderd, which sounds like the odds against anyone but a Philadelphia lawyer understandin' the case.

'But Felix says "Brennan, me boy, we shoodn't have took this case in the first place, we shoodn't have decided it in the second, and we shoodn't be ladlin' out the railroad's money anyway—it ain't becomin' to this high coort." Then Harlan, J., says " Ye're half right, Felix, but ye're wrong there where ye say we shoodn't decide the case; but I dissent from me brother Brennan givin' him the money, too "

' And thin Brennan says " Ye're half right, too, Harlan, and I agree with your Part I ' except insofar as.' " And so Brennan signed Harlan's dissent from Brennan's own opinion, and so did Warren, Black, Douglas and Clark, JJ., the same ones who signed Brennan's opinion in the first place. I tell ye, Hennessy, it's a demoralizin' situation. Here's the highest coort in the land, and they're all half right but none of them are all right, and they're tellin' on each other at that.'

' But what about me friend Stanley Reed? ' asked Mr. Hennessy, ' He didn't sign anybody else's opinion, did he? '

' No, he was the smart wan,' said Mr. Dooley, ' He quit.'

' He *quit*? ' said Mr. Hennessy, ' Just like *that*?'

' Just like that,' said Mr. Dooley, ' He voted loud and clear to back up the Supreme Coort of Missouri—and then he quit. On February 25th he did it, right after they handed down this Rogers case. He walked out of that coort the same day and he hasn't been back since.'

' Well,' said Mr. Hennessy, ' I don't blame him; I'd quit too.'

' That's the trouble with thim jedges, though,' said Mr. Dooley.

' What's that?' asked Mr. Hennessy.

' They don't quit often enough,' said Mr. Dooley."

Alas, there seems to be no English case so neatly various as this. Yet there are instances of what may be termed majority dissents. Thus when in the House of Lords Lord Finlay L.C. laid down two propositions in deciding a case, two of his brethren dissented on one point and the other two on the other, so that he was alone in thinking that his judgment, which in fact settled the law, was wholly right.[5]

---

[5] *Neville* v. *London " Express " Newspaper Ltd.* [1919] A.C. 368. See also *post*, pp. 144, 189.

All Ravished With Gladness

THE famous comment about the prisoner who, when before a judge, "ject un Brickbat a le dit Justice"[1] has a most respectable ancestry. For it appears in the margin of Dyer's Reports, and "the marginal notes in Dyer are good authority; they were written by Lord Chief Justice Treby."[2] A contemporary account of the event from non-judicial sources is that "Judge Richardson, in going the Westerne Circuite, had a great flint stone throwne at his head by a malefactor, then condemned, (who thought it meritorious, and the way to be a benefactor to the Commonwealth, to take away the life of a man so odious,) but leaning low of his elbow, in a lazie recklesse manner, the bullett flew too high and only tooke off his hatt. Soone after, some friends congratulating his deliverance, he replyde, by way of jeast (as his fashion was to make a jeast of every thing), 'You see now, if I had beene an upright Judge (intimating his reclining posture) I had been slaine.'"[3] Perhaps this incident had escaped the mind of Harman J. when delivering judgment in a case in 1957. "It was said by Buckley J. in *In re Davis*[4] that the court will lean towards finding a general charitable intent in the circumstances which he there mentioned. The court has been doing so ever since, and it has leaned so far over that it has become almost prone. I have always had a preference for an upright posture."[5]

There is an old story that when an egg was thrown at Malins V.-C. in court, he observed "That must have been intended for my brother Bacon." No direct confirmation for

---

[1] See 1 Misc. 295.
[2] *Milward* v. *Thatcher* (1787) 2 T.R. 81 at 84, *per* Buller J.; and see *Jones* d. *Henry* v. *Hancock* (1816) 4 Dow 145 at 202, *per* Gibbs C.J.
[3] W. J. Thoms, *Anecdotes and Traditions* (Camden Society, 1st ser., vol. 5, 1839) p. 53, quoting from *Merry Passages and Jests* (Harleian MS. No. 6395), by Sir Nicholas Lestrange (1603–1655), who was connected by marriage to the judge. The story was current table talk in the time of Pepys: see his *Diary* for September 8, 1667.
[4] [1902] 1 Ch. 876 at 884.
[5] *Re Goldschmidt* [1957] 1 W.L.R. 524 at 525.

the remark can be found,[6] though the egg seems authentic enough. One work of authority somewhat coyly records that in 1877 (when Malins and Bacon were both Vice-Chancellors), Malins V.-C. made " an order for the committal of a person (native of the U.S. of America) for throwing a missile at the Judge in open Court": *Re Cosgrave*.[7] Another authority refers to this case as one of " flinging an egg at the judge in court," though no details are given[8]; and a memorandum by Mr. Registrar Lavie in 1893 refers cryptically to " the *Egg Case*" as an instance of personal contempt of court.[9]

However, a contemporary report of the case leaves no doubt. On March 16, 1877, upon Malins V.-C. " rising from his seat to leave the Court at the termination of the day's business a most unprecedented assault was committed by a man in Court throwing an egg at the Judge. The missile passed close to his Lordship's head, and was broken against the wooden canopy behind his seat."[10] Mr. Glasse Q.C., who had something of a privileged position in the court of Malins V.-C. and was at times not far from committing verbal contempt himself, was in court at the time. The following colloquy thereupon took place between the judge, the silk and the man, whose name was Robert Mahon Cosgrave; the judge had recently made a decree against him in the case of *Cosgrave* v. *Woodley*.

V.-C. " What was that? "
Q.C. " An egg."
V.-C. " Where did it come from? "
Q.C. " A hen, I presume."
V.-C. (to Cosgrave, who had been seized by the usher): " Did you throw that egg? "
Cosgrave: " Yes, my lord."
V.-C. " Why did you do it? "
Cosgrave: " Because you insulted me in a case this morning."
V.-C. " I never insulted anyone in my life."

[6] J. F. Oswald, *Contempt of Court* (3rd ed. 1910) p. 42 recounts the story without citing authority.
[7] Seton's *Judgments and Orders* (7th ed. 1912) p. 457.
[8] *Halsbury's Laws of England*, vol. 8 (3rd ed. 1954) p. 5, n. (c).
[9] [1893] 1 Ch. 259n. at 260n.
[10] [1877] *The Times* March 17, p. 13.

Q.C. " Your lordship doesn't propose to *argue* the question with the man? " [11]

Cosgrave, upon whom a loaded pistol was afterwards found, was forthwith committed to prison by an order in the following form : " In the matter of Robert Cosgrave—Forasmuch as this day during the sitting of the Court an egg was thrown with much force against the pannelling behind the seat of the Judge And the above named Robert Cosgrave of No. 3 Great Ormond Street in the County of Middlesex then in the Court (being pointed out as the person throwing and interrogated by the Court) having avowed the act as intentionally done by him, This Court doth adjudge the said Robert Cosgrave to be committed to the custody of the Keeper of Holloway Prison for his contempt in throwing an egg with the intent that the egg so thrown should strike the Judge when acting in his judicial capacity and thereby disturbing the proceedings during the sittings of the Court." [12]

The reports show that Bacon V.-C. was sitting in another court on the same day,[13] but there is nothing to give any authenticity to the remark attributed to Malins V.-C. as to the misdirection of the egg. Cosgrave seems to have remained in prison for over five months, for on August 22, 1877, the following order for his discharge was made : " This Court doth order that the Keeper of Holloway Prison take the said Robert Cosgrave and place him on board the steamship ' Utopia,' Captain Craig, bound from London to New York, or some other ship bound on the same voyage, as soon as conveniently may be, in charge of the Captain of the said ship. And it is ordered that thereupon the said Robert Cosgrave be discharged out of the custody of the Governor of Holloway Prison as to his said contempt." [14] It does not appear whether this order

---

11 Sir John Fox (1922) 38 L.Q.R. 185, repeating the account of an eye witness. True, Vice-Chancellors (and the Master of the Rolls) were traditionally addressed not as " Your Lordship " but as " Your Honor "; but this had not survived the Judicature Act, 1873, s. 5.

12 Sir John Fox, *supra*, at p. 186. The Order was March 16, 1877, A.450 : Seton, *supra*, p. 457. The miscellaneous details can be collected from this, *Seton* and *The Times*.   13 [1877] *The Times* March 17, p. 13.

14 Sir John Fox, *supra*, at p. 186; Order, August 22, 1877, A.1717 : Seton, *supra*, p. 457. *The Times* does not seem to have noticed this order.

was made with Cosgrave's acquiescence, or whether in those days deportation was taken more lightly than it is today.

Contempt may indeed take many forms. An unsuccessful plaintiff in a libel case who had become bankrupt sought to appeal; but on the respondent's application the Court of Appeal [15] ordered the plaintiff, a Mr. Gohoho, to pay £50 into court within twenty-one days by way of security for the costs of the appeal, in default of which the appeal would be dismissed. When this decision was announced, " the plaintiff, removing his jacket, protested and declared that he would be coming to the Court every day. He then lay down on the bench from where litigants in person address the Court. During the hearing of the next application in the Court's list the plaintiff stripped himself of his trousers and underpants and lay naked except for his shirt on the bench. A woman litigant, who had been sitting next to Mr. Gohoho, hurriedly retreated to junior counsels' seats." The court called the tipstaff adjourned the case that was being heard, and rose, directing him to remove the plaintiff for contempt of court. This done, the court returned and announced that a bench warrant had been issued, committing the plaintiff to prison for one week for contempt of court, and also (no doubt so that justice might not even seem to falter) that the plaintiff's time for payment into court had been extended from twenty-one to twenty-eight days.[16]

Some disgruntled litigants prefer words to deeds. In 1669, " the Plaintiff moved to commit the Defendant; for that when the Plaintiff told him he came to serve him with an Order from the Master of the Rolls, the Defendant said, The Master of the Rolls kiss my Arse; but the Master of the Rolls [Sir Harbottle Grimstone] only ordered an Attachment for the Familiarity, but said, He believed the Lord Keeper [Sir Orlando Bridgman] would have committed him." [17] In the next century, " when a rule was served upon the defendant, to shew

---

15 Sellers, Pearson and Russell L.JJ.
16 *Gohoho* v. *Lintas Export Advertising Services Ltd.* [1964] *The Times* Jan. 21.
17 *Witham* v. *Witham* (1669) 3 Rep.Ch. 41. See also a number of instances, without details, mentioned at 8 St.Tr. 49.

cause why an information should not be filed against him; he said, Take the rule back again to those from whom it came, and bid them wipe their backsides with it." The result was a rule absolute for attachment [18]; and so also it was when on service of process on the defendant " the words were G—d d—n the Lord Reeves and the Court, and that he neither cared for him or them." [19] This concept was carried far. Thus in 1723 the Court of King's Bench " declared that a declaration in eject-ment was so far a process of the Court, that they would punish contemptuous words on the delivery of it, as a contempt of this Court." [20]

In the nineteenth century, however, the tide receded a little. On being served with a writ by a sheriff's officer, one defendant "collared him, shook him violently, and ordered him to quit his presence." On these facts, the Court of Common Pleas in 1819 " said, that they would lay down no rule, whether every collaring and shaking of an officer, however improper such conduct were, should or should not be deemed a contempt of Court, it sufficed to say, that no case was here shewn to the Court which disclosed any such obstruction of their process as to call for this summary mode of punishment." [1] Again, it is no contempt to snatch the original writ from the process server and refuse to return it for some while,[2] or to tear up a copy of the writ and throw the pieces at the process server.[3] " The defendant was actually served. If the officer had been prevented from so doing, we might have grounds to interfere." [4] Yet there were limits. In 1664 one Bacon of Gray's Inn, against whom a decree in Chancery had been made, offered a man £100 to kill Grimstone M.R. He was adjudged in contempt of court, and received what in all the circumstances was a modest sentence: he was to be fined 1,000 marks and imprisoned for

---

[18] *R.* v. *Jermy* (1752) Say. 47. For a crude comment upon another rule of court, see *Anon.* (1711) 1 Salk. 84.
[19] *Phillips* v. *Hedges* (1736) Cooke Pr.C. 132; Sir Thomas Reeve was C.J.C.P. in 1736.
[20] *R.* v. *Unitt* (1723) 1 Str. 567.
[1] *Adams* v. *Hughes* (1819) 1 Brod. & B. 24; contrast *Price* v. *Hutchison* (1869) L.R. 9 Eq. 534.
[2] *Weekes* v. *Whitely* (1835) 3 Dowl.Pr. 536.
[3] *Myers* v. *Wills* (1820) 4 Moo.C.P. 147.   [4] *Ibid.*, at p. 148, *per cur.*

three months. He was also bound over to be of good behaviour during his life, and required to make acknowledgment " de son offence al Bar de Chancery." [5]

The legal profession has played a not unexpected part in developing the law of contempt. " Lawyers owe a large, but not an obsequious, duty of respect to the court in its presence." [6] In one case, the Supreme Court of the United States set aside a judge's summary committal of a trial lawyer for ten days for contempt of court. The interchanges between court and counsel, said the Supreme Court, " were marked by expressions and revealed an attitude which hardly reflected the restraints of conventional judicial demeanor." [7] One of the instances cited by the Supreme Court was as follows [8]:

" The Court: Motion denied. Proceed.

    Mr. Offutt: I object to your Honor yelling at me and raising your voice like that.

    The Court: Just a moment. If you say another word I will have the Marshal stick a gag in your mouth."

In discharging the jury, the judge said " I also realize that you had a difficult and disagreeable task in this case. You have been compelled to sit through a disgraceful and disreputable performance on the part of a lawyer who is unworthy of being a member of the profession; and I, as a member of the legal profession, blush that we should have such a specimen in our midst." [9]

" The record," said the Supreme Court, " discloses not a rare flare-up, not a show of evanescent irritation—a modicum of quick temper that must be allowed even judges. The record is persuasive that instead of representing the impersonal authority of law the trial judge permitted himself to become personally embroiled with the petitioner. There was an intermittently continuous wrangle on an unedifying level between

---

[5] *R.* v. *Bacon* (1664) 1 Sid. 230.
[6] *Fisher* v. *Pace*, 336 U.S. 155 at 168 (1949), *per* Rutledge J., dissenting.
[7] *Offutt* v. *United States*, 348 U.S. 11 at 12 (1954), *per* Frankfurter J., speaking for the court.
[8] *Ibid.*, at p. 16n. For other instances, see *Peckham* v. *United States*, 210 F. 2d 693 at 703–706 (1953).
[9] *Offutt* v. *United States*, *supra*, at p. 17n.

75

the two. For one reason or another the judge failed to impose his moral authority on the proceedings. His behavior precluded that atmosphere of austerity which should especially dominate a criminal trial and which is indispensable for an appropriate sense of responsibility on the part of court, counsel and jury." [10] The conviction of the lawyer's client was also quashed by the Court of Appeals by reason of the trial judge's demonstration of " a bias and lack of impartiality which may well have influenced the jury." [11]

In a Scottish case [12] an advocate in Aberdeen had presented on behalf of his client a petition for an interdict in the Sheriff Court. After hearing the case, the Sheriff-Substitute refused the interdict, and was on the point of having his judgment written out by a clerk on the petition when the advocate laid hold of it and said "I withdraw the petition." The Sheriff-Substitute told him that it could not be withdrawn, and ordered him to restore it to the clerk: but the advocate walked out of court with it. A Sheriff's officer was then armed with a " process-caption," issued without notice to the advocate, and was despatched with instructions to get back the document or imprison the advocate; but when the officer entered the advocate's office and demanded the petition, the advocate threw it into the fire. He was thereupon seized and lodged in prison until the next day, when he was released.

The advocate then proceeded against the Sheriff-Substitute and his officers for (*inter alia*) damages; but despite carrying the case to the House of Lords, his claim failed throughout. In the course of argument, Lord Selborne " referred to the case of Chief Justice Gascoigne, who, without a moment's hesitation, and without any prior notification, sent the Prince of Wales instantly to the Fleet Prison for a contempt of Court committed *in praesentiâ*; the heir of the Crown submitting patiently to the sentence, and making reparation for his error by acknowledging it." [13]

---

[10] *Ibid.*, at p. 17, *per* Frankfurter J.
[11] *Peckham* v. *United States, supra*, at p. 702.
[12] *Watt* v. *Ligertwood* (1874) L.R. 2 Sc. & D. 361.
[13] *Ibid.*, at p. 367n.

It was, of course, Falstaff who asked Prince Hal " Shall there be gallows standing in England when thou art king, and resolution thus fobbed as it is with the rusty curb of old father antick the law? " [14] Holinshed's account of Prince Hal's contempt is brief. " Once to hie offence of the king his father, he had with his fist striken the chéefe iustice for sending one of his minions (vpon desert) to prison, when the iustice stoutlie commanded himselfe also streict to ward, & he (then prince) obeied. The king after expelled him out of his priuie councell, banisht him the court, and made the duke of Clarence (his yoonger brother) president of councell in his steed." [15]

Elyot is more ample. " The moste renomed prince, kynge Henry the fifte, late kynge of Englande, durynge the life of his father was noted to be fierce and of wanton courage. It hapned that one of his seruantes whom he well fauored, for felony by hym committed, was arrayned at the kynges benche; wherof he being aduertised, and incensed by light persones about hym, in furious rage came hastily to the barre, where his seruant stode as a prisoner, and commaunded hym to be unygued and sette at libertie, where at all men were abasshed, reserued the chiefe iustice, who humbly exhorted the prince to be contented that his seruaunt mought be ordred accordyng to the auncient lawes of this realme, or if he wolde haue hym saued from the rigour of the lawes, that he shuld optaine, if he moughte, of the kynge, his father, his gracious pardone; wherby no lawe or iustice shulde be derogate. With whiche answere the prince nothynge appeased, but rather more inflamed, endeuored hym selfe to take away his seruaunt. The iuge consideringe the perilous example and inconuenience that moughte therby ensue, with a valiant spirite and courage commaunded the prince upon his alegeance to leue the prisoner and departe his waye. With whiche commandment the prince, being set all in a fury, all chafed, and in a terrible maner, came up to the place of iugement—men thinkyng that he wolde haue slayne the iuge, or haue done to hym some damage; but the iuge sittyng styll,

---

[14] *Henry IV*, Part I, Act 1, sc. 2, l. 66.
[15] Holinshed's *Chronicles* (ed. 1808) vol. III, p. 61.

without mouynge, declarynge the maiestie of the kynges place
of iugement, and with an assured and bolde countenance, hadde
to the prince these words folowyng: Sir, remembre your selfe;
I kepe here the place of the king, your soueraigne lorde and
father, to whom ye owe double obedience, wherfore, eftsones
in his name, I charge you desiste of your wilfulnes and unlaufull
entreprise, and from hensforth gyue good example to those
whiche hereafter shall be your propre subiectes. And nowe for
your contempt and disobedience, go you to the prisone of the
kynges benche, where unto I committe you; and remayne ye
there prisoner untill the pleasure of the kyng, your father, be
further knowen. With whiche wordes beinge abasshed, and
also wondrynge at the meruailous grauitie of that worshipful
Justice, the noble prince, layinge his waipon aparte, doinge
reuerence, departed and went to the kynges benche as he was
commaunded. Wherat his seruants disdainyng, came and
shewed to the kynge all the hole affaire. Wherat he a whiles
studienge, after as a man all rauisshed with gladness, holdyng
his eien and handes up towarde heuen, abrayded, sayinge with
a loude voice, O mercifull god, howe moche am I, aboue all
other men, bounde to your infinite goodnes; specially for that
ye haue gyuen me a iuge, who feareth nat to ministre iustice,
and also a sonne who can suffre semblably and obey iustice? " [16]

It has been asserted that Gascoigne died before Henry IV,
so that Shakespeare's account of Henry V reappointing
Gascoigne to his office as Chief Justice [17] must be fiction. In
fact, he seems to have outlived Henry IV, though he does not
seem to have been reappointed Chief Justice.[18] But quite apart
from this, the whole story rests upon the most doubtful foundations.[19] Other versions recount the striking of the Chief Justice
but substitute removal from the King's Council and exclusion

[16] Sir Thomas Elyot, *The Gouernour* (1531: ed. 1880) vol. 2, p. 61.
[17] *Henry IV*, Part II, Act 5, sc. 2.
[18] See 4 Foss's *Judges* 166–169; and see 1 Camp.C.JJ. 136.
[19] See the learned notes of the editor, H. H. S. Croft, in Elyot, *supra*, at pp.
60–71, 643; A. Luders, *An Essay on the Character of Henry the Fifth when
Prince of Wales* (1813) p. 75 *et seq.* Foss, however, seems to accept it (see
4 Foss's *Judges* 127, 128, 166), and so do Coke (3 Co.Inst. 225), Lord
Campbell (1 Camp.C.JJ. 125–133), and Lord Selborne, *supra*.

from the King's Court as the punishment [20]; and a contemporary version mentions removal from the Council but says nothing of the offence.[1]

The story may be an echo of an incident recounted in 1305. William de Brewes, misliking a judgment pronounced against him by Roger de Hegham B., climbed on the bar, and with gross and contemptuous words found fault with the judgment, and also grossly insulted the judge. This was referred to the King in Council, and the King ordered that William de Brewes should first go bareheaded to the Exchequer, seek the judge's pardon and apologise to him, and that he should then stand committed to the Tower during the King's pleasure. During the course of these proceedings, the King referred to an occasion on which his beloved son, Edward Prince of Wales (later to be Edward II) had uttered gross and bitter words to one of the King's Ministers (perhaps Walter de Langton, Bishop of Lichfield and Coventry [2]). For this, the King had banished the Prince of Wales from the court for nearly six months, and had refused to admit him to his presence until he had made satisfaction to the Minister.[3] These events were about a century old when the Gascoigne incident could have occurred,[4] and not much variation is required for later generations to father on to Edward, Prince of Wales, the conduct and punishment of William de Brewes with which events had associated him, and then to transfer the whole to a later Prince of Wales who seems to have been removed from the Council for some unknown offence.

In more recent days, a member of the Bar who was an M.P., and practised but little, once appeared in the Court of Chancery before Master Brougham as counsel for himself and other petitioners. Later he sent a long letter to Master Brougham, in

[20] Robert Redmayne, *Henrici Quinti Historia* (ed. 1858) p. 11 (translated A. J. Church, *Henry the Fifth* (1906) p. 25). Redmayne wrote late in the reign of Henry VIII: see p. xxviii of the editor's preface to his book.
[1] Thomas Hardyng, citing Church, *supra*, at p. 26.
[2] See 3 Foss's *Judges* 43.
[3] *Coram Rege Roll* No. 182 (Mich. 1305) m. 75d (58 S.S. 152–154; and see p. lxxx); *Abbreviatio Placitorum t.Ric.1–Edw.* 2 (1811) pp. 256, 257.
[4] Gascoigne became C.J.K.B. in 1400; Henry succeeded to the throne in 1414, aged 26 years.

threatening and insulting terms, complaining of his decision and seeking to induce him to change his mind.[5]   This letter was referred to Lord Cottenham L.C., who directed copies of it to be sent to all parties concerned, and adjourned further consideration.   The barrister then wrote a long letter to Lord Cottenham, referring to many matters, including the master's "want of punctuality" and "the reprehensible manner in which he preserves order in his own court,"[6] and asking whether Lord Cottenham "ever knew a person, who called himself a Judge, and who shelters under the purity of the judicial mantle, to have been guilty of the practices with which Master Brougham stands charged by me, and of which I have unquestionable proof?"[7]   He also referred to "the gross irregularity, not to say indecency, that prevailed in the Master's Court."[8]   After further consideration by the Lord Chancellor, and the successful evasion by the barrister of an order to attend and show cause why he should not be committed for contempt, a warrant of committal was issued on November 26, 1836, though not until February 3, 1837, was the barrister apprehended and taken to the Fleet.

Lord Cottenham had in the meantime, on the first day on which Parliament met, informed the Speaker of the warrant, and the barrister had written to the Speaker claiming privilege. A Committee of Privileges was appointed on February 1, 1837, and considered the case, but on February 16, 1837, the committee reported their opinion that the barrister's claim to discharge by reason of privilege ought not to be admitted.   Two days later Lord Cottenham heard a petition by the barrister for release, but refused it, as the petition contained no expression of regret for the attempt to influence the Master.   On February 24, 1837, the barrister tried again, and this time the petition was held, by a narrow margin,[9] to express sufficient contrition; and so after three weeks in the Fleet the barrister was discharged.

Is truth a defence *per se* to a charge of contempt of court by

---

[5] *Mr. Lechmere Charlton's Case* (1837) 2 My. & Cr. 316.
[6] *Ibid.*, at p. 326.
[7] *Ibid.*, at p. 327.
[8] *Ibid.*, at p. 330.   [9] See *ibid.*, at p. 360.

defaming a judge? There seems to be no clear English authority on the point; but such a defence in cases of contempt has been rejected in the United States, where the same rule has been applied as for criminal libel. Thus it has been held that " a publication likely to reach the eyes of a jury, declaring a witness in a pending cause a perjurer, would be none the less a contempt that it was true. It would tend to obstruct the administration of justice, because even a correct conclusion is not to be reached or helped in that way, if our system of trials is to be maintained. The theory of our system is that the conclusions to be reached in a case will be induced only by evidence and argument in open court, and not by any outside influence, whether of private talk or public print." [10] This principle was applicable even where the contempt was an attack on the motives and conduct of judges in cases still pending. At its full width, this doctrine would mean that a person charged with contempt in alleging that a judge had accepted bribes would not be allowed to adduce in his defence even conclusive evidence that his charge was true.[11] On this view, he who seeks to assail a corrupt Francis Bacon must adopt other means.

Excessive zeal has betrayed a number of members of the legal profession into contempt. One solicitor so far espoused the cause of his client in a patent action as to write, under a pseudonym, a number of letters to a paper controverting one of the issues which would fall for decision in the pending action; and for this he was committed.[12] Other solicitors have engaged in the professional misconduct involved in permitting clients to swear affidavits known to be false [13]; and counsel who conspired to put untrue affidavits before the court has been committed.[14]

---

[10] *Patterson* v. *Colorado*, 205 U.S. 454 at 462 (1907), *per* Holmes J., speaking for the court.

[11] Consider *Re K. L. Gauba* (1942) I.L.R. 23 Lah. 411 at 422, *per* Young C.J. ("Any attempt to justify a libel on a Judge by attempting to show that the libel was justified would itself be a fresh contempt"); *M. G. Kadir* v. *Kesri Nrain Jaitly*, I.L.R. [1945] All. 7 at 10, *per* Allsop J. ("It is, indeed, obvious that every attempt to justify must constitute a new offence of contempt committed in the very face of the court.")

[12] *Daw* v. *Eley* (1868) L.R. 7 Eq. 49.

[13] *Re Gray* (1869) 20 L.T. 730; *Re Davies* (1898) 14 T.L.R. 332.

[14] *Linwood* v. *Andrews* (1888) 58 L.T. 612.

It is also highly improper (though not a contempt) for a solicitor, unasked, to put a will into the hands of a witness while he is being examined as to the execution of the will.[15]

Another type of excess of zeal was involved once when Kekewich J. was vacation judge. The solicitor for one of the defendants to an action, on leaving the judge's chambers, assailed the plaintiff's solicitor with foul and offensive names. He called him " a d—d perjured scoundrel," and the plaintiff's solicitor, on reaching the exit door of the Law Courts, not surprisingly applied for protection to some constables standing there. Nevertheless, the defendant's solicitor continued his abuse, and several times " put his hands near the plaintiff's face in a threatening attitude." [16] On the application of the plaintiff and his solicitor to Kekewich J. in court, the defendant's solicitor was committed for contempt; and the Court of Appeal upheld the committal.[17] McMahon M.R. once attached a plaintiff " for horse-whipping the defendant inside the porch of the Rolls court, in consequence of the defendant having by his answer asserted the illegitimacy of the plaintiff " [18]; and he did the same to another plaintiff who, it seemed, " abused, threatened and insulted " the defendant and his counsel in the Master's office.[19] In Australia, there were once noisy hammerings in the proximity of a court in session which disturbed the proceedings, and a refusal to obey the judge's order to desist was held a contempt.[20]

A curious tale from eighteenth-century Ireland concerns a litigant, one Bateman, who had instituted an unsuccessful prosecution, and was also engaged in civil proceedings. He employed a fresh attorney, who asked to see one of Bateman's briefs. These, it was said by a third party, had been left lying about at the court house, and had been taken away by the accused's attorney. Bateman's new attorney then sent a messenger to fetch the briefs, but when he returned it was found that he had

---

15 *Wright* v. *Wilkin* (1858) 6 W.R. 643.
16 *Re Johnson* (1887) 20 Q.B.D. 68 at 69.
17 *Re Johnson* (1887) 20 Q.B.D. 68. Contrast 1 Misc. 21.
18 *O'Reilly* v. *O'Reilly* (n.d.) 1 Hog. 138.
19 *French* v. *French* (1824) 1 Hog. 138; *cf. Parashuram Detaram Shamdasani* v. *King-Emperor* [1945] A.C. 264.
20 *Re Dakin* (1887) 13 V.L.R. 522.

by mistake been given the brief for the accused. Bateman and his attorney thereupon proceeded not only to read it but also to make as public as possible a statement in it which in some degree vindicated Bateman. His attorney also refused to return the brief to its owner. The Court of Exchequer in Ireland ordered the brief to be delivered to an officer of the court, and attached both Bateman and his attorney; and the House of Lords affirmed this decision.[1]

Nearly two centuries later there occurred what might be regarded as a faint English echo of this episode. The power of the Court of Appeal to grant a litigant leave to adduce new evidence is exercised sparingly; amongst other things, it has to be shown that the evidence in question could not have been adduced at the trial by the exercise of due diligence. In 1950 part of the new evidence sought to be introduced consisted of a photograph of the brief that had been delivered to counsel on the other side for the trial. Evershed M.R. conceded that the appellant could not initially have seen this " by any diligence— at any rate, any proper diligence," [2] though on other grounds leave was refused. What was not explained was how the appellant had, between trial and appeal, obtained the photograph of a document that opposing litigants very properly are astute to conceal from each other; possibly the revelation occurred in connection with the taxation of costs. It may be added that a privileged document such as a brief remains privileged indefinitely [3]; but this privilege does not extend to any copies of the document which the other side may have obtained, so that if the privilege is claimed for the original, secondary evidence of its contents may be given, *e.g.*, by proving copies.[4] This is so even if the original from which the copies were made was obtained improperly, *e.g.*, by being stolen.[5]

---

[1] *Bateman* v. *Conway* (1753) 1 Bro.P.C. 519.
[2] *Field* v. *Daily Telegraph Ltd.* (1950) 67 R.P.C. 105 at 107.
[3] See *Hobbs* v. *Hobbs* [1960] P. 112 (brief still privileged on taxation of costs).
[4] *Calcraft* v. *Guest* [1898] 1 Q.B. 759.
[5] *Ibid.*, at p. 764, citing *Lloyd* v. *Mostyn* (1842) 10 M. & W. 478 at 482, *per* Parke B.; and see *Kuruma* v. *R.* [1955] A.C. 197 at 203, citing *R.* v. *Leatham* (1861) 8 Cox C.C. 498 at 501, *per* Crompton J.

Olendorf's New Method of Teaching French

VARIOUS forms of oaths are well enough known, such as the oath of a witness or interpreter. But what oath should be administered to an independent musical expert, chosen by agreement between the parties to play a piano in court to illustrate the arguments in a case alleging infringement of musical copyright? The answer is "I swear by Almighty God that I will, to the best of my ability, skill and knowledge, well and truly interpret and illustrate to the court the music and all such matters and questions as may be required of me." [1]

Occasionally a witness has his own ideas about the oath that he will take. During the "trial" of Queen Caroline, the question was raised whether the oath taken by one of the witnesses qualified him to give evidence. In the ensuing debate, Lord Erskine referred to a case in the King's Bench in which he had been engaged while at the Bar. "A witness came who did not describe himself to be of any particular sect, entitling him to an indulgence, but stating that, from certain ideas in his own mind, he could not swear according to the usual form of the oath; that he would hold up his hand, and would swear, but would not kiss the book. I have no difficulty in saying, that I wished very much to get rid of that witness, and I asked what was his reason for refusing to be sworn in a certain form? He gave a reason which appeared to me a very absurd one, but it strengthens the very matter we are upon—'because it was written in the Revelations that the Angel standing upon the sea held up his hand'—this appeared to me to be no very good reason. I said this does not apply to your case, for, in the first place, you are no angel, secondly, you cannot tell how the Angel would have sworn if he had been on shore. The chief justice sent into the court of Common Pleas to ask the opinion of chief justice Eyre, and the opinion delivered by chief justice Eyre, and which the learned chief justice thought himself bound by was, that though this man could not swear himself to be of a particular sect, yet, if he stated (whether his reason was a good

[1] *Francis Day & Hunter Ltd.* v. *Bron* [1963] Ch. 587 at 597.

or a bad one) that that was the manner consistent with his feelings of the obligation of an oath, and that which would be binding on his conscience, that was the oath which ought to be put to him; and that was administered. The question is what the witness feels himself." [2]

In New York in 1820 a witness had, before the trial, denied a belief in God and the hereafter; he had also said that he did not believe in the scriptures, and had as lief be sworn on a spelling book as the Bible. At the trial he said that he did not know that he had any reason to doubt that there was an after-state of rewards and punishments; and he was sworn. But the Supreme Court held him incompetent, and ordered a new trial.[3] In contrast, at an election in New York, certain inspectors, clerks and voters were unwittingly sworn upon a book that afterwards turned out to be not the Bible but Olendorf's *New Method of Teaching French*, and others were similarly sworn on Watts' *Psalms and Hymns*; but this was held not to invalidate the election.[4]

In England, it was held no objection to a charge of administering an unlawful oath [5] that the oath was taken on what in fact was not a Bible but *The Young Man's Best Companion*. Holroyd J. said that " if the oath administered by the prisoner to the poachers was intended to make the people believe themselves under an engagement, it is equally within the Act whether the book made use of was a Testament or not." [6]   More recently, there were difficulties in a case in the Queen's Bench Division which gave Hallett J. an exercise in comparative theology. " The parties being Hindus, it was found that a copy of their sacred book was not available. By their counsel the parties stated that they believed in one God, and his Lordship directed, with the consent of the parties, that the oath should be administered in the short Scottish form." [7]

---

2 (1820) Hansard (2nd ser.) vol. 2, col. 912. See Revelations, x.5.
3 *Jackson* d. *Tuttle* v. *Gridley*, 18 Johns.Sup. 98 (1820).
4 *People* v. *Cook*, 14 Barb. 259 (1852): see at pp. 295, 299, 310, 320, 323.
5 Under the Unlawful Oaths Act, 1797.
6 *R.* v. *Brodribb* (1816) 6 C. & P. 571 at 575.
7 *Shrinagesh* v. *Kaushal* [1956] *The Times* Oct. 3, not cited in *R.* v. *Pritam Singh* [1958] 1 W.L.R. 143; and see Perjury Act, 1911, s. 15 (1). For authority, see Oaths Act, 1888, s. 5.

One Irish view of the sanctity of the oath was attributed to
the emphasis to be placed on the last three words of the
Commandment, " Thou shalt not bear false witness against thy
neighbour." *Ergo*, thou shalt bear false witness in his favour
if required [8] : what could be clearer? At least three types of
alibi were once in general use, a use so general that there came
into being the word " aliboy " as describing a witness giving
such evidence.[9] In the Kerry alibi, the temporal successor to
the outworn " clock " alibi,[10] all was true save the date. The
events had really happened, but on the day before or the day
after the day to which they were being ascribed. The Achilles'
heel of this was that various other local events might have taken
place on that other day, so that Michael O'Flaherty's funeral,
which had taken place on the Monday, might emerge as part
of the tale of events which, occurring in fact on the Monday,
were being sworn to Tuesday. With this in mind, the police
kept careful records of the dates and times of all such events.[11]
   In another form of alibi (geographically anonymous, it
seems), dates and all else were true; but some friendly stranger
would be imported to impersonate the absent criminal. While
Patrick was away on his unlawful occasion, another man,
preferably a relative stranger, would be present in the company
of as many apparently respectable witnesses as possible, answering to the name of Patrick and doing all that the true Patrick
would have done.[12] A Tipperary alibi, on the other hand,
looked not to the accused but to the witnesses for the prosecution. Once they had been disclosed in the preliminary proceedings before the magistrates, a mass of evidence would be prepared
to show that each of these witnesses was somewhere else than
in the place he had sworn to on the day of the crime.[13]
   There are more ways than one of meeting the problems posed
by oral testimony. When Judge Parry held his first court in a
district from which his predecessor had just resigned, he found

8 A. M. Sullivan, *Old Ireland* (1927) p. 42.
9 A. M. Sullivan, *The Last Serjeant* (1952) p. 109.
10 Sullivan, *Old Ireland*, *supra*, p. 123.
11 M. Healy, *The Old Munster Circuit* (1939) p. 178.
12 See Sullivan, *Old Ireland*, *supra*, at p. 124.
13 Healy, *supra*, p. 180.

that much time was spent in enforcing an order that all witnesses should leave the court. So the new judge sent for the registrar and told him his views.

" ' I don't want all the witnesses out of Court,' I said.

' The late judge always had them out of Court, your Honour.'

' I dare say, but I don't think it's necessary, and it wastes time.'

' Yes, your Honour, but the late judge always had the witnesses out of court,' repeated the registrar.

' Well, I must ask you not to order them out of Court today. It takes a long time to get them out, and longer still to get them back again.'

There was a note of contempt in the registrar's voice as he replied, ' The late judge never had the witnesses back, your Honour.'

I felt that I was in the presence of a procedure invented by a judicial genius." [14]

Not surprisingly, difficulties have arisen in England in cases where a litigant has called his opponent as a witness. Such a move is rare but by no means unknown; indeed, it may even be essential.[15] One consequent disadvantage is that the litigant " by electing to call him as his own witness had disabled himself from impeaching his credit." [16] Nor may the litigant as of right treat the witness as a hostile witness and as such cross-examine him.[17] On the other hand, at the end of the examination-in-chief counsel for the witness-litigant is not entitled as of right to cross-examine his own client, at all events with a view to employing the greater latitude given by cross-examination for the purpose of strengthening his evidence and not impeaching it.[18] Such a witness may thus escape all cross-examination; the matter is one for the discretion of the court.[19]

[14] Sir Edward Parry, *What the Judge Saw* (1912) p. 178, *My Own Way* (1932) p. 227.   [15] See *Bradshaw* v. *Widdrington* (1902) 86 L.T. 726 at 732.
[16] *Scott* v. *Sampson* (1882) 8 Q.B.D. 491 at 498, *per* Cave J.
[17] *Price* v. *Manning* (1884) 42 Ch.D. 373.
[18] *Tedeschi* v. *Singh* [1948] Ch. 319 (plaintiff calls one of two joint defendants).
[19] *Price* v. *Manning, supra*; *Tedeschi* v. *Singh, supra*. In some jurisdictions, the right to call the opposing party as a witness is regulated by statute: see, e.g., *Milk Board* v. *Hillside Farm Dairy Ltd.* (1963) 43 W.W.R. 131 (British Columbia).

Though rare in England, in India the practice seems to have been common; indeed, it appears to have formed part of a regular plan of campaign. In the Judicial Committee Lord Atkinson left no doubt as to the Board's view of the practice. He said " It is one of the artifices of a weak and somewhat paltry kind of advocacy for each litigant to cause his opponent to be summoned as a witness, with the design that each party shall be forced to produce the opponent so summoned as a witness, and thus give the counsel for each litigant the opportunity of cross-examining his own client. It is a practice which their Lordships cannot help thinking all judicial tribunals ought to set themselves to render as abortive as it is objectionable." [20]

A year later Lord Atkinson returned to the attack. He referred to the " species of advocacy tolerated by the Courts of Law in [India], in which the unworthy effort of the advocate on each side is to force his opponent to produce his own client in order that he himself may have the opportunity of cross-examining that client. The result is that, should the opponent refuse to be led into this trap, the parties (the principal witnesses, who possibly could throw light on all these tangled transactions which so perplex those who have to decide these cases) are never examined at all, and the litigation goes forward through tortuous windings to its unsatisfactory and uncertain end. This case is a good example of this practice, for not only was the plaintiff not examined on his own behalf, but the defendant . . . was not examined on her own behalf either. It is a vicious practice, unworthy of a high-toned or reputable system of advocacy. It must embarrass and perplex judicial investigation, and, it is to be feared, too often enables fraud, falsehood, or chicane to baffle justice." [1]

Nearly twenty years later there seems to have been little change for the better. In another appeal, Lord Shaw of Dunfermline referred to the " manoeuvre under which counsel does not call his own client, who is an essential witness, but endeavours to force the other party to call him, and so suffer the discomfiture of having him treated as his, the other party's,

[20] *Kishori Lal* v. *Chunni Lal* (1908) L.R. 36 I.A. 9 at 13.
[1] *Musammat Lal Kunwar* v. *Chiranji Lal* (1909) L.R. 37 I.A. 1 at 4.

own witness. This is thought to be clever, but it is a bad and degrading practice." [2]

In Scotland, apart from the normal rules of evidence, there is a special procedure known as " reference to oath," or " oath of party," whereby one party may, subject to the discretion of the court, require the other to give evidence as to the issue on oath; and if he does this, he is bound by the answers given. " It has been a fixed rule of the law of Scotland for centuries, that a party, pursuer or defender, even after all other methods of discussion or evidence have failed, may say to his adversary before the Court, though I cannot produce other evidence to show the truth, I appeal it to your own oath—to your own conscience as a Christian man. And our law, though different from others, allows this, on the simple principle, that, however strong a case a man may apparently have on documents or apparent evidence, he ought not to be permitted to maintain it against conscience; and that, if he cannot himself swear to the facts as averred by him, and which, if true, must be known to himself, or deny upon oath the material averments of his adversary, though not otherwise proved, he shall not be permitted to avail himself of the appearance of evidence on the one side, or the absence of it on the other, to take a judicial sentence contrary to the truth as revealed by his own conscience." [3] Such a reference may be made at any time before the final decree has been extracted, even though the trial has long been concluded and the House of Lords has given final judgment on the merits.[4]

This Scottish procedure accords due recognition to the hope that in giving evidence the good in man will triumph over temptation. Such a recognition is not confined to Scotland. " Strictly speaking, the court should not instruct the jury that the interest of a witness affects his credit. The better instruction is, that it *may* affect his credit. Interest and truth may go together. Is there, in the world, an honest man who does not

---

[2] *Sardar Gurbakhsh Singh* v. *Gurdial Singh* (1927) 46 Calc.L.J. 272 at 279.
[3] *Pattinson* v. *Robertson*, 1846, 9 D. 226 at 229, *per* Lord Moncrieff.
[4] *Longworth* v. *Yelverton*, 1867, 5 M.(H.L.) 144. See generally *Encyclopaedia of the Law of Scotland*, vol. 10 (1930) pp. 395–415.

know that he can tell the truth against his interest? Interest is felt as a temptation; but corruption reaches to an excess if, yielding to temptation, it succumbs on every occasion. We suppose it does not. Where there is possible doubt as to the effect of villainy upon veracity, the jury ought to be left to decide it. As coming from the average of society, they know best what to think on such a question. Interest is a great rascal; but is not an absolute reprobate. Its doom is not perdition at all events. It has a chance of salvation. It is not obliged to commit perjury." [5]

Laymen do not always realise that lawyers often do not themselves makes the best witnesses. "Every lawyer dislikes to take the witness stand and will do so only for grave reasons. This is partly because it is not his role; he is almost invariably a poor witness. But he steps out of professional character to do it. He regrets it; the profession discourages it." [6] One particular aspect of lawyers as witnesses is the obvious undesirability of a person acting in a case both as advocate and as witness. However, the consequences of acting in such a dual capacity are by no means clear. There have been cases where in an inferior court an attorney, having acted as advocate for his client, has tendered himself as a witness and has given evidence.[7] In such cases new trials have been ordered, for, as Patteson J. said, such a procedure is " not consistent with the proper administration of justice." [8] But some doubt was cast upon this rule by a case in which Lord Campbell C.J. delivered the judgment of the court. In this, it was held that it had been improper for him to have told a litigant that he could not be permitted to address the jury as his own advocate without agreeing to waive his right to give evidence on his own behalf.[9] Such facts, of course, raise rather different questions; but it is certainly " irregular and contrary to practice " for counsel to

---

[5] *Davis* v. *The Central Railroad*, 60 Ga. 329 at 333 (1878), *per* Bleckley J. See also *ante*, p. 19.
[6] *Hickman* v. *Taylor*, 329 U.S. 495 at 517 (1947), *per* Jackson J.
[7] *Stones* v. *Byron* (1846) 16 L.J.Q.B. 32; *Dunn* v. *Packwood* (1847) 2 New Pr.Cas. 65; and see *R.* v. *Brice* (1819) 2 B. & Ald. 606.
[8] *Stones* v. *Byron*, *supra*, at p. 33.
[9] *Corbett* v. *Hudson* (1852) 1 E. & B. 11.

continue to act as an advocate in a case after he has given evidence in it, even if that evidence was merely as to certain aspects of foreign law.[10]

If counsel appears only as a witness, there is nothing to disqualify him from giving evidence of what occurred in court on a previous occasion, even against the interests of his client, provided no breach of professional confidence is involved. Thus in one case a clerk was prosecuted for embezzlement, but the magistrate dismissed the charge. The clerk then sued the prosecutor, who had been his employer, for malicious prosecution; and in those proceedings a question arose as to an entry in a day book. It had been the duty of the clerk to make entries in the book, and the sum in dispute was duly entered in it. The employer, however, contended that the entry had not been in the book at the time of the initial hearing before the magistrate, and that it must have been made by the clerk while he was on bail between the first and second days of the hearing by the magistrate. Before the close of the employer's case in the clerk's action, Jervis C.J. observed that the member of the Bar who had appeared for the clerk in the prosecution was in court. He could clear the matter up, and ought to state what he knew about it. Counsel did not object to testifying, and then gave evidence that he believed that the entry had not been in the book at the first hearing before the magistrate; and on this the clerk's action was dismissed. Subsequently, the Court of Exchequer held that this evidence was properly admitted.[11] On the other hand, where the issue was the accuracy of a newspaper report of what counsel had said in court, Eyre C.J. held that it was at the option of counsel whether or not to give evidence as to what he had said; and counsel, the great Erskine, declined to testify.[12]

Where counsel does give evidence as to what occurred in a case in which he was professionally engaged (and this is often as to the terms of an alleged settlement of that case), there are

10 R. v. *Secretary of State for India in Council, ex p. Ezekiel* [1941] 2 K.B. 169 at 175n.
11 *Brown* v. *Foster* (1857) 1 H. & N. 736.
12 *Curry* v. *Walter* (1796) 1 Esp. 456.

three methods possible. First, he may give evidence from his place in counsel's row, robed but unsworn.[13] Lord Esher M.R. once said " It is not the practice of this Court to allow an affidavit by counsel, as to matters that occurred within his knowledge as counsel at a trial, to be read. The Court places implicit confidence in the statement of a counsel; and when the Court requires information from a learned counsel as to anything that has taken place in a case in which he appeared, our practice is to ask the counsel to attend and state to the Court what occurred." [14]

This occurred in one divorce case in which, after an inter-locutory skirmish in the Court of Appeal,[15] the respondent abandoned her defence on the fourth day of the hearing and the petitioner obtained a decree nisi [16]; but later the Queen's Proctor successfully intervened on the ground of collusion.[17] During the evidence given on the intervention, Sir Frank Lockwood Q.C., who appeared for the Queen's Proctor, said that Sir Edward Clarke Q.C., who had appeared for the petitioner at the trial, was in court, " and although he cannot go into the witness box, he will be glad to make any statement which may assist the Court." At this, Mr. Inderwick Q.C., who was then appearing for the petitioner, said " According to the practice of the Courts for centuries, counsel could not be called upon to give evidence as to how a case had been conducted by him, but I agree that it would be desirable for Sir Edward Clarke to give the Court any information he may have." The report continues " Sir Edward Clarke, Q.C., standing in the Queen's Counsel's row, then stated . . ." [18]

The second possibility is that of counsel giving evidence on oath from the witness box, unrobed, like any other witness.[19] This at least has the advantage of avoiding the crick in the neck

---

[13] See *Kempshall* v. *Holland* (1895) 14 R. 336 at 337; *Hickman* v. *Berens* [1895] 2 Ch. 638 at 640, 641.
[14] *Kempshall* v. *Holland*, *supra*, at p. 337; and see *Iggulden* v. *Terson* (1833) 2 Dowl.Pr. 277.   [15] *Cox* v. *Cox* (1893) 70 L.T. 200.
[16] *Cox* v. *Cox* [1894] *The Times* Nov. 19, 21, 22, 23.
[17] *Cox* v. *Cox* [1895] *The Times* Nov. 20, 21, 22, 23.
[18] *Ibid.*, Nov. 21; and see (1895) 30 L.J.News. 693.
[19] See *Appleby* v. *Errington* [1952] *The Times* Oct. 18; and see *Oxley* v. *Pitts* [1904] *The Times* Dec. 1.

which might well ensue from the cross-examination of a leader in the front row by a junior in the second row, or, perhaps worse still, *vice versa*. The third possibility is an intermediate course, which seems to have little to commend it, namely, that of counsel giving evidence from his place at the bar, robed but on oath.[20] In one case, indeed, Jowitt K.C., at the request of Astbury J., gave evidence thus, while others adopted the first method.[1]

The practice of allowing counsel to give unsworn evidence from his place in court seems to have been applied even where at the time in question he was acting not as counsel but as an arbitrator. Thus when one of the parties to an arbitration alleged that the arbitrator, " a gentleman at the Chancery bar," had refused to look into some accounts, the Court of King's Bench said " We shall not direct him to make an affidavit. He may either personally state to the court what he thinks proper, or he may make an affidavit." Four days later the arbitrator " appeared in court, and stated that he had looked at those accounts," whereupon the court said " We are much obliged to the learned gentleman for his attendance. We are satisfied that justice has been done between the parties." [2]

Judges, too, have been called as witnesses.[3] Thus Hodson L.J. once gave evidence as to a case which he had heard as Hodson J. He testified from the Bench, unrobed and unsworn, sitting beside Vaisey J., who was hearing the action. Vaisey J. said " In no circumstances would I have allowed or invited him to make a statement from the well of the Court, still less would I allow him to make a statement on oath, but I will allow both counsel to put any questions to him." [4] This leaves nicely poised the position of counsel in a case who is promoted to the Bench before the subsequent action is heard. He cannot very well return to counsel's row, and as his status in the case was

---

[20] *Wilding* v. *Sanderson* (1897) 76 L.T. 346 at 347; the report at [1897] 2 Ch. 534 at 539 is not explicit as to robes.

[1] *Owen* v. *Viscount Rothermere* [1927] *The Times* Feb. 12, 16. The others were Sir John Simon K.C., Maugham K.C. and Luxmoore K.C.

[2] *Mansfield* v. *Partington* (1824) 2 L.J.K.B.(O.S.) 153 at 154, a neglected decision.   [3] See also *ante,* p. 13.

[4] *Appleby* v. *Errington, supra.* See also *R.* v. *Baillie* (1779) 21 St.Tr. 1 at 341.

not that of a judge, it might be questioned whether it would
be right for him to do as Hodson L.J. did. In such circumstances, and in the same action as that in which Hodson L.J.
had given evidence, Karminski J. " preferred to give evidence
from the witness box "; and, unrobed and sworn, he in fact
gave it thus.[5] It is perhaps not surprising that at the end of
his evidence Vaisey J. should have asked " Any more Judges? " [6]
Karminski J. was, indeed, no judicial stranger to the witness
box, for less than a year earlier he had been called on subpoena
to give evidence about meetings that had taken place in his
chambers while he was still at the Bar.[7] On the other hand, in
1905 Bargrave Deane J. made an unsworn statement from the
Bench as to certain proceedings in which he had been engaged
as counsel.[8]

One question to which there seems to be no very clear answer
is whether, and how, the reigning sovereign can give evidence
in legal proceedings. There is some authority for two apparently
inconsistent propositions, namely (1) that a certificate by the
sovereign under his sign manual as to what occurred is admissible, and (2) that the sovereign cannot give evidence at all.
The first proposition is open to the obvious objection that such
evidence does not readily admit of cross-examination or any
other method of resolving uncertainties, while the second
proposition is open to the even greater objection that highly
cogent evidence may be excluded. At least it seems probable
that the courts would be reluctant to allow the sovereign to
attend to give *viva voce* evidence in the ordinary way. The
crux of the matter may well be cross-examination: " it would
not be seemly that he should be submitted to such an ordeal." [9]

The leading case on the subject concerned proceedings in
Chancery in the seventeenth century between Lord Abignye
and Lord Clifton on an alleged promise by Lord Clifton to
convey land on the marriage of his daughter. " The King, by
his letters under his signet manuel, certified to the late Lord

[5] *Appleby* v. *Errington, supra.*   [6] *Ibid.*
[7] *Pool* v. *Pool* [1951] P. 470.   [8] (1905) 40 L.J.News. 415.
[9] *The Berkeley Peerage: The Claim of Lord Fitzhardinge* [1891] *The Times*
June 27, *per* Lord Hannen.

Chancellor, and also to this, the manner and substance of the promise, as it was made to His Majesty: in regard whereof, His Majesty gave to the Lord Abignye 18000 pounds in lieu of 1000 per annum in land which he had promised, which certificate was allowed upon the hearing for a proof without exception for so much." [10] In another case at about the same time Sir Henry Lea was committed to the Fleet for disobedience to a decree of the Court of Requests. He had denied having made a promise to the King; "but upon a certificate made by the Kings Majestie, that he made such a promise unto him, the Court of Requests made the said decree, which certificate was mentioned in the body of the said decree." [11] Sir Henry sought prohibition from the Court of Common Pleas, but without apparent success.

These authorities, however, do not appear to have concluded the matter. "Semble que le Roy ne poet estre un testimonie en un cause per son letters desouth son signett manuell. Contra Hobards Reports 288,[12] enter Abigny et Clifton en Chancery allow." [13] Again, "even the certificate of the King under his sign manual of a matter of fact, (except in one old case in Chancery, Hob. 213) has been always refused." [14] On the other hand, others have accepted the principle. "The king may yield a testimony in any cause; for so did king James in many things in the countess of Exeter's cause; and did in chancery by his letters under his signet in lord Auberville's cause." [15] In one sixteenth-century case, indeed, the court seems to have accepted a certificate in the writing of the Earl of Leicester as to words which Queen Elizabeth I uttered.[16]

---

[10] *Abignye* v. *Clifton*, Hob. 213. The King seems to have been James I, and the two Lords Chancellor Ellesmere and Bacon; the date of the case would then be during 1617–21.

[11] *Sir Henry Lea and Henry Leas Case* (1612) Godb. 198 at 199.

[12] *Sic.*

[13] 2 Roll.Abr. 686.

[14] *Omichund* v. *Barker* (1745) Willes 538 at 550, *per* Willes C.J.

[15] W. Hudson, *A Treatise on the Court of Star-Chamber*, 2 *Collectanea Juridica* 1 at 206.

[16] *Mark Steward's Case* (1579) 9 Co.Rep. 99b at 102a, 102b; and see *Sir George Reynel's Case* (1612) 9 Co.Rep. 95a at 98b *et seq.* Contrast *The Berkeley Peerage : The Claim of Lord Fitzhardinge* [1891] *The Times* June 27 (private letter of the Prince Regent rejected by a strong Committee for Privileges).

95

In more modern times, Lord Campbell, writing extra-judicially, stated that "I humbly apprehend that the Sovereign, if so pleased, might be examined as a witness in any case civil or criminal, but must be sworn, although there would be no temporal sanction to the oath." [17] The most recent case in which the point has arisen seems to be *R. v. Mylius* in 1911. In that case the defendant was convicted [18] of a libel in alleging that when George V married Queen Mary in 1893 he already had a wife, namely, a daughter of Admiral Sir Michael Culme-Seymour, whom he had married in Malta in 1880. In fact, the admiral had had two daughters, but in 1880 one was nine and the other seven, and neither had been to Malta until 1893. After sentence,[19] Sir Rufus Isaacs K.C., A.-G., said to Lord Alverstone C.J. that "there is a matter to which I should like to refer, and which I did not think your Lordship would have thought it right for me to mention until after verdict and sentence had been passed. I hold in my hands at this moment a document under the hand of his Majesty the King, from which with your Lordship's permission I will read. I am authorized by his Majesty to state publicly that he was never married except to the Queen and that he never went through any ceremony of marriage except with the Queen. And further that his Majesty would have attended to give evidence to this effect had he not received advice from the Law Officers of the Court that it would be unconstitutional for him to do so. That statement, my Lord, is signed by the King himself." [20]

The Solicitor-General of the day, Sir John Simon K.C., wrote of this case some forty years later. "One interesting question of law had to be investigated—can the reigning Sovereign give evidence as a witness in proceedings in the King's Court? It was a disappointment to His Majesty when I had to advise that this was, on constitutional grounds, impossible. There is, in fact, a precedent to illustrate this proposition derived from

[17] 3 Camp.L.CC. 215.
[18] On what appears to have been the most recent instance of an *ex officio* information: see Archbold's *Criminal Pleading, Evidence and Practice* (35th ed. 1962) p. 117.
[19] 12 months' imprisonment.
[20] *R. v. Mylius* [1911] *The Times* Feb. 2.

ancient times: a man convicted of treason during the Wars of
the Roses had to be released because the sole [1] evidence against
him was the testimony of the King himself." [2]   Unfortunately,
no details of this ancient precedent appear; and one may wonder
why it was preferred to more recent authorities.

The prisoner in a criminal trial has especial difficulties as a
witness. " It is not every one who can safely venture on the
witness stand though entirely innocent of the charge against
him. Excessive timidity, nervousness when facing others and
attempting to explain transactions of a suspicious character, and
offences charged against him, will often confuse and embarrass
him to such a degree as to increase rather than remove prejudices
against him." [3]   In this, there is some echo of the views of
Bentham. In discussing the extent to which a person's evident
confusion upon discovery or accusation may indicate his guilt,
Bentham recounts that " Bolingbroke, after his partial pardon
and return to England, being suspected of harbouring a person
accused of a state crime; his house, and even his bed-chamber,
as he was lying in his bed, were searched by the ministers of
justice. Traitorous bedfellow with him he had none: a bedfellow, however, he had; a female, whose reputation would have
been ruined by the disclosure. Confusion, more or less, he
could not but have betrayed. Had the search ended there, this
confusion would naturally and properly have been regarded as
circumstantial evidence of the crime he was suspected of. His
presence of mind saved him from that mischance. Uncovering
enough of her person to indicate the sex, without betraying the
individual, he preserved himself as well from the imputation of
the crime of which he was not guilty, as from the collateral
misfortune which that imputation was so near bringing on his
head." [4]

Truth does indeed usually prevail, though often after facing

---

[1] The requirement of two witnesses was introduced by the Treason Act, 1695,
s. 2, and abolished by the Treason Act, 1945.
[2] Viscount Simon, *Retrospect* (1952) p. 92. The opinion of Isaacs A.-G. and
Simon S.-G. is printed in full in H. Montgomery Hyde's *Lord Reading*
(1967) pp. 93, 94.
[3] *Wilson* v. *United States*, 149 U.S. 60 at 66 (1893), *per* Field J.
[4] Bentham, *Rationale of Judicial Evidence* (1827) vol. 3, p. 151.

adversity. " Our daily experience apprises us that events are constantly occurring which would, *a priori*, be pronounced in the highest degree improbable. That which is true does not always present the appearance of truth."[5] Yet "Human nature constitutes a part of the evidence in every case. We more easily believe that a person has done what we should have expected under the circumstances; and we require a greater degree of evidence to satisfy us that a person has done something which would be unnatural or improbable."[6]

Human nature plays its part in other ways. All too often it happens that a witness who has given clear and cogent evidence then ventures some additional remark which is so improbable that it deprives his testimony of much of its value. To apply the old saying, the effect of the remark is like that of the thirteenth chime of a crazy clock: it not only is disbelieved in itself but also casts doubt upon all that has gone before.[7] Nevertheless, it must be remembered that " By destroying . . . evidence you do not prove its opposite. If by cross-examination to credit you prove that a man's oath cannot be relied on, and he has sworn that he did not go to Rome on May 1, you do not, therefore, prove that he did go to Rome on May 1; there is simply no evidence on the subject."[8]

Unlike falsehood, "Truth needs no disguise."[9] In one Irish case there was a sharp conflict of evidence between a Mrs. Low, mother of James Low deceased, and a Mr. Holmes, solicitor to Mrs. Low and her son, who made certain claims for himself against the estate of the son. Of Mr. Holmes, Sir Joseph Napier L.C. observed that " of course there is, as in other instances, an appeal made by him to the testimony of the dead, who can neither corroborate nor contradict. I will not insult this lady, nor add one drop more to her cup of sorrow,

5 *United States* v. *Castillero*, 67 U.S. 17 at 276 (1862), *per* Wayne J., dissenting.
6 *Greene* v. *Harris*, 11 R.I. 5 at 17 (1874), *per* Potter J.; and see *ante*, p. 36.
7 A variant of this appears in *R.* v. *Haddock* (1927) Herbert's *Uncommon Law* 24 at 28, *per* Lord Light C.J.
8 *Hobbs* v. *C. T. Tinling & Co. Ltd.* [1929] 2 K.B. 1 at 21, *per* Scrutton L.J.
9 *Hazel-Atlas Glass Co.* v. *Hartford-Empire Co.*, 322 U.S. 238 at 247 (1944), *per* Black J.

still flowing over, by any studied comparison of her testimony with that of Mr. Holmes: it is enough to say, there is an idiom in truth, which falsehood can never imitate; by this, let these contradictions be tested." [10]

A different approach is that of Perrot B.,[11] who is credited (or debited) with what is perhaps the apotheosis of mathematical jurisprudence. In summing-up in a trial at Exeter as to the right to a certain stream of water, he concluded thus: "Gentlemen, there are fifteen witnesses who swear that the watercourse used to flow in a ditch on the north side of the hedge. On the other hand, gentlemen, there are nine witnesses who swear that the watercourse used to flow on the south side of the hedge. Now, gentlemen, if you subtract nine from fifteen, there remain six witnesses wholly uncontradicted; and I recommend you to give your verdict accordingly for the party who called those six witnesses." [12] Perhaps it was an echo of this that was in the mind of Lord Kenyon C.J. when he said " It is a canticle of courts of justice that witnesses *non numerentur sed ponderentur,* they are not to be numbered but weighed." [13]

---

[10] *Low* v. *Holmes* (1858) Dr.*t.*Nap. 290 at 323.
[11] He was on the Bench from 1763 to 1775.
[12] 8 Foss's *Judges* 355, citing no authority.
[13] *R.* v. *Rusby* (1800) Peake Add.Cas. 189 at 193.

The Wisest Thing Under Heaven

FOR many today, a traditional picture of the sixteenth and seventeenth centuries is one of subservience to the Tudors and resistance to the Stuarts. Yet there is at least one instance of stout judicial resistance to the commands of a Tudor. Elizabeth I granted to Richard Cavendish " the making and writing of all Supersedeas's upon exigent issuing out of our Court of common Pleas." The court (then composed of Wray C.J. and Gawdy, Clench and Shute JJ.) declined to admit Cavendish to the office, whereupon the Queen issued under her sign manual first one and then another command to the court to obey, the second being delivered in the presence of Bromley L.C. and the Earl of Leicester. But the court stood firm in defence of the fees of the existing office holders, which this new grant would diminish, with high sounding arguments based on Magna Carta and earlier precedents; and in the end the Queen gave way.[1] An instance of the gulf between the times of Elizabeth I and those of Elizabeth II is provided by a parliamentary report of 1597. " The Lord Keeper having finished his speech, and the queen given the royal assent to 15 private and 28 public bills, which had passed both houses, and refused or quashed 48 several bills, which had passed both houses, the said great officer, by her maj.'s command, dissolved this parliament." [2]

Selden left a terpsichorean picture of the royal courts of his day. " The Court of England has much altered. Att a Solemne dancing, first you have the grave measures, then the Corantoes & the Galliards, & all this is kept upp with ceremony, att length they fall to Trenchmore,[3] & so to the Cushion Dance, Lord & Groome, Lady and Kitchin Maid, no distinction: So in our Court. In Queen Eliz: time, Gravitie & state was kept upp. In King James time things were pretty well But in K. Charles time there has binn nothing but Trenchmore & the

---

[1] *Cavendish's Case* (1587) 1 And. 152; and see J. Manning, *Serviens ad Legem* (1840) p. 306.

[2] (1597) 1 Parl.Hist. (1806) col. 905.　　[3] A boisterous old English country dance.

Cushion dance, Omnium gatherum, totty polly, hoyte come toyte." [4] One of Selden's comments on Charles I is pointed. " The King useing the house of Comons, as hee did in Mr. Pym & his Company, that is chargeing them with treason because they charged my Lord of Canterbury & Sir George Ratcliffe it was just with as much Logick as the boy that would have layen with his Grandmother said to his father, You lay with my Mother & why should I not lye with yours." [5] Lord Campbell's verdict on George IV, uttered while his niece was Queen, was sweeping. " He is detested as the worst of the Georges—as a selfish voluptuary, whose flagrant vices were unredeemed by a single public or private virtue." [6]

Not every lawyer could offhand specify the circumstances in which, without any special Act of Parliament, a person could succeed twice to the throne of England by natural succession. Yet the answer is simple enough. If the King dies, survived by a widow but no son, his eldest daughter or other next heir at once succeeds to the throne. This succession, however, is defeasible and not absolute, though it prevents the Crown from being in abeyance. If a posthumous child of the deceased King is then born, with a superior claim to the throne, that child will on birth displace the defeasible successor. If subsequently that child dies without issue, the defeasible heir (if still living) will once again succeed to the throne, but this time absolutely.

This doctrine was recognised by a statute enacted in 1830,[7] shortly after William IV had succeeded to the throne and while Victoria was heir presumptive. Section 2 provided that if William IV died without issue but was survived by Queen Adelaide (as in fact occurred) Victoria should be proclaimed sovereign in the customary form, " but subject to and saving the Rights of any Issue of His said Majesty which may afterwards be born of Her said Majesty " [8]; and any oath, declaration or

---

[4] Selden, *Table Talk* 64.   [5] *Ibid.*, p. 65.
[6] Campbell, *Lives of Lord Lyndhurst and Lord Brougham* (1869) p. 323.
[7] 1 Will. 4, c. 2, 1830.
[8] As in fact was done: see *Annual Register*, 1837, **Chronicle**, p. 61; but compare p. 65. See also *The Greville Diary*, ed. P. W. Wilson (1927) vol. 1, p. 526. But in 1952 Elizabeth II was proclaimed without any such saving: see Supplement to London Gazette Extraordinary No. 39,458 (1952).

assurance of allegiance was to be qualified in a similar way.
The statute also provided that for a number of purposes any
such posthumous child of William IV should on birth succeed
to the throne in the same way as if there had been a demise of
Victoria, "and as Her Heir,"[9] so that to some extent each
could have succeeded as heir of the other. Much, indeed, had
happened since 1321, when one " Johannes de Crombewelle,"
Constable of the Tower of London, had very properly been
deprived of his office because he had allowed the Queen's bed-
chamber there to fall out of repair to such an extent that the
rain came in upon the Queen while she was giving birth to a
princess.[10]

The death of William IV gave rise to one problem. Acting
under statutory powers, he had granted to trustees for Queen
Adelaide an annuity of £100,000 a year, payable quarterly in
arrear after his death. The annuity was paid for some twelve
years, and then Queen Adelaide died, two-thirds of the way
through a quarter. Lord Brougham, the surviving trustee,
thereupon sought payment of an apportioned part of the
annuity, but failed. As the first instalment had been paid in
full, even though William IV had died only ten days before a
quarter day, this seems not unreasonable; but the arguments
appear to have ranged wide. In the words of Lord Campbell
C.J., " Finally, reliance is placed on the exalted rank of Her
Majesty. We are at a loss to know how this should influence
the construction of the language by which provision is made
for her: we might as well be told of her exemplary virtues
while living, and of her saintlike death, which will ever make
her memory cherished with affection and reverence by the
English nation: these we are ready to acknowledge; but we sit
here merely as Judges to interpret an Act of Parliament." [11]

A different activity of the ever-active Lord Brougham was

[9] 1 Will. 4, c. 2, 1830, s. 5.
[10] *Munimenta Gildhallae Londoniensis : Liber Custumarum* (R.S., 1860), vol.
II, Part I, p. 409 (" Quia pluviebat super lectum Reginae Angliae, puellam,
nomine ' Johannam,' parturientis ibidem "). The Queen was Isabella, wife
of Edward II, and the princess married the future David II of Scotland.
[11] *R. v. Lords Commissioners of the Treasury, ex p. Henry Lord Brougham
and Vaux* (1851) 16 Q.B. 357 at 366.

discussed by Lord Campbell in critical terms. Lord Campbell referred to " William Courtenay, whom Lord Chancellor Brougham, *proprio vigore*, created Earl of Devon. He was the undoubted male heir to the Courtenays, Earls of Devon, but only collaterally. Now the title had been limited to the grantee and *his heirs male*. This limitation, by the law of England, was only to heirs male descended from his body, and not to heirs male collateral, descended from a common ancestor. Therefore, when heirs male of the body of the grantee failed, the title was extinct. So it was universally understood ever since the last Earl died, ages ago, and the true representative of the family laying no claim to the earldom, had been created Viscount Courtenay to him and his heirs male. The Viscount's heirs male becoming extinct, William Courtenay, eldest son of the Bishop of Exeter, bred to the bar, made a Master in Chancery, and afterwards Clerk Assistant in the House of Lords, became the representative of this illustrious house. He made out his pedigree very satisfactorily, and (as he himself told me) he petitioned the Crown that he might have a writ sent to him as Earl of Devon, not with any thought of being entitled to this peerage, but in the hope that, his pedigree being clear, he might be created a peer by favour of the Crown, on account of his distinguished lineage, being of the same blood as the Bourbons and the Emperors of the East. It was referred by the Queen to the House of Lords, and coming before a Committee of Privileges (to the astonishment of all mankind, and particularly of the claimant) Lord Chancellor Brougham expressed a clear opinion that the point was well founded. Unfortunately for Brougham the point was defectively argued by Sir Thomas Denman, then Attorney General, who knew nothing of the subject, and omitted to cite the Prince's case from Lord Coke's Reports,[12] which would have been quite decisive against the claim." [13]

Lord Campbell adds " I have often rallied Brougham upon his creating William Courtenay Earl of Devon. He says that

---

[12] (1606) 8 Co.Rep. 1a.
[13] Campbell, *Lives of Lord Lyndhurst and Lord Brougham* (1869) p. 524.

he consulted Lord Chief Justice Tenterden, who agreed with
him in thinking the claim well founded. But Lord Chief
Justice Tenterden knew nothing of *Peerage law,* and must have
come to a contrary conclusion if he had heard the question
properly argued. If the limitation had been ' to the grantee *and
his heirs,*' it is allowed that the collateral heir male could not
have taken; and the limitation ' to the grantee and his heirs
male ' could not let in the collateral heir." [14]

These passages suggest that Lord Campbell was stronger on
his law than on his facts. As to the latter, doubts creep in at
once. Thus how could the peerage claim have been referred
by " the Queen " to the House of Lords and be considered by
a Committee " of " Privileges which included " Lord Chancellor
Brougham "? For Brougham was Lord Chancellor only in the
reign of William IV, and lost the Great Seal some three years
before Victoria became Queen. In fact, the Devon Peerage
Claim was decided in 1831.[15] On Lord Campbell's own
account it could not have been later than 1832, for in that year
Lord Tenterden died, Denman leapt from A.-G. to C.J.K.B.,
and Campbell himself in consequence became S.-G. But the
main point lies in the circumstantial detail given as to Mr.
William Courtenay, son of the Bishop of Exeter, petitioning
the Crown that a writ might be sent to him as Earl of Devon.
In fact, the claim was made not by him but by his third cousin,
William, Viscount Courtenay; and it was the viscount who on
May 14, 1831, was declared Earl of Devon.[16] Not until he
died on June 12, 1835, when Brougham held the Great Seal no
more, did Mr. William Courtenay become Earl of Devon, though
no doubt it was with the probability of this succession in mind
that he had been the moving spirit in his cousin's claim to the
peerage.[17]

The Earldom in question was the creation of September 3,
1553, in favour of Edward Courtenay, " to him and his heirs
male for ever." [18] In 1556 he died without issue, and for the

[14] *Ibid.*, p. 525. [15] *The Devon Peerage Claim* (1831) 5 Bli.N.S. 220.
[16] *Ibid.* See also Sir Harris Nicolas, *Claim to the Earldom of Devon* (1837).
[17] See *The Complete Peerage*, vol. 4 (1916) p. 336; and see 1 Misc. 12.
[18] " Et heredibus suis masculis imperpetuum ": *Devon Peerage Claim, supra,*
at p. 221.

next 275 years the peerage was generally regarded as being extinct. Indeed, the title of Earl of Devon was conferred on a Blount (Lord Mountjoy) in 1603, and after that peerage also had become extinct, on a Cavendish in 1618, whence the Dukes of Devonshire.[19] However, when the Committee for Privileges spoke in 1831, it was revealed that there had apparently been seven Earls of Devon who had died without realising their true rank, and that it sufficed for a claimant to the creation of 1553 to show that he and the first earl had a male ancestor in common who had died as far back as May 2, 1377.[20] Truly on Lord Brougham's law the word " male " was potent: limit a peerage to a man " and his heirs " and by the settled law of peerage only his descendants can inherit; " this limitation is practically equivalent to 'heirs of the body.' "[1] Add the word " male," and this not only drives out the females (as might be expected), but also nullifies the implication of " of the body," and lets in all heirs, however remote.

Lord Brougham's law of peerage did not long endure, however, for the law was established in the sense stated by Lord Campbell in the same year as that of the publication of his book containing the passages quoted above. This occurred in the *Wiltes Peerage Case*,[2] in which the proceedings occupied eight days spread out over nearly seven years. However, Lord Campbell could not have known of this case, for he had died in 1861, before the hearings began.

Much of Lord Campbell's extensive writings would have offended against Standing Order 113 of the House of Lords, made in 1721. Under this, " Any person presuming to publish the life, or will, of any deceased Peer, without the consent of his heir or executors, is guilty of a breach of the privileges of the House." This order remained in force until in 1845 Lord Campbell procured its repeal so as to make possible the publica-

---

[19] *The Complete Peerage, supra,* pp. 332, 339.
[20] *Ibid.,* pp. 322–324, 335.
[1] *Halsbury's Laws of England,* vol. 25 (2nd ed. 1937) p. 44.
[2] *The Wiltes Claim of Peerage* (1869) L.R. 4 H.L. 126; see *per* Lord Chelmsford. But Lord Redesdale and Lord Colonsay put the decision primarily on *res judicata.*

tion of his *Lives of the Chancellors*.[3] In days past there were other unexpected means of preserving privacy. In 1761 an information was granted against the printer of *Lloyd's Evening Post* for printing a " ludicrous paragraph " giving an account of a marriage in Dublin between the Earl of Clanricard [4] (a married man) and an actress. For in the view of the Court of King's Bench " It is high time to put a stop to this intermeddling in private families " [5]; and it mattered not that the earl was not a peer of Great Britain, for " it is a high offence, even against a commoner." [6]

It is the Habeas Corpus Act, 1679, that is reputed, with some apparent justification, to have received its third reading in the House of Lords in unusual circumstances. Lord Grey was teller for the Ayes, and Lord Norris for the Noes. " Lord Norris, being a man subject to vapours, was not at all times attentive to what he was doing: so a very fat lord coming in, lord Grey counted him for ten, as a jest at first: but seeing lord Norris had not observed it, he went on with this mis-reckoning of ten: so it was reported to the house, and declared that they who were for the bill were the majority, though it indeed went on the other side: and by this means the bill passed." [7] As the third reading was carried by 57 votes to 55 (a total of 112 votes), the story at least derives some support from the fact that only 107 peers were entered as being present, and only 101 had taken part in an earlier division.[8] But as Lord Campbell later pointed out, before any error was suspected the Lord Chancellor probably would have put the further motion " that this bill do pass "; and in view of the apparent majority on the third reading, this would have been assented to without a division.[9] This would have cured all, albeit by false pretences.

---

[3] 5 Camp.L.CC. 118 and 6 *ibid.*, 221 (stating the Order in various forms); Hansard (3rd ser.) vol. 82, cols. 1131–1134 (1845).

[4] *Sic*: probably John, 11th Earl of Clanricarde, of the Peerage of Ireland.

[5] *R.* v. *Kinnersley* (1761) 1 Wm.Bl. 294 at 295.

[6] *Ibid.*, at p. 294.

[7] Burnet's *History of His Own Time* (2nd ed. 1833) vol. 2, p. 256. Today, there are improved techniques: consider the Electrical Trades Union ballot-rigging case in 1961 (*Byrne* v. *Foulkes*), summarised in C. H. Rolph, *All Those in Favour?* (1962).

[8] See Holdsworth's *History of English Law*, vol. 9 (3rd ed. 1944) p. 117.

[9] See 4 Camp.L.CC. 204.

It may be added that when a teller in the House of Lords reported the result of a division by saying "The Noes were one," he defended himself from the ensuing criticism of his grammar by pointing out that he could not very well have said "The Noes was one." [10]

The statement that "parliament can do every thing, *except* making a woman a man, or a man a woman*"* is nearly always attributed to de Lolme, as any student of English constitutional law will avow. It is indeed to be found in his writings,[11] though only in a footnote. What is less well known is that the saying was well over a century old in his day. In 1648 the Earl of Pembroke and Montgomery is reported as attributing it to his father, Henry Herbert, second Earl of Pembroke: "My father said, that a Parliament could do any thing but make a man a woman, and a woman a man." [12] Some twenty years later, Wilde J. observed that "In regard to all civil acceptations, an Act of Parliament can do any thing, as, . . . it may make a woman mayor or justice of the peace, for they are the creatures of men, but it cannot alter the course of nature." [13] Kay L.J. turned to real property and mathematics. "Even an Act of Parliament cannot make a freehold estate in land an easement, any more than it could make two plus two equal to five." [14] But to Scrutton L.J. this was heresy. "I respectfully disagree with him, and think that 'for the purposes of the Act' it can effect both these statutory results." [15] And that seems to be that.

Yet is it? Look at *Green* v. *Mortimer*.[16] In that case, a private Act called Carew's Estate Act, 1857,[17] provided by section 46 that on the application of a tenant for life or the

[10] 8 Camp.L.CC. 105.
[11] de Lolme, *Constitution of England* (ed. 1807) p. 132n.
[12] Philip Herbert, fourth Earl of Pembroke and Montgomery, in a speech at Oxford on April 11, 1648, set out in a lampoon printed at Montgomery, 1648: 5 *Harleian Miscellany* (1810) 112 at 113.
[13] *Crow* v. *Ramsey* (1671) T.Jo. 10 at 12.
[14] *Metropolitan Railway Co.* v. *Fowler* [1892] 1 Q.B. 165 at 183; and see *Weston* v. *Arnold* (1873) 8 Ch.App. 1084 at 1089, *per* James L.J. (squaring the circle).
[15] *Taff Vale Railway Co.* v. *Cardiff Railway Co.* [1917] 1 Ch. 299 at 317.
[16] (1861) 3 L.T. 642.
[17] See *Statutes at Large*, 1857, 20 & 21 Vict., p. xv, No. 6.

trustees of the settlement the Court of Chancery might, in accordance with the provisions of the Act and in so far as the rules of law and equity and the jurisdiction and authority of the court would admit, make any order or give any directions which the court might think fit, so as to insure that the whole of the income of the settled property to be paid to the tenant for life should be inalienable by him, and from time to time when it became payable should be applied solely for his exclusive enjoyment. On the application of the tenant for life, an order providing that the income should be inalienable by him was accordingly made by Romilly M.R. Despite this, the tenant for life soon afterwards assigned his life interest by way of charge, and the assignee obtained a judgment by consent against the tenant for life for the money due. However, the trustees demurred at paying the assignee the moneys due under the judgment, on the understandable ground that the Act and the order of the court had made the interest of the tenant for life inalienable. Counsel for the trustees argued in support of this demurrer, but the full Court of Appeal in Chancery had so little doubt that they were wrong that counsel for the assignee were not even called upon to argue.

The brief report of the judgments is worth reproducing in full.[18] Lord Campbell L.C. " expressed his great surprise that such an Act should appear upon the statute-book; it must have passed *per incuriam*. The House of Lords had the advantage of the superintendence of one of its most competent and diligent members over all private Bills in their passage through the House; but his attention could not have been drawn to this Act. The present Act contained something which was quite absurd, and in terms gave the court power to do that which was quite impossible; for it was clear that it could have no power to do that which the Act of Parliament professed to empower it to do. The order by which the declared intentions of the Act were to be carried out, was *ultra vires* of this court, for there could be no power to give such a qualification to the defendant's interest. There must be the same power in the

18 *Green* v. *Mortimer* (1861) 3 L.T. 642 at 643.

defendant to incumber his life-estate as if the Act had never passed, and therefore he was of opinion that the demurrer must be overruled." Lord Justice Knight Bruce " said, that, in the particular position of the trustees, there was no blame to be imputed to them for filing this demurrer; but it was clear that the demurrer must be overruled." Lord Justice Turner merely " intimated his agreement with the other members of the court." No doubt much in the case may be explained; yet does not some suspicion remain that the court perceived well enough what was the expressed intention of Parliament, and yet said it nay?

In more recent times, one valorous litigant in person was a Mr. Norman, whose cause of complaint was the lack of any income tax allowance or deduction in respect of a cold caught by him while taking notes as a shorthand writer for the Inland Revenue.[19] In the words of Lord Greene M.R., he even argued that " the Finance Act, 1942, was not competently passed, because the prolongation by Parliament of its own life was not valid.[20] He has obviously spent a great deal of time in interesting research into various constitutional matters in this country, but I do not think I should be justified in doing more, while paying a tribute to his industry, than to say that to argue before this court that Parliament is not entitled to prolong its own life is really an argument which does not call for any reasoned refutation. It is fundamental in this country that Parliament can do what it pleases. The Parliament which prolonged its own life was a living Parliament, constituted and existing lawfully at the time; it lawfully prolonged its own life, and the argument, with all respect to Mr. Norman, is quite untenable." [1] Such a splendid attack upon one of the basic principles of the constitution surely deserved better than to be excluded from most of the reports of the case.[2]

---

[19] *Norman* v. *Golder* (1944) 26 T.C. 293 at 300; and see 1 Misc. 177; *ante*, p. 55.
[20] See Septennial Act, 1715; Parliament Act, 1911, s. 7; Prolongation of Parliament Acts, 1940, 1941, 1942: 26 T.C. at p. 296.
[1] *Norman* v. *Golder* (1944) 171 L.T. 369 at 371; 26 T.C. 293 at 299.
[2] See [1944] 1 All E.R. 632; [1945] 1 All E.R. 352; [1944] W.N. 116, 222; 114 L.J.K.B. 108. The report at 23 A.T.C. 361 has an uneasy foot in each camp: the headnote deals with the point, but this promise is not fulfilled by the reports of the judgments, which wholly ignore it.

Some repeals are more emphatic than others. "An act of parliament made in the time of King R. 3, bastardised all the the children of E. 4, this act was not repealed, but taken off the files of Chancery and burnt; (by the advice of all the judges in England) that no memory might remain to posterity of such a horrible falsehood. The King had pardoned the Bishop of Bath & Wells, who had contrived this act; the lords not knowing this, were proceeding in the upper House of Parliament to punish this wicked crime: but upon notice of the said pardon, the prosecution vanished.

"Beneficium principis debet esse mansurum." [3]

A marginal note points out that it is a "strange mistake" to say that the Act was not repealed, since "the year-book says, the judges advised a repeal by mentioning in the act of repeal only a few words of the beginning of Richard's act, instead of reciting the substance of it." Although the Record Commissioners' edition of the statutes includes no such repealing Act,[4] the year books record the substance of it. It directs the Act and Record of Richard III to be "annulled and utterly destroyed," to be "taken out of the Roll of Parliament, and be cancelled and burnt, and be put in perpetual oblivion. Also the said Bill, with all the appendancy, &c." [5]

The "perpetual oblivion" decreed for the Act of Richard III, however, was not complete; for the Act is set out *in extenso* [6] in a chapter in Speed's *History* which was "for the most part written by Sir Thomas Moore." [7] The Act recites that Edward IV "was and stood married, and troth-plight to one Dame Elienor Butler daughter of the old Earle of Shrewsbury with whom the same Edward had made a precontract of Matrimonie long time before hee made the saide pretended marriage with the said Elizabeth Gray," so that the issue of Edward IV and Queen Elizabeth were all bastards.[8] The Act then proceeded to declare that Richard was "the very undoubted King of this

---

[3] *Case XXVI*, Jenk. 168 (" The benefit of a prince ought to be lasting ").
[4] See vol. 2, p. 499 *et seq.*
[5] Y.B. 1 Hen. 7, Hil., pl. 1 (1486).
[6] John Speed, *History of Great Britain* (1611) pp. 711–713.
[7] *Ibid.*, p. 710.
[8] *Ibid.*, p. 712. The Act is sometimes called Titulus Regis, 1483.

Realme of England," and that the "Crowne and royall dignity
of this Realme . . . rest and abide" in Richard and after his
decease in the heirs of his body begotten.

Some descriptions of the common law suggest that there
could be little left for Parliament to do. "Reason is the life of
the law, nay the common law itselfe is nothing else but reason;
which is to be understood of an artificiall perfection of reason,
gotten by long study, observation, and experience, and not of
every man's naturall reason; for, *Nemo nascitur artifex*.[9] This
legal reason *est summa ratio*.[10]   And therefore if all the reason
that is dispersed into so many severall heads, were united into
one, yet could he not make such a law as the law in England is;
because by many successions of ages it hath beene fined and
refined by an infinite number of grave and learned men, and
by long experience growne to such a perfection, for the government of this realme, as the old rule may be justly verified of it,
Neminem oportet esse sapientiorem legibus: no man out of his
own private reason ought to be wiser than the law, which is
the perfection of reason."[11]   The claim, indeed, could be put
even higher. "The law of England is the law of God . . . the
law of England is no written law: It is the law that hath been
maintained by our ancestors, by the tried rules of reason, and
the prime laws of nature; for it does not depend upon statutes,
or written and declared words or lines. And this is our laws,
that have been maintained by our ancestors, and is subordinate
to the law and will of God: Therefore I say again, the law of
England is pure primitive reason, uncorrupted and unpolluted
by human humours, or human corruptions, wits, or wills: That
is the law of England."[12]

Yet there were other views. "We must remember, that
lawes were not made for their own sakes, but for the sake of
those who were to be guided by them; and though it is true
they are and ought to be sacred, yet, if they be or are become
unusefull for their end, they must either be amended if it may

[9] "Nobody is born an artificer."
[10] "Is the highest reason."
[11] Co.Litt. 97b; and see *post*, p. 187.
[12] *Trial of Lt.-Colonel J. Lilburne* (1649) 4 St.Tr. 1269 at 1289, *per* Jermyn J.

be, or new lawes be substituted, and the old repealed, so it be
done regularly, deliberately, and so far forth only as the
exigence or convenience justly demands it. And in this respect
the saying is true, *salus populi suprema lex esto.*[13] . . . He, that
thinks a state can be exactly steered by the same lawes in every
kind, as it was two or three hundred years since, may as well
imagine, that the cloaths that fitted him when he was a child
should serve him when he is grown a man. The matter
changeth the custom; the contracts the commerce; the dispositions education and tempers of men and societies change in a
long tract of time; and so must their lawes in some measure be
changed, or they will not be usefull for their state and condition.
And besides all this, as I before said, time is the wisest thing
under heaven. These very lawes, which at first seemed the
wisest constitution under heaven, have some flawes and defects
discovered in them by time. As manufactures, mechanical arts,
architecture and building, and philosophy itself, receive new
advantages and discoveries by time and experience; so much
more do lawes, which concern the manners and customs of
men." [14]

Again, " Time works changes, brings into existence new
conditions and purposes. Therefore a principle to be vital must
be capable of wider application than the mischief which gave
it birth. This is peculiarly true of constitutions. They are not
ephemeral enactments, designed to meet passing occasions.
They are, to use the words of Chief Justice Marshall, ' designed
to approach immortality as nearly as human institutions can
approach it.' The future is their care and provision for events
of good and bad tendencies of which no prophecy can be made.
In the application of a constitution, therefore, our contemplation
cannot be only of what has been but of what may be. Under
any other rule a constitution would indeed be as easy of application as it would be deficient in efficacy and power. Its general
principles would have little value and be converted by precedent

---

[13] " Let the welfare of the people be the paramount law."
[14] Hale C.J., *Considerations touching the Amendment or Alteration of Lawes,*
printed in Hargrave's *Law Tracts* (1787) p. 269.

into impotent and lifeless formulas. Rights declared in words might be lost in reality." [15]

Modern appreciations of the law vary. In one case, Diplock L.J. concurred in allowing an appeal, " although the legal route which has led me to this conclusion is not at all points identical with that traversed by the Master of the Rolls.[16] After all, that is the beauty of the common law; it is a maze and not a motorway." [17] But arguments may be otherwise. " This argument completely misses the highway of logic and enters on a secondary road of complete irrelevancy." [18] Logic indeed plays an uncertain role. " Many English procedures are logically insupportable but work admirably in practice—John Bull being traditionally more disposed to ask ' Does it work? ' than to enquire ' Is it logical? ' " [19] Bailhache J. once referred to Lord Halsbury's dictum that the law is not always logical,[20] and added " If the law is not logical, public policy is even less logical." [1]

Beyond public policy lie international affairs. Certain letters exchanged between the President of the United States and the Russian People's Commissar for Foreign Affairs were once described as " characteristically delicate and elusive expressions of diplomacy. The draftsmen of such notes must save sensibilities and avoid the explicitness on which diplomatic negotiations so easily founder." [2] It may, moreover, be remembered that some say of the two kinds of International Law, Private and Public, that one is not international and the other is not law.

[15] *Weems* v. *United States*, 217 U.S. 349 at 373 (1910), *per* McKenna J.
[16] Lord Denning.
[17] *Morris* v. *C. W. Martin & Sons Ltd.* [1966] 1 Q.B. 716 at 730.
[18] *Great Lakes Forwarding Corp.* v. *Pennsylvania R. Co.*, 100 A. 2d 612 at 618 (1953), *per* Musmanno J., dissenting.
[19] *Ex p. Nel*, 1957 (1) S.A. 216 at 218, *per* Holmes J.
[20] See 1 Misc. 304.
[1] *Tinline* v. *White Cross Insurance Association Ltd.* [1921] 3 K.B. 327 at 331.
[2] *United States* v. *Pink*, 315 U.S. 203 at 241 (1942), *per* Frankfurter J.

II

Semanticity

Soldiers of Cadmus

THE importance of law reports and the unreliability of many of them were matters which formerly attracted much attention, not least from those who produced the reports. The analogies were various. Bulstrode turned to the sea. "Truly, without the Reports of the learned Judges, that have formerly sate at the Helm, the Law by this time had been almost like a Ship without Ballast, for that the Cases of Modern Experience, are fled from those that were adjudged and ruled in former Times. But of late, we have found so many wandring and masterless REPORTS (like the Soldiers of *Cadmus*) daily rising up, and justling each other, that our learned Judges have been forced to provide against their multiplicity, by disallowing of some Posthumous Reports; well considering, That as Laws are the Anchors of the Republique, so the Reports are as the Anchors of Laws, and therefore ought well to be weighed before put out." [1]

On the other hand, Style put the emphasis on legitimacy. He proclaimed: "It may be objected, that the Press hath been very fertile in thisour Age, and hath brought forth many, if not too many births of this nature. I must confess this Truth; but how legitimate most of them are, let the Learned judge: This I am sure of, there is not a father alive to own many of them, and they speak so plain in the Language of *Ashdod*,[2] that a knowing-man cannot believe they ever sprung from *Israelitish-Parents*, but by their pronouncing of *Siboleth* insteed of *Shiboleth*,[3] may easily collect of what extract they are. What I here present you with, is, (though a Homely, yet) a lawfull Issue, and I dare call it mine own, and that (I believe) I may do with as good a right as any ever might a work of the like nature, having had as little (if not less) assistance from others in the

---

[1] 2 Bulstr. viii, Epistle Dedicatory.
[2] See Nehemiah xiii, 23, 24.
[3] See Judges xii, 6 (Sibboleth, Shibboleth); see also *post*, p. 200.

bringing it forth, as any that have travelled in this kind before me." [4]

Others wrote in similar terms. " Soon after the martyrdom of King Charles the First, there came forth a flying squadron of thin Reports, of which Mr. March led the van, most of them very good." [5] The editor of Gouldsborough Reports pointed out to the reader that " thou hast not here a spurious deformed Brat, falsly fathered upon the name of a dead man, too usuall a trick, played by the subtile Gamesters of this Serpentine Age; but thou hast presented to thee, though I cannot say the Issue of the Learned Gouldsborough's own Brain, yet I daresay, the Work of his own Hand; and that, which were he living, he would not blush to own." [6] Again, " The cases in Winch are in general well reported; but in the Preface to Benloe's and Dalison's Reports it seems as if those were not really the reports of Sir H. Winch; for it is there said, ' the book called Winch's Reports, but improperly enough ascribed to that learned Judge.' And indeed it appears that several of the cases in that book were decided after Sir H. Winch's death." [7]

Nevertheless, patent paternity was no guarantee of honour. Many series of reports have been judicially castigated. The best known of these is probably Espinasse, perhaps due to the possibilities of facile jest offered by his name. It was Pollock C.B. who, in speaking of his reports, was reputed to have said " Mr. Espinasse was deaf. He heard one half of a case and reported the other." [8] Pollock does not stand alone. Blackburn J. thought that Espinasse had not " such a character for intelligence and accuracy as to make it at all certain that the facts are correctly stated, or that the opinion of the judge was rightly understood." [9] Indeed, when the future Lord Chelmsford L.C. and the future Lord Penzance relied upon a decision reported by Espinasse, Lord Denman C.J. was gentle but firm in his

---

[4] Sty., p. iv, Epistle Dedicatory.
[5] 5 Mod. viii.
[6] Gould. (2nd ed. 1682) p. iv.
[7] *Troward* v. *Cailland* (1795) 6 T.R. 439 at 441, *per* Lord Kenyon C.J.
[8] T. Mathew (1938) 54 L.Q.R. 368; and see *Warren* v. *Keen* [1954] 1 Q.B. 15 at 21, *per* Denning L.J.
[9] *Readhead* v. *Midland Railway Co.* (1867) L.R. 2 Q.B. 412 at 437, putting Carrington & Payne's Reports into the same gallery.

reproof. " I am tempted to remark for the benefit of the profession that Espinasse's Reports, in days nearer their own time, when their want of accuracy was better known that it is now, were never quoted without doubt and hesitation; and a special reason was often given as an apology for citing that particular case. Now they are often cited as if counsel thought them of equal authority with Lord Coke's Reports." [10]

But Espinasse does not lack companions in shame. Some series of reports have been castigated as being of " no authority." These include Fitzgibbon [11] (by whom the cases " are very incorrectly reported " [12]), Reports in Chancery,[13] and Holt's King's Bench.[14] The " somewhat loose compilation " [15] of reports entitled " Modern " have also attracted much condemnation, both collectively and individually. It was Pollock C.B. who proclaimed that " You may find authority in the Modern Reports for many propositions that are not law." [16] Volume 8 is " a miserably bad book," [17] which is " notoriously inaccurate and of no authority " [18]; and in one case the Court of King's Bench treated it " with the contempt that it deserves." [19] One report in it has been said to be " totally mistaken there, as indeed are nine cases out of ten in that book." [20]

Volume 9 fared little better. " There are no reports upon which less reliance can be placed." [1] It is " a book of very questionable authority," [2] for " the ninth Mod. is worse than the tenth," [3] which " is of little authority." [4] " 11th Modern

[10] *Small* v. *Nairne* (1849) 13 Q.B. 840 at 844.
[11] *Harvey* v. *Ashley* (1748) 3 Atk. 607 at 610, *per* Lord Hardwicke L.C.
[12] *Ashburnham* v. *Bradshaw* (1740) West *t.*Hard. 505 at 509, *per* Parker C.B.
[13] *Reynish* v. *Martin* (1746) 3 Atk. 330 at 334, *per* Lord Hardwicke L.C.
[14] *Taylor* d. *Atkyns* v. *Horde* (1755) 1 Keny. 143 at 178, *per* Ryder C.J.; and see *R.* v. *Bishop of London* (1743) 1 Wils.K.B. 11 at 15, *per* Lee C.J.
[15] *R.* v. *Allen* (1862) 8 Jur.N.S. 230 at 231, *per* Blackburn J.
[16] *Hodgins* v. *Hancock* (1845) 14 M. & W. 120 at 123.
[17] *R.* v. *Williams* (1757) 1 Burr. 385 at 386n., *per* the reporter.
[18] *R.* v. *Williams* (1828) 3 Man. & Ry. 402 at 405, *per* Bayley J.
[19] *R.* v. *Harrison* (1762) 3 Burr. 1322 at 1326n.
[20] *R.* v. *Harris* (1797) 7 T.R. 238 at 239, *per* Lord Kenyon C.J., quoting a judgment of Wilmot J.
[1] *In b. Spitty* (1852) 16 Jur. 92, *per* Dr. Lushington.
[2] *Marquis Cholmondeley* v. *Lord Clinton* (1820) 2 Jac. & W. 1 at 171, *per* Plumer M.R.
[3] *Doe* d. *Mayhew* v. *Asby* (1839) 10 A. & E. 71 at 73, *per* Littledale J.
[4] *Chandler* v. *Roberts* (1779) 1 Doug.K.B. 58 at 61, *per* Buller J.

Reports is not esteemed a book of authority," and 12 Modern is "not a book of any authority." [6] Indeed, it was this series that attracted one of the best-known judicial outbursts on the reports. One report in the series states that the court answered a particular objection by saying that the party concerned ought to plead it,[7] whereas in fact the point had been fully pleaded and there was no ground for the objection. When this was subsequently pointed out, Holt C.J. ejaculated "See the inconveniences of these scambling reports: they will make us appear to posterity for a parcel of blockheads." [8]

These reports are by no means alone in disgrace. Thus the authority of Popham is "none" [9]; and Noy "has always been considered as a bad authority." [10] Twisden J. once "wholly rejected" the volume of Noy's Reports, "for it was but an abridgment of cases by Serjeant Size, who when he was a student borrowed Noy's Reports, and abridged them for his own use." [11] Atkyns' Reports "must not be cited as authority" [12]; they are "extremely inaccurate," [13] and one case in them was said to be "miserably reported." [14] Again, "It must . . . be admitted that Keble is of no high repute as an accurate reporter: and the court would be slow to act on a case in that book, if it were unsupported by others." [15] Lord Mansfield C.J. called Keble "a bad reporter," [16] and Lord Kenyon C.J. not only concurred [17] but also stigmatised him as "a feeble reporter," [18]

---

[5] *Jones* v. *Jones* (1823) 1 Bing. 249 at 250, *per* Park and Burrough JJ.
[6] *R.* v. *Mayor & Burgesses of Lyme Regis* (1779) 1 Doug.K.B. 79 at 83, *per* Buller J.
[7] *Hodge* v. *Clare* (1691) 4 Mod. 14.
[8] *Slater* v. *May* (1704) 2 Ld.Raym. 1071 at 1072; see 1 Misc. 293.
[9] *R.* v. *Starling* (1664) 1 Keb. 675 at 676, *per* Hyde C.J.; and see *Fisher* v. *Wigg* (1700) 1 Ld.Raym. 622 at 626; *Dean & Chapter of Westminster's Case* (1664) Carth. 9 at 15.
[10] *Petrie* v. *Hannay* (1789) 3 T.R. 418 at 424, *per* Buller J.
[11] *Freeman* v. *Banes* (1670) 1 Ventr. 80 at 81.
[12] *La Vie* v. *Philips* (1765) 1 Wm.Bl. 570 at 571, *per cur.* (Lord Mansfield C.J., Wilmot, Yates and Aston JJ.).
[13] *Olive* v. *Smith* (1813) 5 Taunt. 56 at 64, *per* Mansfield C.J.
[14] *Lickbarrow* v. *Mason* (1793) 6 East 21n. at 29n., *per* Buller J.
[15] *Farrall* v. *Hilditch* (1859) 5 C.B.N.S. 840 at 853, *per* Williams J.
[16] *Jones* v. *Maunsell* (1779) 1 Doug.K.B. 302 at 305.
[17] *Doe* d. *Shore* v. *Porter* (1789) 3 T.R. 13 at 17.
[18] *Colonel Pitt's Case* (1734) Ridg.*t.*Hard. 91 at 100, *per* the reporter.

who, said Willes C.J., "seldom enlightens any thing." [19] Park J., too, once recounted that "Lord Kenyon reprimanded me when I was at the bar for citing Keble." [20] However, even Lord Kenyon mellowed in his views to "that reporter is not always accurate" [1]; and Lord Hardwicke C.J. conceded that Keble, "though very far from being an accurate, is a pretty good register." [2] Williams J. asserted that "more is to be said for the character of this reporter, as a ' tolerable historian of the law,' than from the remarks made upon him from time to time might have supposed." [3] This, no doubt, refers to the succinct verdict of Burnet J. that Keble was "an inaccurate reporter, yet a tolerable historian of the law." [4]

Bunbury also had his critics. Lord Mansfield C.J. said that "Mr. Bunbury never meant that those cases should have been published: they are very loose notes" [5]; and Plumer V.-C. said that Bunbury was of "no great authority." [6] Subsequently, however, the Court of Exchequer rehabilitated the reports. Platt B. said that "Although Lord Mansfield . . . cast some imputation on Bunbury's notes, the learned Serjeant who edited them gives them a very different character; and it may be doubted whether the observations attributed to Lord Mansfield were not the result of some hasty expressions on his part, before he was fully aware of the value of the notes. Now Serjeant Wilson, who edited Bunbury's Reports, speaks thus about them: ' The learned author attended Westminster Hall above forty years, chiefly at the Exchequer bar, but for the last thirty years thereof in that Court only. He retired in the year 1743, and when he took leave of the Court had been many years postman [7] there. His long experience in the several branches of business in the Exchequer induced gentlemen of the profession to desire

---

[19] *Huggins* v. *Bambridge* (1740) Willes 241 at 245.
[20] *Adams* v. *Gibney* (1830) 6 Bing. 656 at 664.
[1] *Farr* v. *Newman* (1792) 4 T.R. 621 at 649.
[2] *Colonel Pitt's Case* (1734) Ridg.*t*.Hard. 91 at 100; Fort. 159 at 162 (" who. tho' he was a bad reporter, was a good register ").
[3] *Farrall* v. *Hilditch* (1859) 5 C.B.N.S. 840 at 855.
[4] *Batchelor* v. *Bigg* (1772) 3 Wils.K.B. 319 at 330.
[5] *Tinkler* v. *Poole* (1770) 5 Burr. 2657 at 2658.
[6] *Nash* v. *Nash* (1817) 2 Madd. 133 at 140.
[7] For " postman," see *post*, p. 122.

his notes, which in his lifetime were all or the greatest part of them transcribed, are in many hands, and frequently cited in Westminster Hall. From some apprehensions that these cases might get into the press improperly, and come out imperfect, and, indeed, by the desire of some gentlemen eminent in the profession, the editor was persuaded to give the public a true copy of such cases only as the author took in Court with his own hand, and are settled and corrected by himself from his notes.' These notes having been corrected and published under such circumstances, and by persons of such experience and learning, it certainly appears to me rather a rash proceeding to give them the character which Lord Mansfield is represented to have done. The learned editor proceeds to say: 'All the marginal notes in this book are the author's own, except one on page 302 of *Walker* v. *Jackson*, coram Lord Chancellor Hardwicke, July 22nd, 1743.' Since the expressions of Lord Mansfield have been alluded to, I have thought it right thus to bring before the Court the character given to these very notes by the learned Serjeant who had the responsibility of publishing them, he himself bearing as high character as any member of the bar." [8] Today, Bunbury's position as "postman" [9] perhaps merits a word of explanation. The postman was an experienced member of the junior Bar who had a place in the Court of Exchequer by the post anciently used as a measure of length in excise cases. He had precedence in motions over all other juniors; the "tubman," whose place was next to the tub used as a measure of capacity, came next.

Lord Manners L.C. had mild words for Barnardiston. "Although Barnardiston is not considered a very correct Reporter, yet some of his Cases are very accurately reported." [10] Lord Eldon was of a similar disposition. "Lord Mansfield, then Mr. Murray, argued that case [11] before Lord Hardwicke, and Mr. Barnardiston was at the bar at the same time, although afterwards, when Mr. Murray had become Lord Mansfield,

---

[8] *R.* v. *Edwards* (1853) 9 Exch. 32 at 51; and see at p. 53, *per* Parke B.
[9] *Supra.*
[10] *Boardman* v. *Jackson* (1813) 2 Ball & B. 382 at 386.
[11] *Richard* v. *Syms* (1740) Barn.Ch. 90.

when Mr. Barnardiston's Reports were cited, his lordship used
to say, 'Barnard—what you call him.' In that book, however,
my Lords, there are some reports of great value." [12]   It was said
of Lord Mansfield that he absolutely forbade the citing of the
volume of Barnardiston's Reports in Chancery, "for it would
only be misleading students, to put them upon reading it. He
said, it was marvellous however, to such as knew the serjeant
and his manner of taking notes, that he should so often stumble
upon what was right: but yet, that there was not one case in
his book, which was so throughout." [13]   Lord Kenyon C.J. was
more blunt; he simply dismissed Barnardiston as "a bad
reporter," [14] whereas Stuart V.-C. more mildly said that
"Barnardiston is not a reporter to be relied upon in all cases." [15]

Barnardiston's volume of King's Bench Reports stands in
little better case; it is "not a book of much authority in
general." [16]   One explanation of his disrepute, at law as well
as in equity, is reputed to have been given by Lord Lyndhurst,
though it did not remain unanswered. When Preston once
cited a case from Barnardiston's King's Bench Reports, Lord
Lyndhurst exclaimed "Barnardiston, Mr. Preston! I fear that
is a book of no great authority; I recollect, in my younger days,
it was said of Barnardiston, that he was accustomed to slumber
over his note-book, and the wags in the rear took the opportunity of scribbling nonsense in it." Preston answered "There
are some cases, my Lord, in Barnardiston, which, in my
experience (and having had frequent occasion to compare that
reporter's cases with the same cases elsewhere), I have found to
be the only sensible and intelligent reports; and I trust I shall
show your Lordship that it may be said of Barnardiston, '*non
omnibus dormio*'." [17]

---

[12] *Duffield* v. *Hicks* (1827) 1 Dow & Cl. 1 at 11; cp. the case as reported *sub
nom. Duffield* v. *Elwes* (1827) 1 Bli.N.S. 497 at 538.
[13] *Zouch* d. *Woolston* v. *Woolston* (1760) 2 Burr. 1136 at 1142n., *semble per*
the reporter.
[14] *R.* v. *Stone* (1801) 1 East 639 at 642n.
[15] *Holland* v. *Holland* (1869) 4 Ch.App. 450n. at 453n.
[16] *Salt* v. *Salt* (1798) 8 T.R. 47 at 48, *per* Lord Kenyon C.J.
[17] J. W. Wallace, *The Reporters* (4th ed. 1882) pp. 424, 425 ("I am not
oblivious to all"). For the matrimonial doctrine of *non omnibus dormio*,
see *Lovering* v. *Lovering* (1792) 3 Hagg.Ecc. 85 at 87.

Dickens has attracted a variety of comments. Stuart V.-C., after referring to one case that he reported,[18] observed that "the accuracy of his reports is not to be relied upon, and this case is a remarkable instance of inaccuracy."[19] Lord Cottenham L.C. had "so little faith" in a report in Dickens that he had the records of the court searched.[20] However, Lord Redesdale L.C. was less sweeping. "Mr. Dickens was a very attentive and diligent Register, but his notes, being rather loose, were not considered as of very high authority; he was constantly applied to, to know if he had any thing on such and such subjects in his notes; but if he had, the Register's books were always referred to."[1]

Yet Lord Cottenham L.C. differentiated. "Much may, no doubt, be said against the accuracy of many of the reports in Dickens; but there are many of them, in which he himself interfered and made suggestions to the Court. And I have always considered these cases of higher authority than the rest, because you have there an opportunity of seeing what was suggested by a very experienced officer, and what the Court did in consequence."[2] This view echoed the reference of Lord Eldon L.C. to "Mr. Dickens, who from his long experience in this Court had a great knowledge of the practice."[3] In more modern times, discrimination is also necessary in using Beavan. His thirty-six volumes, spread over twenty-eight years, got no better as time passed, nor were the later vintages of Sir John Romilly M.R. (whom Beavan reported from 1851 to 1866, in volumes 14 to 36) as dependable as the earlier. " Late Beavan " is thus frail support[4]; as Harman L.J. once pointed out, " Those who rely on reports in 33 Beavan are sometimes said to be in the last ditch."[5]

---

[18] *Bailey* v. *Ekins* (1784) 2 Dick. 632.
[19] *Holland* v. *Holland* (1869) 4 Ch.App. 450n. at 453n.
[20] *Neate* v. *Duke of Marlborough* (1838) 3 My. & Cr. 407 at 420.
[1] *Smith* v. *Hibernian Mine Co.* (1803) 1 Sch. & Lef. 238 at 240; and see *Adair* v. *Shaw* (1803) 1 Sch. & Lef. 243 at 259.
[2] *Fisher* v. *Fisher* (1847) 2 Ph. 236 at 240.
[3] *Norway* v. *Rowe* (1812) 19 Ves. 144 at 153.
[4] *Quaere* how late is " late " for this purpose. Harman L.J. used to say extra-curially that volume 27 was the earliest Beavan to be " late."
[5] *Beesley* v. *Hallwood Estates Ltd.* [1961] Ch. 105 at 118.

Opinions about Moseley's Reports have differed. Lord Mansfield C.J. said that they should not be cited,[6] for, as Thomson B. observed, "the authority of that book is very small."[7] But the cautious Lord Eldon L.C. said "I myself think very differently from Lord Mansfield on that subject, having always considered Moseley's Reports as a book possessing a very considerable degree of accuracy,"[8] and containing "many good cases."[9] But even this did not prevent Shadwell V.-C. from describing Moseley as being "not a reporter of very great authority."[10]

Eminence in the law is no guarantee of skill as a reporter. In the words of Lord Mansfield C.J., "We must not always rely on the words of reports, though under great names: Mr. Justice Blackstone's Reports are not very accurate."[11] Again, "Levinz, though a good lawyer, was sometimes a very careless reporter."[12] One case in his reports[13] was said by Willes C.J. to have been "so imperfectly reported that it is difficult to know what to make of it. But, if taken to be as reported by Levintz, it is so absurd an opinion that I can lay no weight at all on it."[14]

Of one case in 1698 in Lord Raymond's Reports,[15] Lord Mansfield C.J. said "These notes were taken in 10 W. 3, when Lord Raymond was young, as short hints for his own use: but they are too incorrect and inaccurate, to be relied on as authorities."[16] Lord Kenyon C.J., too, commented on a report[17] of another case in the same year as being "a short note taken by Lord Raymond when he was very young."[18] Raymond was in fact twenty-five years old at the time, and as Bolland B.

6 *Quantock* v. *England* (1770) 5 Burr. 2628 at 2629.
7 *Rootham* v. *Dawson* (1797) 3 Anstr. 859 at 861.
8 *Mills* v. *Farmer* (1815) 1 Mer. 55 at 92.
9 *Parkhurst* v. *Lowten* (1819) 2 Swans. 194n., *per* Lord Eldon L.C.
10 *Browne* v. *Lockhart* (1840) 10 Sim. 420 at 425.
11 *Devon* v. *Watts* (1779) 1 Doug.K.B. 86 at 93.
12 *Tomkyns* v. *Ladbroke* (1755) 2 Ves.Sen. 591 at 595, *per* Lord Hardwicke L.C.
13 *Ellis* v. *Ruddle* (1675) 2 Lev. 151; *sub nom. Ellis* v. *Audle*, 3 Keb. 552; *sub nom. Ellis* v. *Nelson*, 3 Keb. 659, 678.
14 *Huggins* v. *Bambridge* (1740) Willes 241 at 245.
15 *Cole* v. *Davies* (1698) 1 Ld.Raym. 724.
16 *Cooper* v. *Chitty* (1756) 1 Burr. 20 at 36.
17 Of *Young* v. —— (1698) 1 Ld.Raym. 725.
18 *Ball* v. *Herbert* (1789) 3 T.R. 253 at 261.

observed subsequently in relation to one of these cases,[19] decided
by Holt C.J., "With the highest respect for every opinion
delivered by so great a man as Lord Mansfield, I must take the
liberty of saying that the four resolutions in Lord Raymond's
Report, of which that I have extracted is the first, appear, as far
as the reporter is concerned, to bear the stamp of accuracy; the
positions laid down are plain and simple, and such as even a
young man of so much talent as Lord Raymond could readily
comprehend."[20] Further, "The case was tried by Lord Holt
in 1698. Lord Raymond, after twenty-six years' practice from
that time, was elevated to the bench, and presided as Chief
Justice for nine years: so that ample time and opportunity were
afforded to his lordship to have corrected his MS. of the report,
if it had been liable to the imputation of inaccuracy by which
Lord Mansfield attacked and destroyed its authority."[1] Lord
Denman C.J., too, said "Is it really possible to believe that Lord
Raymond was too young to understand what he heard? If not,
his youth is immaterial in this argument; and are we then to
discard as inaccurate and incorrect all that he reported in the
first half of his first volume during the five years preceding?
I cannot refrain from saying, that we can rely upon none of our
reports, if we admit a doubt that Raymond has recorded Holt's
genuine doctrine, and that he understood it fully."[2]

Another reporter who has been under fire is Comberbach.
His volume of reports has been called "a book that is very
incorrect."[3] Lord Mansfield C.J., when referring to a case
reported in Shower and in Comberbach,[4] said "Comberbach,
in giving the judgment of the court, which is the only sensible
part of his whole report, (for it is plain to me, that he did not
understand the former argument on the former day, which is

[19] *Cole* v. *Davies, supra.*
[20] *Garland* v. *Carlisle* (1833) 2 Cr. & M. 31 at 59; and see *ibid.*, at p. 86, *per* Vaughan B., and at p. 105, *per* Bayley B.
[1] *Garland* v. *Carlisle* (1837) 4 Cl. & F. 693 at 761, *per* Bolland B.
[2] *Garland* v. *Carlisle* (1833) 2 Cr. & M. 31 at 115. 149 E.R. 696 makes two mistakes in reprinting this passage ("impossible" for "possible," and "accorded" for "recorded").
[3] *Fonnereau* v. *Fonnereau* (1745) 3 Atk. 315 at 318, *per* Lord Hardwicke L.C.
[4] *Letchmere* v. *Thorowgood* (1689) 1 Show.K.B. 12; *sub nom. Lechmere* v. *Thorowgood*, Comb. 123.

the first part of his report of the case,) agrees with Shower. . . .
But he must be mistaken in the first part of this report: for
Lord Ch.Just.Holt could never say '. . .'." [5] Lord Kenyon
C.J., however, would not have this. In *Rorke* v. *Dayrell* [6] he
said: " With respect to what is supposed to have been said by
Lord Mansfield in *Cooper* v. *Chitty* [7] of Comberbach's having
mistaken Lord Holt's opinion in *Lechmere* v. *Thoroughgood*,[8]
it is as probable that the report of that observation is mis-stated."
This, of course, struck at Sir James Burrow, who had made the
report of *Cooper* v. *Chitty*.

Yet the biter was bit; for Lord Kenyon, too, had played the
law reporter. Forty years later, Vaughan B. advised the House
of Lords that " If Lord Kenyon, before he delivered his judgment in *Rorke* v. *Dayrell,* had fortunately referred to his own
note of *Cooper* v. *Chitty*,[9] which has since been published by
Mr. Hanmer, from his Lordship's original manuscript, instead
of impeaching, he must have borne testimony to the accuracy of
Sir James Burrow's report of Lord Mansfield's judgment in that
particular. The notes of Lord Kenyon and of Sir J. Burrow on
this point are in such perfect harmony, that the one may be
considered a *fac simile* of the other." [10] This restores Comberbach to the status of disfavour to which Lord Ellenborough C.J.
also assigned him. " The comparative accuracy of Comberbatch
as a reporter may be judged of by referring to his short report
of [*Smallcomb* v. *Cross* [11]] under the name of *Smallcorn* v.
Vic.Lond.,[12] in which report the facts, point, and names of
parties are all mistated." [13] As for Shower, Holt C.J. would not
allow volume I of his King's Bench Reports as an authority [14];
and Lord Abinger C.B. referred to one case in that volume as

---

[5] *Cooper* v. *Chitty* (1756) I Burr. 20 at 36.
[6] (1791) 4 T.R. 402 at 412.
[7] *Supra.*
[8] *Supra.*
[9] See *Cooper* v. *Chitty* (1756) I Keny. 395 at 422, *per* Lord Mansfield C.J.:
Comberbach " makes Lord Holt say what he could never say."
[10] *Giles* v. *Grover* (1832) I Cl. & F. 72 at 144.
[11] (1697) I Ld.Raym. 251; *sub nom. Smallcomb* v. *Buckingham*, I Salk. 320;
sub nom. Smalcomb v. *Buckingham*, I Comyns 35.
[12] (1697) Comb. 428.
[13] *Payne* v. *Drewe* (1804) 4 East 523 at 540.
[14] *Tate* v. *Whiting* (1708) 11 Mod. 196.

" resting perhaps on the authority of a doubtful reporter, who might not have heard accurately what was said." [15]

Cases in Chancery is " a book of very doubtful authority." [16] The reports are " very incorrect," [17] and are " not entitled to any great attention." [18] Of one case reported in volume 2, Lord Loughborough C.J. said that it was, " as most of the others are in the same book, grossly misreported; no such determination was made, and both the state of the case and the decision are perfectly mistaken." [19] Volume 2 of Equity Cases Abridged is " not a book of the first authority." [20] Sir Thomas Plumer twice called it a book " of no great authority," once as Vice-Chancellor [1] and again as Master of the Rolls [2]; and Lord Manners L.C. echoed the phrase.[3] Lord Eldon said that it was " of no very high character," and " not so high in character " as volume 1.[4] One report in it [5] has been called " a very loose note " and " very inaccurate; as most of the cases in that book are." [6]

Dolben J. considered Siderfin's reports " fit to be burned, being taken by him, when a student, and unworthily done by them that printed it." [7] " Ay," said Holt C.J., " many good cases are spoil'd in Siderfin, neither reported with that truth, nor with that spirit which the case required." [8] And when Carter's Reports were cited, Holt C.J. said that he " did not know that Carter, nor would allow that report for any authority." [9] The volume of Reports *t.* Finch is " a book of no

[15] *Sunbolf* v. *Alford* (1838) 3 M. & W. 248 at 253.
[16] *Leonard* v. *Leonard* (1812) 2 Ball & B. 171 at 183, *per* Lord Manners L.C.; and see *M'Mahon* v. *Burchell* (1846) 1 Coop.*t.*Cott. 457 at 518.
[17] *Ruscombe* v. *Hare* (1818) 6 Dow 1 at 9, *per* Lord Redesdale.
[18] *Richards* v. *Chambers* (1805) 10 Ves. 580 at 582, *per* Grant M.R.
[19] *Garforth* v. *Fearon* (1787) 1 Hy.Bl. 327 at 332.
[20] *Pierson* v. *Garnet* (1786) 2 Bro.C.C. 38 at 45, *per* Kenyon M.R.
[1] *Nash* v. *Nash* (1817) 2 Madd. 133 at 140.
[2] *Martin* v. *Mitchell* (1820) 2 Jac. & W. 413 at 428.
[3] *Palmer* v. *Wheeler* (1811) 2 Ball & B. 18 at 28.
[4] *Duffield* v. *Elwes* (1827) 1 Bli.N.S. 497 at 539.
[5] *Allen* v. *Harding* (1708) 2 Eq.Ca.Abr. 17.
[6] *Mosely* v. *Virgin* (1796) 3 Ves. 184 at 185, *per* Lord Loughborough L.C.
[7] *R.* v. *Lee* (1691) 1 Show.K.B. 251 at 252; and see *Symonds* v. *Cudmore* (1693) 4 Mod. 1 at 6; 12 Mod. 32 at 33; Carth. 257 at 261.
[8] *Hayward* v. *Wilson* (1696) Comb. 377.
[9] *Pennoyer* v. *Brace* (1697) Comb. 441 at 442.

authority," [10] which is " not entitled to any great attention." [11] A case in these reports was said to be " of no authority, the book from which it is cited not containing Lord Nottingham's own reports." [12]

Volume 8 of Taunton " is of but doubtful authority, as the cases were not reported by Mr. Taunton himself." [13] The volume is " an apocryphal authority. It was made up from Mr. Justice Taunton's notes, and was not revised by him." [14] Again, " Lewin was not an accurate reporter " [15]; and " You may find in *Barnes* rules absolute for any thing." [16] Yet these reports escaped lightly when compared with Wentworth's *Pleader*. This " is a book of no authority; it is a collection of very vicious precedents," which are " in a great measure extremely incorrect: and it cannot be assumed that there is the least authority to be derived from his statement." [17]

Vernon's Reports have an unusual origin. The manuscripts were found in his London house after his death, and Chancery litigation ensued. It was contended that the manuscripts " did belong to the heir at law, as guardian of the reputation of his ancestor. It was said, that if the tomb or monument of an ancestor be defaced or destroyed, an action lies for the heir at law; and by parity of reason, as these manuscripts were intended by the testator as a monument to transmit his learning and reputation to posterity, the law would intrust the heir with the care of them, that they should be printed in such a manner as would be most for the honour of Mr. Vernon's memory. The printing, or not printing these papers, may as much affect the reputation of Mr. Vernon as any monument or tomb. Possibly, they are not fit to be printed; possibly they were never intended to be printed." However, " the Court decided nothing in this

[10] *Reynish* v. *Martin* (1746) 3 Atk. 330 at 334, *per* Lord Hardwicke L.C.; *Elton* v. *Elton* (1747) 1 Wils.K.B. 159 at 162, *per* Lord Hardwicke L.C.
[11] *Richards* v. *Chambers* (1805) 10 Ves. 580 at 582, *per* Grant M.R.
[12] *Hall* v. *Terry* (1738) West *t.*Hard. 500 at 504.
[13] *Hadley* v. *Baxendale* (1854) 9 Exch. 341 at 347, *per* Parke B.
[14] S.C., 23 L.J.Ex. 179 at 180, *per* Parke B.; and see S.C., 18 Jur. 358.
[15] *R.* v. *Francis* (1874) 43 L.J.M.C. 97 at 100, *per* Blackburn J.
[16] *Doe* d. *Simons* v. *Masters* (1819) 1 Chit.Pr. 233, *per* Abbott C.J.
[17] *Sunbolf* v. *Alford* (1838) 3 M. & W. 248 at 251, 254, *per* Lord Abinger C.B.

affair, because all consented to have them printed under the direction of the Court, without making any profit of them." [18]

Vernon was " one of the ablest men in his profession, though his notes are sometimes loose." [19]   His reports were edited by Peere Williams, the distinguished reporter, and Melmoth.[20] Nevertheless, the Bench was critical. Willes C.J. merely said that Vernon was not " a very exact reporter," [1] but Lord Loughborough C.J. spoke of " the usual inaccuracy of the cases in Vernon," [2] and Lord Brougham L.C. said " There is certainly a want of accuracy in that reporter." [3] Arden M.R. observed that 2 Vernon was " a book of no great accuracy," [4] and Lord Kenyon C.J. called one report in that volume " very unsatisfactory." [5] Of another case,[6] Lord Hardwicke L.C. said that he had ordered the Register to be searched, and as the case was there stated, it was impossible that the point reported could have been in issue in the case; and he added " I am very sorry to find that the reports of so able a man should be so imperfect, and come out in this manner." [7] However, as Farwell J. pointed out, " Mr. Vernon, who was a most learned lawyer, did not publish his own reports, and is believed to have made the notes, which were published after his death, as memoranda merely for his own use." [8] And early in the nineteenth century there appeared what Lord Eldon L.C. called " that very valuable edition (edition by Mr. Raithby) of Vernon, lately published." [9] Indeed, much depends upon editing. The preface to the fifth edition of Hobart's Reports complains that previously they had been published " deformed, without any Correction: Which,

18 *Atcherley* v. *Vernon* (1723) 10 Mod. 518 at 529, 531; and see *Atcherley* v. *Vernon* (1723) 9 Mod. 68.
19 *Winter* v. *White* (1819) 1 Brod. & B. 350 at 369, *per* Park J., quoting Lord Kenyon.
20 *Winter* v. *White, supra,* at p. 369, *per* Park J.
1 *Carr* d. *Dagwel* v. *Singer* (1750) 2 Ves.Sen. 603 at 610, *per* Willes C.J.
2 *Parsons* v. *Thompson* (1790) 1 Hy.Bl. 322 at 326.
3 *A.-G.* v. *Hope* (1834) 1 Cr.M. & R. 530 at 538.
4 *Crickett* v. *Dolby* (1795) 3 Ves. 10 at 14.
5 *Hadley* v. *Clarke* (1799) 8 T.R. 259 at 266, *per* Lord Kenyon C.J.
6 *Cave* v. *Cave* (1705) 2 Vern. 508.
7 *Boycot* v. *Cotton* (1738) 1 Atk. 552 at 556.
8 *Re Willatts* [1905] 1 Ch. 378 at 383.
9 *Bax* v. *Whitbread* (1809) 16 Ves. 15 at 24.

when Extant, seemed Beauteous in their Confusion." [10]   The editor's labours were rewarded seventy years later when Lord Kenyon C.J. referred to Hobart's "excellent volume of reports." [11]

One of the unsolved puzzles of this list of condemnations is the status of a criticism of A's Reports contained in a case reported in B's Reports if B's Reports have themselves been said to be worthless; there are many examples of this.   A further puzzle is the status of a case which is reported by two bad reporters and not only one; but on this Lord Mansfield C.J. has spoken.   "There is an express authority of a case of *Rex* versus *King*,[12] reported in two books, each of which states the case in the same way.   It is objected, however, that these are books of no authority: but if both the reporters were the worst that ever reported, if substantially they report a case in the same way, it is demonstration of the truth of what they report, or they could not agree." [13]

Nisi prius decisions, on the other hand, were beyond redemption.   "Very likely," said Bayley J., "one's first thoughts at Nisi Prius may be wrong, and I am extremely sorry that they are ever reported, and still more so that they are ever mentioned again, at least so far as my Nisi Prius decisions are concerned, because I think they are entitled to very little weight.   What is said by a judge upon a trial is merely the first impression of his mind on a point coming suddenly before him, and which he had no opportunity of considering beforehand." [14]   Nevertheless, the future Lord Campbell's path to the Woolsack was much smoothed by the four volumes of his *nisi prius* reports, a bold venture for a barrister of less than two years' standing.   The reports earned much praise.   Blackburn J., who was not given to easy compliments, once contrasted him with certain other reporters, and said " We may depend on the accuracy of this

[10] (1724) p. iv; and see 5 Mod. (5th ed. 1794) p. viii, attributing a similar remark to Finch L.C.
[11] *Troward* v. *Cailland* (1795) 6 T.R. 439 at 441.
[12] (1673) 3 Keb. 230; Free.K.B. 348.
[13] *R.* v. *Genge* (1774) 1 Cowp. 13 at 16, *per* Lord Mansfield C.J.
[14] *Doe* d. *James* v. *Staunton* (1819) 1 Chit.Pr. 118 at 121.

reporter." [15] Lord Cranworth L.C., too, once said "On all occasions I have found, on looking at the reports, by the late Lord Campbell, of Lord Ellenborough's decisions, that they really do, in the fewest possible words, lay down the law, very often more distinctly and more accurately than it is to be found in many lengthened reports." [16]

Let Lord Campbell himself give an explanation. "When I was a nisi prius reporter I had a drawer marked 'Bad Law' into which I threw all the cases which seemed to me improperly ruled. I was flattered to hear Sir James Mansfield C.J. say, 'Whoever reads Campbell's reports must be astonished to find how uniformly Lord Ellenborough's decisions were right.' My rejected cases, which I had kept as a curiosity—not maliciously— were all burnt in the great fire in the Temple when I was Attorney-General." [17] There was, it seems, enough "bad Ellenborough law" to form an additional volume of reports.[18] Yet even if all the "right" were right, who can say how many of the "bad" were not in fact good?

The reference to Sir James Mansfield C.J. seems to be to a case of 1813 in which Sir James is reported as having said of a decision of Lord Ellenborough's that "It is utterly impossible for any Judge, whatever his learning and abilities may be, to decide at once rightly upon every point which comes before him at Nisi Prius; and whoever looks through Campbell's Reports, will be greatly surprized to see, among such an immense number of questions, many of them of the most important kind, which come before that noble and learned Judge, not that there are mistakes, but that he is in by far the most of the causes so wonderfully right, beyond the proportion of any other Judges." [19] Many years later Darling J. made use of Campbell's reports to be a little coy about an unreported decision of his own. It was argued that certain dicta in the Court of Appeal were *obiter* and in conflict with his decision. But this was not enough. "Such

---

[15] *Readhead* v. *Midland Railway Co.* (1867) L.R. 2 Q.B. 412 at 438.
[16] *Williams* v. *Bailey* (1866) L.R. 1 H.L. 200 at 213.
[17] 5 Camp.L.CC. 376.
[18] 2 *Atlay* 138.
[19] *Fentum* v. *Pocock* (1813) 5 Taunt. 192 at 195. Yet many of the judgments reported were by judges other than Lord Ellenborough.

decisions at nisi prius as had the good fortune to be reported by Lord Campbell are admittedly of high authority; but I cannot bring myself to attribute to that particular decision of a court of first instance which has been pressed upon me an authority overbearing the opinions of the Lords Justices, obiter dicta though they be." [20]

The Mother of Repose

MUCH has been written and spoken on the doctrine of judicial precedent, and doubtless much more is still to come. At one extreme lies the goal of such certainty in the law as to obviate virtually all litigation save on disputed questions of fact; and the price to be paid is that of injustice in unforeseen cases. At the other extreme there is the goal of perfect hand-tailored justice in every case, at the price of great uncertainty in the law, and a flood of litigation. Each price is too great; and inevitably the greatest of judges have differed in their views as to the point between the extremes at which the line is to be drawn. Those who feel most assured that they are wiser than their fathers are the most bold.

If the doctrine of precedent is not followed, " The law becomes not a chart to govern conduct but a game of chance; instead of settling rights and liabilities it unsettles them. Counsel and parties will bring and prosecute actions in the teeth of the decisions that such actions are not maintainable on the not improbable chance that the asserted rule will be thrown overboard. Defendants will not know whether to litigate or to settle for they will have no assurance that a declared rule will be followed. But the more deplorable consequence will inevitably be that the administration of justice will fall into disrepute. Respect for tribunals must fall when the bar and the public come to understand that nothing that has been said in prior adjudication has force in a current controversy." [1] " Little respect will be paid to our judgments if we overthrow that one day, which we resolved the day before." [2] " Before overruling a precedent in any case it is the duty of the Court to make certain that more harm will not be done in rejecting than in retaining a rule of even dubious validity." [3]

---

[1] *Mahnich* v. *Southern Steamship Co.*, 321 U.S. 96 at 112 (1944), *per* Roberts J., dissenting.
[2] *R.* v. *Inhabitants de Haughton* (1718) 1 Str. 83 at 84, *per* Pratt J.
[3] *United States* v. *South-Eastern Underwriters Association*, 322 U.S. 533 at 580 (1944), *per* Stone C.J., dissenting.

Sugden L.C. once said, "I do not sit here to make new rules, but to administer the settled rules of property, and to keep the land-marks of the law sacred."[4] "In questions which respect the rights of property, it is better to adhere to principles once fixed, though, originally, they might not have been perfectly free from all objection, than to unsettle the law, in order to render it more consistent with the dictates of sound reason."[5] Property apart, there are many unsettled points of law of which it can well be said that "it is highly proper the law should be settled one way or other in this case, though no great matter which way, so it be but known."[6] In the words of Lord Blackburn, "I believe it to be of more consequence that this point should be settled than how it is settled."[7] And when such a point is settled, it is well to follow the decision, even if it produces consequences less perfect than were expected. "When once a rule has been laid down, it is best to abide by it. We cannot always be speculating what would have been the best decision in the first instance."[8] Lord Eldon was of the same mind, too. "It is better the law should be certain, than that every Judge should speculate upon improvements in it"[9]; for "certainty is the mother of repose."[10] "Peace and concord is the end of all laws, and . . . the law was ordained for the sake of peace. . . . And therefore those laws which bring the greatest peace are the most estimable."[11]

This doctrine is particularly welcome when the grounds for the rule are obscure. As Lord Eldon once frankly said, "From the mischief of changing continually I have thought it right to follow that practice; not exactly understanding the principle."[12] So too in America. "Mistakes may occur and sometimes do occur, but it is better that they should be endured than that, in

4 *Marjoribanks* v. *Hovenden* (1843) Dr.*t*.Sugd. 11 at 21.
5 *Marine Insurance Co. of Alexandria* v. *Tucker*, 7 U.S. 357 at 388 (1806), *per* Washington J.
6 *Farrington* v. *Knightley* (1719) 1 P.Wms. 544 at 549, *per* Lord Parker L.C.
7 *Tiverton & North Devon Railway Co.* v. *Loosemore* (1884) 9 App.Cas. 480 at 499.
8 *Rayner* v. *Mowbray* (1791) 3 Bro.C.C. 234 at 235, *per* Lord Thurlow L.C.
9 *Sheddon* v. *Goodrich* (1803) 8 Ves. 481 at 497.
10 *Walton* v. *Tryon* (1753) Dick. 244 at 245, *per* Lord Hardwicke L.C.; *post*, p. 235. 11 *Stowel* v. *Lord Zouch* (1569) 1 Plowd. 353 at 368, *per* Dyer C.J.
12 *Paxton* v. *Douglas* (1803) 8 Ves. 520.

a vain search for infallibility, questions shall remain open indefinitely." [13] " It is almost as important that the law should be settled permanently, as that it should be settled correctly." [14] Some have gone further. "It is usually more important that a rule of law be settled, than that it be settled right. Even where the error in declaring the rule is a matter of serious concern, it is ordinarily better to seek correction by legislation. Often this is true although the question is a constitutional one. The human experience embodied in the doctrine of *stare decisis* teaches us, also, that often it is better to follow a precedent, although it does not involve the declaration of a rule. That is usually true so far as concerns a particular statute whether the error was made in construing it or in passing upon its validity. But the doctrine of *stare decisis* does not command that we err again when we have occasion to pass upon a different statute." [15] Further, "I see no reason why I should be consciously wrong today because I was unconsciously wrong yesterday." [16]

"To me," said Viscount Simonds, "heterodoxy, or, as some might say, heresy, is not the more attractive because it is dignified by the name of reform. Nor will I easily be led by an undiscerning zeal for some abstract kind of justice to ignore our first duty, which is to administer justice according to law, the law which is established for us by Act of Parliament or the binding authority of precedent. The law is developed by the application of old principles to new circumstances. Therein lies its genius. Its reform by the abrogation of those principles is the task not of the courts of law but of Parliament." [17] To this may be added a genealogical postscript by Diplock L.J.: " The common law evolves not merely by breeding new principles but also, when they are fully grown, by burying their progenitors." [18]

[13] *Tilt* v. *Kelsey*, 207 U.S. 43 at 56 (1907), *per* Moody J.
[14] *Gilman* v. *Philadelphia*, 70 U.S. 713 at 724 (1865), *per* Swayne J.
[15] *Di Santo* v. *Pennsylvania*, 273 U.S. 34 at 42 (1927), *per* Brandeis J., dissenting.
[16] *Massachusetts* v. *United States*, 333 U.S. 611 at 639 (1948), *per* Jackson J., dissenting.
[17] *Scruttons Ltd.* v. *Midland Silicones Ltd.* [1962] A.C. 446 at 467.
[18] *Hongkong Fir Shipping Co. Ltd.* v. *Kawasaki Kisen Kaisha Ltd.* [1962] 2 Q.B. 26 at 71.

At times, the self-confidence of those who hold opposing views may be overwhelming. "Every direct authority known to us is against us. Nevertheless, we are right, and these authorities are all wrong, as time and further judicial study of the subject will manifest."[19] Sometimes authorities meet authorities, and set the court free. "It will be observed, that I have cited no cases in support of this opinion; not that I have not read, and considered, and puzzled myself with, the multitude that were commented on in the argument; but because, finding them like the swiss troops, fighting on both sides, I have laid them aside, and gone upon what seems to me the true spirit of the law."[20] It has even been said in dissent that the majority view itself provides support for both sides. "The Court's opinion marshals every argument in favor of state aid and puts the case in its most favorable light, but much of its reasoning confirms my conclusions that there are no good grounds upon which to support the present legislation. In fact, the under-tones of the opinion, advocating complete and uncompromising separation of Church from State, seem utterly discordant with its conclusion yielding support to their commingling in educational matters. The case which irresistibly comes to mind as the most fitting precedent is that of Julia who, according to Byron's reports,[1] 'whispering "I will ne'er consent,"— consented '."[2]

Sometimes, however, the difference is plainly one of principle. Thus where a group insurance scheme made provision for any "descendant" of the assured, the question arose whether the term included a man's illegitimate child. Despite the authorities, Lord Denning M.R. held that it did; but Diplock and Russell L.JJ. held the contrary. Russell L.J. ended his judgment with these words: "I may perhaps be forgiven for

[19] *Green* v. *Coast Line R.Co.*, 24 S.E. 814 at 822 (1895), *per* Simmons C.J. (delivering for the Supreme Court of Georgia a judgment written by Bleckley ex-C.J.: see at p. 814).
[20] *Watkins* v. *Crouch & Co.*, 5 Leigh 522 at 530 (Va. 1834), *per* Carr J.
[1] *Don Juan*, c. I, cxvii.
[2] *Everson* v. *Board of Education of the Township of Ewing*, 330 U.S. 1 at 19 (1947), *per* Jackson J., dissenting.

saying that it appears to me that Lord Denning M.R. has acceded to the appeal of Bassanio in the Merchant of Venice.

> *Bassanio*: 'And, I beseech you,
>> Wrest once the law to your authority:
>> To do a great right, do a little wrong.'

But Portia retorted:

> *Portia*: 'It must not be; there is no power in Venice
>> Can alter a decree establishéd:
>> 'Twill be recorded for a precedent,
>> And many an error, by the same example,
>> Will rush into the State: it cannot be.'

I am a Portia man." [3]

Yet there is a middle course. "*Stare decisis* is ordinarily a wise rule of action. But it is not a universal, inexorable command." [4] "The maxim which, taken literally, requires courts to follow decided cases, is shown by the thousands of overruled decisions, to be a figurative expression requiring only a reasonable respect for decided cases." [5] In one case in 1959 the House of Lords was confronted with a decision of its own [6] made some twelve years earlier. That decision was not directly in point, but it was not easy to distinguish it in principle. Lord Denning's view was that "The doctrine of precedent does not compel your Lordships to follow the wrong path until you fall over the edge of the cliff. As soon as you find that you are going in the wrong direction, you must at least be permitted to strike off in the right direction, even if you are not allowed to retrace your steps. And that is what I would ask your Lordships to do." [7] As, however, all the other law lords had already expressed agreement, independently of any question of authority, with the result that would be produced by applying the precedent,

---

3 *Sydall* v. *Castings Ltd.* [1967] 1 Q.B. 302 at 321.
4 *State of Washington* v. *W. C. Dawson & Co.*, 264 U.S. 219 at 238 (1924), *per* Brandeis J., dissenting.
5 *Lisbon* v. *Lyman*, 49 N.H. 553 at 602 (1870), *per* Doe J.
6 *Inland Revenue Commissioners* v. *Australian Mutual Provident Society* [1947] A.C. 605.
7 *Ostime* v. *Australian Mutual Provident Society* [1960] A.C. 459 at 489.

Lord Denning's invitation, based as it was on the direction being wrong and not right, fell on unreceptive soil.

The Bench, indeed, is not always as grateful as it might be for the doctrine of precedent. Lord Lyndhurst L.C. pointed out that " Lord Chief Justice Gibbs used to say that he could get authorities in the Year Books for any side in any thing." [8] Manisty J. had similar views. He is reported as saying " But for the authorities I should have no doubt at all. There is nothing too absurd but what authority can be found for it." [9] In the Law Reports, however, these words became " Common sense is a better guide in such matters than authority." [10] A. L. Smith L.J. was of the same school. Speaking of a covenant, he said " It is so clear that, unless one embrangles it with cases, you cannot miss the intention of the parties." [11]

Some judicial tributes to counsel, too, barely conceal the barbs. Lord Esher M.R. once observed that " every case upon the subject that industry could find and ingenuity could torture was brought before us." [12] " Doubtless," said Cave J., " no form of words has ever yet been framed by human ingenuity with regard to which some ingenious counsel could not suggest a difficulty." [13] So too Bowen L.J. " The distinguished counsel [14] who argued this case before us have, I think, drawn three red herrings across the path of the Court, in the hope that we should be drawn off the scent." [15] A different piscine approach is to describe the argument of counsel as " A most skilful presentation of a highly attractive fly " [16]; but like many of his predecessors that trout rose without biting. There are other ways of putting it. " Mr. Geoffrey Cross [17] destroyed the argu-

---

8 *Gray* v. *R.* (1844) 11 Cl. & F. 427 at 441.
9 *Henderson* v. *Preston* (1888) 4 T.L.R. 632 at 633.
10 *Ibid.*, 21 Q.B.D. 362 at 365; and see the compromise version at 59 L.T. 335.
11 *Re Floyd* [1897] 1 Ch. 633 at 638.
12 *Turner* v. *Mersey Docks & Harbour Board* [1892] P. 285 at 297.
13 *Pratt* v. *South Eastern Railway Co.* [1897] 1 Q.B. 718 at 721.
14 Ince Q.C. and Buckley.
15 *Re Blackburn and District Benefit Building Society* (1883) 24 Ch.D. 421 at 436.
16 *Paxton* v. *Allsopp* [1971] 1 W.L.R. 1310 at 1320, *per* Karminski L.J.
17 Now Lord Cross of Chelsea.

ments of Mr. Russell [18] and Mr. Megarry [19] in one sentence
when he said that they had raised the dust and then claimed that
we could not see through it. Our eyes, however, are not blinded
by dust of that kind." [20]   *Quaere*, one may ask, as to the kind
of dust that would succeed.

In America, the doctrine of precedent has led to some prolonged battles. *Hole* v. *Rittenhouse* [1] was a curious case concerning the title to land. In 1851 the plaintiff succeeded in an
action for ejectment in the Common Pleas of Columbia County
in Pennsylvania. On a writ of error the judgment was reversed
in the State Supreme Court by a majority of three to two, and
a new trial was ordered. In the leading judgment for the
majority, Black C.J. affirmed the rule in *Waggoner* v. *Hastings*,[2]
with Lowrie and Gibson JJ. concurring, whereas Lewis and
Woodward JJ. dissented on this point.[3] The new trial duly
took place in 1854 and after the trial judge, Conyngham P.J., had
instructed the jury in accordance with the rule in *Waggoner* v.
Hastings,[4] the jury found for the plaintiff again, though only
for part of the land.

Again the defendant sued out a writ of error, but this time
the Supreme Court was differently constituted. Lewis J., one
of the former dissentients, had become C.J., and Black C.J. had
sunk to the rank of J. Over the sole dissent of Black J., the
court overruled *Waggoner* v. *Hastings*, reversed the judgment,
and again ordered a new trial.[5] Of the two former allies of
Black J., one, Gibson J., was dead,[6] and the other, Lowrie J.,
deserted him.

The third trial took place in 1858, and again the plaintiff's
claim to the part of the land for which he had had the verdict
in the second trial was successful. Once again the defendant

[18] Now Russell L.J.
[19] [Advert.]
[20] *Tithe Redemption Commission* v. *Runcorn U.D.C.* [1954] Ch. 383 at 407, *per* Denning L.J.
[1] See *Hole* v. *Rittenhouse*, 37 Pa. 116 (1860) for a summary of the course of proceedings.
[2] 5 Pa. 300 (1847).
[3] *Hole* v. *Rittenhouse*, 19 Pa. 305 (1852).
[4] See *Hole* v. *Rittenhouse*, 25 Pa. 491 at 492 (1855).
[5] *Hole* v. *Rittenhouse*, 25 Pa. 491 (1855).   [6] See 19 Pa. iii.

sued out a writ of error, and this time the Supreme Court was unanimous. Black J. had resigned in 1857,[7] and the judgment of the court was delivered by the other of the dissentients in the first appeal, Woodward J. Once again the judgment was reversed, but this time no new trial was ordered,[8] and the plaintiff's discomfiture was complete; even a Supreme Court may be driven into saying " We have spoken three times, and thrice is enough."

The State Reports say no more of the dissent of Black J. in the second appeal than " Black, J., dissented." [9] But another series of reports has preserved his dissent. It was forceful. After discussing the line of authorities supporting *Waggoner* v. *Hastings*, the judge said: " I could say much by way of proving that the rule I contend for is wholesome in its operation, and that no other rule equally just and simple can be substituted in its place. But that is surely not necessary. When a principle of law is established by a long series of decisions without a single case on the other side: to carry it out in plain good faith, is as sacred a duty as any Judge has to perform. His own notion that it ought to be otherwise is not entitled to a moment's consideration. It is no part of our office to tinker at the law and patch it up with new materials of our own making. Suitors are entitled to it just as it is. Bad laws can be borne; but the *jus vagum aut incertum*—the law that shifts and changes every time it passes through the Courts is as sore an evil and as heavy a curse as any people can suffer; and no people who are fit for self-government will suffer it long. Even a legislator, if he is wise and thoughtful, will make no change which is not absolutely necessary. Legislative changes however are prospective, and disturb nothing that is past. But Judge-made laws sweep away all the rights which may have been acquired on the faith of previous rules. For such wrongs even the legislature can furnish no redress. When the scales of justice are shaken by the hands that hold them here, there is no power elsewhere to adjust them. A simple man who has invested his money in the purchase of a

[7] See 27 Pa. iii.
[8] *Hole* v. *Rittenhouse*, 37 Pa. 116 (1860).
[9] *Hole* v. *Rittenhouse*, 25 Pa. 491 at 502 (1855).

title solemnly pronounced indefeasible in half a dozen cases decided by the highest tribunal of the State, may wake up from his dream of security to find himself ruined by a contrary ruling of the very same question.

" The judgment now about to be given, is one of 'death's doings.' No one can doubt that if Judge Gibson and Judge Coulter [10] had lived, the plaintiff could not have been thus deprived of his property; and thousands of other men would have been saved from the imminent danger to which they are now exposed of losing the homes they have labored and paid for. But they are dead; and the law which should have protected those sacred rights has died with them. It is a melancholy reflection, that the property of a citizen should be held by a tenure so frail. But 'new lords, new laws' is the order of the day. Hereafter if any man be offered a title which the Supreme Court has decided to be good, let him not buy if the Judges who made the decision are dead; if they are living let him get an insurance on their lives; for ye know not what a day or an hour may bring forth.

" The majority of this Court changes on the average once every nine years, without counting the chances of death and resignation. If each new set of Judges shall consider themselves at liberty to overthrow the doctrines of their predecessors, our system of jurisprudence (if system it can be called) would be the most fickle, uncertain and vicious that the civilized world ever saw. A French constitution, or a South American republic, or a Mexican administration would be an immortal thing in comparison to the short-lived principles of Pennsylvania law. The rules of property which ought to be as steadfast as the hills, will become as unstable as the waves. To avoid this great calamity, I know of no resource but that of *stare decisis*. I claim nothing for the great men who have gone before us on the score of their marked and manifest superiority. But I would stand by their decisions, because they have passed into the law

---

[10] Gibson C.J. had delivered the judgment of the court in *Waggoner* v. *Hastings, supra,* and had concurred with Black C.J. in the first appeal in *Hole* v. *Rittenhouse, supra.* Coulter J. was a member of the court in *Waggoner* v. *Hastings, supra.*

and become a part of it—have been relied and acted on—and rights have grown up under them which it is unjust and cruel to take away." [11]

In England, a decision that gave rise to much difficulty was *Hutton* v. *Upfill*.[12] The question was whether a person who was a member of the provisional committee on the formation of a joint stock company, and had accepted shares in the company, thereby became liable as a contributory when the company failed. Master Brougham answered "Yes," but Knight Bruce V.-C. said "No,"[13] and the case was taken to the House of Lords. The only law lord present was Lord Brougham, and counsel for the respondent said that "he was instructed most respectfully to state that an application was intended to be made to request the Lord Chancellor to attend—," whereat Lord Brougham intervened to say that "he had the greatest respect for his noble and learned friend, the Lord Chancellor. He had just taken his seat in the Court of Chancery, and was not yet much conversant with these cases. Were he, however, to attend, he would be here like any other peer. It was not proper that a suitor here should solicit the attendance of any peer. If the parties did not wish for delay, then their objection was that only one Law Lord was present. That was not new; for he himself, when he held the Great Seal, and also after resigning it, often was the only Law Lord present to hear appeals." [14]

Lord Truro, who had been C.J.C.P. until he attained the Woolsack less than a month earlier, cannot have read these comments with any great enthusiasm; but the hearing proceeded. In due course Lord Brougham delivered judgment allowing the appeal and restoring the decision of the Master; he was "his favourite brother," and he had appointed him to office nearly twenty years earlier.[15] No other speech is recorded, though Lord Brougham, after saying that "Lord Lyndhurst has unfor-

---

[11] *Hole* v. *Rittenhouse*, 25 Pa. 491 (1855), as reported at 2 Phila.Rep. (13 *Legal Intelligencer*) 411 at 417, *per* Black J., dissenting.
[12] (1850) 2 H.L.C. 674.
[13] *Ibid.*, at p. 677.
[14] *Ibid.*, at p. 681.
[15] Campbell, *Lives of Lord Lyndhurst and Lord Brougham* (1869) p. 408; J. Haydn, *Book of Dignities* (1890) pp. 358, 397.

tunately left town, so that I cannot state how he would view the matter," added "I have communicated [16] with my noble and learned friend Lord Cottenham upon this subject, and he takes exactly the same view that I do." [17]

Two years later *Bright* v. *Hutton* [18] was carried to the House of Lords. Once again on similar facts Master Brougham had put the shareholder on the list of contributories, and in obedience to *Hutton* v. *Upfill* Lord Cranworth V.-C. had affirmed the decision, though very strongly doubting whether *Hutton* v. *Upfill* was right. [19] This time there was legal talent in plenty in the House. Lord St. Leonards L.C. presided, with Lord Brougham, Lord Campbell and Lord Cranworth present [20]; and nine judges were in attendance. [1] The judges unanimously advised that they considered *Hutton* v. *Upfill* binding on all inferior courts, though "but for that case, we, upon other decisions, should have been of a contrary opinion." [2] Their lordships unanimously accepted this advice, though in differing terms. Lord St. Leonards thought the House was not bound by its own decisions on a point of law, [3] whereas Lord Campbell thought that it was bound, though what Lord Brougham had decided in *Hutton* v. *Upfill* had been fact not law. [4] Lord Brougham was plainly in difficulties, but his escape was by much the same route, [5] while Lord Cranworth, jubilant at reversing his own constrained decision, concurred in this. [6]

The House of Lords may also demonstrate how procedure can control substance. It is at least theoretically possible that in a case before the House of Lords, the appellant may have five distinct grounds of appeal, success on any one of which will bring him victory on the whole case. What, then, is his position if on each of the five grounds there is one law lord in his favour

---

[16] He had a letter from Lord Cottenham: see *Bright* v. *Hutton* (1852) 3 H.L.C. 341 at 390.
[17] *Hutton* v. *Upfill, supra*, at p. 694.
[18] (1852) 3 H.L.C. 341.
[19] *Ibid.*, at p. 393.
[20] Lord Truro left before the end.
[1] *Bright* v. *Hutton* (1852) 3 H.L.C. 341 at 372; two others left before the end.
[2] *Ibid.*, at p. 387.
[3] *Ibid.*, at p. 391.
[4] *Ibid.*, at p. 392.
[5] *Ibid.*, at p. 391.
[6] *Ibid.*, at p. 393.

and four against? The answer appears to be that if it is an English case the appeal will be unanimously allowed, whereas if it is a Scottish case the appeal will be unanimously dismissed.

The reason for this distinction is procedural. The English case would be treated as a whole, and as each law lord is in favour of the appellant on a ground sufficient by itself for success, each will vote for allowing the appeal. In Scotland, each point will constitute a separate plea in law. On each plea, there will be a majority of four to one against the appellant, and so his appeal will fail.[7] The contrast would be enhanced if all five law lords averred that the law of England was the same as the law of Scotland on all five points. The extent to which such a case would form a binding precedent is also not without interest. Presumably any subsequent litigant in England whose case exhibited any three of the five points would, on a mathematical basis, be assured of success, for he could muster three out of the five law lords in his favour.[8] In Scotland, on the other hand, he would be doomed to failure in any event.

A problem sometimes arises when the junior member of the Court of Appeal utters no more than a few words in which he simply expresses his concurrence with the other two judgments. Does he thereby make authoritative all that was said in the second judgment? Counsel[9] once argued before Birkett L.J. that this was so as regards an earlier case[10] in which Denning L.J. had delivered the second judgment and Birkett J. the third; but Birkett L.J. answered "It is difficult in a concurring judgment to say that you agree with most of what has been said. I agreed with the result. . . ."[11]

When the judges of a court were equally divided, a practice sometimes followed in the past was for the junior judge to withdraw his judgment. Indeed, towards the end of the last

---

[7] See (1950) 66 L.Q.R. 298; and see *per* Asquith L.J., (1950) 1 J.S.P.T.L.(N.S.) 358.
[8] And see *ante*, p. 69.
[9] Megarry.
[10] *Littlechild* v. *Holt* [1950] 1 K.B. 1.
[11] *Wright* v. *Walford* [1955] 1 Q.B. 363 at 367. See the discussion in the Presidential Address to the Holdsworth Club, 1969, by Russell L.J., *Behind the Appellate Curtain.*

century this had become the settled practice in the Queen's
Bench Division. Lopes L.J. had no doubts. " But surely Mr.
Justice Grantham withdrew his judgment? It is always the
custom for the junior judge to do so." [12] The answer was that
he had not done so : he had not been asked to do it. But in most
cases the practice seems to have been observed, at times with
somewhat odd results on appeal. Thus in 1913 a King's Bench
Divisional Court was divided in an appeal from the appeal
tribunal under the London Building Act, 1894.[13] Judgment
was reserved, and then Lush J. delivered a ten-page judgment
in favour of allowing the appeal, while Ridley J., in four pages
less, was for dismissing it. " Lush J., as the junior judge, withdrew his judgment, and judgment was given for the respondents." [14] The Court of Appeal, however, held that Lush J.
had been right,[15] though this decision was afterwards reversed
by the House of Lords.[16]

Later in the same year Lush J. again found himself in a
similar position. Bray J. was in favour of allowing an appeal
from the county court, whereas Lush J. was in favour of dismissing it. Lush J. then withdrew his judgment and the appeal
was allowed.[17] However, a few days later the respondent made
an application to the court for Lush J. to withdraw his with-
drawal, on the ground that he had no power to make it in the
first place; but Bray J. held that Lush J. had a discretion
whether or not to withdraw it, and Lush J. considered that it
was better to leave matters as they were.[18] Again the case was
carried to the Court of Appeal, and again Lush J. was held to
be right [19]; and this time there was no further appeal. In his
judgment Phillimore L.J. doubted whether Lush J. had been
right in withdrawing his judgment, and referred to a case [20] in
which Stephen and Hawkins JJ. had differed on whether

[12] *Bound* v. *Lawrence* [1892] 1 Q.B. 226, as reported (1891) 8 T.L.R. 1. For
another example, see *ante*, p. 36.
[13] *Clode* v. *London County Council* [1914] 3 K.B. 852.
[14] *Ibid.*, at p. 874.   [15] *Ibid.*
[16] *London County Council* v. *Clode* [1915] A.C. 947.
[17] *Poulton* v. *Moore* (1913) 83 L.J.K.B. 875.
[18] *Ibid.*, at p. 884.
[19] *Poulton* v. *Moore* [1915] 1 K.B. 400.
[20] *R.* v. *Bishop of London* [1891] 2 Q.B. 48.

mandamus should issue. " I happen to remember that, upon it being suggested that Stephen J. should withdraw his judgment, that learned judge refused with considerable emphasis." [1] (His judgment was duly upheld by the Court of Appeal and House of Lords.[2]) With these words of Phillimore L.J. the practice of the junior judge withdrawing his judgment seems to have expired,[3] if, indeed, it was not already dead.[4]

Today, courts usually avoid the possibility of equal division by sitting with an uneven number of judges, thus ensuring a majority and minority, at least in the result. It was Cardozo J. who illuminated the difference in style between a majority judgment and a dissent. " Comparatively speaking at least, the dissenter is irresponsible. The spokesman of the court is cautious, timid, fearful of the vivid word, the heightened phrase. He dreams of an unworthy brood of scions, the spawn of careless dicta, disowned by the *ratio decidendi*, to which all legitimate offspring must be able to trace their lineage. The result is to cramp and paralyze. One fears to say anything when the peril of misunderstanding puts a warning finger to the lips. Not so, however, the dissenter. He has laid aside the role of the hierophant, which he will be only too glad to resume when the chances of war make him again the spokesman of the majority. For the moment, he is the gladiator making a last stand against the lions. The poor man must be forgiven a freedom of expression, tinged at rare moments with a touch of bitterness, which magnanimity as well as caution would reject for one triumphant." [5]

Hughes C.J. put similar views a little differently. " Dissent-

---

[1] *Poulton* v. *Moore* [1915] 1 K.B. 400 at 416.

[2] *R.* v. *Bishop of London, supra, sub nom. Lighton* v. *Lord Bishop of London* [1891] A.C. 666; 61 L.J.Q.B. 62.

[3] See also *Metropolitan Water Board* v. *Johnson & Co.* [1913] 3 K.B. 900 at 904, where Channell and Avory JJ. differed, but Channell J. ruled that the proper course was to dismiss the appeal and not for the junior judge to withdraw his judgment. In due course the Court of Appeal allowed the appeal, as Channell J. would have done.

[4] It is believed that a resolution to this effect in relation to county court appeals was moved by Lush J. at a meeting of King's Bench judges on January 12, 1914, and was carried.

[5] *Selected Writings of Benjamin Nathan Cardozo* (1947) p. 353, reprinting " Law and Literature " from *The Yale Law Review* for July 1925.

ing opinions enable a judge to express his individuality. He is not under the compulsion of speaking for the court and thus of securing the concurrence of a majority. In dissenting, he is a free lance. A dissent in a court of last resort is an appeal to the brooding spirit of the law, to the intelligence of a future day, when a later decision may possibly correct the error into which the dissenting judge believes the court to have been betrayed." [6] It has even been said of an intermediate court that "a Lord Justice has refused to read a prepared dissenting judgment on the ground that its sole function was to give the defeated party ammunition for a further appeal." [7] The case cited, however, does not support the allegation of so unsporting an attitude; the dominant consideration seems to have been not the deprivation of munitions but the call of the table. What Diplock L.J. said of his judgment was "If I read it it would not be completed before the luncheon adjournment and I do not think that any useful purpose is served by reading it now." [8] He then summarised his conclusions, and in due course the judgment appeared *in extenso* in the Weekly Law Reports, assisting, no doubt, in the production of the many variant views that were taken in the House of Lords. [9]

A dissent may be decorous without losing its force. "I know that this, like every other case, will become the parent stock from which a motley progeny will spring. In those after years when this case, elevated to high authority by the cold finality of the printed page, is quoted with the customary, 'It has been said' perchance another court will say, 'Mayhaps the potter's hand trembled at the wheel.' Possibly when that moment comes these words may give the court a chance to say, 'Yea, and a workman standing hard by saw the vase as it cracked.'" [10]

Opinions vary on the value of dissents. "There has been

[6] Hughes C.J., *The Supreme Court of the United States* (1928) p. 68.
[7] R. F. V. Heuston, *Judges and Biographers* (1967) p. 23.
[8] *Hardwick Game Farm* v. *Suffolk Agricultural Poultry Producers Association* [1966] 1 W.L.R. 287 at 320.
[9] *Henry Kendall & Sons* v. *William Lillico & Sons Ltd.* [1969] 2 A.C. 31, in the result affirming the decision below.
[10] *Oliver* v. *City of Raleigh*, 193 S.E. 853 at 857 (1937), *per* Clarkson J., dissenting.

much undiscriminating eulogy of dissenting opinions. It is said they clarify the issues. Often they do the exact opposite. The technique of the dissenter often is to exaggerate the holding of the Court beyond the meaning of the majority and then to blast away at the excess. So the poor lawyer with a similar case does not know whether the majority opinion meant what it seemed to say or what the minority said it meant. Then, too, dissenters frequently force the majority to take positions more extreme than was originally intended. The classic example is the *Dred Scott Case*,[11] in which Chief Justice Taney's extreme statements were absent in his original draft and were inserted only after Mr. Justice McLean, then a more than passive candidate for the presidency, raised the issue in dissent.

"The *right of dissent* is a valuable one. Wisely used on well-chosen occasions, it has been of great service to the profession and to the law. But there is nothing good, for either the Court or the dissenter, in dissenting per se. Each dissenting opinion is a confession of failure to convince the writer's colleagues, and the true test of a judge is his influence in leading, not in opposing, his court."[12]

The absence of any precedent at all is a spur to valour. In 1588 counsel said that "he had searched all the books, and there is not one case where he which is named in the writ, may be resceived"[13]; whereat Anderson C.J. said "What of that? shall not we give judgement because it is not adjudged in the bookes before? wee will give judgement according to reason, and if there bee no reason in the bookes, I will not regard them."[14] Nearly three centuries later, Doe C.J. was of the same mind. In his pregnant phrase, "As there was a time when there were no common-law precedents, everything that can be done with them could be done without them."[15] Yet "could" does not

[11] *Dred Scott* v. *Sandford*, 60 U.S. 393 (1856).
[12] R. H. Jackson J., *The Supreme Court in the American System of Government* (1955) p. 18. Dissenters may even get answered back: see *Bradley Egg Farm Ltd.* v. *Clifford* [1943] 2 All E.R. 378 at 386.
[13] "Resceit" was the receiving of C to plead his right in an action brought by A against B.
[14] *Anon.* (1588) Goulds. 96. See also *Candler* v. *Crane, Christmas & Co.* [1951] 2 K.B. 164 at 178, *per* Denning L.J.
[15] *Metcalf* v. *Gilmore*, 59 N.H. 417 at 433 (1879).

always mean " would." " Every precedent had first a commencement," [16] said Lord Ellesmere L.C. But, replied Coke C.J., " When authority and precedent is wanting, there is need of great consideration, before that any thing of novelty shall be established." [17]

[16] *Case of Proclamations* (1610) 12 Co.Rep. 74.
[17] *Ibid.*, at p. 75.

The Devil

THREE dicta from three centuries may set the scene. "Needless verbosity is the mother of difficulty."[1] "One half the doubts in life arise from the defects of language."[2] "Most of the disputes in the world arise from words."[3] Dictionaries often solve little. "All construction is the ascertainment of meaning. And literalness may strangle meaning."[4] Hence dictionaries are "the last resort of the baffled judge."[5] "It is one of the surest indexes of a mature and developed jurisprudence not to make a fortress out of the dictionary; but to remember that statutes always have some purpose or object to accomplish, whose sympathetic and imaginative discovery is the surest guide to their meaning."[6] Yet "while for the purpose of judicial decision dictionary definitions often are not controlling, they are at least persuasive that meanings which they do not embrace are not common."[7] Words and phrases alike may provide barriers to thought. "When things are called by the same name it is easy for the mind to slide into an assumption that the verbal identity is accompanied in all its sequences by identity of meaning."[8] Similarly, "It is one of the misfortunes of the law that ideas become encysted in phrases and thereafter for a long time cease to provoke further analysis."[9]

The difficulties are well known. "Few words possess the

[1] *Good's Case* (1627) Poph. 211 at 212, *per cur.* (*semble*, Hyde C.J., Doderidge, Jones and Whitelocke JJ.).
[2] *Gibbons* v. *Ogden*, 22 U.S. 1 at 232 (1824), *per* Johnson J.
[3] *Morgan* v. *Jones* (1773) Lofft 160 at 176, *per* Lord Mansfield C.J.
[4] *Utah Junk Co.* v. *Porter*, 328 U.S. 39 at 44 (1946), *per* Frankfurter J.
[5] *Jordan* v. *De George*, 341 U.S. 227 at 234 (1957), *per* Jackson J., dissenting.
[6] *Cabell* v. *Markham*, 148 F. 2d 737 at 739 (1945), *per* Learned Hand J., cited in part in *Farmers Reservoir and Irrigation Co.* v. *McCourt*, 337 U.S. 755 at 764 (1949), *per* Vinson C.J.
[7] *Aschenbrenner* v. *United States Fidelity & Guaranty Co.*, 292 U.S. 80 at 85 (1934), *per* Stone J.
[8] *Lowden* v. *Northwestern National Bank & Trust Co.*, 298 U.S. 160 at 165 (1936), *per* Cardozo J.
[9] *Hyde* v. *United States*, 225 U.S. 347 at 391 (1912), *per* Holmes J., dissenting.

precision of mathematical symbols." [10] "Language draws a
series of mental pictures in the mind of the person hearing the
words spoken. Those pictures are sometimes fairly well defined,
and sometimes blurred in outline, but they are never very precise.
Language is a medium which disdains mathematical rules." [11]
There is an old warning: "Words are but pictures of things,
and he who employs himself about the embellishments of language, seems to be in love with the picture, and to neglect the
life." [12] On the difficulties in this sphere, judges far removed
from each other in space and thought have concurred. Lord
Halsbury L.C. once said "I doubt whether any one of us has
not more than once found that human language is but an
imperfect instrument for the expression of human thought." [13]
Holmes J. was brief. "Ideas are not often hard but words are
the devil." [14]

Metaphors have a special position. Lord Mansfield C.J. once
remarked that "Nothing in law is so apt to mislead as a metaphor." [15] So too "A rule of law should not be drawn from a
figure of speech." [16] Lord Kenyon C.J. has often been derided
both for the frailty of his Latin and for his weakness for mixed
metaphors. No doubt some of the instances are apocryphal.
It seems impossible to authenticate the account of his allocution
when sentencing a butler convicted of stealing his master's wine:
"Dead to every claim of natural affection, and blind to your
own real interest, you burst through all the restraints of religion
and morality, and have for many years been feathering your nest
with your master's bottles." [17] But some unquestionable

---

[10] *Boyce Motor Lines Inc.* v. *United States*, 342 U.S. 337 at 340 (1952), *per*
Clark J.

[11] *Re Coates* [1955] Ch. 495 at 498, *per* Roxburgh J.

[12] Lilly, *Assize* (1719) p. xxix.

[13] *Tubes Ltd.* v. *Perfecta Seamless Steel Tube Co. Ltd.* (1902) 20 R.P.C. 77
at 96.

[14] I *Holmes-Laski Letters* p. 542.

[15] *Knox* v. *Gye* (1872) L.R. 5 H.L. 656 at 676, *per* Lord Westbury, citing no
source for the remark.

[16] *Illinois ex rel. McCollom* v. *Board of Education of School District No. 71,
Champaign County, Illinois*, 333 U.S. 203 at 247 (1948), *per* Reed J.,
dissenting.

[17] A. H. Engelbach, *Anecdotes of Bench and Bar* (1913) p. 184; and see
Croake James, *Curiosities of Law and Lawyers* (1896) p. 636.

examples are to be found in the reports. Thus Lord Kenyon once intervened in a dispute between counsel to say " *Modus in rebus*—there must be an end of things." [18] Lord Campbell's comment was that " this classical quotation his Lordship was in the habit of introducing when he thought it was full time to put an end to any discussion." [19] Lord Campbell also observes that when Lord Kenyon " declared that there was palpable fraud in a case, he would add ' apparently *latet anguis in herbâ* '." [20] An alternative version (though to much the same effect) is that when Lord Kenyon wished " to illustrate in a strong manner the conclusiveness of some fact, [he] thus addressed the Jury, ' Why, Gentlemen of the Jury, it is as plain as the noses upon your faces!—*Latet anguis in herbâ*! ' " [1]

Perhaps the tale is exaggerated, or perhaps Lord Kenyon learned. Certainly after he had been C.J.K.B. for less than six years he is reported as saying " There may be morality and virtue in this paper: and yet, apparently, *latet anguis in herbâ*. There may be much that is good in it, and yet there may be much to censure." [2] But it was Serjeant Marryat and not Lord Kenyon who one day spoke of moving for " a brace of man-dami " [3]; and it was the future Lord Cairns L.C., ever chaste of tongue, who while still Sir Hugh Cairns gravely informed the House of Commons that " It is always dangerous to pin yourself to one horn of a dilemma until you have heard the other." [4]

Constitutional issues seem to have tempted Lord Kenyon to multi-metaphor. " If an individual can break down any of those safeguards, which the constitution has so wisely and so cautiously erected, by poisoning the minds of the jury at a time when they are called upon to decide, he will stab the administration of justice in its most vital parts." [5] Again, when summing

[18] *R.* v. *Dean of St. Asaph* (1783) 21 St.Tr. 847 at 875 (" Moderation in all things "). [19] 3 Camp.C.JJ. 24.
[20] 3 Camp.C.JJ. 44 (" A snake lies hidden in the grass ").
[1] 3 *Westminster Hall* (1825) p. 156.
[2] *R.* v. *Lambert* (1793) 22 St.Tr. 953 at 1018, *per* Lord Kenyon C.J. in his charge to the jury.
[3] 2 *Atlay* 90.   [4] (1864) Hansard (3rd ser.) vol. 173, col. 989.
[5] W. C. Townsend, *Lives of Twelve Eminent Judges* (1846), vol. 1, p. 79, citing Lord Kenyon C.J. as reported in the Term Reports, but without specifying any volume or page.

Semanticity

up in a prosecution for seditious libel, Lord Kenyon said "A
great deal has been said respecting a reform of parliament, that
is, an alteration of parliament. If I were called upon to decide
on that point, before I would pull down the fabric, or presume to
disturb one stone in the structure, I would consider what those
benefits are which it seeks, and whether they, to the extent to
which they are asked, ought to be hazarded; whether any
imaginary reform ought to be adopted, however virtuous the
breast, or however able the head, that might attempt such a
reform. I should be a little afraid, that when the water was let
out, nobody could tell how to stop it; if the lion was once let
into the house, who would be found to shut the door?" [6]

It cannot be said that in twentieth-century England the
tradition lives on, though there is an occasional spark. "I
suppose, Mr. Sims," Crossman J. once said to counsel, "the
parties in this case are sitting on the fence to see which way the
cat jumps?" "No, my Lord," was the grave reply, "they
are sitting on the fence to see which side their bread is buttered." [7]
It must be admitted that in some respects, at least, Lord Kenyon's
mantle, transcending time and space, passed to Musmanno J., of
Pennsylvania, after a respectful pause in transit at the tomb
of Amanda M'Kittrick Ros of Northern Ireland, author of
Delina Delaney, Irene Iddesleigh and *Fumes of Formation*.
One case concerned the damage caused by a boat on a navigable
river striking a submarine cable. The majority of the Supreme
Court of Pennsylvania reversed the decision below and held
the owners of the boat not liable; but Musmanno J. dissented.
"The reasoning which would defeat the plaintiff's verdict, fairly
and squarely won in the assizes, is a reasoning which would
upset any decision because it uses theory for facts and supposition
for logic. The river of conjecture flowing on to the sea of presumption can carry on its boundless bosom fleets of hypotheses
and armadas of surmise, but they will never reach the port of
reality and never sail into the harbor of objective revelation. To
wipe out the promontory of fact in this case and substitute for it

[6] *R. v. Lambert* (1793) 22 St.Tr. 953 at 1016.
[7] K. R. A. Hart, *A Spastic Wins Through* (1955) p. 101.

154

the mirage of speculation is to deny the plaintiff company of its
constitutional right of trial by jury. . . . Not only in the interests
of justice but in appreciation of the very reassuring laws of cause
and effect which impart order and stability to this whirling
world of awesome phenomena, I would keep hands off a verdict
which is intelligent, fair, honest and just." [8]

Again, the view of Musmanno J. was that " To say that a
court does not have the right to revoke a decree is like saying
that a general has no right to change a military order; that a
ship's captain may not alter the course of his vessel; that an
aviator may not deviate from the scheduled orbit of his flight
though a strange aircraft appear before him; that a doctor may
not rewrite a prescription even though new symptoms dictate a
different treatment. Under this line of reasoning a judge may
not change a punishment even though newly revealed facts and
renewed reflection convince him that the first sentence was
unjust. This type of reasoning rips from the ship of dutiful
performance the rudder of responsibility; it tears from the
ordnance of correction the guiding sight of accuracy." [9]

Many a Musmannodict was uttered in dissent; and the
majority was made to pay for its temerity in prevailing. "In
an attempt to find authority for its position, the Majority beats
the bushes of the law and frightens out several rabbits of
decision which at the mere appearance of reason scamper back
into their holes of irrelevancy, from which they might as well
have never emerged." [10] Again, " The defendant, the Superior
Court which reversed the lower Court's awarding of a new trial,
and this Court which sustains that reversal, have all demonstrated an attitude of fault-finding which, it seems to me, aims
at a ship and misses the ocean. . . . The Majority Opinion said
that in order to award a new trial, the ' injustice of the verdict
should stand forth like a beacon.' A beacon of injustice would
hardly be of much use to mariners seeking an open sea of safety

[8] *Bell Telephone Co. of Pennsylvania* v. *Dravo Corp.*, 88 Atl. 2d 737 at 741
(1952).
[9] *Sherman* v. *Yiddisher Kultur Farband*, 99 Atl. 2d 868 at 872 (1953), *per*
Musmanno J., dissenting.
[10] *Zilka* v. *Sanctis Construction, Inc.*, 186 A. 2d 897 at 905 (1963), *per*
Musmanno J., dissenting.

and truth. The lower court was guided, not by the beacon of injustice, but by the beacon of *justice*. And for this Court to ignore the beams of that beacon is to substitute picayune for precedent, theory for tabulation, and penalty for pain; and, in doing so, to write on the books of the law an illustration of how in straining for gnats, a court can produce a good-sized camel of injustice." [11]

Road, rail and sea all made their contribution. " Since law is intended to be the application of common sense and fundamental logic to life in all its tangible truths, the section of the Vehicle Code quoted by the Majority should not be studied and analyzed in a scholar's study under the lamp of abstract meditation. It should be read on the highways where the illumination of purpose comes from the headlights of reality, and legislative intent is to be found in the spinning wheels of fact." [12] Again, " The argument in the Majority Opinion sweeps like an express train over a high-speed main track of jurisprudence, hauling precedents and dicta which have nothing to do with the question before us. The controversy in this litigation involves a single-track spur track of the law which has its own rules, its own precedents and its own fitting appreciation of the unusual facts involved." [13] " The decision of the majority leaves the litigation in this case in the midstream of indecision. . . . These questions, I fear, will outfit further vessels of contention to sail the heavy seas of dubious litigation." [14]

Logic, it seems, has died a manifold death in Pennsylvania. " The path of law and logic is invaded by the foliage of irrelevancy when the Majority Opinion says . . ." [15] Further, the lower court's " powers of reflection were not routed by the forces of emotion. It courageously held the line of reason at the

11 *Elza* v. *Chovan*, 152 A. 2d 238 at 245, 246 (1959), *per* Musmanno J., dissenting.
12 *Notarianni* v. *Ross*, 119 A. 2d 792 at 796 (1956), *per* Musmanno J., dissenting.
13 *Scibelli* v. *Pennsylvania Railroad Co.*, 108 A. 2d 348 at 353 (1954), *per* Musmanno J., dissenting.
14 *School Dist. of Borough of Irwin* v. *School Dist. of North Huntingdon Tp.*, 97 A. 2d 96 at 103, 104 (1953), *per* Musmanno J., dissenting.
15 *Commonwealth of Pennsylvania* v. *Green*, 128 A. 2d 577 at 579 (1957), *per* Musmanno J., dissenting.

Thermopylae of logic and did not give way at the Gettysburg of fact. But the Majority here retreats from logic, abandons precedent, and treats the words of a very clear statute as empty vessels into which any meaning may be poured." [16] Indeed, "Here the Majority Opinion completely inters logic in a deep grave and buries precedent in a bottomless crypt." [17] Too often discord triumphed. "Such a situation does not strike a very melodious chord on the piano of justice which I always try to keep tuned in the living room of my mind and heart." [18]

The powerful combination of Latin and tort has proved difficult. After referring to a contention that in a certain statutory provision " cause " meant " effective cause," Willmer J. once observed " I am aware that the practice of attaching epithets to the word ' cause ' has been frowned on by no less an authority than Lord Sumner . . . but at least one may be permitted to hold that a cause is something which causes." [19] That, indeed, seems to have been the view of Lord Sumner himself; for in the passage referred to, he said " It is surprising how many epithets eminent judges have applied to the cause, which has to be ascertained for this judicial purpose of determining liability, and how many more to other acts and incidents, which for this purpose are not the cause at all. ' Efficient or effective cause,' ' real cause,' ' proximate cause,' ' direct cause,' ' decisive cause,' ' immediate cause,' ' causa causans,' on the one hand, as against, on the other, ' causa sine qua non,' ' occasional cause,' ' remote cause,' ' contributory cause,' ' inducing cause,' ' condition,' and so on. No doubt in the particular cases in which they occur they were thought to be useful or they would not have been used, but the repetition of terms without examination in other cases has often led to confusion, and it might be better, after pointing out that the inquiry is an investigation into responsibi-

[16] *Commonwealth of Pennsylvania* v. *Thomas*, 117 A. 2d 204 at 223 (1955), *per* Musmanno J., dissenting.
[17] *Appeal of the Catholic Cemeteries Association of the Diocese of Pittsburgh*, 109 A. 2d 537 at 545 (1954), *per* Musmanno J., dissenting. *Usque ad inferos?*
[18] *Vega* v. *Borough of Burgettstown*, 147 A. 2d 620 at 625 (1958), *per* Musmanno J., dissenting.
[19] *Day* v. *Day* [1957] P. 202 at 211.

lity, to be content with speaking of the cause of the injury simply and without qualification." [20]

Again, in one case a man was injured while trying to help in preventing a horse from bolting. The Court of Appeal held that he could not recover damages from the owner of the horse, and in so doing, Scrutton and Slesser L.JJ. used phrases such as *volenti non fit injuria, post hoc propter hoc, causa sine qua non, causa causans,* and *novus actus interveniens.*[1] The judgment of the third member of the court, Eve J., was brief: " I agree, and in order not to fall behind my learned brethren in Latinity, I express my conclusion in this way: that the injuries sustained by the respondent were due to a course which he adopted ex mero motu." [2]

A few years later Lord Wright added his howitzer to the rapier of Eve J. In a marine case he said that counsel had " strenuously contended on behalf of the appellants, that the master's action, whether or not negligent, was ' novus actus interveniens,' which broke the nexus or chain of causation, and reduced the unseaworthiness from ' causa causans ' to ' causa sine qua non.' I cannot help deprecating the use of Latin or so-called Latin phrases in this way. They only distract the mind from the true problem which is to apply the principles of English law to the realities of the case. ' Causa causans ' is supposed to mean a cause which causes, while ' causa sine qua non ' means, I suppose, a cause which does not, in the sense material to the particular case, cause, but is merely an incident which precedes in the history or narrative of events, but as a cause is not in at the death, and hence is irrelevant. English law can furnish in its own language expressions which will more fitly state the problem in any case of this type." [3] Lord Wright's reference to " a cause which causes " perhaps invokes Bacon. " It were infinite for the law to judge the causes of causes, and their impulsions one of another; therefore it contenteth it self with the

---

[20] *British Columbia Electric Railway Co. Ltd.* v. *Loach* [1916] 1 A.C. 719 at 727.

[1] *Cutler* v. *United Dairies (London) Ltd.* [1933] 2 K.B. 297 at 303–306.

[2] *Ibid.*, at p. 307 (" from his mere motion," " of his free will ").

[3] *Smith, Hogg & Co. Ltd.* v. *Black Sea and Baltic General Insurance Co. Ltd.* [1940] A.C. 997 at 1003; and see *post*, p. 329.

immediate cause, and judgeth of acts by that, without looking to
any farther degree."[4]   Nevertheless, Lord Wright notwithstanding, "*causa causans*" and "*causa sine qua non*" have
gone marching on in the House of Lords, at all events in tax
cases,[5] though these may perhaps be a law unto themselves.

Latin, indeed, is far from dead in the law, however great
the hopes of some. A hope remains no more than a hope, even
though the speaker has "tried to conceal its nakedness and
exalt its status with a threadbare mantle of Latinity by calling
it a spes."[6]   But let the last word in this field be Australia's.
" An examination of such cases as I have been able to discover
. . . in which the expression *causa causans* was used makes me
think that either it has no certain meaning for legal purposes or,
if it has, that its use in some cases was catachrestic. It can be
a dress for what would otherwise be a naked *petitio principii*."[7]

Other legacies from Rome have been ungratefully received.
Eyre C.J. once referred to the word "quasi" as "senseless
jargon," as applied to certain estates in land. It is "a term used
to denote something which is supposed to be neither the old
estate nor a new estate, but something between both, something
perfectly anomalous and unintelligible, with no legal qualities
attached to it, and wholly inoperative, except for the mischievous
purposes of disappointing a will."[8]   The years have not brought
honour to the word. It is one which may be difficult to avoid,
" but it seldom conduces to clarity of exposition to call X which
is not Y a ' quasi-Y '; this comment applies particularly where
none of the essential elements of Y can be found in X except
in the form of opposites. Easements essentially require passive
sufferance, and to call a duty to expend effort or money a ' quasi-
easement ' involves a confusion of concepts sometimes categorised

[4] Bacon, *Maxims of the Law* (Bacon's *Law Tracts* (2nd ed. 1741) p. 35).
[5] See, *e.g.*, *Hochstrasser* v. *Mayes* [1960] A.C. 376 at 389, 395, *per* Viscount Simonds and Lord Cohen respectively; *Laidler* v. *Perry* [1966] A.C. 16 at 32, *per* Lord Reid.
[6] *Commissioners of Customs and Excise* v. *Gallaher Ltd.* [1971] A.C. 43 at 63, *per* Lord Pearce, dissenting.
[7] *National Insurance Co. of New Zealand Ltd.* v. *Espagne* (1961) 105 C.L.R. 569 at 590, *per* Windeyer J. (" begging the question "). See also 1 Misc. 27; *Pritchard* v. *Arundale* [1972] Ch. 229 at 237.
[8] *Goodtitle* d. *Holford* v. *Otway* (1796) 1 B. & P. 576 at 595, dissenting.

by grammarians as a 'lucus a non lucendo'." [9] "The mere retreat to the qualifying 'quasi' is implicit with confession that all recognized classifications have broken down, and 'quasi' is a smooth cover which we draw over our confusion as we might use a counterpane to conceal a disordered bed." [10]

Of words themselves, there is no end. It has been said that " floccinaucinihilipilification " is the longest word in the English language. The mere recording of this fact may, however, be itself regarded as a floccinaucinihilipilification; and the word's proud title must yield to some technical terms, such as pneumonoultramicroscopicsilicovolcanokoniosis.[11] The triumphant flexibility of English orthography, too, may be illustrated by the consideration that, quite soberly, it may be contended that " ghoti " is one way of spelling " fish ": " gh " as in " enough," " o " as in " women," and " ti " as in " nation." Today, puns enjoy little favour; but a triple is better than a double or single. Thus a father who bought a cattle ranch for his two sons called it " Focus "; for, he said, " That is where the sun's rays meet." A *lapsus calami* [12] which makes the eye hesitate may yet fail to deceive the ear. Thus the catchwords to one report of a case read " Sale of land—Doctrine of unjust in Richmond." [13] Again, a report of the argument of counsel on a point of statutory construction showed him as referring to " the 'just and generous' rule." [14]

In the United States, the saga of the nonesuch word " choate " [15] has been developing over the years. True, the Supreme Court does not seem to have advanced beyond cautious discussions whether certain liens had " become choate " [16]; but

---

[9] *Jones* v. *Price* [1965] 2 Q.B. 618 at 643, *per* Winn L.J. (" A grove is called ' lucus ' because it excludes the light " (*lucus*)).
[10] *Federal Trade Commission* v. *Ruberoid Co.*, 343 U.S. 470 at 487 (1952), *per* Jackson J., dissenting.
[11] See (1962) 48 A.B.A.J. 49.
[12] " Slip of the pen."
[13] (1963) 21 *The Advocate* 179 (unjust enrichment).
[14] *Brampton Jersey Enterprises Ltd.* v. *The Milk Control Board of Ontario* [1956] O.R. 1 at 3 (*ejusdem generis*: " of the same kind ").
[15] See 1 Misc. 33.
[16] *Illinois* v. *Campbell*, 329 U.S. 362 at 371 (1946), *per* Rutledge J.; *United States* v. *City of New Britain*, 347 U.S. 81 at 86 (1954), *per* Minton J.; *Crest Finance Co. Inc.* v. *United States*, 368 U.S. 347 (1961), *per curiam*.

some of the States have been more vigorous. Thus in Michigan there has been a twenty-page discussion of the " choate lien doctrine," [17] and in Oregon there has been judicial talk of a " choate status," and " the requirements of choateness." [18] Even here, however, there has been a note of timidity: for it has been discussed whether one lien is " more choate " than another, instead of making a courageous use of " choate, choater, choatest." Again, would not " choatitude " be more elegant than the squalid " choateness "? And if adjective and noun, why not a verb, so that it can be asserted that " X thereby choated his lien "? The English " cohate," [19] it must be added, mercifully does not seem to have been exported, though transatlantic choate-lovers will doubtless soon turn their attention to the analogies of promoting flation and encouraging the flammable [20]; and once they begin, who knows where they will gin? [1]

In Scotland, Lord Mackay was noted for an individual linguistic style. At times, his touch was light: could delicacy be carried further than to say of the wife, in a matrimonial case in which adultery and condonation were in issue, " She admits that, on one occasion, her husband proposed that they should enjoy conjugal felicity." [2]? Yet more often there was complexity and weight. Thus in a death duty case concerning a gift *inter vivos* and an increase in the value of the shares that had been given, Lord Mackay sought an answer " to the simple question: Is, for the purposes of the tax of death duty, appreciation in the interim between gift date and death date, or depreciation between the same dates, intended by the statutes to be the subject, in addition or in subtraction, from the actual subject which did in hard fact proceed from one to the other at first? I feel that this alleged problem is simple. . . . I find for myself a quite clear answer, good, as I think it ought to be, for, and

[17] See (1956) 54 Mich.L.Rev. 829–848.
[18] *Gower* v. *State Tax Commission of Oregon*, 295 Pac. 2d 162 at 165, 166 (1956), *per* Latourette J.   [19] 1 Misc. 33.
[20] A pretender which, for reasons of safety for the semi-literate, has over the last decade in the U.S.A. now succeeded in ousting the legitimate; and England is infected: see Highly Flammable Liquids and Liquefied Petroleum Gases Regulations 1972.
[1] See Professor A. F. Conard (1956) 42 A.B.A.J. 608.
[2] *Paterson* v. *Paterson*, 1938 S.C. 251 at 259.

Semanticity

in, all the forms which 'gift' may adopt. It is that such
appreciation or depreciation due to the actings, wise or foolish,
of the direct donee, or of the donee, if one may be allowed a
non-committal term, from one holding in trust for another, with
the subject actually and at first transferred, is not intended to
inflate or deflate that by which the deceased's estate (say four
years before) was diminished and someone else's (still donee's
estate) was enhanced. Generally speaking, it is a great
simplification this." [3]

Stretching through the centuries, the law reports form a
linguistic gold-mine; yet the gold is not unmixed with dross.
"Parallelity" is a word of no especial attraction ("There is no
parallelity or necessary mutual dependence between the two
inquiries" [4]); but there is a rotund ring about the ancient but
little-used "frustraneous" ("It was essential to the ends of
justice to allow a new trial, on the pursuer's paying the defender's
frustraneous expenses of the previous trial" [5]). There is little
to be said, however, for "precisionise" ("It is not necessary for
me to precisionise what the second defendant's position was in
relation to the hospital board" [6]); and to its honour one series of
reports substituted "ascertain precisely." [7] "Difficulted," though
inelegant, is legitimate, at any rate north of the Tweed, and has
its uses ("We have been difficulted in this case, by the terms in
which the statement of facts is drawn up" [8]); but the phrase
"*Personal Obsception*" in the catchwords to a report can most
charitably be ascribed to a misprint, for the case concerned
"*personali exceptione.*" [9]

There is a simple charm in the seventeenth-century definition
of "idiot." [10] "Ideot is hee that is a foole naturall from his
birth, and knoweth not how to account or number twentie pence,

---

[3] *Hetherington's Trustees* v. *Lord Advocate*, 1953 S.C. 66 at 77, in a
dissenting judgment.
[4] *Ballantyne* v. *Douglas*, 1953 S.C. 285 at 290, *per* Lord Mackay.
[5] Headnote to *Wallace* v. *Gray* (1836) 14 D. 541.
[6] *Higgins* v. *North West Metropolitan Regional Hospital Board* [1954] 1
All E.R. 414 at 422, *per* Pilcher J.
[7] *Ibid.*, [1954] 1 W.L.R. 411 at 423.
[8] *M'Whir* v. *Oswald* (1833) 11 S. 552 at 554, *per* Lord President Hope and
Lord Gillies.   [9] *Macdougall* v. *Stevenson* (1834) 13 S. 55.
[10] *Les Termes de La Ley* (1629) p. 224.

or cannot name his father, or mother, nor of what age himself is, or such like easy and common matters, so that it appeareth hee hath no manner of understanding of reason or governement of himselfe, what is for his profit or disprofit, &c. But if he have so much knowledg that he can read, or learne to read by instruction and information of others, or can measure an Ell of Cloath, or name the dayes of the weeke, or beget a Child, Sonne, or Daughter, or such like, whereby it may appeare that hee hath some light of reason, then such a one is no Ideot naturally." Later ages, though subscribing fully to the principles of sex-equality indicated by the meticulous reference to son or daughter, perhaps attach less weight to a capacity for paternity as an indication of mental ability: for often the feeble-minded have proved notably fertile and philoprogenitive. Lord Tenterden C.J., indeed, justly observed that " the strict legal definition of an idiot is very narrow." [11]

Looking further back, the claim of law French to be a language of precision (" Really the Law is scarcely expressible properly in English " [12]) still left poverty-stricken corners. As Maitland has taught us, it would not have been impossible for the Year Books to contain a sentence such as " Il counte que le counte ad counte un counte vers luy en le counte ": " He counts that the earl has counted a count against him in the county," [13] or, in a more modern idiom, " He pleads that the earl has pleaded a case against him in the county court." Perhaps one of the derivations from " counte " is " cuntey cuntey," which is " a kind of Trial, as appears by Bract. in these Words: The Matter in this Case shall be ended by *Cuntey Cuntey*, as between Co-heirs, lib. 4, Tr. 3, cap. 18. And again in the same Place; In a writ of Right the Business shall be determined by *Cuntey Cuntey*. And thirdly, lib. 4, Tr. 4, cap. 2. The Cause shall be tried by Writ of Right, neither by Battel, nor by the great Assize, but by *Cuntey Cuntey* only; which seems to be as much as by an ordinary Jury." [14]

[11] *Ball* v. *Mannin* (1829) Sm. & Bat. 454 at 460.
[12] R. North, *A Discourse on the Study of the Laws* (1824) p. 13.
[13] S.S. vol. 17 (1903) p. lxxxiv.
[14] *Termes de la Ley* (1721 ed.) p. 205.

Some children of the past live unsettled lives today. He who seeks rectification of a contract must, in the words of Lord Thurlow L.C., adduce "strong irrefragable evidence." [15] Doubtless the second adjective was in more general use two centuries ago than it is today (*e.g.*, Bentham's reference to Blackstone's "irrefragable plea for obstinacy" [16]). In recent years, however, its pronunciation has caused some difficulty. In 1955 leading counsel pronounced it irrefrăggable, but Harman J. asserted that it was irrefrăyggable; and thus it was for the rest of the case.[17]   However, on appeal (on another point) one of the juniors invoked the *Oxford English Dictionary*, and his leader persuaded a reluctant and suspicious Court of Appeal to shift the accent from the third syllable to the second, and pronounce the word "irrefrăggăbl." [18]

In one case under the Road Traffic Act, 1930, dealing with driving a car while under the influence of "drink or a drug," Lord Goddard C.J. said that he did not think it necessary to deal with an ingenious point as to "whether a non-alcoholic beverage is drink within the meaning of the Act. If that were so, I should be inclined to apply the dictum of Martin B.[19] where the bailiff was sworn to keep the jury without meat or drink, or any light but candlelight, and a juryman asked if he might have a glass of water. Martin B. said: 'Well, it is certainly not meat and I should not call it drink. He can have it.' I think 'drink' means alcoholic drink." [20]   After all, there cannot be many who drive under the influence of water.

There are, however, other approaches. A point that a

---

15 *Countess of Shelburne* v. *Earl of Inchiquin* (1784) 1 Bro.C.C. 338 at 341; and see *Simpson* v. *Lord Howden* (1837) 3 My. & Cr. 97 at 103, *per* Lord Cottenham L.C.   Contrast *Joscelyne* v. *Nissen* [1970] 2 Q.B. 86 at 98.

16 Bentham, *A Comment on the Commentaries* (ed. C. W. Everett, 1928) p. 194; see also a Cabinet Memorandum by Lord Brougham L.C. quoted in 1 *Atlay* 325.

17 *North Thames Gas Board* v. *Sunbury U.D.C.*, unrep., Ch.D., March 1, 1955.

18 *Ibid.*, unrep., C.A., June 7, 1955, *cor.* Evershed M.R. and Jenkins and Parker L.JJ., *ex rel.* the then Reader in Equity in the Inns of Court.

19 *Quaere* whether it was not Maule J.: see R. Walton, *Random Recollections of the Midland Circuit, Second Series* (1873) p. 74; E. Bowen-Rowlands, *Seventy-Two Years at the Bar* (1924) p. 256; *Manson* 196.

20 *Armstrong* v. *Clark* [1957] 2 Q.B. 391 at 394.

Divisional Court had kept open in 1915 [1] was resolved the next year, in a decision bearing a headnote of splendid brevity: " Ice-cream is not ' meat ' within s. 3 of the Sunday Observance Act, 1677." [2] Darling J. observed that many judges had disliked this type of legislation, as he did, and had " tried to get out of the statute by holding or suggesting that all kinds of things might be ' meat ' although they were not. That is not an effective way of getting rid of the statute. In my opinion the best way to attain that object is to construe it strictly, in the way the Puritans who procured it would have construed it; if that is done it will very soon be repealed." [3] This seems to be an unconscious echo of an earlier and more general statement. " Perhaps the most efficacious mode of procuring good laws, certainly the only one allowable to a court of justice, is to act fully up to the spirit and language of bad ones, and to let their inconvenience be fully felt, by giving them their full effect." [4] Still, it must be remembered that " words, like men, grow an individuality; their character changes with years and with use." [5]

In discussing the meaning of " contributory " under the Companies Act, 1948, Roxburgh J. once referred to decisions which showed that shareholders who in fact could not be called upon to make contributions because their shares were fully paid up could nevertheless be " contributories." After citing a passage from a judgment of Turner L.J. referring to " every person liable under this Act to contribute," [6] Roxburgh J. said " By this I understand the Lord Justice to mean liable, not in the events which have happened, but in the events which might happen, in the same way in which a certain college porch is named ' Jumbo ' because the college would have to keep an elephant there if it had one." [7] The college is King's College, Cambridge. [8]

Few readers of the newspapers can be unaware of the curious convention whereby for many years past the word " person "

---

[1] In *Amorette* v. *James* [1915] 1 K.B. 124.
[2] *Slater* v. *Evans* [1916] 2 K.B. 403. [3] *Ibid.*, at p. 405.
[4] *Pocock* v. *Pickering* (1852) 18 Q.B. 789 at 798, *per* Coleridge J.
[5] *Adler* v. *Deegan*, 167 N.E. 705 at 706 (1929), *per* Crane J.
[6] *Re National Savings Bank Association* (1866) 1 Ch.App. 547 at 551.
[7] *Re Phoenix Oil and Transport Co. Ltd.* [1958] Ch. 560 at 564.
[8] (1958) 74 L.Q.R. 14.

was used anatomically in prosecutions for indecency. Yet he who consulted Stroud's *Judicial Dictionary*,[9] or Burrows' *Words and Phrases Judicially Defined*,[10] or Jowitt's *Dictionary of English Law* [11] would find under "person" nothing save a chaste silence on the subject. Nevertheless, the point has been taken, and the word sufficiently defined. When in 1853 an indictment for a common law misdemeanour charged that the accused "did expose . . . the body and person " of the accused in an omnibus, the defence objected that the offence charged was not stated with sufficient certainty. During the argument, Maule J. asked "What do you mean in law by exposing his *person?* The indictment should have been for exposing his *private parts*." [12] However, he is also reported as in effect answering his own question by saying "' The person,' in Old Bailey language, means ' private parts ' "; and Lord Campbell C.J. added "The word is modern slang." [13] This condemnation was doubtless uttered in forgetfulness of Parliament's choice of language some thirty years earlier, imposing penalties in certain circumstances upon a man for "exposing his person." [14] Nor did Lord Campbell's views on the point prevent either him [15] or Talfourd J.[16] from using the word in the criticised sense during the hearing. Not until 1972 did the courts firmly decide that "person" means "penis," no more and no less.[17] Perhaps legislative drafting has improved over the years; for the Food Hygiene Regulations, 1955, innocently provide that a person engaged in the handling of food must "keep any open cut or abrasion on any exposed part of his person covered with a suitable waterproof dressing." [18]

[9] (3rd ed. 1953) vol. 3, pp. 2167–2174.
[10] (1944) vol. 4, pp. 224–229; (2nd ed. 1969) vol. 4, pp. 111–114.
[11] (1959) pp. 1334, 1335.
[12] *R.* v. *Holmes* (1853) 22 L.J.M.C. 122 at 123.
[13] *Ibid.*, as reported 1 W.R. 416; see also S.C. as reported 1 C.L.R. 487 at 488.
[14] Vagrancy Act, 1824, s. 4, a provision which lives on today: see, *e.g.*, *Ford* v. *Falcone* [1971] 1 W.L.R. 809.
[15] *R.* v. *Holmes*, *supra*, as reported Dears. 207 at 208; 3 C. & K. 360 at 362.
[16] *Ibid.*, as reported 17 J.P. 390 at 391. The reports of the case at 21 L.T.O.S. 160, 17 Jur. 562 and 6 Cox C.C. 216 contribute nothing of value on this point.
[17] *Evans* v. *Ewels* [1972] 1 W.L.R. 671. Yet *quaere* as to the rest of the genital area; " private parts " still has something to commend it.
[18] S.I. 1955 No. 1906, r. 9 (c).

Even when there is no difficulty about the meaning of the
words used, all in public life know that by a process of judicious
selection, coupled with a little *suppressio veri*, the most innocent
remark can be given a sinister twist. Thus there is the old story
of the bishop, visiting New York for the first time, who on
arrival was asked by a reporter " Are you going to see a night
club? " His innocent reply " What, are there any night clubs
here? " was greeted next day by the headlines " Bishop's first
question: Are there any night clubs here? " And a purported
retraction may double an insult, as where a man says that an
acquaintance " has manners not fit for a pig," and then retracts
the statement by saying that " his manners are fit for a pig." [19]
This technique was well known in Scotland early in the nineteenth century. A junior member of the Scottish Bar who had
lost a case was heard by the Bench to exclaim that he was surprised at the decision; and for this he was ordered to attend
at the bar next morning. He consulted John Clerk (later Lord
Eldin), who agreed to appear and apologise for him. He did
so, saying " He is extremely penitent, and you will kindly ascribe
his unintentional insult to his ignorance. You will see at once
that it did not originate in that: he said he was surprised at the
decision of your lordships. Now, if he had not been very
ignorant of what takes place in this Court every day; had he
known your Lordships but half so long as I have done, he would
not be surprised at anything you did." [20]

Towards the end of the eighteenth century in Ireland, there
was no love lost between Lord Fitzgibbon L.C. and Curran,
later to be M.R. During argument before him, the Chancellor
said to Curran, " To me the words you seek to differentiate,
' also ' and ' likewise,' seem clearly synonymous." The answer
was prompt and crushing. " No fanciful distinction, my Lord.
My Lord, the great Lord Lifford for many years presided over
this court. You *also* preside, but not *likewise*." [1] A similar
tale runs in Scotland, as between John Clerk (later Lord Eldin)

[19] Winfield, *Tort* (6th ed. 1954) p. 361.
[20] G. A. Morton and D. M. Mallock, *Law and Laughter* (1913) p. 169; and see
Croke James, *Curiosities of Law and Lawyers* (1896) p. 177.
[1] Leslie Hale, *John Philpot Curran* (1958) p. 72.

Semanticity

and the second Lord Meadowbank as compared with his father [2]; England seems to have no counterpart.

In multilingual countries, the courts sometimes face problems unknown in England. Thus in one case in Natal, " the applicant's affidavits were in English and his counsel addressed the Court in English. The first respondent's affidavit was in Afrikaans and counsel for the respondents addressed the Court in Afrikaans. In which language then should the Court give judgment? One's experience is that the winner is usually content to know merely that he has won. But the loser likes to know the reasons why he has lost. I proceed therefore to give judgment in the language of the losers." [3]

This problem is one which does not seem likely to arise in England, where the proceedings are in English, and a litigant in person has no right to make a speech in his native tongue and have it translated to the court by an interpreter [4]; this, of course, is quite distinct from giving evidence in some foreign tongue and having it translated by a sworn interpreter. In Wales and Monmouthshire, however, the Welsh Courts Act, 1942, at first sight suggested that the problem might arise; for that Act authorised the use of Welsh in any court in Wales or Monmouthshire by " any party or witness who considers that he would otherwise be at a disadvantage by reason of his natural language of communication being Welsh." [5]   However, if the question had arisen the solution might have been different; for the Act required the translation into English of anything spoken or written in Welsh unless this was unnecessary for the due administration of justice,[6] but it made no corresponding provision for the translation of English into Welsh.[7] A monoglot Welshman whose English opponent understood no Welsh might well have contended that even if he was the victor judgment ought to be given in Welsh, for only thus could both understand it. For

---

[2] Henry Cockburn, *Memorials of His Time* (ed. 1909) p. 142; Croke James, *Curiosities of Law and Lawyers* (1896) p. 58; G. A. Morton and D. M. Mallock, *Law and Laughter* (1913) p. 169.
[3] *Martin* v. *Kiesbeampte, Newcastle Afdeling, en 'n Ander*, 1958 (2) S.A. 649 at 650, *per* Holmes J. (the rest of the judgment was in Afrikaans).
[4] See *Re Trepca Mines Ltd.* [1960] 1 W.L.R. 24 (Serbo-Croat and French rejected).
[5] s. 1.
[6] s. 3 (2).
[7] But see the delphic s. 3 (1).

English judges, this prospect can hardly have added to the
attractions of going circuit in Wales, though they might have
escaped by pointing out that the Act gave authority to use Welsh
only to " any party or witness." However, the Welsh Language
Act 1967 has now swept away most of the doubts and difficulties
by providing that " in any legal proceeding in Wales or Monmouthshire the Welsh language may be spoken by any party,
witness or other person who desires to use it " [8]; and presumably
" other person " embraces a judge, though he may be able to
argue that for this purpose he is a bull.[9] There is also now a
wide authority for " any necessary provision for interpretation." [10]

Oratio obliqua usually adds its own peculiar difficulties,
though of course " To generalize is to omit." [11] An immigration
officer's visit to the bridge of a ship while the captain was
engaged in an intricate stage of navigation in the Royal Dock
at Grimsby ended in proceedings in court for assault, duly
reported in *The Times*. In his judgment Lord Goddard C.J.
said that " When the navigation was tricky the immigration
officer came on to the bridge and interrupted the Captain. The
Captain was a bit choleric and told him to get off. The immigration officer added fuel to the fire by saying that he would go
if he were asked properly. Well! His (his Lordship's) good-
ness gracious: he did not wonder that the Captain lost his
temper. He was going to throw him down the stairs when—he
(his Lordship) did not know whether he should say fortunately
or unfortunately—the Captain's glasses came off." [12] Perhaps
the most appropriate comment comes from Pennsylvania. " Odd
and peculiar as at times seem the ways of the world, irrationaliza-
tion has not so seized the human race that rivulets of anger
control glaciers of thought and that flea bites destroy intellect." [13]

[8] s. 1 (1).
[9] Consider *Ex p. Hill* (1827) 3 C. & P. 225 (a statutory provision relating to
  any " ox, cow, heifer, steer, sheep, or other cattle " does not include a
  bull, as being a beast of superior degree).
[10] Welsh Language Act 1967, s. 1 (1).
[11] *Donnell* v. *Herring-Hall-Marvin Safe Co.*, 208 U.S. 267 at 273 (1908),
  per Holmes J.
[12] *Haddleton* v. *Holwerda* [1956] *The Times* Apr. 19.
[13] *Obici* v. *Third National Bank & Trust Co. of Scranton*, 112 A. 2d 94 at 98
  (1955), *per* Musmanno J., dissenting.

Poisson d'Avril

THE statute book is not the most praised of all our institutions. " As a collection our statute book might be summed up as beyond the average citizen's pocket to purchase, beyond his book-shelves to accommodate, beyond his leisure to study and beyond his intellect to comprehend." [1] The courts have at times been both sweeping and forthright. When considering the terms of a local Act, Kindersley V.-C. once said " I have carefully gone through this Act of Parliament, and to say that it might have been made more clear and precise than it is, or even to say that there is at least one passage in it which is absolute nonsense, is only to say of this Act what I am afraid may be predicated [2] of perhaps nine out of ten Acts of Parliament which come before Courts of Justice for their consideration." [3]

The causes of disaster are many and varied. Sometimes it has been the course of the Parliamentary process. Thus the Rating and Valuation Act, 1928, with its modest five sections and two schedules, occupies a mere six pages of the statute book; but initially, as a Bill, it contained a clause which, passed by the House of Commons, disappeared in the House of Lords in a cloud of smoke. The clause authorised the Minister of Health to refer to the High Court any " substantial question of law " relating to the valuation for rating purposes of hereditaments or any class of hereditaments if in the absence of an authoritative determination a " want of uniformity or inequality in valuation " might result; and the High Court was to be obliged to give its opinion on the question. [4] The peers, and especially the law lords, set about this provision with a fine vigour. The basic objection was that the clause gave the Minister the power to require the courts to express opinions on abstract points; but

---

[1] Sir Cecil Carr, *Delegated Legislation* (1921) p. 7.
[2] " Predicted " in the report.
[3] *Trevillian* v. *Mayor etc. of Exeter* (1854) 5 De G.M. & G. 828 at 831.
[4] The clause is conveniently set out in Lord Hewart, *The New Despotism* (1929) p. 119, and by C. K. Allen at (1931) 47 L.Q.R. 44.

there was other ammunition. Viscount Haldane, Lord Merrivale, Lord Hanworth, Lord Atkin and Lord Carson were all in the hunt[5]; and Lord Hewart C.J. described the clause as being "without exception the worst clause of its kind which has ever appeared. I say that having in mind Section 29 of the Local Government Act of 1888, and Section 70 of the Local Government Act of 1894."[6] On the third reading Lord Hailsham L.C. not surprisingly bowed to the storm and withdrew the clause[7]; the judges had triumphed. Yet that was not the end; the triumph was not complete. Apparently unnoticed by Lord Hewart and others, words were left standing in the long title to the Act which proclaimed that it was an Act "to provide for obtaining decisions on points of law with a view to securing uniformity in valuation." The Act is a rare example of a statutory promise devoid of any fulfilment even in law.

Rules now long buried have also made their contributions. In January 1777 an annuity was granted for value. Nearly four months later the Royal Assent was given to an Act which made void any annuity granted "after the passing of this Act" unless it was registered within twenty days of the grant.[8] Naturally enough, the annuity did not comply with the requirements of this Act. Nevertheless, it was held that as the Act took effect from the commencement of the Parliamentary session in which it was passed, the annuity was void for want of registration.[9] This decision was reached in obedience to earlier decisions of the House of Lords to the effect that a statute increasing the rate of import duties made importers liable for the higher rate of tax on all goods imported since the session began, even though full duty at the rates existing at the time of import had been paid.[10] It is pleasant to relate that a year after the annuity case had been decided an Act was passed which recited that the rule was " liable

[5] See (1928) Hansard (5th ser.) H.L., vol. 70, cols. 609–642, 756–780, 794–806, 914–928. Passages which make good reading are quoted in Hewart, *supra*, at pp. 120–140, and Allen, *supra*, at pp. 44–47.
[6] Hansard, *supra*, col. 920.
[7] Hansard, *supra*, cols. 915–918.
[8] 17 Geo. 3, c. 26, 1777, s. 1.
[9] *Latless* v. *Holmes* (1792) 4 T.R. 660.
[10] *Panter* v. *Att.-Gen.* (1772) 6 Bro.P.C. 486; *Vickars* v. *Att.-Gen. of Ireland* (1779) 6 Bro.P.C. 491.

to produce great and manifest injustice," and established in its place the modern rule that unless otherwise provided every Act should commence on the day of the Royal Assent, as endorsed on the Act by the Clerk of the Parliaments.[11] No longer could the old rule make a man a criminal for an act which, though innocent when done on the first day of a Parliamentary session, had become criminal under a statute passed on the last day of that session.

Excessive zeal, too, may be to blame. Subject to certain exceptions, the Royal Marriages Act, 1772, prohibits the marriage of descendants of George II without the consent of the Sovereign. In 1793, the Duke of Sussex married Lady Augusta Murray in Rome and again in London, but without the requisite consent. In 1794 the Dean of the Arches declared the marriage void [12]; and after the Duke's death the Committee for Privileges of the House of Lords reached the same conclusion.[13] However, quite apart from these proceedings it seems that George III referred the matter to the Privy Council when he discovered the facts. Lord Thurlow L.C. angrily asked the future Lord Eldon, then Solicitor-General, why " all the parties concerned in this abominable Marriage " had not been prosecuted; for by s. 3 all who solemnise, assist or are present at such a marriage are guilty of *praemunire*.[14] The Solicitor-General replied that it was a difficult business to prosecute, for as all concerned were guilty of felony, and none could prove a marriage except persons present at it, there could be no prosecution; for none present could be compelled to be a witness. As Thurlow had been partly responsible for drafting the Act, it is not surprising that this answer seems to have silenced him.[15] The Act, indeed, had a somewhat unusual genesis; for during the debate on the Bill in the House of Lords, the judges were summoned to attend. They were asked, and through Smythe B. answered, a number of questions on the existing law; and in due course the House

---

[11] Acts of Parliament (Commencement) Act, 1793.
[12] *Heseltine* v. *Lady Augusta Murray* (1794) 2 Add. 400n.
[13] *The Sussex Peerage Case* (1844) 11 Cl. & F. 85.
[14] Under the Statute of Praemunire, 1392.
[15] *Lord Eldon's Anecdote Book* (1960) pp. 39, 40.

directed two of the judges to carry down the Bill to the House
of Commons for the concurrence of that House in the Bill.[16]

Fact and fiction sometimes join hands. There are many
stories of nonsensical and contradictory provisions in Acts of
Parliament; but they nearly all share a coy failure to identify any
statute that in fact exhibits the frailties alleged. Thus it is said
that " in the Irish Bank Bill passed in June, 1808, there was a
clause providing ' That the profits shall be equally divided, and
that the residue should go to the Governor.' "[17] There was
indeed a statute which extended the powers of the Bank of
Ireland and received the Royal Assent on June 25, 1808[18]; but,
alas, it is innocent of any provision to the effect suggested.

Again, there is a tradition of a Bill in the time of George III
which provided for a pecuniary penalty for an offence, with one
half to go to His Majesty and one half to the informer. The
Bill was altered in Committee; and when it received the Royal
Assent the destination of the penalty was unchanged, but the
penalty itself had become whipping and imprisonment.[19]
Other versions state the substituted penalty as being fourteen
years' transportation,[20] or put the poor of the parish in place of
His Majesty.[1]

Possibly the statute 52 Geo. 3, c. 3, 1812, is the foundation of
this legend. This is an excise Act which by s. 24 provides that
an offender shall " forfeit the sum of fifty pounds, and in default
of payment shall suffer three months imprisonment "; and s. 33,
after providing for the mode of recovering " all fines, penalties
and forfeitures," enacts that " one moiety of every such fine,
penalty or forfeiture shall be to His Majesty, his Heirs and
Successors, and the other moiety to him or them who shall
inform, discover or sue for the same."

Other candidates revert to Ireland. Thus an Irish Bill to

---

[16] See (1772) 33 Lds.Jnl. 263, 266, 270, 279.
[17] J. Willock, *Legal Facetiae* (1887) p. 88.
[18] 48 Geo. 3, c. 103, 1808.
[19] J. Larwood, *Humour of the Law* (1903) p. 132; F. F. Heard, *Oddities of the Law* (1921) p. 162.
[20] *Law and Lawyers* (1840) vol. 2, p. 56 (stating that Lord Stanhope mentioned the Act in a speech in the House of Lords in 1816).
[1] H. Cohen, *Spirit of Our Laws* (3rd ed. 1932) p. 19, suggesting that the Act was passed in 1812.

limit the privilege of franking letters is said to have contained a clause providing that any Member of Parliament who from illness or any other cause was unable to write might authorise another by writing under his hand to frank letters for him.[2] Again, " In a Bill for pulling down the Old Newgate in Dublin, and rebuilding it on the same spot, ' it was enacted that the prisoners should remain in the old jail till the new one was completed.' " [3] This might readily be dismissed as gross exaggeration or pure fiction, were it not for Lord Eldon. True, he lifts the discredit across the Irish Sea, but otherwise it is substantially the same story; and none would take lightly any assertion from such a source. He says that " Many Absurdities have been noticed in Irish Acts of Parliament. Perhaps none greater than what, I think, may be found in an English Act of Parliament. There was an Act for rebuilding Chelmsford Gaol: by one Enactment the New Gaol was to be built by the Materials of the Old Gaol: by another the Prisoners were to be kept in the Old Gaol till the New Gaol was finished." [4]

Here again, materials for identifying the Act are slender. However, at Chelmsford a " new and elegant County Gaol, erected upon a very liberal plan, at the expence of the County, was finished and inhabited in the year 1777." [5] This, no doubt, was the prison which the statute 10 Geo. 3, c. 28, 1770, authorised the justices of the County of Essex to build; and there seems little doubt that this is the statute that Lord Eldon had in mind. Section 5 seems to be most in point. This, *inter alia,* enacted that the sheriff of the county should have the power, " when the said gaol is made fit for the reception and safe keeping of prisoners, to remove thither all such prisoners as shall then be in his custody; which removal shall not be deemed or taken to be an escape; and that after such removal, it shall and may be lawful

---

[2] F. F. Heard, *Oddities of the Law* (1921) p. 102, giving " May, 1874 " as the date when the Bill was sent for the Royal Assent. Perhaps May, 1784, was meant; but there seems to have been no such Act at that date.

[3] J. Willock, *Legal Facetiae* (1887) p. 78; F. F. Heard, *Oddities of the Law* (1921) p. 110.

[4] *Lord Eldon's Anecdote Book* (1960) p. 76; and see Rob. 229, referring to this as a " celebrated instance," and ascribing the result to a section being added " at the last moment."

[5] J. Neild, *State of the Prisons in England, Scotland & Wales* (1812) p. 118.

to and for the said justices at their said general quarter-sessions, to cause the present gaol, situate at or near Chelmsford aforesaid, to be pulled down or taken down, and the materials thereof, or any part thereof, either to use or cause to be used in or about the building or finishing such new gaol, or the same to sell or cause to be sold; and the money arising thereby, to apply towards the expence and charge of building and finishing such new gaol."

It seems improbable that Lord Eldon can have had another statute in mind; and, unless he did, it must be confessed that his account is, unusually for him, a little highly coloured. The absurdity is not that the prisoners *must* be kept in the old gaol until the new is finished, and that the new *must* be built from the materials of the old; at most it is that the power to remove prisoners from the old to the new is not to arise until the new is "made fit," and that thereafter the old *may* be demolished and the materials *may* be used for "building or finishing" the new. The new prison might well be "fit" for the custody of prisoners even before it was complete; and the materials of the old prison could then be used for "finishing" the new. In the end, Lord Eldon's "absurdity" seems to stand or fall by the word "building"; if the new gaol is fit to receive prisoners, it seems a little late then to begin using the materials of the old for the "building" of the new.

Lord Eldon's account of another statutory blunder is as follows. "When the Dog Act passed, which was brought into the House by Sir Thomas Clavering, and by the Enactments of which the person, convicted of Stealing a Dog before a Justice of Peace, was to be forthwith whipped, but, nevertheless, was to have the benefit of an Appeal to the Quarter Sessions, which should be held next after he had been whipped, the Judge who was upon the Northern Circuit—I think Baron Perrett [6] was the Judge, in giving his Charge to the Grand Jury at Durham stated that it was his Habit to give the Grand Jury the most useful Information he could respecting the Cases in the Calendar and to explain the several Acts, which had passed in the preceeding Sessions of Parliament, relative to Offences. He then went

[6] Perrot B. seems to be the only possible candidate.

thro' several with Observations, and concluded by adverting to the Dog Act. This, he said, he and his chosen Brethren, the Judges, had endeavoured to understand, but they were unable to comprehend it—a Thing he should have much lamented, if he did not perceive that the Gentleman, who brought the Bill into Parliament, was their Foreman, and who could of course, inform them what was the Value of an Appeal against being whipped, after the Whipping had been inflicted." [7]

The answer of Sir Thomas might with some justice have been " Read the Act." It seems clear enough that the Act was 10 Geo. 3, c. 18, 1770, for it dealt with dog stealing and was of about the right date. [8] The most relevant provisions appear to be as follows. By s. 1, the penalty for a second or subsequent offence was a sum of not less than £30 nor more than £50, half to go to the informer and half to the poor of the parish. If this penalty was not paid, the offender was to be sent to prison for not less than twelve nor more than eighteen months, and the justices were to " order the said Offender to be publickly whipped, within Three Days after such Commitment . . . between the hours of Twelve and One of the Clock." Section 4 gave to any person who thought himself " aggrieved by any Thing done in pursuance of this Act " a right of appeal to " the next General Quarter-session of the Peace to be held for the County or Place wherein the Cause of Complaint shall arise, and within Four Days after the Cause of such Complaint shall have arisen." The vital words in Lord Eldon's account (" which should be held next after he had been whipped ") find no support in the statute book, save, perhaps, for a person who found cause for complaint not in an order that he should be whipped but only in the actual whipping.

The attitude of the courts sometimes defies analysis. Ridley J. once refused costs to a defendant who had successfully pleaded the Gaming Acts; but the Court of Appeal held this to be wrong. " To say that the Acts should not be pleaded looks like a reflection on the Legislature." [9] Yet the courts have not uniformly

---

[7] *Lord Eldon's Anecdote Book* (1960) p. 76.
[8] Perrot B. was on the Bench from 1763 to 1775.
[9] *Granville & Co.* v. *Firth* (1903) 19 T.L.R. 213, *per* Lord Halsbury L.C.

abstained from reflecting on the legislature. Thus during the course of an argument on the statute 7 & 8 Vict. c. 76, 1844, s. 4, which required leases to be made by deed, Maule J. said "The 7 & 8 Vict. c. 76,[10] was a notorious statutory blunder. It was incongruous and impossible of operation; and its absurdities were so great that the framers themselves had no very distinct notion of its meaning." [11] Again, sections 30 and 31 of the Wills Act, 1837, appear to represent an accidental statutory duplication, now well over a century old. "The 31st section is probably another drafting of the 30th. . . . I believe the real history of the two sections is, that they are two drafts dealing with the same subject, though both remain in the Act of Parliament." [12] In 1916, too, the Secretary of State for War told the House of Commons that " owing to a misprint, the word ' prisoner ' in the Criminal Lunatics Act, 1884, became ' person '—a mistake which was copied into the Irish Lunacy Act, 1901,[13] the consequences being that soldiers committed as dangerous lunatics to asylums in Ireland, whether they are prisoners or not, become chargeable to the Prison Vote instead of to the rates." [14]

Another infelicity of the statute book is an Act of 1873 which began with the words "Whereas a person who is accessory before or after the fact, or counsels, procures, commands, aids, or abets the commission of any indictable offence, is by English law liable to be tried and punished as if he were the principal offender. . . ." [15] This, as any law student would have pointed out, was quite untrue in regard to accessories after the fact, for whom (with certain exceptions) the maximum penalty was two years' imprisonment.[16] Yet for twenty years [17] Parliament was content to leave this patent blemish undisturbed on the statute book. An Act of 1898 which is still in force achieves distinction

---

[10] The Transfer of Property Act, 1844.
[11] *Stratton* v. *Pettit* (1855) 16 C.B. 420 at 432.
[12] *Freme* v. *Clement* (1881) 18 Ch.D. 499 at 514, *per* Jessel M.R.
[13] Lunacy (Ireland) Act, 1901.
[14] Hansard (5th ser.) H.C., vol. 84, col. 1001. No specific sections are mentioned: but see ss. 8, 9, 10, 16 of the Act of 1884, and ss. 3, 6 of the Act of 1901.
[15] Extradition Act, 1873, s. 3.
[16] See Accessories and Abettors Act, 1861, s. 4.
[17] The Statute Law Revision (No. 2) Act, 1893, deleted the offending words.

in another way: it provides that the spouse of a person charged with certain offences " may be called as a witness either for the prosecution or defence and without the consent of the person charged." [18] It is perhaps possible to doubt the need for providing for a witness to be called for the defence without the consent of the person charged.

In one case,[19] the court was called upon to construe the statutory phrase " unless judgment shall have been signed, or execution issued." [20] " We have here," said Lord Denman C.J., " words which, as they stand, are useless; a circumstance, perhaps, not altogether unprecedented. But, to give an effectual meaning, we must alter, not only ' or ' into ' and,' but ' issued ' into ' levied.' It is extremely probable that this would express what the Legislature meant. But we cannot supply it." [1] It would be, said Williams J., " so violent a change that it amounts to framing a new section, instead of interpreting what we find. We are not authorized to do this. It is much safer to say that the words have really no meaning." [2] Another Act of the same year,[3] dealing with receiving stolen securities, was held to be so inaccurately penned that no conviction under it ought to take place.[4]

" As if " clauses, too, have their perils.[5] A Natal statute gave natural-born subjects of the United Kingdom all rights to dispose by will of both real and personal property " as if such natural-born subject resided in England." [6] Even if " resided " meant " were domiciled," the phrase would not have enabled such testators to escape the general rule that a devise of land must comply with the local law; for this rule applied even to those domiciled abroad. Yet the plain intention of the legislature, as appearing elsewhere in the statute, was to make such compliance unnecessary. Ultimately, a puzzled Judicial Committee of the

---

[18] Criminal Evidence Act, 1898, s. 4 (1).
[19] *Green* v. *Wood* (1845) 7 Q.B. 178.
[20] 3 Geo. 4, c. 39, 1822, s. 2.
[1] *Green* v. *Wood, supra,* at p. 185.
[2] *Ibid.,* at p. 186.
[3] 3 Geo. 4, c. 24, 1822.
[4] *R.* v. *King* (1826) 2 C. & P. 412.
[5] See *Re Lawrence's Will Trusts* [1972] Ch. 418 at 434.
[6] Natal Ordinance No. 1, 1856, s. 1.

Privy Council gave effect to the general sense of the statute and rejected the troublesome nine words.[7]

Lord Goddard C.J. once observed " It is no part of my functions, and indeed it would be contrary to good practice, to criticize an Act of Parliament, but I may perhaps be allowed to say—and I think in this respect I speak for my Brethren—that I have found this an extraordinarily difficult Act[8] to construe. It is perhaps unfortunate that such an obscure Act should have been passed in relation to people like costermongers and small traders who trade in the street and who, to discover their rights, and to find out whether they are committing an offence, should have to read provisions of this Act which are quite impossible for any of them to understand. I have spent some hours in trying to understand the Act, and I think that I have some glimmering about it, but I am still far from satisfied that I do understand it; but, having regard to the fact that the Long Vacation is immediately approaching, and as this involves the livelihood of these three street traders, it is desirable that we should give a decision at once and not delay until October."[9] Singleton J. added his agreement with " what the Lord Chief Justice has said as to the confused nature of the law on this subject as expressed in part IV of the London County Council (General Powers) Act, 1947. While listening to the argument in this case I thought of a ditty of many years ago:

> " I thought when I learned my letters
> That all my troubles were done,
> But I find I am sadly mistaken,
> They have only just begun."[10]

Ambiguities raise different problems. It is well settled that where the words of a statute are ambiguous, in the sense that they are fairly and equally open to divers meanings, subsequent legislation on the same subject may be looked at in order to resolve the ambiguity. If, then, judges differ in the interpreta-

[7] *Salmon* v. *Duncombe* (1886) 11 App.Cas. 627.
[8] London County Council (General Powers) Act, 1947.
[9] *Southwark Borough Council* v. *Nightingale* (1948) 64 T.L.R. 563 at 565.
[10] *Ibid.*

tion to be put on the words in the earlier Act, does not this *per se* show that those words are ambiguous? The answer is No. " Each one of us has the task of deciding what the relevant words mean. In coming to that decision he will necessarily give great weight to the opinion of others, but if at the end of the day he forms his own clear judgment and does not think that the words are ' fairly and equally open to divers meanings ' he is not entitled to say that there is an ambiguity. For him at least there is no ambiguity." [11] The result is that if some judges think that the words clearly mean X and others that they clearly mean Y, there is no ambiguity but instead certainty in the sense which has the majority; whereas if the judges unanimously hold that the words may well mean X or may well mean Y, but on the whole probably mean X, there is ambiguity despite the unanimity. The quality of certainty must not be confused with the particular meaning of words; judges may agree that the first is present even though they differ sharply on the second. The House of Lords may thus be unanimous in holding that an expression is unambiguous but divided in deciding what that expression means. [12]

Sometimes exceptions will be implied. " When laws or statutes are made, yet there are certain things which are exempted and excepted out of the provision of the same by the law of reason, although they are not expressly excepted. As the breaking of prison is felony in the prisoner himself by the Statute de Frangentibus Prisonam [13] : yet if the prison be on fire, and they who are in break the prison to save their lives, this shall be excused by the law of reason, and yet the words of the statute are against it." [14] The cautious Coke restricts this proposition by qualifying the words " on fire " by " unlesse it be by the privity of the prisoner." [15]

No doubt this is what Field J. had in mind three centuries later in a case in which a sheriff who, in obedience to a bench

---

[11] *Kirkness* v. *John Hudson & Co. Ltd*. [1955] A.C. 696 at 712, *per* Viscount Simonds.
[12] See, *e.g.*, *Ellerman Lines Ltd*. v. *Murray* [1925] A.C. 126.
[13] 1 Ed. 2, St. 2, 1307.
[14] *Reniger* v. *Fogossa* (1550) 1 Plowd. 1 at 13, *per* Robert Brook, *arguendo*.
[15] See 2 Co.Inst. 590.

warrant, had arrested a carrier of the U.S. mails on a charge of murder was himself charged with knowingly and wilfully obstructing the passage of the mails. " The common sense of man approves the judgment mentioned by Puffendorf,[16] that the Bolognian law which enacted, ' that whoever drew blood in the streets should be punished with the utmost severity,' did not extend to the surgeon who opened the vein of a person that fell down in the street in a fit. The same common sense accepts the ruling, cited by Plowden, that the statute of 1st Edward II, which enacts that a prisoner who breaks prison shall be guilty of felony, does not extend to a prisoner who breaks out when the prison is on fire—' for he is not to be hanged because he would not stay to be burnt.' " [17]

Omissions have impressed different courts in different ways. " The difficulties of so-called interpretation arise when the legislature has had no meaning at all; when the question which is raised on the statute never occurred to it; when what the judges have to do is, not to determine what the legislature did mean on a point which was present to its mind, but to guess what it would have intended on a point not present to its mind, if the point had been present." [18] Yet " the judicial function is that of interpretation; it does not include the power of amendment under the guise of interpretation." [19] " We are not at liberty to revise while professing to construe." [20] Further, " I think this court ought not to interject what it can only suppose the lawmakers would have inserted if they had thought long enough." [1] In short, " A *casus omissus* does not justify judicial legislation." [2]

---

[16] *Sic*: see Pufendorf, *Of the Law of Nature and Nations*, Bk. 5, c. 12, s. 8 (1934 ed., vol. 2, p. 802); and see 1 Bl.Comm. 61; Maxwell, *Interpretation of Statutes* (11th ed. 1962) p. 17 (omitted from 12th ed. 1969).

[17] *United States* v. *Kirby*, 74 U.S. 482 at 487 (1868).

[18] J. C. Gray, *Nature and Sources of the Law* (2nd ed. 1927) p. 173, quoted by Cardozo J., *The Nature of the Judicial Process* (1921) p. 15.

[19] *West Coast Hotel Co.* v. *Parrish*, 300 U.S. 379 at 404 (1937), *per* Sutherland J., dissenting.

[20] *Sun Printing & Publishing Ass'n.* v. *Remington Paper & Power Co. Inc.*, 139 N.E. 470 at 471 (1923), *per* Cardozo J. (of a contract).

[1] *Federal Trade Commission* v. *Klesner*, 274 U.S. 145 at 159 (1927), *per* McReynolds J., dissenting.

[2] *Ebert* v. *Poston*, 266 U.S. 548 at 554 (1925), *per* Brandeis J.

Learned Hand J. put the point with force. "The issue involves the baffling question which comes up so often in the interpretation of all kinds of writings: how far is it proper to read the words out of their literal meaning in order to realize their overriding purpose? It is idle to add to the acres of paper and streams of ink that have been devoted to the discussion. When we ask what Congress ' intended,' usually there can be no answer, if what we mean is that what any person or group of persons actually had in mind. Flinch as we may, what we do, and must do, is to project ourselves, as best we can, into the position of those who uttered the words, and to impute to them how they would have dealt with the concrete occasion. He who supposes that he can be certain of the result is the least fitted for the attempt." [3]

This view is not unrelated to some words uttered by Denning L.J. a few years earlier. "It would certainly save judges trouble if Acts of Parliament were drafted with divine prescience and perfect clarity. In the absence of it, when a defect appears a judge cannot simply fold his hands and blame the draftsman. He must set to work on the constructive task of finding the intention of Parliament, and he must do this not only from the language of the statute, but also from a consideration of the social conditions which gave rise to it, and of the mischief which it was passed to remedy, and then he must supplement the written word so as to give ' force and life ' to the intention of the legislature. . . . Put into homely metaphor it is this: A judge should ask himself the question: If the makers of the Act had themselves come across this ruck in the texture of it, how would they have straightened it out? He must then do as they would have done. A judge must not alter the material of which it is woven, but he can and should iron out the creases." [4]

Next year, this approach was applied to a statute and to an Order made by a Minister,[5] only to be condemned by the House

[3] *United States* v. *Klinger*, 199 F. 2d 645 at 648 (1952).
[4] *Seaford Court Estates Ltd.* v. *Asher* [1949] 2 K.B. 481 at 499, welcomed at (1950) 66 L.Q.R. 19.
[5] In *Magor and St. Mellons Rural District Council* v. *Newport Corporation* [1950] 2 All E.R. 1226 at 1236, *per* Denning L.J., dissenting.

of Lords. " The general proposition that it is the duty of the
court to find out the intention of Parliament—and not only of
Parliament but of Ministers also—cannot by any means be
supported. The duty of the court is to interpret the words that
the legislature has used; those words may be ambiguous, but,
even if they are, the power and duty of the court to travel outside
them on a voyage of discovery are strictly limited. . . ." [6] The
proposition was that " the court, having discovered the intention
of Parliament and of Ministers too, must proceed to fill in the
gaps. What the legislature has not written, the court must
write. This proposition . . . cannot be supported. It appears to
me to be a naked usurpation of the legislative function under the
thin disguise of interpretation. And it is the less justifiable when
it is guesswork with what material the legislature would, if it
had discovered the gap, have filled it in. If a gap is disclosed, the
remedy lies in an amending Act." [7] The views of Denning L.J.
on this point may well find more fertile soil across the waters;
but at home they bear no lawful fruit, though still held by Lord
Denning.[8]

Apart from the *casus omissus*, there is sometimes a simple
clerical slip. " Criminal conversation," as such, died over a
century ago[9]; but in recent years the Ontario legislature has
bravely committed itself to a concept of progenitive correspondence by enacting provisions relating to " letters parent." [10]
Again, publication of the banns of marriage in Manitoba is regulated by a statute which makes provision, *inter alia*, for the case
of parties who are " in the habit of attending whorship at
different churches "; who can speak with certainty as to the

---

[6] *Ibid.*, [1952] A.C. 189 at 191, *per* Lord Simonds.
[7] *Ibid.*, *per* Lord Simonds. The views of Lord Goddard, Lord Morton of
Henryton and Lord Tucker were similar: see [1951] 2 All E.R. 839 at 841,
847, 850. See also *St. Aubyn* v. *Att.-Gen.* [1952] A.C. 15 at 32.
[8] See *Ministry of Housing and Local Government* v. *Sharp* [1970] 2 Q.B. 223
at 264 (" We do not now in this court stick to the letter of a statute. We
go by its true intent. We fill in the gaps. We follow what I said in
Seaford Court Estates Ltd. v. *Asher* [1949] 2 K.B. 481 at 498–499 ").
[9] Matrimonial Causes Act, 1857, s. 59.
[10] Conveyancing and Law of Property Act (R.S.O. 1960, c. 66), s. 13 (1);
contrast Conveyancing and Law of Property Act (R.S.O. 1950, c. 68),
s. 12 (1) (" letters patent ").

course of religious observance in Manitoba? [11]   Conceivably this
is an outcropping of Canada's recognition that for some purposes,
at all events, it has at least four sexes.   Certain Regulations [12]
provide that unless the context otherwise requires, "words of
one gender include all other genders."   The legislative authority
obviously appreciated that neither " the other gender " nor " both
other genders " would do: nothing short of " all other genders "
is wide enough to embrace Canada's sexual diversities.   Yet
again, there is a statutory instrument which provided that in
certain cases a notice was to be added to a writ " informing the
defendant that he can apply to have the action transferred to
the County Court in which he resides or carries on business." [13]
Perhaps there are but few of such defendants; but modern
legislation seeks to provide for every conceivable case.

The happiest example comes from the United States.   At
first blush, Act 17 of 1945 of the State of Arkansas is innocent
enough.   Its title is " AN ACT to Authorize and Permit Cities
of First and Second Class and Incorporated Towns to Vacate
Public Streets and Alleys in the Public Interest."   Sections 1 to
7 duly proceed to develop this theme; but then there is s. 8.   It is
short and far-reaching.   "All laws and parts of laws, and
particularly Act 311 of the Acts of 1941, are hereby repealed."
The broad sweep of the legislative brush is not impeded by the
pusillanimous insertion of any phrase after " parts of laws "
such as " in conflict herewith," or " inconsistent with this Act."
The only other section of the Act, s. 9, appropriately concludes
with the words "and an emergency is hereby declared and this
Act shall be in full force and effect from and after its passage."
This is promising material: yet s. 8 had to wait for over twenty-
three years before, in a wide-ranging case,[14] it attracted the

---

11 Marriage Act (c.M50: Revised Statutes of Manitoba 1970), s. 8 (2) (b).
   (The loose-leaf volume is more strait-laced.)
12 The Atomic Energy Regulations of Canada, r. 101 (1) (m), made under the
   Atomic Energy Control Act, 1946.
13 The Salford Hundred Court of Record (Extension of Jurisdiction) Rules,
   1955 (S.I. 1955 No. 1295 (L.9)), r. 2, adding a new r. 3B to Order II of
   the Salford Hundred Court of Record Rules, 1912, as amended.
14 *Poisson* v. *d'Avril*, 244 Ark. 478A (1968), discussed sympathetically by Jasper
   Bogus McClodd and Pepe le Peu at 22 Ark. Law Rev. 724 (1969).

detailed attention of the Supreme Court of Arkansas. The report of the decision merits reproduction in full.

"J. R. POISSON v. Etienne d'AVRIL

" 6-5253

" Opinion delivered April 1, 1968

" STATUTES—REPEAL OF ALL LAWS.—Legislative act repealing all laws and parts of laws is construed to apply only to statutes, leaving all judge-made law unmonkeyed with.

" Appeal from Hot Springs Chancery Court, *Burl R. Hutch*, Chancellor; reversed.

" *J. R. Poisson,* pro se.

" *Etienne d'Avril,* pro se.

" George Rose Smith, Justice. This case—on the surface a routine suit for specific performance of an oral contract for the sale of land—presents, when probed in depth (as we have probed it), the most far-reaching question ever submitted to this court, perhaps to any court in the English-speaking world. The awesome issue confronting us is that of determining to what extent, if any, the common law and the statute law of this State were set aside and annulled by what we will call the Omnibus Repealer, adopted by the legislature in 1945.

" The facts are wholly insignificant. Poisson brought this suit against d'Avril to enforce an oral agreement by which d'Avril sold Poisson forty acres of bottom land in the Hot Springs Mountains. D'Avril, as might be expected, pleaded the Statute of Frauds, insisting that under that statute an oral contract for the sale of land cannot be enforced. But Poisson countered by dropping a judicial bombshell. He alleged that the venerable Statute of Frauds, which was adopted in 1838— soon after Arkansas became a State—had been nullified (along with the rest of our laws) by the Omnibus Repealer of 1945. The learned chancellor, appalled by the enormity of the question presented to him, took the case under advisement and finally delivered an opinion rejecting Poisson's sweeping contention, thereby preserving the status quo pending this appeal. The case has now been submitted to us for final decision.

" The Omnibus Repealer was appended to Act 17 of 1945—

an otherwise innocuous bit of legislation—and reads as follows: 'All laws and parts of laws, and particularly Act 311 of the Acts of 1941, are hereby repealed.' Period.

"Fundamentally, the Repealer hardly calls for judicial interpretation. The legislature has spoken: plainly, clearly, unmistakably, decisively. 'All laws and parts of laws . . . are hereby repealed.' Under many prior decisions of this court it is unquestionably our solemn duty to give effect to the General Assembly's magnificently comprehensive command. It will suffice to quote two of our earlier pronouncements on the subject.

"'It is a well-settled rule of law that, where the will of the Legislature is clearly expressed, the court should adhere to the literal expression of the enactment *without regard to consequences,* and every construction derived from a consideration of its reason and spirit should be *discarded,* for it is *dangerous* to interpret a statute contrary to its express words, where it is not obvious that the makers meant something different from what they have said.' (Italics supplied.) *Walker* v. *Allred,* 179 Ark. 1104, 20 S.W. 2d 116 (1929).

"'There are certain elemental rules of construction to be observed in the interpretation of statutes from which we will *not* depart. One is that, where a law is plain and unambiguous, there is no room left for construction, and neither the exigencies of the case nor a resort to extrinsic facts will be permitted to alter the meaning of the language used in the statute. *Even where a literal interpretation of the language used will lead to harsh or absurd consequences,* that meaning can not be departed from unless the whole of the statute furnishes some other guide.' (Italics supplied.) *Cunningham* v. *Keeshan,* 110 Ark. 99, 161 S.W. 170 (1913).

"Our duty is clear. 'We shall not,' in Churchill's words (nor in anyone else's), 'flag or fail.' Nonetheless, it does occur to us that the pivotal word 'law' in the Omnibus Repealer is open to two interpretations. On the one hand, giving 'laws' a strict construction, it may be said to mean statutes only, leaving all judge-made law unmonkeyed with. On the other hand, the word 'laws,' if given a broad and liberal connotation, may well encompass the common law as well as the digest of statutes, annotated.

" In the study of this question we have devotedly worked our law clerks to the bone and, indeed, have lost some sleep ourselves. As far as our research discloses, no other legislative body has ever taken the bold course of repealing all laws—and parts of laws. The nearest parallel we have been able to find, which is persuasive but not binding, is an observation by the great French [15] essayist Montaigne in Chapter 13 of his essay, Of Experience : ' I am further of opinion that it would be better for us to have no laws at all than to have them in so prodigious numbers as we have.'

" After much anxious study we have concluded that the legislature intended for the Omnibus Repealer to apply only to statutes, not to the common law. We are simply unable to believe that the General Assembly would do away with judge-made law. That law is obviously too wonderful to be lightly tampered with. In the immortal words of Lord Coke (himself, as it happens, a judge) : ' Reason is the life of the law; nay, the common law itself is nothing else but reason. . . . The law, which is perfection of reason.' See Bartlett's Familiar Quotations, p. 110 (13th Ed. 1955).[16]

" In reaching our conclusion we attach much weight to the legislature's use of the plural ' laws ' rather than the singular ' law.' Had the act undertaken to repeal ' all law,' it might well be argued that the intent was to abrogate the common law as well as the statutes. But in the Omnibus Repealer, which gives every indication of careful draftsmanship, the lawmakers were careful to refer to ' laws ' rather than to ' law.' Thus it may well be true that the letter ' s ' in ' laws ' is the most significant ' s ' in legal literature. At least, counsel have not cited a more significant ' s,' nor has our own research disclosed one.

" Both reason and authority support our interpretation of the Repealer. It is essential that the common law be preserved if we are to avoid anarchy—that state of society where there is no

---

[15] " As it happens, the parties to this suit are, significantly, French."
[16] See Co.Litt. 97b (which is slightly misquoted here : see *ante*, p. 111).

law. The statutory law is not equally essential. Indeed, it will be found that the statutes which were on the books when the Omnibus Repealer was adopted in 1945 can, for the most part, be spared. This is true simply because the common law, always fluid in nature, will at once seep into the temporary vacancy left by the evaporation of the statutes and keep the ship of state safely on the right track.

" Counsel for the appellee made the usual last-ditch arguments that are so frequently heard when a court is called upon to perform its stern duty, despite the demands of expediency and wishy-washiness. All sorts of imaginary perils are conjured up. It is said, for instance, that to give full effect to the Omnibus Repealer (hereinafter called the Omnibus Repealer) will nullify such pillars of government as the sales tax law and the income tax law, both of which antedated 1945. We dare-say, however, that the general public can and will face that catastrophe with that serene equanimity born of courage. Again, it is argued, with a veiled threat, that wholesome recreational activities such as horse racing will be abolished by the Repealer. Not so! In its wisdom the common law permits such contests, prohibiting only the secondary practice of betting on the outcome of the races. We need not extend this opinion by discussing one by one the various bugbears envisaged by counsel's vivid imagination. The truth is that in nearly every instance the purposes served by the Omnibus Repealer are praiseworthy and beneficent. We are calling the act to the attention of the Commissioners on Uniform Laws, who may well be inclined to make similar model legislation available to all the states.

" The decree must be reversed.

" HARRIS, C.J., would affirm the decree.

" JOHN A. FOGLEMAN, Justice, dissenting. I dissent because I disagree.

" WARD, BROWN, and JONES, JJ., concur in the dissent.

" BYRD, J., disqualified."

Splendid though this decision plainly is, it must be admitted that it has not set all doubts at rest. It could hardly be suggested that the authority of the judgment was diminished merely because there was a dissent by five of the six judges sitting.[17] Indeed, the fact that four of them in terms expressed themselves as dissenting shows that they recognised to the full the authority of the judgment from which they were dissenting. But where both parties are reported as having argued their cases in person, the references in the judgment to " counsel " and " counsel for the appellee " must throw some suspicion on the judicial process. Further, there was no need to decide whether the repeal was of both common law and statute law or only of statute law; for on either footing the Statute of Frauds had gone. Much of the judgment was thus *obiter*; perhaps that is why the dissenters merely dissented. It would also, no doubt, be captious to object that the case contains no reference to an earlier decision by the court on the same section which had dismissed the matter in a single sentence to the opposite effect (" No doubt the legislature meant to repeal all laws in conflict with that act, and, by error of the author or the typist, left out the usual words ' in conflict herewith,' which we will imply by necessary construction " [18]). At all events, the case stands, perhaps alone, as an example of how the minority view, *obiter* and *per incuriam*, may be elevated into the *ratio decidendi*.

The course of events seems to have been that Smith J., the senior associate justice of the court, composed and circulated his judgment without the benefit of argument or, for that matter, any actual case, giving it a title and date which seemed appropriate. The report somehow found its way into the advance sheets of the State Reports, though with a pagination (pp. 478A–478E) which facilitated the exclusion of the report from the bound volume, an exclusion which, not unexpectedly, in fact occurred. In the meantime, the initial report appears to have had an impact on some members of the profession which can only be described as remarkable.[19] Perhaps in Arkansas, as elsewhere, due tribute is not always paid to the sound advice " Read it all before you speak "; first impressions do not always endure.

[17] For a unanimous dissent, see *ante*, p. 66.

[18] *Cernauskas* v. *Fletcher*, 201 S.W. 2d 999 at 1000 (1947), *per* McHaney J.

[19] It may be added that there was a Hot Spring (not Springs) Chancery Court, but no chancellor there called Burl R. Hutch; and Poisson d'Avril is a name to be linked with no date other than that of the judgment.

III

Vile Bodies

The Constable Has Blundered

" The condition upon which God hath given liberty to man is eternal vigilance; which condition if he break, servitude is at once the consequence of his crime, and the punishment of his guilt." [1] " It is a fair summary of history to say that the safeguards of liberty have frequently been forged in controversies involving not very nice people." [2] The warning is plain. " Do the people of this land—in the providence of God, favored, as they sometimes boast, above all others in the plenitude of their liberties—desire to preserve those so carefully protected by the First Amendment: liberty of religious worship, freedom of speech and of the press, and the right as freemen peaceably to assemble and petition their government for a redress of grievances? If so, let them withstand all *beginnings* of encroachment. For the saddest epitaph which can be carved in memory of a vanished liberty is that it was lost because its possessors failed to stretch forth a saving hand while yet there was time." [3]

In the Supreme Court of the United States, much law has flowed from disturbances in public places. " This Court has gone far toward accepting the doctrine that civil liberty means the removal of all restraints from these crowds and that all local attempts to maintain order are impairments of the liberty of the citizen. The choice is not between order and liberty. It is between liberty with order and anarchy without either. There is danger that, if the Court does not temper its doctrinaire logic with a little practical wisdom, it will convert the constitutional Bill of Rights into a suicide pact." [4] Yet " Unless we make the requirements for administrative action strict and demanding, *expertise*, the strength of modern government, can become a

---

[1] John Philpot Curran, 1790 (*Speeches*, 4th ed. 1815, p. 4).
[2] *United States* v. *Rabinowitz*, 339 U.S. 56 at 69 (1950), *per* Frankfurter J., dissenting.
[3] *Associated Press* v. *National Labor Relations Board*, 301 U.S. 103 at 141 (1937), *per* Sutherland J., dissenting.
[4] *Terminiello* v. *Chicago*, 337 U.S. 1 at 37 (1949), *per* Jackson J., dissenting.

monster which rules with no practical limits on its discretion.
Absolute discretion, like corruption, marks the beginning of the
end of liberty. . . . The standard set for men of good will is
even more useful to the venal." [5]

In one of the " war brides " cases, Jackson J. said " This
American citizen is told he cannot bring his wife to the United
States, but he will not be told why. He must abandon his bride
to live in his own country or forsake his country to live with his
bride. So he went to court and sought a writ of *habeas corpus*,
which we never tire of citing to Europe as the unanswerable
evidence that our free country permits no arbitrary official detention. And the Government tells the Court that not even a court
can find out why the girl is excluded. But it says we must find
that Congress authorized this treatment of war brides and, even
if we cannot get any reasons for it, we must say it is legal;
security requires it.

" Security is like liberty in that many are the crimes committed in its name. The menace to the security of this country,
be it great as it may, from this girl's admission is as nothing compared to the menace to free institutions inherent in procedures
of this pattern. In the name of security the police state justifies
its arbitrary oppressions on evidence that is secret, because
security might be prejudiced if it were brought to light in hearings. The plea that evidence of guilt must be secret is abhor-
rent to free men, because it provides a cloak for the malevolent,
the misinformed, the meddlesome, and the corrupt to play the
role of informer undetected and uncorrected." [6]

Within the United States, citizens, however poor, may move
freely from State to State, and " unless this Court is willing to
say that citizenship of the United States means at least this much
to the citizen, then our heritage of constitutional privileges and
immunities is only a promise to the ear to be broken to the hope,
a teasing illusion like a munificent bequest in a pauper's will." [7]

[5] *New York* v. *United States*, 342 U.S. 882 at 884 (1951), *per* Douglas J.,
dissenting (minor revisions have been made to the punctuation).
[6] *United States ex rel. Knauff* v. *Shaughnessy*, 338 U.S. 537 at 550 (1950),
per Jackson J., dissenting.
[7] *Edwards* v. *California*, 314 U.S. 160 at 186 (1941), *per* Jackson J.

Rights are enduring, too: they may be released, but they do not die. " Of such an high estimation is right in the eye of the law, as the law preserveth it from death and destruction: trodden downe it may bee, but never trodden out." [8] Yet war changes much. As Lord Sumner pointed out in 1920, " Experience in the present war must have taught us that many things are done in the name of the Executive in such times purporting to be for the common good, which Englishmen have been too patriotic to contest. When the precedents of this war come to be relied on in wars to come, it must never be forgotten that much was voluntarily submitted to which might have been disputed, and that the absence of contest and even of protest is by no means always an admission of the right." [9]

There are, of course, limits even to the claims of liberty. " An old proverb warns us to take heed lest we ' walk into a well from looking at the stars.' " [10] Again, " The price of freedom of religion or of speech or of the press is that we must put up with, and even pay for, a good deal of rubbish." [11] Commercial exploitation, too, must be kept within bounds. In Oklahoma, a husband and wife who carried on business in partnership attempted to have their business included in a telephone directory under the title AAAAAAAAAAA- AAAAAAAAAAAA, thereby assuring themselves an impregnable alphabetical priority; but the telephone company rejected the application. Nothing daunted, the couple then formed a company under the title AAAAAAAAAAAAAAAAAAAAAAAA Inc., and caused the company to apply for a similar entry in the directory; but again the application failed. An application to the State's Corporation Commission for a direction to the telephone company to make the entry had no greater success; and, on appeal, the State Supreme Court held that there had been no unlawful discrimination against the company, and that the telephone company had not acted arbitrarily, unjustly or unreasonably. All that the company had to show for its alpha-

[8] Co.Litt. 279b.
[9] *Att.-Gen.* v. *De Keyser's Royal Hotel Ltd.* [1920] A.C. 508 at 563.
[10] *Terminiello* v. *Chicago*, 337 U.S. 1 at 14 (1949), *per* Jackson J., dissenting.
[11] *United States* v. *Ballard*, 332 U.S. 78 at 95 (1944), *per* Jackson J., dissenting.

betical efforts was an undoubted priority in the tables of cases in reports and textbooks.[12]

The jury, of course, plays a large part in liberty; but it is for the Bench to protect the jury. It was the judgment of Vaughan C.J. in *Bushell's Case*[13] that finally established the immunity of the jury from punishment for reaching a verdict with which the Bench did not agree. As might be expected, there is much crabbed learning in the judgment: but there are also powerful ideas and fine language. " I would know whether any thing be more common, than for two men students, barristers, or Judges, to deduce contrary and opposite conclusions out of the same case in law? And is there any difference that two men should inferr distinct conclusions from the same testimony: Is any thing more known than that the same author, and place in that author, is forcibly urg'd to maintain contrary conclusions, and the decision hard, which is in the right? Is any thing more frequent in the controversies of religion, than to press the same text for opposite tenents? How then comes it to pass that two persons may not apprehend with reason and honesty, what a witness, or many, say, to prove in the understanding of one plainly one thing, but in the apprehension of the other, clearly the contrary thing: must therefore one of these merit fine and imprisonment, because he doth that which he cannot otherwise do, preserving his oath and integrity? And this often is the case of the Judge and jury." [14] The same idea is pursued later in the judgment. " A man cannot see by anothers eye, nor hear by anothers ear, no more can a man conclude or inferr the thing to be resolv'd by anothers understanding or reasoning; and though the verdict be right the jury give, yet they being not assur'd it is so from their own understanding, are forsworn, at least in foro conscientiae." [15]

Personal liberty takes many forms; and times have changed. In 1658, when Oliver Cromwell was Protector, and had " laid

[12] *AAAAAAAAAAAAAAAAAAAAAAAA Inc.* v. *Southwestern Bell Telephone Co.*, 373 P. 2d 31 (1962). See its proud place, *post*, p. 353.
[13] (1670) Vaugh. 135.
[14] *Ibid.*, at p. 141.
[15] *Ibid.*, at p. 148 (" before the tribunal of conscience ").

some very extraordinary Tax upon the City, one *Cony*, an
eminent Fanatick, and one who had heretofore served him very
notably, positively refused to pay his part; and loudly disswaded
others from submitting to it ' as an imposition notoriously against
the Law, and the Property of the Subject, which all honest Men
were bound to defend.' *Cromwell* sent for him, and cajoled
him with the memory of ' the old kindness, and friendship, that
had been between them. . . .' When *Cromwell* saw that he
could not convert him, he told him ' that he had a will as stub-
born as His, and he would try which of them two should be
Master.' Thereupon, with some expressions of reproach and
contempt, he committed the Man to prison; whose courage was
nothing abated by it; but assoon as the Term came, he brought
his *Habeas Corpus* in the King's Bench, which they then called
the *Upper* Bench.

" *Maynard*, who was of Council with the Prisoner, demanded
his Liberty with great confidence, both upon the illegality of
the Commitment, and the illegality of the imposition, as being
laid without any lawful Authority. The Judges could not maintain or defend either, and enough declared what their Sentence
would be; and therefore the Protector's Atturney required a
farther day, to answer what had been urged. Before that day,
Maynard was committed to the Tower, for presuming to question
or make doubt of his Authority; and the Judges were sent for,
and severely reprehended for suffering that Licence; when they,
with all humility, mention'd the Law and Magna Charta, Cromwell told them, with terms of contempt, and derision, ' their
Magna F— should not controle his Actions; which he knew
were for the safety of the Common-wealth.' He asked them,
' who made them Judges? whether they had any Authority to sit
there, but what He gave them? and if his Authority were at
an end, they knew well enough, what would become of themselves; and therefore advised them to be more tender of that
which could only preserve them; and so dismissed them with
caution, that they should not suffer the Lawyers to prate what it
would not become Them to hear.'

" Thus he subdued a spirit that had been often troublesome

to the most Soveraign power, and made *Westminster*-Hall as
obedient, and subservient to his Commands, as any of the rest
of his Quarters. In all other matters, which did not concern the
life of his Jurisdiction, he seem'd to have great reverence for the
Law, rarely interposing between Party and Party. As he proceeded with this kind of indignation, and haughtiness, with
those who were refractory, and durst contend with his greatness,
so towards all who complied with his good pleasure, and courted
his Protection, he used great civility, generosity, and bounty." [16]

Cromwell's phrase seems to have survived for a while: for
when Magna Carta was cited a few years later to Kelyng C.J.,[17]
who was committing a man in a very arbitrary way, " the only
answer given by my Lord Chief Justice of England was to
repeat, with a loud voice, Cromwell's rhyme, ' MAGNA CHARTA—
MAGNA ——A." [18]

Slavery, too, has long been dead in English law. The celebrated phrase in *Sommersett's Case*,[19] " This air is too pure for a
slave to breathe in," [20] was already ancient when Serjeant Davy
uttered it *arguendo* in 1772; for it was in 1569 that it was said
that " England was too pure an Air for Slaves to breathe in." [1]
By comparison, the year 1815 is modern. In that year, some
slaves escaped from the United States and were taken on board
British warships. The owner of the slaves sued the command-
ing officers for wrongfully harbouring his property, but his
claim failed.

The keynote of the judgment of Best J. was that " proceedings in our Courts are founded upon the law of England, and
that law is again founded upon the law of nature and the
revealed law of God." [2] "Slavery," he said, " is a local law,
and, therefore, if a man wishes to preserve his slaves, let him
attach them to him by affection, or make fast the bars of their
prison, or rivet well their chains, for the instant they get beyond

[16] Clarendon, *History of the Rebellion* (1707) vol. III, p. 506.
[17] 1663–1671.
[18] 1 Camp.C.JJ. 509.
[19] (1772) 20 St.Tr. 1.
[20] *Ibid.*, at col. 79: see 1 Misc. 127, 128.
[1] See *Cartwright's Case* (1569) 2 Rushworth's Hist.Coll. (1721) p. 468.
[2] *Forbes* v. *Cochrane* (1824) 2 B. & C. 448 at 471.

the limits where slavery is recognised by the local law, they have broken their chains, they have escaped from their prison, and are free." [3] He added "It is a matter of pride to me to recollect that whilst economists and politicians were recommending to the Legislature the protection of this traffic, and senators were framing statutes for its protection and declaring it a benefit to the country, the Judges of the land, above the age in which they lived, standing upon the high ground of natural right, and disdaining to bend to the lower doctrine of expediency, declared that slavery was inconsistent with the genius of the English constitution, and that human beings could not be the subject matter of property. As a lawyer I speak of that early determination, when a different doctrine was prevailing in the senate, with a considerable degree of professional pride." [4]

The outcroppings of liberty defy classification. The United States Supreme Court once held that it was right to deny naturalisation to a woman who on religious grounds was unwilling to take up arms in defence of the country. Holmes J. dissented, and concluded his judgment [5] by saying "I would suggest that the Quakers have done their share to make this country what it is, that many citizens agree with the applicant's belief and that I had not supposed hitherto that we regretted our inability to expel them because they believe more than some of us do in the teachings of the Sermon on the Mount." [6] The court has also held that under the Constitution a conviction obtained on evidence disclosed by an unlawful arrest or an unlawful search cannot stand; but many State courts, construing the constitutions of the individual States, have held otherwise. Indeed, Cardozo J. once described the Federal rule as being one by which "the criminal is to go free because the constable has blundered." [7]

In Scotland, when considering the right of the police forcibly to take the finger-prints of a person under arrest, Lord Sands

---

[3] *Ibid.*, at p. 467.
[4] *Ibid.*, at p. 470.
[5] Which later prevailed: see *Girouard* v. *United States*, 328 U.S. 61 (1946).
[6] *United States* v. *Schwimmer*, 279 U.S. 644 at 655 (1929).
[7] *People* v. *Defore*, 242 N.Y. 13 at 21 (1926).

dealt with the argument that no man can be compelled to supply evidence against himself. "If a man's finger-prints could not be obtained without some voluntary action on his part, and were to be obtained only by tormenting him until he agreed to give them, I could understand the argument. But, if, as I am led to believe, finger-prints can be obtained with very moderate force *nolens volens* of the patient, and if this is done when he refuses to give them, then there is no question of the man being compelled to supply evidence against himself. An Ephraimite who was compelled at the point of the Gileadite's sword to pronounce the word Shibboleth [8] might perhaps have complained that he was compelled to incriminate himself. But not so the man whose finger-prints are forcibly taken. He is entirely passive, and he is not compelled to do anything requiring any exercise of his own will or control of his body." [9]

Today, a home is still a home. "An Englishman's house, though a hovel, is his castle, precisely because the law secures freedom from fear of intrusion by the police except under carefully safeguarded authorization by a magistrate." [10] Further, "It is not now, and never has been the law that a man assailed in his own dwelling, is bound to retreat. If assailed there, he may stand his ground, and resist the attack.[11] He is under no duty to take to the fields and highways, a fugitive from his own home. . . . Flight is for sanctuary and shelter, and shelter, if not sanctuary, is in the home." [12] "Uncontrolled search and seizure is one of the first and most effective weapons in the arsenal of every arbitrary government. And one need only briefly to have dwelt and worked among a people possessed of many admirable qualities but deprived of these rights to know that the human personality deteriorates and dignity and self-reliance disappear where homes, persons and possessions are

---

8 Judges, xii, 6; and see also *ante*, p. 117.
9 *Adair* v. *M'Garry*, 1933 J.C. 72 at 88.
10 *Harris* v. *United States*, 331 U.S. 145 at 164 (1947), *per* Frankfurter J., dissenting.
11 So too may his geese if assailed by minks: *Aldrich* v. *Wright*, 53 N.H. 398 (1873).
12 *People of the State of New York* v. *Tomlins*, 213 N.Y. 240 at 243 (1914), *per* Cardozo J.

subject at any hour to unheralded search and seizure by the police." [13] Again, " A search is not to be made legal by what it turns up. In law it is good or bad when it starts and does not change character from its success." [14]

The link between civilisation and freedom of thought and of speech is plain. " To have doubted one's own first principles is the mark of a civilized man." [15] " Too many settled beliefs have in time been rejected to justify this generation in refusing a hearing to its own dissentients." [16] " Compulsory unification of opinion achieves only the unanimity of the graveyard." [17] The thought is not new. " Conscience is not controlable by human laws, nor amenable to human tribunals. Persecution, or attempts to force consciences, will never produce conviction; and are only calculated to make hypocrites, or martyrs." [18]

" Intellectual freedom means the right to re-examine much that has long been taken for granted. A free man must be a reasoning man, and he must dare to doubt what a legislative or electoral majority may most passionately assert. The danger that citizens will think wrongly is serious, but less dangerous than atrophy from not thinking at all. . . . Thought control is a copyright of totalitarianism, and we have no claim to it. It is not the function of our Government to keep the citizen from falling into error; it is the function of the citizen to keep the Government from falling into error. We could justify any censorship only when the censors are better shielded against error than the censored." [19] " Under our Constitution men are punished for what they do or fail to do and not for what they think and believe." [20] Yet " Liberty of thought soon shrivels without freedom of expression. Nor can truth be pursued in an

[13] *Brinegar* v. *United States*, 338 U.S. 160 at 180 (1949), *per* Jackson J., dissenting.
[14] *United States* v. *Di Re*, 332 U.S. 581 at 595 (1948), *per* Jackson J.
[15] (1915) 10 Ill.L.R. 1 at 3, *per* Holmes J.
[16] *Jones* v. *Opelika*, 316 U.S. 584 at 594 (1942), *per* Reed J.
[17] *West Virginia State Board of Education* v. *Barnette*, 319 U.S. 624 at 641 (1943), *per* Jackson J.
[18] *Chamberlain of London* v. *Evans* (1767) 16 Parl.Hist. 313 at 325, *per* Lord Mansfield C.J. (*sub nom. Harrison* v. *Evans* (1767) 3 Bro.P.C. 465).
[19] *American Communications Assn.* v. *Douds*, 339 U.S. 382 at 442 (1950), *per* Jackson J.
[20] *Re Summers*, 325 U.S. 561 at 578 (1945), *per* Black J., dissenting.

atmosphere hostile to the endeavor or under dangers which are hazarded only by heroes." [1]

Law, too, is not all. "Civil liberties draw at best only limited strength from legal guaranties. Preoccupation by our people with the constitutionality, instead of with the wisdom, of legislation or of executive action is preoccupation with a false value. Even those who would most freely use the judicial brake on the democratic process by invalidating legislation that goes deeply against their grain, acknowledge, at least by paying lip service, that constitutionality does not exact a sense of proportion or the sanity of humor or an absence of fear. Focusing attention on constitutionality tends to make constitutionality synonymous with wisdom. When legislation touches freedom of thought and freedom of speech, such a tendency is a formidable enemy of the free spirit. Much that should be rejected as illiberal, because repressive and envenoming, may well be not unconstitutional. The ultimate reliance for the deepest needs of civilization must be found outside their vindication in courts of law; apart from all else, judges, howsoever they may conscientiously seek to discipline themselves against it, unconsciously are too apt to be moved by the deep undercurrents of public feeling. A persistent, positive translation of the liberating faith into the feelings and thoughts and actions of men and women is the real protection against attempts to strait-jacket the human mind. Such temptations will have their way, if fear and hatred are not exorcised. The mark of a truly civilized man is confidence in the strength and security derived from the inquiring mind. We may be grateful for such honest comforts as it supports, but we must be unafraid of its incertitudes. Without open minds there can be no open society. And if society be not open the spirit of man is mutilated and becomes enslaved." [2]

The fine words of Brandeis J. on freedom of speech are often cited. "Those who won our independence believed that the final end of the State was to make men free to develop their faculties; and that in its government the deliberative forces

---

[1] *Dennis* v. *United States*, 341 U.S. 494 at 550 (1951), *per* Frankfurter J.
[2] *Ibid*., at p. 555, *per* Frankfurter J.

should prevail over the arbitrary. They valued liberty both as an end and as a means. They believed liberty to be the secret of happiness and courage to be the secret of liberty. They believed that freedom to think as you will and to speak as you think are means indispensable to the discovery and spread of political truth; that without free speech and assembly discussion would be futile; that with them, discussion affords ordinarily adequate protection against the dissemination of noxious doctrine; that the greatest menace to freedom is an inert people; that public discussion is a political duty; and that this should be a fundamental principle of the American government. They recognized the risks to which all human institutions are subject. But they knew that order cannot be secured merely through fear of punishment for its infraction; that it is hazardous to discourage thought, hope and imagination; that fear breeds repression; that repression breeds hate; that hate menaces stable government; that the path of safety lies in the opportunity to discuss freely supposed grievances and proposed remedies; and that the fitting remedy for evil counsels is good ones. Believing in the power of reason as applied through public discussion, they eschewed silence coerced by law—the argument of force in its worst form. Recognizing the occasional tyrannies of governing majorities, they amended the Constitution so that free speech and assembly should be guaranteed.

"Fear of serious injury cannot alone justify suppression of free speech and assembly. Men feared witches and burned women. It is the function of speech to free men from the bondage of irrational fears. To justify suppression of free speech there must be reasonable ground to fear that serious evil will result if free speech is practiced. There must be reasonable ground to believe that the danger apprehended is imminent. There must be reasonable ground to believe that the evil to be prevented is a serious one. Every denunciation of existing law tends in some measure to increase the probability that there will be violation of it. Condonation of a breach enhances the probability. Expressions of approval add to the probability. Propagation of the criminal state of mind by teaching syndicalism

increases it. Advocacy of law-breaking heightens it still further.
But even advocacy of violation, however reprehensible morally, is
not a justification for denying free speech where the advocacy
falls short of incitement and there is nothing to indicate that the
advocacy would be immediately acted on. The wide difference
between advocacy and incitement, between preparation and
attempt, between assembling and conspiracy, must be borne in
mind. In order to support a finding of clear and present danger
it must be shown either that immediate serious violence was to
be expected or was advocated, or that the past conduct furnished
reason to believe that such advocacy was then contemplated.

" Those who won our independence by revolution were not
cowards. They did not fear political change. They did not
exalt order at the cost of liberty. To courageous, self-reliant
men, with confidence in the power of free and fearless reasoning
applied through the processes of popular government, no danger
flowing from speech can be deemed clear and present, unless
the incidence of the evil apprehended is so imminent that it
may befall before there is opportunity for full discussion. If
there be time to expose through discussion the falsehood and
fallacies, to avert the evil by the processes of education, the
remedy to be applied is more speech, not enforced silence. Only
an emergency can justify repression. Such must be the rule if
authority is to be reconciled with freedom. Such, in my
opinion, is the command of the Constitution. It is therefore
always open to Americans to challenge a law abridging free
speech and assembly by showing that there was no emergency
justifying it." [3] " The law knows no finer hour than when it
cuts through formal concepts and transitory emotions to protect
unpopular citizens against discrimination and persecution." [4]

In this sphere, schools have played a large part. " Scholar-
ship cannot flourish in an atmosphere of suspicion and distrust.
Teachers and students must always remain free to inquire, to
study and to evaluate, to gain new maturity and understanding;

[3] *Whitney* v. *California*, 274 U.S. 357 at 375 (1927), Holmes J. concurring.
(On p. 203, *ante*, I have substituted " burned " for " burnt ".)
[4] *Falbo* v. *United States*, 320 U.S. 549 at 561 (1944), *per* Murphy J.,
dissenting.

otherwise our civilization will stagnate and die." [5] Without this freedom, " a problem can no longer be pursued with impunity to its edges. Fear stalks the classroom. The teacher is no longer a stimulant to adventurous thinking; she becomes instead a pipe line for safe and sound information. A deadening dogma takes the place of free inquiry. Instruction tends to become sterile; pursuit of knowledge is discouraged; discussion often leaves off where it should begin. This, I think, is what happens when a censor looks over a teacher's shoulder. . . . A school system producing students trained as robots threatens to rob a generation of the versatility that has been perhaps our greatest distinction." [6]

Where is the line to be drawn? " We can afford no liberties with liberty itself." [7] " The character of every act depends upon the circumstances in which it is done.[8] The most stringent protection of free speech would not protect a man in falsely shouting fire in a theater and causing a panic." [9] " Utterance in a context of violence can lose its significance as an appeal to reason and become part of an instrument of force." [10] " That utterances inciting to the overthrow of organized government by unlawful means, present a sufficient danger of substantive evil to bring their punishment within the range of legislative discretion, is clear. Such utterances, by their very nature, involve danger to the public peace and to the security of the State. They threaten breaches of the peace and ultimate revolution. And the immediate danger is none the less real and substantial, because the effect of a given utterance cannot be accurately foreseen. The State cannot reasonably be required to measure the danger from every such utterance in the nice balance of a jeweler's scale. A single revolutionary spark may kindle a fire that, smouldering

[5] *Sweezy* v. *New Hampshire*, 354 U.S. 234 at 250 (1957), *per* Warren C.J.
[6] *Adler* v. *Board of Education of the City of New York*, 342 U.S. 485 at 510, 511 (1952), *per* Douglas J., dissenting.
[7] *United States* v. *Spector*, 343 U.S. 169 at 180 (1952), *per* Jackson J., dissenting.
[8] " *Gompers* v. *Bucks Stove and Range Co.*, 221 U.S. 418, 439."
[9] *Schenck* v. *United States*, 249 U.S. 47 at 52 (1919), *per* Holmes J., cited by Latham C.J. in *Adelaide Company of Jehovah's Witnesses Incorporated* v. *The Commonwealth* (1943) 67 C.L.R. 116 at 127.
[10] *Milk Wagon Drivers Union of Chicago, Local 753* v. *Meadowmoor Dairies, Inc.*, 312 U.S. 287 at 293 (1941), *per* Frankfurter J.

for a time, may burst into a sweeping and destructive conflagration." [11]

It was the judgment of Holmes J. in *Schenck* v. *United States* [12] that gave rise to the test of " clear and present danger " for determining whether restrictions on liberty would be held constitutional. Some thirty years after Holmes had delivered his judgment, Jackson J. observed that " All agree that it means something very important, but no two seem to agree on what it is." [13] In one case the issue was whether a conviction for " criminal anarchy " in publishing a left-wing " Manifesto " was good, or whether the statute authorising it was unconstitutional. The case was argued in the Supreme Court in April 1923, and reargued in November 1923; but not until more than a year and a half later were the reserved judgments delivered, affirming the conviction, with Holmes and Brandeis JJ. dissenting. In his judgment, Holmes J. took the view that the manifesto gave rise to no clear and present danger. " It is said that this manifesto was more than a theory, that it was an incitement. Every idea is an incitement. It offers itself for belief and if believed it is acted on unless some other belief outweighs it or some failure of energy stifles the movement at its birth. The only difference between the expression of an opinion and an incitement in the narrower sense is the speaker's enthusiasm for the result. Eloquence may set fire to reason. But whatever may be thought of the redundant discourse before us it had no chance of starting a present conflagration." [14]

In referring to the right of the people to meet to petition for the redress of grievances, Brandeis J. once said " Full and free exercise of this right by the citizen is ordinarily also his duty; for its exercise is more important to the Nation than it is to himself. Like the course of the heavenly bodies, harmony in national life is a resultant of the struggle between contending forces. In frank expression of conflicting opinion lies the greatest promise of wisdom in governmental action; and in suppression lies

[11] *Gitlow* v. *People of New York*, 268 U.S. 652 at 669 (1925), *per* Sanford J.
[12] 249 U.S. 47 at 52 (1919).
[13] *Dennis* v. *United States*, 341 U.S. 494 at 567 (1951).
[14] *Gitlow* v. *People of New York*, 268 U.S. 652 at 673 (1925).

ordinarily the greatest peril. There are times when those charged with the responsibility of Government, faced with clear and present danger, may conclude that suppression of divergent opinion is imperative; because the emergency does not permit reliance upon the slower conquest of error by truth. And in such emergencies the power to suppress exists." [15]

In one case, where evidence for the prosecution had been obtained by wire-tapping (as listening to the telephone conversations of others by means of a connection to the telephone wire is sometimes called), the United States Supreme Court, by a majority of one, held the evidence admissible. Brandeis J. expressed his dissent in wide terms. " The makers of our Constitution undertook to secure conditions favorable to the pursuit of happiness. They recognized the significance of man's spiritual nature, of his feelings and of his intellect. They knew that only a part of the pain, pleasure and satisfactions of life are to be found in material things. They sought to protect Americans in their beliefs, their thoughts, their emotions and their sensations. They conferred, as against the Government, the right to be let alone—the most comprehensive of rights and the right most valued by civilized men." [16] It was immaterial, he said, " that the intrusion was in aid of law enforcement. Experience should teach us to be most on our guard to protect liberty when the Government's purposes are beneficent. Men born to freedom are naturally alert to repel invasion of their liberty by evil-minded rulers. The greatest dangers to liberty lurk in insidious encroachment by men of zeal, well-meaning but without understanding." [17] Further, " decency, security and liberty alike demand that government officials shall be subjected to the same rules of conduct that are commands to the citizen. In a government of laws, existence of the government will be imperilled if it fails to observe the law scrupulously. Our Government is the potent, the omnipresent teacher. For good or for ill, it teaches the whole people by its example. Crime is contagious. If the Government becomes a law-breaker, it breeds contempt for law;

[15] *Gilbert* v. *State of Minnesota*, 254 U.S. 325 at 338 (1920), dissenting.
[16] *Olmstead* v. *United States*, 277 U.S. 438 at 478 (1928).
[17] *Ibid.*, at p. 479.

it invites every man to become a law unto himself; it invites anarchy. To declare that in the administration of the criminal law the end justifies the means—to declare that the Government may commit crimes in order to secure the conviction of a private criminal—would bring terrible retribution. Against that pernicious doctrine this Court should resolutely set its face." [18]

Deeds may lend eloquence to words. In *James Bagg's Case* [19] the main issue was whether one of the chief burgesses or magistrates of Plymouth [20] could be removed from his position by his brethren for an assortment of insulting expressions spoken of successive mayors. Thus in the mayoralty of Thomas Fowens, James Bagg, in the presence and hearing of the Mayor and many others and " in contempt and disdain " of the Mayor, " turning the hinder part of his body in an inhuman and uncivil manner towards the aforesaid Thomas Fowens, scoffingly, contemptuously, and uncivilly, with a loud voice, said to the aforesaid Thomas Fowens, these words following, that is to say, (' Come and kiss ')." [1] The Court of King's Bench held that such insults as these were no ground for removal, and awarded a writ for his restoration to office.

With the years have come changes in technique but not in principle. In 1963 a Manchester United goalkeeper, playing in a football match at Sheffield, saved a penalty kick, whereupon he was alleged to have " raised two fingers to the crowd in a derogatory manner "; the sign with two fingers was said to be " not intended as a ' V for Victory ' sign." However, the penalty kick had to be taken again, and this time the home side scored. At this, the goalkeeper was said to have " dropped his shorts and waggled his bare buttocks at the spectators." A prosecution for using an insulting gesture likely to cause a breach of the peace was launched, but the goalkeeper, who " told the court that he had to hoist his pants, which came down after the dive to save the penalty," secured a triumphant acquittal. [2]

[18] *Ibid.*, at p. 485.　　　　　　　　　　[19] (1615) 11 Co.Rep. 93b.
[20] Hayes J. inexplicably makes Surrebutter B. assent to Edward Crogate's ascription of the episode to Ipswich instead of Plymouth: see *Hayesiana*, pp. 15, 16 (where the reference to 11 Rep. 97 should be to 11 Rep. 95b).
[1] *James Bagg's Case, supra*, at p. 95b.
[2] *The Guardian* [1963] Feb. 26, p. 11.

A Crazy Quilt

THERE are many ways under many laws in which marriage may be constituted. Usually, no doubt, it is preceded by a proposal of marriage, duly accepted; but not all proposals are orthodox. As Lord Wheatley observed in giving judgment in 1959, " In the course of experience one has encountered many strange circumstances, but in my personal experience, and I should imagine in the experience of the Court, this is the first time a proposal of marriage has been made under cross-examination." [1] It seems that marriage had never even been discussed between the defender in a divorce action and his paramour until he proposed marriage to her from the witness box.

Scotland is rich in marriage lore. A note to one Scottish report sets out an epitome of the old Scots law of marriage in the form of seven eight-line verses, with a chorus, composed by Lord Neaves.[2] (He also wrote some pleasantly ironic verses on the claim that Lord Monboddo, another Scottish judge, had anticipated Darwin in his theory of evolution).[3] The now extinct[4] form of Scottish marriage known as marriage by promise *subsequente copula*[5] required *copula* which took place upon the faith of a promise of marriage, and was founded on a presumption of there being a consent to present marriage during the *copula*; a mere intention of future marriage would not suffice. The act of *copula* thus drew with it a rebuttable presumption of present consent to marry. " If the knight kneels before the lady and kisses her hand but no words are spoken, that is not marriage. But, if the knight has intercourse with the lady, that may be marriage, because by a legal fiction, the words are taken as exchanged." [6]

---

[1] *McEwan or Williamson* v. *Williamson* [1959] *Glasgow Herald* Nov. 21.
[2] *M'Adam* v. *Walker* (1813) 1 Dow 148, as reported 14 R.R. 48.
[3] W. F. Gray, *Some Old Scots Judges* (1914) p. 71.
[4] Marriage (Scotland) Act, 1939, s. 5.
[5] See 1 Misc. 126.
[6] *N.* v. *C.*, 1933 S.C. 492 at 500, *per* Lord Sands.

However, " the doctrine of marriage by promise *subsequente copula* has never sunk into the Scottish mind as have some others of our legal doctrines in regard to personal and domestic relations. This perhaps accounts for puzzles which surround the question. According to the theory of the law, when two persons who are engaged to be married indulge in sexual intercourse, presumably they there and then exchange matrimonial consent and become married persons. But, according to the view which prevails in those sections of community in which antenuptial fornication is most apt to occur, they do nothing of the kind. They yield to desire and indulge in immoral intercourse, robbed doubtless of some of its danger by the prospect of future marriage. There was at one time a custom in certain parts of the country, where the child of an engaged couple had actually been born before the celebration of the marriage, to place it under the mother's petticoats during the ceremony. The intention was to make the child fictionally one which had come forth *after* wedlock." [7]

The so-called " common law marriage," little known in England save as a polite verbal cloak for fornication or adultery of the less ephemeral type, has a respectable ancestry in America. " The validity of a common-law marriage is well established in our law. It took root there when the conditions in Texas justified it. The sparse settlements, the long distance to places of record, bad roads, difficulties of travel, made access to officers or ministers difficult for some of our residents, lack of education in the English language produced unfamiliarity with the laws, and, in the small settlements it was more difficult to dignify an illicit association with the name of marriage than in one of our large cities where all of us are strangers to the private life of most of its residents. We do not say that all the reasons for upholding common-law marriages have disappeared. We do say that the courts should review with care a common-law marriage claimed to have been contracted in the shadow of the county clerk's office and within the sound of church bells." [8]

[7] *Ibid.*, at p. 501, *per* Lord Sands.
[8] *McChesney* v. *Johnson*, 79 S.W. 2d 658 at 659 (1935), *per* Lattimore J.

Some jurisdictions in the United States have unleashed upon the law matrimonial a doctrine of estoppel that produces remarkable results. Suppose that H procures an invalid Reno divorce from his wife, W_1. He then marries W_2, and subsequently W_1 validly divorces him on account of his adultery with W_2. Tiring of W_2 but not bothering to obtain any further divorce, H then marries W_3; and W_2 then sues him on account of his adultery with W_3. H's defence is that W_2 cannot divorce him, for he was never married to W_2; the ceremony of marriage to her produced no marriage, he says, for at the time the Reno divorce had failed to put an end to his marriage with W_1. " The question is, can he be heard to assert the invalidity of a divorce he himself induced the court to grant? This question has been precisely and authoritatively answered in the negative." [9] H's defence thus fails, and W_2 succeeds in her claim for divorce.[10]

But what of W_3? There is nothing to prevent her from asserting that H was still the husband of W_1 when he married W_2, and therefore that he was never married to W_2; and as W_1 conveniently divorced H before he married W_3, W_3 is H's wife. " Her marriage being entirely valid, she is naturally free from any imputation of adulterous conduct." [11] Whether H and W_3 are married thus depends on who is speaking; if it is H, they are merely man and mistress, whereas if it is W_3, they are husband and wife. The same acts, too, amount to lawful marital intercourse *quoad* W_3 but illicit and adulterous copulation *quoad* H. Perhaps W_3, guiltless of the crime of adultery in her own proper person, is guilty as a principal in H's criminal acts. Any issue of the union would be legitimate, for no estoppel binds them [12]; yet if one of them addressed H as " Father," in law H's answer should, it seems, be " Yes, bastard? " Indeed, what has been called a " crazy quilt of divorce laws " in the United States (of which the Nevada divorce is so conspicuous a feature) has been

---

[9] *Stewart* v. *Stewart*, 67 N.Y.S. 2d 799 (1947), *per* Steuer J.
[10] *Ibid.*
[11] *Ibid.*, at p. 800, *per* Steuer J.
[12] See *Re Lindgren's Estate*, 55 N.E. 2d 849 (1944); *Urquhart* v. *Urquhart*, 69 N.Y.S. 2d 57 (1947); *Urquhart* v. *Urquhart*, 92 N.Y.S. 2d 484 (1949).

said to permit a " divisible divorce by which the parties are half-bound and half-free," permitting a man to " have a wife who cannot become his widow and to leave a widow who is no longer his wife." [13] Truly, " if there is one thing that the people are entitled to expect from their lawmakers, it is rules of law that will enable individuals to tell whether they are married and, if so, to whom." [14]

To come rather nearer home, it is a sober reflection that probably few who marry according to the Church of England service know when in law they became man and wife. The day and the approximate hour may for ever be fixed in their memories: but can they say at what precise moment in the service the marriage was constituted? In an Australian case, the parties had exchanged their promises of marriage, but while the groom was putting the ring on the bride's finger and it had reached her knuckle, she pulled it off, threw it to the ground, and, saying " I will not marry you," ran from the premises. The ceremony was thus abruptly ended, without any joining of hands or pronouncement by the minister that the parties were man and wife. Were they married? Herring C.J. held that they were not, on the ground that there was no marriage until the ceremony was complete. But Martin and Smith JJ. held that there was a marriage as soon as the parties had exchanged their consents,[15] and so the two were one. The moment of marriage is thus the second " I do."

The problems involved in the separate marriages of female siamese twins seem never to have come before a court. But there is a full report of the arguments (by Dr. Penny-feather and Dr. Leather-head) and the decision in a fictional case on this subject. The judge of the consistory court held that the marriages were valid, and ordered both husbands " to cohabit with your Wives, and to lie in bed each on the side of his own Wife. I hope, Gentlemen, you will seriously consider that you are under a stricter tye than common Brothers-in-law; that being, as it were, Joint Proprietors of one common Tenement, you will so behave

---

[13] *Rice* v. *Rice*, 336 U.S. 674 at 680 (1949), *per* Jackson J., dissenting.
[14] *Estin* v. *Estin*, 334 U.S. 541 at 553 (1948), *per* Jackson J., dissenting.
[15] *Quick* v. *Quick otherwise O'Connell* [1953] V.L.R. 224.

as good Fellow-lodgers ought to do, and with great modesty
each to his respective Sister-in-law, abstaining from all further
Familiarities than what Conjugal Duties do naturally oblige you
to.   Consider also by how small limits the Duty and the Trespass
is divided; lest, while ye discharge the duty of Matrimony, ye
heedlessly slide into the sin of Adultery."

This decision was affirmed by the Court of Arches, but the
Commission of Delegates annulled the marriages, on the ground
that " allowing the manner of Cohabitation enjoined to be practi-
cable (though highly inconvenient), yet the *Jus petendi* and
reddendi Debitum conjugale being at all times equal in both
Husbands and both Wives, and at the same time impossible in
more than one, two Persons could not have a Right to the entire
possession of the same thing at the same time; nor could one so
enjoy his property, as to debar another from the use of his, who
has an equal right.   So much as to the *Debitum petendi*, and as
to the *Debitum reddendi, nemo tenetur ad impossibile*." [16]

There are jurisdictions in which nullity of marriage is somewhat less confined in its scope than it is in England.   Thus in
one South African case,[17] a marriage was annulled on the ground
that the husband had in all innocence married a woman who
was three months pregnant by another man.   Resort was made
to Voet, who had pointed out that a man could not have his
marriage annulled merely because his wife is portionless and he
married her believing her to be wealthy, for " he has himself to
blame for not inquiring better beforehand; but in the case of a
man marrying a woman deflowered, if he had the eyes of Argus
himself, could he have discovered the secret amours of persons
studying to deceive, if possible, the omniscience even of the
Deity? " [18]

The court was, however, sceptical of the doctrine that a mere
lack of virginity, unaccompanied by pregnancy, would suffice.
" There does not seem any authority in the law, or perhaps in

[16] *Memoirs of Martinus Scriblerus*, ch. 13, *Works of Pope* (ed. Warton, 1797)
vol. 6, pp. 180, 181. (" The right of seeking "; " the obligation of conjugal
yielding "; " nobody is required to do the impossible.") The last word
appears in the original as *impossible.*"
[17] *Horak* v. *Horak* (1860) 3 Searle 389.
[18] *Ibid.*, at p. 397, *per* Bell J.

principle, for saying that virginity, and still less chastity, is a
condition precedent to marriage; and inquiry as to the state of
fact in either respect would obviously lead to the most inconvenient discussions and to inquiries which might be subversive
of marriage altogether. Indeed the inquiry will generally be as
unnecessary as it would be inconvenient; for the learned author
(*Voet*), betrayed, as he sometimes, though but seldom, is by
enthusiasm, into eloquence in support of his positions, forgets
that jealousy is Argus-eyed, and that secret amours will generally
reveal themselves by the absence of that modesty and chariness
of manner in the woman, which nature has given her not only
as her protection against lasciviousness, but as the surest outward
indication to the other sex that the jewel is equal to its setting,
but which nature withdraws when the woman has been tempted
to ' stoop to folly,' and protection is no longer required for that
which has ceased to exist." [19] It was another matter, however,
where a lack of virginity was compounded by an undisclosed
pregnancy by another man.

Again, where a professional thief induced a young woman to
become his wife by representing himself to be honest and
industrious, a New York court granted the wife a decree of
nullity. "Companionship, with its reciprocal duties, is the
basis of marriage, and no respectable young woman should be
obliged to divide the life companionship of a husband between
herself and the penal institutions of the state." [20] On the other
hand, no success attended a husband who sought a decree of
nullity in Massachusetts on the ground that he had been induced
to marry his wife by her representation that until they had first
enjoyed ante-nuptial intercourse some three or four days earlier
she had been a virgin, and that as a result of that intercourse she
was already pregnant. She had, it seems, employed " a certain
artifice, which need not here be described," to convince her lover
of her virginity. Artifice does indeed appear to have been
requisite; for in fact, at the time in question, " she had pending
in the Superior Court four actions, in each of which allegations

[19] *Ibid.*, at p. 398, *per* Bell J.
[20] *Keyes* v. *Keyes*, 26 N.Y.S. 910 at 911 (1893), *per* McAdam J.

were made by her that one of the defendants had had intercourse with her with resulting pregnancy, and against other defendants that they had performed an abortion upon her at the persuasion of the first defendant without her knowledge or consent." [21]

In England, the courts seem somewhat more sceptical. After over fourteen years of marriage, a husband petitioned for a decree of nullity on the ground that, despite frequent attempts on his part, his wife was incapable of consummating the marriage. Langton J., however, dismissed the petition on the ground that the only safe conclusion that he could reach in the conflict of evidence was that, " although a very great deal of the petitioner's evidence is quite likely to be true, in the course of this very unhappily married life he had more success than he imagines." [1] Again, on a wife's petition for a decree of nullity on the ground of her husband's impotence, the court held that the report of the medical inspectors who had examined his virile member was insufficient to support a decree. In the delicate words of the judge, Dr. Calvert, " They could only say it appeared soft and short which does not always continue." [2]

In the nineteenth century judicial views of masculine virility seem to have been somewhat restricted. Thus it was said that " A man of sixty who marries a woman of fifty-two should be contented to take her ' tanquam soror.' " [3] While it may no doubt be said that at such ages " the passions are subdued," it seems a little strong to continue " and marriage is contracted only for comfortable society." [4] Nor will every man of forty agree that he is " approaching to the period when a philosopher has stated, that desires are no longer in a state of unsubdued provocation, but must be held to be under reasonable controul," so that if by his marriage to a woman of forty-eight he attains no joys of the flesh " he therefore may be fairly left to just reflection, and more placid gratifications." [5]

---

[21] *Levy* v. *Levy*, 34 N.E. 2d 650 at 651 (1941), *per* Dolan J.
[1] *T.* v. *T.* (*otherwise J.*) (1931) 146 L.T. 18 at 21.
[2] *Grimbaldeston otherwise Anderson* v. *Anderson* (1778) 3 Phil. 155.
[3] *Brown* v. *Brown* (1828) 1 Hagg.Ecc. 523 at 524, *per* Sir John Nicholl (" as if a sister "); but see *W.* v. *H.* (1861) 2 Sw. & Tr. 240 at 244.
[4] *Briggs* v. *Morgan* (1820) 3 Phill. 325 at 331, *per* Sir William Scott.
[5] *Ibid.*, at p. 321, *per* Sir William Scott.

Sometimes those about to marry seek to define their respective rights and duties in marriage by entering into some kind of agreement. One such form that has been unaccountably overlooked by those who compile books of precedents is the document that came before the court in *Dagg* v. *Dagg* in 1882.[6] The relevant facts are succinctly stated in the report. " This was a petition by William Pritchard Dagg, a pianoforte tuner, for dissolution of his marriage by reason of his wife's adultery. Neither the respondent nor co-respondent appeared.

" In 1867, the petitioner was a porter, and the respondent cook at a hydropathic hospital, and, she being with child by him, they agreed to be married. Before the marriage, the following document in the handwriting of the petitioner, was signed by the parties, viz. :

" ' This is to certify that whereas the undersigned parties do agree that they will marry, and that only to save the female of us from shaming her friends or telling a lie, and that the said marriage shall be no more thought of, except to tell her friends that she is married (unless she should arrive at the following accomplishments—viz., piano, singing, reading, writing, speaking, and deportment); and whereas these said accomplishments have in no way been sought after, much less mastered, therefore the aforesaid marriage shall be and is null and void; and whereas we agree that the male of us shall keep his harmonium in the aforesaid female's sitting room, we agree that it shall be there no more than four months, and that from that time the aforesaid and undersigned shall be free in every respect whatsoever of the aforesaid and undersigned female, as witness our hands this 1st of ——, 1867.

' Catherine L. H. Jeffries.
' William Pritchard Dagg.'

" A month after the marriage the respondent was delivered of a child, at a lodging taken for her by the petitioner; but he had had no further intercourse with her. He paid her 2s. 6d. a week until recently, when he discovered that she had been for some years living in adultery with another man." Hannen P. dis-

[6] 7 P.D. 17.

216

missed the petition on the ground that the agreement had been obtained by the husband " without the real concurrence of his wife and without justification. Knowing her frailty it was his duty, when he became her husband, not to have left her to those chances of falling, to which, abandoned as she was by him, she must have been exposed. . . . He withdrew from her that protection to which, as his wife, she was entitled, and it is not to be wondered at that she fell with another man." [7]

Another unprecedented precedent was conceived in respect of a marriage at Brentford Register Office on October 10, 1933, between a Miss Estella Blitz, who was aged eighteen years and was domiciled in England, and a Mr. Mohamed Hussein, an Egyptian railway official. Before the ceremony the husband prevailed upon the wife to sign a document which read as follows:

" I undersigned Estella agree to marry Mohamed on the following conditions: (1) I know well that he is an old-fashioned Egyptian and I know all about the Egyptian habits and character and I promise to follow all these habits and character without any exceptions; (2) I promise not to go out anywhere without my husband; (3) I will never have men or boy friends of me nor ask any man or boy to visit me at home nor see any man or boy outside or have any appointments; (4) I promise not to write to anybody friend of mine in Egypt or anywhere else abroad, man, boy, girl or lady; (5) I promise not to dance with any man or boy at home or at any other home or at any dancing hall in any feast or in any other circumstance; (6) I know well that Mohamed is not rich at all and he can't promise anything except just keeping me comfortably; (7) I confess that I write these conditions with my own wish and without any obligation from any side, and that I am conscious and responsible, and if I break any of these conditions I have to separate, and have no right to claim any penny from Mohamed at any Court, whether Egyptian or English."

On allegations that the husband had brought about the marriage (which was never consummated) by, *inter alia*, threatening to

---

[7] *Ibid.*, at p. 18.

kill the wife, Henn Collins J. granted a decree of nullity some four and a half years later.[8]

The precedent books are also unaccountably deficient in providing forms for a husband to sell and convey his wife. Authorities, though not lacking, seem to be little known today. Thus *Paynel* v. *The King* is an unforgettable though forgotten decision of 1302. The wife of Sir John de Cameys had eloped with Sir William Paynel; and Sir John then executed a deed of gift of his wife, Margaret, with her goods and chattels, to Sir William. This deed provided, *inter alia*, " Noveritis, me tradidisse et dismisisse spontanea voluntate mea Domino Willo Paynel, Militi, Margaretam de Cameys . . . Uxorem meam; Et etiam dedisse et concessisse eidem Domino Willo, relaxasse, et quietum clamasse, omnia bona et catalla que ipsa Margareta habet." [9] Modern conveyancing, one feels, would have made more of the occasion. A habendum (" to have and to hold," or at least " to hold unto the purchaser "), and a covenant for quiet enjoyment, would surely have been more than usually appropriate, unless, of course, Sir John would have felt as diffident about giving the covenants as he would have felt a recital of seisin to be misplaced.

Some time after executing the deed, Sir John died, Sir William married Margaret, and together they claimed dower out of Sir John's lands. However, the Statute of Westminster II, 1285,[10] had dealt with the point. Elegantly sandwiched between words making rape a felony and words imposing a penalty of three years' imprisonment for abducting a nun, there was a provision that " if a Wife willingly leave her Husband, and go away, and continue with her Advouterer, she shall be barred for ever of Action to demand her Dower, that she ought to have of her Husband's Lands, if she shall be convict thereupon, except that

[8] *Hussein otherwise Blitz* v. *Hussein* [1938] P. 159.
[9] I Rot.Parl. 146; and see 2 Co.Inst. 435 for a slightly variant version, where, *inter alia*, the surname is given as " Camoys." There is a translation in *Haworth* v. *Herbert* (1554) Dy. 106b (n.), the relevant parts of which are, in substance: " Know that I have delivered and committed of my free-will to the Lord William Paynel, Knight, Margaret of Commoys my wife; and have also given and granted, and to the same Lord William released and quitclaimed, all the goods and chattels which the said Margaret has."
[10] c. 34; see I *Statutes of the Realm* (1810) p. 87.

her Husband willingly, and without Coercion of the Church, reconcile her, and suffer her to dwell with him; in which Case she shall be restored to her Action." [11] All this, as Coke observes, " is comprehended shortly in two hexameters,

> Sponte virum mulier fugiens, et adultera facta,
> Dote sua careat, nisi sponsi sponte retracta." [12]

Sir William and Margaret contended that the deed of grant had saved the dower, that the ecclesiastical courts had acquitted them of adultery, and that they were willing to submit the issue of adultery to a jury. But none of these contentions sufficed: " and therefore it is considered that William and Margaret do take nothing by their petition but be in mercy for their false claim." [13]

Nearly four centuries later a similar point arose. " In dower, the defendant pleaded elopement in the wife: the wife replied, that her husband had bargained and sold her to the adulterer; and held bad." [14] Some fifty years later there was " a cause in the Court of Chancery, wherein it appeared, that a man had formally assigned his wife over to another man: and Lord Hardwicke directed a prosecution for that transaction, as being notoriously and grossly against public decency and good manners." [15] In Victorian days *Paynel's Case* had still not ceased to be an authority: for in *Woodward* v. *Dowse* [16] the Court of Common Pleas held that the adulterous widow was barred of her dower even if her initial departure from her husband had been caused by his cruelty. This case was argued shortly after a lady had, in circumstances of some notoriety, eloped with one of her husband's servants; and when *Paynel's Case* was cited by Serjeant Hayes, who was opposing the widow's claim, Byles J. sought further information about it. " Did the lady lie in *grant* or in *livery*, Brother? " he said. " A nice question, My Lord! "

---

[11] There was no corresponding statutory provision making a husband's adulterous departure a bar to curtesy: see *Sidney* v. *Sidney* (1734) 3 P.Wms. 269 at 276.
[12] Co.Litt. 32b.
[13] 2 Pollock and Maitland's *History* (2nd ed. 1898) p. 396.
[14] *Coot* v. *Berty* (1698) 12 Mod. 232, a case apparently overlooked by Kenny at (1929) 45 L.Q.R. 494; see also the unreported instance of 1766 cited by Kenny at p. 496. Kenny also gives some information about wife-selling at market.
[15] *R.* v. *Delaval* (1763) 3 Burr. 1434 at 1438, *per* Lord Mansfield C.J., in a case concerning the assignment for immoral purposes of an apprenticeship of an infant female singer.   [16] (1861) 10 C.B.N.S. 722.

Vile Bodies

was the ready answer, "unless the grantee *were the footman*, in which case, I apprehend, there would be no doubt as to the answer." [17]

Such sales were no monopoly of the wealthy. In *Bye* v. *Kowatski*,[18] decided in the City of London Court in (it seems) the 1860s, a Mr. Camera advertised for a wife, and the plaintiff answered the advertisement. Mr. Camera then "sold" her to the defendant for £27, for which sum the defendant gave a bill. Unfortunately the defendant was merely a head cook at a City tavern, and the plaintiff refused to marry "a common cook." Mr. Camera then reduced the price to £5, and in place of the bill for £27 took an I.O.U. from the defendant for £5 to be paid if the plaintiff changed her mind and married the defendant. Mr. Camera, who owed the plaintiff £15 for wages as a barmaid, then gave her the I.O.U. as part payment, and subsequently she sued on this. The claim failed, however, apparently on the ground that no consideration had been given for the I.O.U.

Much used to be said of the unity of man and wife. It was Maule J. who once observed "In the eyes of the law, no doubt, man and wife are for many purposes one: but that is a strong figurative expression, and cannot be so dealt with as that all the consequences must follow which would result from its being literally true." [19] An extra-judicial comment from the same source puts the point even more strongly. "People talk about a man and wife being one. It is all nonsense; I do not believe that, under the most favourable circumstances, they can be considered less than two. For instance, if a man murders his wife, did ever anybody hear of the charge against him being one of suicide?" [20] Indeed,

> Suppose in matrimonial strife
> A man should basely slay his wife,
> Sits there a court that would decree
> That either was *felo de se*?

[17] *Hayesiana* (1892) p. vii.
[18] G. Pitt-Lewis, *Commissioner Kerr* (1903) p. 196. For an American example, see (1973) 92 Law Notes 171.
[19] *Wenman* v. *Ash* (1853) 13 C.B. 836 at 844, *per* Maule J. (cited 1 Misc. 112). See also *ante*, p. 48.
[20] Rob. 123, as slightly varied. See now Homicide Act, 1957, s. 4; Suicide Act, 1961.

220

In days now past,[1] when a man was liable for the torts of his wife, the consequences were sometimes striking. If Mrs. A enticed away Mrs. B's husband, and Mrs. B sued for damages, then although Mrs. A had gravely wronged her husband by leaving him to live in adultery, " according to our law, he has to pay for that—*he* has to pay." [2]

Not the least of the achievements of the judicial mind is the ability to discover excellent reasons for retaining the law unaltered. Yet not all forebodings of the perils of change carry conviction, at all events when surveyed a century later. Thus in 1858, the question was raised in Pennsylvania whether an Act of 1848 which was intended to protect the property of a married woman from the creditors of her husband had made it possible for a wife to sue her husband in contract. Woodward J., speaking for the Supreme Court of the State, said that " one of the favourite maxims of the common law is, that marriage makes the man and woman one person in law, and of course it excludes the possibility of a civil suit between them. Now this characteristic of the contract may be considered a fiction, an absurdity, a fossil, or whatever else the necessities of the new era may denominate it, but it is in exact accordance with the revealed will of God, was designed for the protection of the woman, and leads to that identification of sympathies and interests, which secures to families and neighbourhoods the blessings of harmony and good order.

" It is doubtless competent for the legislative power to change and modify the qualities of the marriage relation, perhaps to abolish it altogether; but if the history of the human race teaches any lesson whatever, it is, that concubinage is the alternative of marriage. In just so far as you impair the one, you encourage the other. In just so far as you sever the material interests of husband and wife, you destroy the sympathies which constitute the oneness of the relation, and degrade the divine institution to mere concubinage.

" Nothing could so complete that severance and degradation,

---

[1] Before the Law Reform (Married Women and Tortfeasors) Act, 1935.
[2] *Newton* v. *Hardy* (1933) 149 L.T. 165 at 168, *per* Swift J.

as to throw open litigation to the parties. The maddest advocate for woman's rights, and for the abolition on earth of all divine institutions, could wish for no more decisive blow from the courts than this. The flames which litigation would kindle on the domestic hearth would consume in an instant the conjugal bond, and bring on a new era indeed—an era of universal discord, of unchastity, of bastardy, of dissoluteness, of violence, cruelty, and murders.

"But will the courts expose this fundamental relation to the consequences of unbridled litigation? Never. If it is to be done, it must be by the legislature, and then by no indirection, or inferential consequence, but by direct, plain, unmistakable English."[3] And so the wife's claim for $1065.00 was dismissed, and the State was preserved from a sudden access of universal discord, unchastity, bastardy, dissoluteness, violence, cruelty and murder.

Not all matrimonial litigation is *inter partes*. Sometimes there is a touching alliance in affliction, whatever the source. "Mrs. Barber is the kind of wife who stands by her husband in all the troubles he would not have had if he had not married her."[4] In one case in Illinois in 1958, a wife had shot and killed her husband after he had returned home drunk. He had, she said, threatened her and chased her round their apartment; and when he grabbed a chair and lifted it, she "must have shot, I don't remember that." The widow sued the store that had sold the liquor to her husband, and an award of $10,000.00 damages was upheld on appeal.[5]

In Nevada, on the other hand, a wife was less successful. She sued a corporation which carried on a gambling room for $5,000.00 damages for enticing her husband to play poker, "whereby she was deprived of the companionship of her husband, and of the money upon which she relied for her support, which caused her many hours of worry, humiliation, and sickness, and lessened her enjoyment of life, to her great

[3] *Ritter* v. *Ritter*, 31 Pa. 396 at 398 (1858). Thompson J. dissented.
[4] *Bondarchuk* v. *Barber*, 38 A. 2d 872 (1944), *per* Jayne V.-C.
[5] *Kiriluk* v. *Cohn*, 148 N.E. 2d 607 (1958).

damage." It was held that no cause of action had been disclosed, in that it had not been alleged that the corporation knew that the husband was a married man.[6] Sanders C.J., indeed, refused to confine his decision to this narrow point, and found it difficult to consider the action seriously. " A husband is exposed to the temptations, enticements, and allurements of the world, which easily withdraw him from the society of his wife, and the wife had reason to expect all these things when she entered the marriage relation, and her right to his society has all these conditions." [7]

In Nova Scotia, the spouses in another case had joined forces. They agreed with a solicitor that he should commence a suit for divorce against the wife on the ground of her adultery with a named person. The wife gave the names of several other persons with whom she said she had committed adultery; these were to be threatened with legal proceedings, any money extracted from them was to be applied towards the solicitor's costs, and the balance was to be used for the benefit of the husband and wife, or one of them. The plan prospered. A decree of divorce was obtained " illegally and collusively, and about $900.00 extracted from the pockets of those persons with whom the [wife] alleged she had committed adultery, by threats of legal proceedings, involving publicity to the parties named. The partition of the spoils, as made by [the solicitor], not being satisfactory to the other parties, the [wife] brought this action to recover the share to which she considered herself entitled." [8]

On these facts, McDonald C.J. " held that there was a cause of action, but that the evidence was insufficient to justify a verdict for the plaintiff." [9] Not surprisingly, on appeal the Supreme Court of Nova Scotia held that the action was of such an illegal or immoral character that the court would not entertain it.[10] Nothing daunted, the wife appealed to the Supreme Court of Canada. On this, " the judgment of the court *en banc*

[6] *Anderson* v. *McGill Club*, 266 Pac. 913 (1928).
[7] *Ibid.*, at p. 914.
[8] *Byron* v. *Tremaine* (1898) 31 N.S.R. 425 at 426, *per* Ritchie J.
[9] *Byron* v. *Tremaine* (1898) 29 S.C.R. 445.
[10] *Byron* v. *Tremaine* (1898) 31 N.S.R. 425.

was not attacked but the appellant urged that on the evidence given at the trial, she should have had a verdict. The court however agreed with the trial judge that there was not sufficient evidence and dismissed the appeal." [11] It would indeed have been remarkable if, as this account perhaps suggests, the Supreme Court of Canada had held that the case failed not because the court would not hear such an action but because the evidence was too weak. Yet the report is very brief, and the court may well have disposed of the case on the footing that whether or not such an action would be heard, it must fail.

[11] *Byron* v. *Tremaine* (1898) 29 S.C.R. 445 at 446.

De Ventre Inspiciendo

A CHILD has long been presumed to be legitimate if conceived or born during wedlock. The presumption is, of course, rebuttable; and it "does not consecrate as truth the extravagantly improbable, which may be one, for ends juridical, with the indubitably false." [1] There are, indeed, "breaths of human nature at which presumptions shrink and wither." [2] The presumption has been responsible for many a shot-gun marriage; and in one such case in Arkansas it was said that "It appears very highly probable that if there had not been a wedding, there would have been a funeral." [3]

There are even occasions when the presumption may produce a superfluity of legitimacy. Thus if a widow remarries three months after her husband's death, and bears a child three months later, what is the status of the child? In Blackstone's happy phrase, the child "is said to be more than ordinarily legitimate" [4]; and there was an old rule, soon doubted, [5] that on reaching years of discretion the child might elect whether to claim the first or second husband as his father. [6] Another suggestion was that the child might be the child of two fathers [7]; yet this too was soon disapproved. [8] Solutions abounded: as one book said, "Wherein how many Heads, so many Wits; how many Men, so many Minds; and no Man which hath not somewhat to say, as well for the Defence of his own Opinion, as for the Confutation of the contrary." [9] The true position in such

---

[1] *Matter of Findlay*, 253 N.Y. 1 at 8 (1930), *per* Cardozo C.J.

[2] *Ibid.*, at p. 11.

[3] *Lee* v. *Lee*, 3 S.W. 2d 672 at 673 (1928), *per* Smith J.

[4] 1 Bl.Comm. 456, 457; and see generally W. Hooper, *The Law of Illegitimacy* (1911) pp. 11, 12.

[5] See Brooke Abr., tit. Bastard, pl. 18 (1347); Y.B. 21 Edw. 3, Mich., pl. 40 (1347); Co.Litt. 8a.

[6] Y.B. 21 Edw. 3, Mich., pl. 40 (1347); Fitzherbert Abr., tit. Bastard, 22 (1309) (the point is not mentioned in *Halstede* v. *Gravashale* (1309) Y.B. 2 & 3 Edw. 2 (S.S. vol. 19) 53, which seems to be the same case: see p. 53, n. 1).

[7] *Re Heath* [1945] Ch. 417 at 422 (suggested also in *Swinburne on Testaments* (6th ed. 1743) p. 303).

[8] *Re Overbury* [1955] Ch. 122 at 126.   [9] Swinburne, *loc. cit.*

cases can hardly be ascertained by any rigid rule of law. Thus
in one case the wife may have been on terms of enmity with her
first husband, who died after a long illness; in another case the
first marriage may have been happy and vigorous until the first
husband was instantly killed in an accident, and poverty may
have impelled the wife into a marriage of convenience with an
elderly second husband. Indeed, there may be many reasons for
a prompt remarriage. One pointed out by Stephen was that in
days past in India the widow of a soldier was obliged to give up
her quarters if she had not remarried within six months or
(later) a year.[10]

In one case in 1394, a woman remarried immediately after
the death of her first husband, and had issue 40 weeks and 11
days after the first husband's death; and this was held to be issue
of the second husband.[11] In another case, Thecar married " a
lewd woman, but she does not cohabit with him, and is suspected
of incontinency with Duncomb; Thecar dies; Duncomb within
three weeks after the death of Thecar marries her; two hundred
and eighty one days and sixteen hours after his death she is
delivered of a son." Evidence of the non-cohabitation with
Thecar was excluded, and it was held that the son [12] was
Thecar's.[13]

The medieval rule was in the end made to turn on whether
or not at the time of the second marriage the widow's pregnancy
was so far advanced as to be indisputable. If she was then
grossement enceinte, the father was the second husband; if not,
it was the first husband.[14] On some statements, this rule seems
to have operated without regard to paternity, so that even if the
wife was great with child when her first husband died, the second

10 Stephen's *Digest of the Law of Evidence* (11th ed. 1930) p. 115, excised from
the 12th ed. (1936) and subsequent editions.
11 *Anon.* (1394) Co.Litt. 123b, n. 1.
12 A daughter, according to other reports: see *Theaker's Case* (1624) Cro.Jac.
686 (proceedings in C.P. on writ *de ventre inspiciendo*: *Theakers Case* (1624)
Winch. 71 is solely concerned with this); *Thecar's Case* (1628) Litt.R. 177.
See generally Sir Harris Nicolas, *A Treatise on the law of Adulterine Bastardy*
(1836) p. 74.
13 *Thecar's Case* (1627) Co.Litt. 123b, n. 1, K.B.; and see *Alsop* v. *Stacy* (1619)
Palm. 9, Co.Litt. 123b, n. 1; *sub nom. Alsop* v. *Bowtrell* (1619) Cro.Jac. 541.
14 See *Termes de la Ley* (1629) p. 43.

husband was adjudged the father.[15]   But other statements qualified the rule by excepting from it the case of a wife great with
child by her husband at his death (as distinct from an unmarried
woman great with child), in which case the child was the
husband's even if the wife remarried before the child's birth.[16]

Across the Atlantic, one court in the nineteenth century held
a child to be a child of the first husband even though she was
born nearly eight months after the marriage had been terminated
by divorce on the ground of desertion by reason of refusal of
sexual intercourse for nearly two years.[17]   The second marriage
took place some five months before the child's birth, but the
decision, which denied curtesy in the wife's land to the second
husband, was reached by refusing to admit the evidence of non-
access on the ground that it would bastardise issue.[18]   This seems
a somewhat severe conclusion which even before the statutory
reversal [19] of the rule in *Russell* v. *Russell* [20] was unlikely to
appeal to the English courts.   In *Viscount Ingestre* v. *Attorney-
General*,[1] a wife had remarried a month after her first marriage
had been terminated by a decree absolute of divorce, and her son,
born a month and a half later after more than eleven months of
cohabitation between the wife and her second husband, was held
a legitimate son of the second husband and so the heir apparent
to an earldom.

In a more recent case,[2] Harman J. said that " there appears to
be no authority on this subject, for in Stephen's *Digest of the
Law of Evidence* (1936) 12th ed., I find this note on p. 133: ' I
am not aware of any decision as to the paternity of a child born
say, six months after the death of one husband and three months
after the mother's marriage to another husband.' " [3]   This some-

15 See *Ludlow's Case*, cited by Bereford J. in *Halstede* v. *Gravashale* (1309) Y.B.
  2 & 3 Edw. 2 (S.S. vol. 19) 53 at 54, 55.
16 *Termes de la Ley* (1629) p. 43; and see Sir Harris Nicolas, *supra*, p. 75.
17 *Re Shuman's Estate*, 53 N.W. 455 (1892).
18 Under the rule known in England as the rule in *Russell* v. *Russell* [1924]
  A.C. 657.
19 By the Law Reform (Miscellaneous Provisions) Act, 1949, s. 7.
20 [1924] A.C. 657.
1 [1913] *The Times* Oct. 14, noted by Charles Sweet at (1914) 30 L.Q.R. 153.
2 *Re Overbury* [1955] Ch. 122.
3 *Ibid.*, at p. 126.

what overstates the paucity of authority. The facts of the case were that the first husband died from an accident some six months after the marriage. Almost exactly six months later, the widow remarried, and almost exactly nine months after the first husband's death a child was born. There were some rather in-conclusive indications of paternity on either side, but in the end the learned judge decided in favour of the improbability of a wife of six months' standing not only having ceased to have any marital intercourse but also having embarked upon an adulterous intrigue.

The writ *de ventre inspiciendo* is little known today. Formerly it was employed when a widow gave out that she was with child by her deceased husband, and such a child might dis-place those upon whom some or all of his property would other-wise devolve. The object was to prevent a supposititious birth. The most recent reported case in which the writ was ordered to issue seems to have been in 1845,[4] but formerly it was by no means rare. At common law, two writs issued, the first to ascertain whether the widow was with child and when she would be delivered, and the second, if she was enceinte, directing her removal to a castle where the sheriff was to keep her safely.[5] Under the first writ, the inspection was carried out by " twelve women in the presence of twelve knights," and under the second some of the twelve women were to view the widow daily, and some were to be with her at the birth.[6]

With the years, however, the procedure was modified, allowing residence at a more convenient place, and periodical inspection, upon reasonable notice, merely by two women nominated by those who would be displaced.[7] Again, the writ might be ordered to lie in the office for fourteen days, and if during that time the widow submitted to examination by two midwives appointed by the applicants, the writ was not to go until further order.[8] Where it was suggested that the widow's

---

4 *Re Blakemore* (1845) 14 L.J.Ch. 336.
5 *Theaker's Case* (1624) Cro.Jac. 686; *Ex p. Aiscough* (1730) 2 P.Wms. 591 at 592, 594n.; and see Co.Litt. 8b, 123b, n. 1.
6 *Willoughby's Case* (1597) Cro.Eliz. 566.
7 *Ex p. Aiscough, supra,* at p. 593; Mos. 391 at 394.
8 *Ex p. Wallop* (1792) 4 Bro.C.C. 90.

mother was also with child and so was not a proper person with whom the widow should reside (no doubt lest the mother might pass off her child as her daughter's), it was ordered that the mother should only be allowed to visit the widow.[9]   But if the widow had remarried and was enceinte, she was not removed from the custody of her husband, but instead was left with him, subject to his entering into a recognisance that she should not remove from their house, and that " one or two of the women returned by the sheriff should see her every day, and that two or three of them should be present at her travail." [10]   In one case [11] " James Baron married his maid servant, who in three weeks after marriage was brought to bed of a dead child."   Four months later the husband died, and the widow alleged that she was again with child.   The circumstances " naturally induced the family to look upon her with suspicious eyes," [12] and a writ was applied for and issued.

In a bastardy case, Rickhill J. quoted the old saying " Who that bulleth my Cow, the calf is mine." [13]   Over a century earlier, Metingham C.J. had uttered the same adage, in more ancient form:

> " Hwo so boleyth myn kyn
> Ewere is the calf myn." [14]

Devised for the regulation of property rights in farmyard and stable, the sentiment is less suitable when pressed into service for the determination of human rights of succession, as it has been, both in law report and drama.   Thus King John to Faulconbridge, of the Bastard—

> " In sooth, good friend, your father might have kept
> This calf, bred from his cow, from all the world." [15]

[9] *Ascough* v. *Lady Chaplin* (1730) Cooke C.P. 62.
[10] *Theaker's Case, supra*, at p. 686.
[11] *Ex p. Bellett* (1786) 1 Cox Eq. 297.
[12] *Ibid.*, at p. 299, *per* Kenyon M.R.
[13] Y.B. 7 Hen. 4, Hil., pl. 13, fo. 9 (1406).
[14] Y.B. 15 Edw. 1 (1288), as cited by W. C. Bolland, *The Year Books* (1921) p. 76.   Yet the *Register of Year Books* (Selden Society, 1956) p. 1 discloses not even a manuscript year book for 15 Edw. 1; and Metingham, though previously a puisne, did not become C.J. (of the Common Pleas) until 1290.
[15] *King John*, Act 1, sc. 1, lines 123, 124.

Vile Bodies

Peerage claims have sometimes begotten extravagant contentions. Thus in one unsuccessful claim to an earldom, Sir Vicary Gibbs A.-G. argued that " Age may not be proof of impotency, but it is evidence of it. The probability of the Earl's begetting a child at eighty is very slight, and it is not increased by the appearance of another child two years later. Instances have been adduced of these extraordinary births, but none have been cited, in which a man at eighty-two having begotten a son, had concealed the birth of such son. Would not he seek publication rather than concealment? Besides, at the birth of children in families of distinction, it is generally an object of much anxiety to have the event authenticated. Some registry is made of it. None has been found here after the most diligent search. If the register is lost, the date may always be supplied by the banquets and festivities with which it is contemporaneous. Why! the whole county would have resounded with the ringing of bells; you would have had processions of old men upon the anniversary of such a prodigy. It would have excited as much surprise as if a mule had been brought to bed! ... In no register, in no will, in no document is there any notice of this wonderful production. And then, not content with one, the miracle must be multiplied. It was not enough that one child should be born to a man at eighty-two; he must have another when he was eighty-four. And nature consummated her prodigality, by lavishing on these children the strength and vigour, which she usually denies to the offspring of imbecility." [16]

In the *Lovat Peerage* case, the claimant's argument depended upon establishing the identity of one Alexander Fraser who died in 1776 with another Alexander Fraser. This led the claimant into difficulties, for on this footing " Alexander must have been born in or before the year 1663, and therefore in the year when he is supposed to have died he must have been at least 113 years old. That is not an impossibility, but it is an eminent improbability; the probabilities are millions upon millions to one against

---

[16] *The Claim to the Earldom of Banbury* (1811), Le Marchant's *Proceedings on the Claims to the Barony of Gardner* (1828) 389 at 427, 428; and see Sir Harris Nicolas, *A Treatise on the Law of Adulterine Bastardy* (1836) pp. 452, 453, which prints this passage with critical footnotes.

its being true. Not only that, but he must have been working at daily wages of 1s. 4d., I think the year before he died; that is to say, he must have been working at manual labour, manifestly from the entry, when he was at least 112 years old. That is eminently improbable. He must have remained unmarried until the year 1738, when he was at least seventy-five years of age, and then he is said to have eloped with a young woman. One does not wish to create a smile, but certainly that is not an age at which one would suppose that a young woman of respectable family, as she is stated to have been, would have eloped with a miner in the condition of this man. After his marriage in 1738, when he was seventy-five years old or more, he must have had four children, the last of whom was born in the year 1759, when the father must have been at least ninety-five years old. Now, it is not one improbability only, but this is positively a congeries of improbabilities so utterly unlikely that it is impossible to suppose that they could have existed in the case of one man." [17]

A problem that has sometimes arisen in assessing damages, valuing annuities and so on, is how long a widowhood will continue.[18] In America, it has long been recognised that the difficulties are great. "How can any calculation be made in regard to the continuance of widowhood when there are no tables and no statistics by which to calculate such contingency? How can a valuation of a probable continuance of widowhood be made? Who can say what the probability of remarrying is in regard to any particular widow? We know what some of the factors might be in the question; inclination, age, health, property, attractiveness, children. These would at least enter into the question as to the probability of continuance of widowhood, and yet there are no statistics which can be gathered which would tend in the slightest degree to aid in the solving of the question." [19]

[17] *The Lovat Peerage* (1885) 10 App.Cas. 763 at 803, *per* Lord Bramwell. For an explanation, see (1886) 2 L.Q.R. 497 (" The Origin of the Lovat Myth," by G. F. Richardson).
[18] In the limited but important field of a widow's action for damages under the Fatal Accidents Acts 1846 to 1959 the problem now no longer arises: Law Reform (Miscellaneous Provisions) Act, 1971, s. 4.
[19] *Dunbar* v. *Dunbar*, 190 U.S. 340 at 345 (1903), *per* Peckham J.

In England, on the other hand, the Court of Appeal had earlier held that it was possible to make a fair estimation of the value of a woman's life interest *dum casta* [20] *et sola* [1]; and the delicacy of the former can hardly have been less than the difficulty of the latter. Perhaps the English courts were more bold, or, as some would say, more foolhardy; but the answer may lie in the statement in one of the cases that it was arranged that the matter should be referred to an actuary, who would first value the annuity as a simple life annuity, and then deduct from that value " such a sum as he should estimate to be the proper deduction for the contingency." [2] " In other words," said Peckham J., " it was left to the actuary to guess the proper amount to be deducted " [3]; and that, it must be admitted, is fair comment.

There are also difficulties in assessing maintenance. In considering the phrase " adequate provision for the proper maintenance " of a person, it has been said that " What is proper maintenance in any given case depends on all the circumstances, and it is difficult to relegate any circumstance to complete irrelevancy. Proper maintenance is (if circumstances permit) something more than a provision to keep the wolf from the door—it should at least be sufficient to keep the wolf from pattering round the house or lurking in some outhouse in the back yard—it should be sufficient to free the mind from any reasonable fear of any insufficiency as age increases and health and strength gradually fail." [4]

As to liability, in South Africa a child had to be maintained by his parents or, if they were unable to do so, by his grandparents. In one case a grandparent had died, and the question was whether his undistributed estate was liable to contribute to the support of grandchildren of his whose surviving parent were unable to support them. This claim was resisted on the ground, *inter alia*, that " a father is directly responsible for the existence of his offspring and it would accordingly be *contra bonos mores* to allow a father to bring children into the world and avoid

[20] *Re Batey* (1880) 14 Ch.D. 579.
[1] *Re Blakemore* (1877) 5 Ch.D. 372 (" while chaste and unmarried ").
[2] *Re Blakemore, supra,* at p. 375. [3] *Dunbar* v. *Dunbar, supra,* at p. 349.
[4] *Re Harris* [1936] S.A.S.R. 497 at 501, *per* Cleland J.

responsibility for them by himself departing from the world." [5]
Such an argument, hinting at a jurisdiction to grant injunctions
against dying, has at least its full share of difficulties; and it met
with no success.

In England, statute in 1925 destroyed any preferential claim
of a father as against the mother to the custody of their children.[6]
In Ireland, there was no corresponding provision, and the
father's rights were held still to prevail.[7] This doctrine, however, was held not to apply where there was an effective ante-
nuptial agreement between the parties, *e.g.*, as to the religious
education of the children; and authority for this view was found
in certain articles of the Constitution. "The strong language of
these articles arrests attention; it must have been chosen of set
purpose, because the grave subject-matter demanded that Ireland
to-day should define her position in unequivocal terms. Thus,
for religion, for marriage, for the family and the children, we
have laid our own foundations. Much of the resultant policy is
both remote from British precedent and alien to the English way
of life, and, when the powerful torch of transmarine legal
authority is flashed across our path to show us the way we should
go, that disconformity may point decisively another way." [8]

The appropriate education for a ward of court is sometimes
hotly disputed, though few of such cases are reported. However, in one case which found its way into the reports, Fitz-
Gibbon J. did not hesitate to enter into an open discussion of the
comparative merits of certain English and Irish public schools,
with a number of references to the personal acquaintance of himself and members of his family with some of them, as governor,
as parents or as pupils.[9] It was an Earl of Ilchester who in a
memorandum relating to his son expressed the wish that he
" should go first to a small school and afterwards at a proper
age to Eton," adding the cautious proviso " should that school
be then in good repute." [10]

---

[5] *Lloyd* v. *Menzies*, 1956 (2) S.A.L.R. 97 at 102.
[6] Guardianship of Infants Act, 1925, s. 1.
[7] *Re Frost* [1947] I.R. 3.
[8] *Re Tilson* [1951] I.R. 1 at 15, *per* Gavan Duffy P.
[9] *Re Westby Minors (No. 2)* [1934] I.R. 311 at 325, 326.
[10] *Ex p. Earl of Ilchester* (1803) 7 Ves. 348 at 350.

At an even more exalted level, the reluctance of Princess Charlotte, the daughter of George IV, to marry the Prince of Orange in 1814 is well known. In the end, she succeeded in resisting her father's pressure, which had taken strange forms. "An attempt had even been made through one of his law officers to persuade her that after receiving some presents, and saying things construed into promises, she could be compelled, by a Court of Equity, to perform the contract. This strange doctrine, this new kind of Equity, she had met with admirable presence of mind, and indeed skill, declaring her ignorance of the law, but offering to believe the proposition thus (by way of threat) laid down—provided, to prevent all mistakes, they who stated it would put it in writing and sign their names to it, that she might show it to Mr. Brougham, with whom she had been advising. Accordingly, as may well be supposed, nothing more was heard of this equitable novelty, this extension of the doctrine of specific performance." [11]

Yet although equity would not compel, it might make smooth the path. In 1573 Margaret Boothe's father was the main obstacle to her marriage to Edward Trafford; and, by Royal Command, Sir Nicholas Bacon L.K. intervened. Margaret's father asserted that the couple did not, and could not, like each other sufficiently to justify a marriage. "Whereupon the said Lord Keeper, understanding the said Margaret to have accomplished the full age of twelve years, and wishing to be informed of the truth of this objection before he should proceed to any decree, doth require and enjoin Thomas Stanley, Esq., in whose indifferent custody the said Margaret now is," to arrange that the couple should "have meeting, talk, and conference the one with the other, two or three several times before the term of St. Michael next coming," in the presence of Thomas Stanley.

Two such meetings accordingly took place, and Thomas Stanley, having obeyed the Lord Keeper's direction to ascertain "what liking the said parties shall have of each other," duly certified to the Lord Keeper that the couple liked each other well enough and were content to marry. On November 8, the

[11] 1 *Law Review* (1845) p. 282.

De Ventre Inspiciendo

Lord Keeper accordingly made a final decree for the delivery
of Margaret to Edward's father, to the end that the couple
should be married. This, however, was subject to a proviso
that if Margaret changed her mind she was to be delivered
back into the custody of her own father.[12]

In days past, the family provided the law with many an
analogue. "Certaintie is the mother of quietnesse and repose."[13]
Again, "In truth justice is the daughter of the law, for the law
bringeth her forth."[14] So also "Trusts are children of equity;
and in a court of equity they are at home—under the family
roof-tree, and around the hearth of their ancestor."[15] There
was also a taste for asserting unusual human relationships.
Thus it was said that in a manner it was possible for a man to be
his own grandfather and for a woman to be her own grandmother. Suppose a widower and his son to intermarry with a
widow and her daughter, the widow as bride of the son and the
daughter as bride of the widower. The son then becomes the
stepfather-in-law of his father, and so the step-grandfather-in-
law of his father's children, including himself; and correspond-
ingly for the daughter.[16] Perhaps such intermarriages seem
improbable; but humanity being what it is, who can assert their
impossibility?

---

[12] 2 Camp.L.CC. 233, citing Reg.Lib.A. 1573, p. 71.
[13] Co.Litt. 212a; and see *ante*, p. 135.
[14] Co.Litt. 142a.
[15] *Kupferman* v. *McGehee*, 63 Ga. 250 at 256 (1879), *per* Bleckley J.
[16] See (1858) 5 *Notes and Queries* (2nd ser.) 454, 504.

Nul Home en Engleterre

A SERIES of statutes [1] kept alive whatever rights John Dutton of Dutton in the County of Chester and his heirs and assigns might have by royal charter, prescription or otherwise in the County Palatine and the County of the City of Chester. The language varies from a vague generality to a more specific claim to the right to license minstrels. The origin of the claim seems to have been as follows. "*Randall Blundeville*, Earl of *Chester*, towards the latter End of the Reign of King *Richard* I, being suddenly besieged by the *Welsh* in the Castle of *Ruthelent* in *Flintshire*, sent to his Constable of *Cheshire*, one *Roger Lacy* (for his Fierceness surnamed *Hell*) to hasten with what Force he could to his Relief,

"It happened to be on *Midsummer-Day*, and a great Fair then held at *Chester*; whereupon *Roger* immediately got together a great lawless Mob of Fidlers, Players, Coblers, and the like, and marched instantly towards the Earl; and the *Welch* perceiving a great Multitude approaching, raised the Siege and fled.

"The Earl being thus freed, comes back with his Constable to *Chester*; and in Memory of this Service, by a Charter grants to *Roger Lacy* and his Heirs, Power over all the Fidlers, Letchers, Whores, and Coblers in *Chester*.

"About the latter End of the Reign of King *John*, or Beginning of King *Henry* III, *Roger Lacy*, being dead, his Son, *John Lacy*, by the following Deed, granted to one *Hugh Dutton* his Steward, and to his Heirs, the Rule and Authority over all the Letchers and Whores in the County, viz.

'Know all Men present and to come, that I *John*, Constable of *Chester*, have given and granted, and by this my present Charter have confirmed to *Hugh de Dutton* and his Heirs, the Government of all the *Letchers* and *Whores* of

---

[1] 14 Eliz. 1, c. 5, 1572, s. 42; 39 Eliz. 1, c. 4, 1598, s. 10; 43 Eliz. 1, c. 9, 1601, s. 2; 1 Jac. 1, c. 25, 1604, s. 1; 17 Geo. 2, c. 5, 1744, s. 29.

all *Cheshire*, as freely as I hold that Government of the Earl, saving my Right to me and my Heirs.'

" Though the original Grant makes no Mention of giving Rule over Fidlers and Minstrels, yet antient Custom has now reduced it only to the Ministrelsey; for probably, the Rout, which the Constable brought to the Rescue of the Earl, were debauched Persons drinking with their Sweet-hearts at the Fair, the Fidlers that attended them, and such loose Persons as he could get.

" In the 14th *Henry VII* a *Quo Warranto* was brought against *Lawrence Dutton* of *Dutton*, Esquire, to shew why he claimed all the Minstrels of *Cheshire* and the City of *Chester* to appear before him or his Steward at *Chester*, yearly, on the Feast of *Saint John Baptist*, and to give him at the said Feast, four Flaggons of Wine and a Lance, and also every Minstrel then to pay him Fourpence Halfpenny, and why he claimed from every Whore in *Cheshire*, and the City of *Chester*, exercising her Trade, Fourpence, to be paid yearly at the Feast aforesaid. To which he pleaded Prescription." [2]

The outcome of the writ is not stated, but at least in some degree Lawrence Dutton seems to have triumphed. For in 1679 it was said that " The Heirs of the said *Hugh Dutton* enjoy the same Power and Authority over the Minstrelsy of *Cheshire*, even to this Day, and keep a Court every Year upon the Feast of *St. John Baptist* at *Chester*, being the Fair-Day, where all the Minstrels of the County and City do attend and play before the Lord of *Dutton* upon their several Instruments; he or his Deputy then riding through the City, thus attended, to the Church of *St. John Baptist*, many Gentlemen of the County accompanying him, and one walking before him in a *Surcoat* of his *Arms*, depicted upon *Taffata*; and after Divine Service ended, holds his Court in the City, where he or his Steward renews the old Licences granted to the Minstrels, and gives such new ones as he thinks fit, under the Hand and Seal of himself or his Steward, none presuming to exercise that Faculty there,

[2] T. Blount, *Fragmenta Antiquitatis* (2nd ed. 1784) p. 298.

without it. But now this Dominion or Privilege is by a Daughter and Heir of *Thomas Dutton*, devolved to the Lord Gerard of *Gerard-Bromley* in *Staffordshire*." [3] The process whereby whores and letchers were somewhat unexpectedly transmuted into minstrels remains unexplained; at least the grievance of the world of music must be less than it would have been had the conversion proceeded in the reverse direction.

One may turn to beggars and churls. First, the beggar. "An hungry beggar espying daintie cheere in a cookes shop, hasted thither, and being set down, did eat a small piece of his own bread, and incontinentiy receiued such wonderful comfort by the sweet smell of the cookes cates and sauces, whereof he tasted no bit, that he confessed, that his eager stomacke was as well satisfied therewith, and had as good a repast, as if he had indeed stuffed his paunch with the best cheere there: which the cooke hearing, straightwaies with a sterne countenance bids the poore caytife pay for his breakefast, whereat the simple guest was mightily amazed, and the craftie cooke so much the more earnest, insomuch that this poore man and the cooke were content therein to abide the award of him that should next passe by: no sooner was the submission made, but thither cometh a most notorious naturall foole, to whom as their iudge, they rehearsed the matter, which being heard, the Ideot caused the poore man to put so much mony betweene two basons as the couetous cooke exacted, and to shake them in the cookes hearing: which done, this arbitrator awarded, that as the cooke had fed the poore man with the only smell of cates, so the poore man should pay him therfore with the only sound of his coine, which sentence was highly approued of all the hearers." [4]

Next, the churl. There was once "a couetous churle, who sorrowed extremely, for that hee had lost a purse with one and twenty angels [5] in it. But an honest man hauing found the same, of meere conscience deliuered it to the same churle, who not once thanking him that was the bringer, fals to account his coine, and finding only xx angels in the purce, with great rigour

[3] *Ibid.*, at p. 302.
[4] W. West, *Symboleography*, Part II (1606) p. 164b.
[5] An angel had a value which varied between 6s. 8d. and 10s.

exacted the od angel, and because the honest man denied the
finding therof, he conuented him before a Magistrate of a corporation, whose wealth and authoritie farre exceeded his wit (as
in such places commonly happeneth, for that affection and
simplicitie be their ordinarie Electors.) The plaintife sweareth,
they were one and twentie angels in the purse which hee lost:
the defendant, that there were onely twentie in that which hee
found: Whereupon the Magistrate pronounced, that the purse
found was not the plaintifes, and therefore adiudged him to
restore unto the defendant the purse with twenty angels, leauing
the plaintife to good fortune for the finding againe of his purse
with one and twenty angels. I thinke a man may trie a
thousand fooles in the like cases, before he receiue the like
sentence." [6]

The bounds of humanity to those of ancient days at times
seem strange to modern eyes. " If the Testator make thee his
Executor, or do bequeath unto thee any Legacy conditionally,
if he shall have no Issue, and afterwards his Wife do bring forth
a Monster, or mis-shapen Creature, having peradventure a Head
like unto a Dog's Head, or to the Head of an Ass, or a Raven,
or Duck, or of some other Beast or Bird: Such monstrous
Creature, though it should live, (as commonly none do) yet it is
not accounted amongst the Testator's Children: For the law doth
not presume that Creature to have the Soul of a Man, which hath
a Form and Shape so strange and different from the Shape of
a Man. For by the Law of this Realm, if the Wife be delivered
of a Monster, which hath not the Shape of Mankind; this is no
Issue in Law. But although the Issue hath some Deformity in
any Part of his Body; yet if he hath human Shape, this sufficeth.
. . . As having six Fingers on either Hand; or on the contrary,
wanting some of the ordinary Members, as having but one
Hand, or one Foot: Such Creature is not excluded, but is to
be accounted for the Testator's Child. What if there be Duplication of notable Members, as to have four Arms, or two
Heads, or Disorder in the principal Members, as the Face stand-

[6] W. West, *loc. cit.*

ing backwards, or in the Breast? In this Case I suppose much to be attributed to the Discretion of the Judge." [7]

The unquestionably human were nevertheless sometimes remarkable in their achievements. In 1839, one " David Elwin Colombine, a solicitor practising in London, and acting as a money scrivener and bill-broker," [8] began to cohabit with one Amy Miles. They " sent the usual wedding cards as if just married " [9]; and over two years later a daughter was born to them. When in 1847 insolvency pressed them hard, they belatedly resorted to the desperate device of marriage, having prudently first executed a marriage settlement of all the husband's property, " with a very few and trifling exceptions." [10] How few and trifling these were may be judged from the fact that the settlement included the whole of the furniture and fixtures of the house in which they lived, " including the most minute articles, such as pieces of India matting, tooth-brush, &c. The settlement also included other articles: paintings in the dining and drawing-rooms, a turning lathe by Holtzappfel, a carriage, wearing apparel, jewelry, china, linen, coal in the cellar, twelve dozen of old Madeira and bottles of spirits, French wine, &c., in the wine cellar, plants in the greenhouse, Newfoundland dog and kennel, &c." [11]

Two days after the settlement was made, the marriage was celebrated; and on the nuptial day the parties exercised a joint power of appointment under the settlement in favour of their daughter, then aged five; but the daughter took subject to the right of her mother for life to hold and enjoy the settled property, and receive the income. Difficulties nevertheless came thick and fast. " Mr. Colombine had negotiated among his clients several bills of exchange for Lord Cantilupe,[12] to the amount of £5,000, and had received from the noble lord the amount due upon such bills, but neglected to repay those persons who had contributed the loan "; and in addition to his obliga-

[7] *Swinburne on Testaments* (6th ed. 1743) p. 305.
[8] *Colombine* v. *Penhall* (1853) 1 Sm. & G. 228 at 229.
[9] *Ibid.*, at p. 238.
[10] *Ibid.*, at p. 235.
[11] *Ibid.*, at p. 234.
[12] Probably Viscount Cantelupe, the heir to the Earldom de la Warr.

tions to these and other creditors, he was overdrawn at one of his banks to the extent of £922.[13] The trustees of the settlement, too, had refused to act; and bankruptcy proceedings were soon taken. Litigation then broke out all round, in the Court of Review, before Knight-Bruce V.-C., before Lord Denman C.J. and a special jury in the Court of Queen's Bench, and before Wilde C.J. and a special jury in the Court of Common Pleas.[14]

Finally, a bill and cross-bill came before Stuart V.-C.; and the creditors alleged that the settlement was fraudulent and void. Part of the evidence which was relied upon to show fraud was a draft of a settlement found among the husband's papers. This " purported to be a settlement between Henry Edward Lloyd and Agnes Miles, widow, comprised the same property, declared the same trusts, and specified one of the same trustees—the names of the other two being represented as A.B. and C.D. It was approved by counsel in January 1846, a year before the marriage. Mr. Colombine explained that the fictitious names used in the draft were employed to conceal the real parties from the pupils in the chambers of the conveyancer by whom the draft was settled." [15]

Stuart V.-C. expressed no opinion about this ingenious contention. He considered, however, not only the state of indebtedness of Mr. Colombine when he married, but also the extent of the property settled and the trusts of the settlement in favour of his wife. " Every article necessary for continuing his establishment, so as to live in comfort, is put at her disposal for her separate use, with a power when she pleased to appoint in his favour, or in favour of anyone else. So that, by the operation which the settlement would have, Mr. Colombine, living with this lady as his wife, might continue to have the enjoyment of the property." [16] And so the settlement was duly held fraudulent and void, Madeira, plants, dog, kennel, tooth brush and all, down to the last lump of coal in the cellar.[17]

One may turn to schools. Two eighteenth-century reports

[13] *Colombine* v. *Penhall, supra*, at p. 237.
[14] *Ibid.*, at pp. 236, 237.
[15] *Ibid.*, at p. 238.
[16] *Ibid.*, at p. 255.   [17] See also *Penhall* v. *Elwin* (1853) 1 Sm. & G. 258.

show how relatively dull they have become today. The reports are brief. " The Court was moved for leave to file an information against the defendant, who was about fifteen years old, and a scholar at Winchester-School, for assaulting, beating, and challenging, one Eyres, a clergyman, who was then second master of that school, for no other cause, but that the said schoolmaster reproved the defendant for something done at school. A rule was made for the defendant to shew cause." [18] The other report is a little more complex. " An indictment was against several of the boys of Christ's-Hospital, for a riot upon the prosecutor.

" It was proved that two of them beat her, and that the rest only hallooed.

" Holt, Chief Justice. As many as hallooed are abettors, and therefore principals in the case.

" But the jury acquitted all but two, whereupon the plaintiff's counsel desired they should be all acquitted; for two alone cannot be guilty of a riot, but there must be three at least, and battery cannot be found upon this indictment." [19]

Another sad story is a century earlier. " Two boyes did contend and fight near unto their houses, and the one stroke the other, so he did bleed; who went and complained to his father, who having a rod with him, came to the other boy, and beat him; upon which he died And the opinion of the whole Court was, that it was not murder." [20]

Girls, too, will be girls. " Upon a motion for leave to bring a book into Court, for the conversion of which an action of trover was brought, it appeared; that the book, entitled Memoirs of a Woman of Pleasure,[1] had been lent by a bookseller to some young ladies at a boarding school; that the defendant's wife, who was mistress of the school, took it from them and sent it to the bookseller, with a request that it might not be again lent to the young ladies; and that the book being afterwards found in the possession of one of the young ladies, the defendant's wife took

[18] R. v. *Sir Charles Holloway* (1724) 8 Mod. 283.
[19] *Anon.* (1701) 12 Mod. 509.
[20] *Royley & Dormer's Case* (1612) Godb. 182.
[1] Probably John Cleland's notorious *Fanny Hill, or the Memoirs of a Woman of Pleasure*: see G. R. Scott, *Into Whose Hands* (1945) pp. 143–145; N. St. John-Stevas, *Obscenity and the Law* (1956) p. 25.

it from her and kept it. A rule was made to shew cause, why, upon bringing the book into Court, the proceedings should not be stayed; and it is probable, that the plaintiff thereupon agreed to drop his action; for the Court never heard any more of the rule." [2]

On the qualities of man, many dicta are to be found. " Secret charities are often, if not uniformly, a genuine index of the real character of the donor." [3] " Masterly inactivity may be prudence to one man, desperate rashness to another." [4] Yet as Holmes J. once said, " No man can go far who never sets down his foot until he knows that the sidewalk is under it." [5] Human failings play a full part. In determining whether or not wages paid by a local authority to some of its employees were excessive, Scrutton L.J. pointed out that " Good faith is not in my view sufficient by itself; some of the most honest people are the most unreasonable; and some excesses may be sincerely believed in, but yet quite beyond the limits of reasonableness." [6] So too it has been said that " Obstinacy is the strength of mind of a weak person " [7]; and " A man once broken in will does not readily, if ever, recover from the breaking." [8] Again, " A self-made man usually hasn't made much " [9]; yet " We can forgive a man the defects of his qualities, if only he has the qualities of his defects." [10]

Temptations abound. " It is common knowledge that nothing is more alluring than the expectation of receiving large returns on small investments." [11] Yet " One is not incompetent, within the meaning of the statute, to manage one's affairs because one is lacking in the sagacity that makes for success in busi-

[2] *Catling* v. *Bowling* (1753) Sayer 80.
[3] *Applegate* v. *McFadin*, 20 S.W. 2d 396 at 398 (1929), *per* Baugh J.
[4] *Re Liverpool Household Stores Association Ltd.* (1890) 59 L.J.Ch. 616 at 618, *per* Kekewich J.
[5] *The Occasional Speeches of Justice Oliver Wendell Holmes* (ed. M. de W. Howe, 1962) p. 157 (a speech made on December 3, 1902).
[6] *R.* v. *Roberts, ex p. Scurr* [1924] 2 K.B. 695 at 712 (reversed *sub nom. Roberts* v. *Hopwood* [1925] A.C. 578).
[7] Sir Reginald Poole, (1934) 13 *Bell Yard* 34 at 36.
[8] *Malinski* v. *New York*, 324 U.S. 401 at 428 (1945), *per* Rutledge J.
[9] *Per* Holmes J., H. B. Phillips, *Felix Frankfurter Reminisces* (1960) p. 11.
[10] *Per* Holmes J., cited by Learned Hand J., *The Spirit of Liberty* (1954) p. 270.
[11] *Durland* v. *United States*, 161 U.S. 306 at 313 (1896), *per* Brewer J.

ness." [12] Nor are the universities immune. H. J. Laski once observed of the Cambridge don that " He cultivates his little garden; but I don't think he experiments enough with new seeds." [13] The score was balanced by H. G. Wells' description of the Oxford don as " a person who lies in wait to wreak his vengeance on the footnotes of the book that he had hoped to write." [14] Mercifully, recollection is selective. " Memory spreads a floor of light from summit to summit of our experience, across which our vision moves easily and uninterrupted. Between them there lie broad valleys wrapped in darkness, and many men wrapped in sleep. But we see them not." [15]

Women, of course, play their full part. Masculine incompetence in judging feminine age was as firmly established six centuries ago as it is today, when there is often the added hazard of resolving the sex as well. When in 1376 counsel tried to persuade the court to judge by inspection whether or not a woman was of full age, the Bench was prudent. " Il n'ad nul home en Engleterre que luy adjudge a droit deins age ou de plein age, car ascun femes que sont de age de xxx. ans, voile apperer d'age de xviii. ans." [16] At times chivalry is a little muted. " Maude at the relevant date was 39 years old and was still unmarried. According to the evidence she was attractive, and it was regarded by those who knew her as surprising that she had not married. A photograph, taken in the pattern of her age, was exhibited, at which we did not look but Mr. Buckley told us that had we done so we might have been disappointed." [17]

The law has usually moved more slowly than the times. Thus some thirty years back a court in South Africa was concerned with the benefits conferred upon women by the Senatus

---

12 *In the Matter of Case*, 214 N.Y. 199 at 203 (1915), *per* Cardozo J.
13 1 *Holmes-Laski Letters*, p. 460.
14 *Ibid.*, at p. 465. I have revised this a little (". . . a book he hoped to write.").
15 Holmes J., *The Occasional Speeches of Justice Oliver Wendell Holmes* (ed. M. de W. Howe, 1962) p. 1.
16 Y.B. 50 Edw. 3, Hil., pl. 12, fo. 5 at fo. 6, *per* Cavendish J. (" There is no man in England who can rightly judge whether she is an infant or of full age, for all women who are thirty years old wish to appear to be eighteen.").
17 *Re Tacon* [1958] 2 W.L.R. 66 at 72, *per* Lord Evershed M.R. (The report in [1958] Ch. 447 at 456 omits the latter part of the third sentence.)

Consultum Velleianum, concerning suretyship and loans by women on behalf of others. Even to this there were limits. " One of the incongruities of this inconsequent age is the fact that women, while enjoying full rights of citizenship, including that of making or marring policies of the State as effectively as any male, are able in their private affairs to invoke a defence based on their innate fecklessness and incapacity and so avoid liability in respect of obligations which they have deliberately assumed. We have to administer the law as we find it. On the other hand our law in this respect is a recognised anomaly, a fossil left over from a dispensation in which it was deemed reprehensible in a woman to engage in anything so masculine as the undertaking of suretyship. We should not be astute, therefore, to extend the scope of the legal benefits by analogy or to restrict the operation of statutes designed to curtail them. . . . Ulpian tells us that [the Senatus Consultum] was passed to protect women against *sexus imbecillitatem*." [18]

Some years later there were muted echoes of this approach in Oregon. Statute had provided that " No person other than a person of the male sex shall participate in or be licensed to participate in any wrestling competition or wrestling exhibition." [19] A lady wrestler, Miss Jerry Hunter, was prosecuted for violating this statute. The information ran as follows: " Jerry Hunter is accused by W. L. Bradshaw, District Attorney, by this Complaint of the Crime of Person of Female Sex Participating in Wrestling Competition and Exhibition committed as follows: The said Jerry Hunter on the 25th day of October, A.D., 1955, in the County of Clackamas and State of Oregon, then and there being a person not of the male sex, to-wit: of the female sex, did then and there unlawfully and wilfully participate in a wrestling competition and wrestling competition [20] and wrestling exhibition, said act of defendant being contrary to the statute in such cases made and provided, and against the peace and dignity of the State of Oregon." The accused stood upon her con-

---

[18] *Van Rensburg* v. *Minnie*, 1942 O.P.D. 257 at 259, 262, *per* van den Heever J. (" the weakness of their sex ").
[19] ORS 463.130.
[20] *Sic.*

stitutional rights, and contended that the statute operated as an unjustifiable denial to women of the equal protection of the laws.

The Supreme Court of Oregon, however, held the classification to be reasonable, and upheld the conviction. " In addition to the protection of the public health, morals, safety, and welfare, what other considerations might have entered the legislative mind in enacting the statute in question? We believe that we are justified in taking judicial notice of the fact that the membership of the legislative assembly which enacted this statute was predominately masculine. That fact is important in determining what the legislature might have had in mind with respect to this particular statute, in addition to its concern for the public weal. It seems to us that its purpose, although somewhat selfish in nature, stands out in the statute like a sore thumb. Obviously it intended that there should be at least one island on the sea of life reserved for man that would be impregnable to the assault of woman. It had watched her emerge from long tresses and demure ways to bobbed hair and almost complete sophistication; from a creature needing and depending upon the protection and chivalry of man to one asserting complete independence. She had already invaded practically every activity formerly considered suitable and appropriate for men only. In the field of sports she had taken up, among other games, baseball, basketball, golf, bowling, hockey, long distance swimming, and racing, in all of which she had become more or less proficient, and in some had excelled. In the business and industrial fields as an employe or as an executive, in the professions, in politics, as well as in almost every other line of human endeavor, she had matched her wits and prowess with those of mere man, and, we are frank to concede, in many instances had outdone him.

" In these circumstances, is it any wonder that the legislative assembly took advantage of the police power of the state in its decision to halt this ever-increasing feminine encroachment upon what for ages had been considered strictly as manly arts and privileges? Was the Act an unjust and unconstitutional discrimination against woman? Have her civil or political rights been unconstitutionally denied her? Under the circumstances, we think not."[1] Doubtless Dr. Johnson would have approved. His view was that "Nature has given women so much power that the law has very wisely given them little."[2]

There are other authorities, too, which deny any complete approximation between man and woman. "The fact that women may now have achieved the virtues that men have long claimed as their prerogatives and now indulge in vices that men have long practiced, does not preclude the States from drawing a sharp line between the sexes, in such matters as the regulation of the liquor traffic."[3] Again, "It will need more than the Nineteenth Amendment[4] to convince me that there are no differences between men and women, or that legislation cannot take those differences into account."[5] "The truth is that the two sexes are not fungible; a community made up exclusively of one is different from a community composed of both; the subtle interplay of influence one on the other is among the imponderables."[6]

In some ways, however, little has changed. When a tenant was sued for possession of the demised premises on the ground that he had sub-let them without the landlord's consent, Harman L.J. observed that there was adequate evidence admissible against the tenant to show that a Miss Blank was a sub-tenant of his. He added: "She was a versatile lady. She was his mistress; she managed the property for him; and she paid him rent, either in meal or in malt—I do not know which. She had a rent book. One would have liked to see what was in it."[7] The familiar forensic phrase "in meal or in malt" is old in the law. Its origin (or an origin) may perhaps lie in a statute of 1576 which prohibited certain colleges and schools from granting leases of their lands except on the terms that at least one third of the rent

[1] *State of Oregon* v. *Hunter*, 300 P. 2d 455 at 457 (1956), *per* Tooze J.
[2] Letter dated August 18, 1763, to Rev. Dr. Taylor, (1882) 5 *Notes & Queries* (6th ser.) 342.
[3] *Goesaert* v. *Cleary*, 335 U.S. 464 at 466 (1948), *per* Frankfurter J.
[4] Prohibiting the denial or abridgment of the right to vote on account of sex.
[5] *Adkins* v. *Children's Hospital of the District of Columbia*, 261 U.S. 525 at 569 (1923), *per* Holmes J., dissenting (a minimum wages case).
[6] *Ballard* v. *United States*, 329 U.S. 187 at 193 (1946), *per* Douglas J.
[7] *Finkle* v. *Strzelczyk* [1961] E.G.D. 261 at 265 (omitted from the reports at [1961] 1 W.L.R. 1201; [1961] 3 All E.R. 409).

should be reserved and paid in corn, "that is to say, in good wheat after six shillings and eight pence the quarter or under, and good malt at five shillings the quarter or under," or in the money equivalent.[8] In times of depreciating currency, this did much to maintain the income of the schools and colleges in question.[9]

Versatility apart, it is perhaps in the adroitly feathered verbal shaft that one of woman's superlatives still lies. On meeting the wife of Holmes J. shortly after his appointment to the United States Supreme Court, President Theodore Roosevelt inquired kindly whether she had met many people in Washington. Quite a number of Congressmen's wives had called upon her, she replied politely, though with a veiled note in her voice. "You found the ladies pleasant?" the President inquired. Her answer is celebrated: "Washington is full of famous men and the women they married when they were young."[10]

Brute creation has been said to bring out the best in man; but few rules are absolute. In 1956 there was spirited litigation before Harman J. about the affairs of the National Canine Defence League. The main issue was the validity of the election of the chairman and members of the council of the League at the annual general meeting in 1954. A far from happy situation had resulted from a combination of inept rules, internal dissension, unsatisfactory procedure, and the attendance at the meeting of many non-members of the League as the result of what was called "The Hampton Court plot."[11] As the learned judge said, "this case bristles with so many irregularities that one does not know where to begin."[12] During the argument, counsel[13] said that the meeting had gone on from 2.30 p.m. until 6.30 p.m.

"*His Lordship.* No cups of tea?

"*Counsel.* The irony was that tea was ordered and was on

---

[8] 18 Eliz. I, c. 6, 1576, s. 1.
[9] See M. Dewar, *Sir Thomas Smith* (1964) p. 185.
[10] C. D. Bowen, *Yankee from Olympus* (1944) p. 362.
[11] *Currie* v. *Moore* [1956] *The Times* June 14, *per* Harman J.
[12] *Ibid.*
[13] Geoffrey Lawrence, Q.C. (afterwards Lawrence J.).

the agenda, but it was never served. That gives your Lordship some indication . . .

"*His Lordship.* Of the extreme acrimony of the situation, no tea!" [14]

In giving judgment declaring all the elections void, Harman J. said that in the course of the somewhat protracted hearing of this unhappy suit, there had occurred to him a little poem by Isaac Watts which he had been forced to learn in the nursery:

> " Let dogs delight to bark and bite,
>   For God hath made them so;
> Let bears and lions growl and fight,
>   For 'tis their nature too.
> But, children, you should never let
>   Such angry passions rise;
> Your little hands were never made
>   To tear each other's eyes." [15]

Oddly enough, Serjeant Hayes had cited this verse to Lord Campbell C.J. almost exactly a century earlier,[16] and in the same year W. F. Allen J. had quoted it in a judgment in New York.[17] It is improbable that Eliot J. would have been a member of the League even if it had existed in his day; for it was he who in 1520 uttered the infamous condemnation " Chien est un vermiñ." [18] Doubtless the League would have trained its members' dogs to make, whenever passing the judge's house, the appropriate canine gesture of disdain.

Propinquity may be a blessing or a curse. Lord Sorn once observed that the case before the court " affords a good illustration of the saying that ' good fences make good neighbours,' because it has clearly demonstrated the contrary proposition that bad fences make bad neighbours." [19] A landowner had shot a

---

[14] *Currie* v. *Moore* [1956] *The Times* June 12.
[15] *Currie* v. *Moore* [1956] *The Times* June 15. The verse appears in Isaac Watts' *Divine Songs for Children*, XVI, Against Quarrelling.
[16] *Emery* v. *Peake* (1856) R. Walton, *Random Recollections of the Midland Circuit* (1869) 171 at 175.
[17] *Wiley* v. *Slater*, 22 Barb. 506 at 508 (1856).
[18] *Filow's Case* (1520) Y.B. 12 Hen. 8, Trin., pl. 3, fo. 3 at 4.
[19] *Clark* v. *Syme*, 1957 J.C. 1 at 6.

trespassing sheep of his neighbour's. He had given due warning, but this was held to be no defence. " A misconception of legal rights, however gross, will never justify the substitution of the law of the jungle for rules of civilised behaviour or even of common sense." [20] The saying has an ecclesiastical application, too. " If nowhere else, in the relation between Church and State, ' good fences make good neighbors '." [1]

There are dangers, however, in neighbours (and others) being neighbourly; and the law recognises this. " It is the wise policy of the law, not to construe acts of charity, though continued and repeated for never so many years, in such a manner as to make them the foundation of legal obligation." [2] Indeed, " Nothing worse can happen in a free country than to force people to be churlish about their rights for fear that their indulgence may be abused, and to drive them to prevent the enjoyment of things which, although they are matters of private property, naturally give pleasure to many others besides the owners, under the fear that their good nature may be misunderstood. . . . However continuous, however lengthy, the indulgence may have been, a jury ought to be warned against extracting out of it an inference unfavourable to the person who has granted the indulgence." [3] It was Lord Selborne who " once said that if all men pressed their legal rights to the extreme limit on all occasions life would be unbearable." [4]

Lastly, one may turn from actuality to hypothesis. In rating cases, an important figure is the Hypothetical Tenant; for the rent that he would be prepared to pay under a yearly tenancy of

---

[20] *Ibid.*, at p. 5, *per* Lord Justice-General Clyde.

[1] *Illinois ex rel. McCollom* v. *Board of Education of School District No. 71, Champaign County, Illinois,* 333 U.S. 203 at 232 (1948), *per* Frankfurter J.

[2] *Steel* v. *Houghton* (1788) 1 Hy.Bl. 51 at 60, *per* Heath J., cited by Lord Selborne L.C. in *Neill* v. *Duke of Devonshire* (1882) 8 App.Cas. 135 at 156, where, as Lord Selborne observed at p. 138, there had been two actions and seven trials; in three, the juries had not agreed, in two they had held against the respondent and in two they had been in his favour. It was, after all, an Irish appeal.

[3] *Blount* v. *Layard* (1888) [1891] 2 Ch. 681n. at 691n., *per* Bowen L.J. See, *e.g., Behrens* v. *Richards* [1905] 2 Ch. 614 at 620.

[4] *Corelli* v. *Wall* (1906) 22 T.L.R. 532, *per* Swinfen Eady J. *Quaere* whether this was an imperfectly remembered reference to *Neill* v. *Duke of Devonshire, supra.*

the premises in question is a touchstone of the rateable value. In one case, a tenant sought a reduction in the rateable value of his house on the ground of its proximity to a railway. Mr. John Watson, F.R.I.C.S., sitting as the Lands Tribunal, said " This is no ordinary railway running behind a street of houses; it is a shunting yard of mammoth proportions. I believe the appellant when he complains of noise and smoke and dirt, and I am satisfied from my own observation that the noises are less penetrating when heard from the other side of the road. The back garden of the appeal property is only about 25 ft. long and the yard is immediately below. I find it difficult to believe that the appellant does not suffer more from smoke and dirt than the occupants of the houses opposite. Questioned by the Tribunal, the valuation officer said that if he personally had to choose between one side of the road and the other he would take a house on the west side so that he could see the trains. I intend no disrespect to an experienced valuer when I say that every small boy in the country would whole-heartedly agree with him. But the hypothetical tenant, if I correctly interpret the authorities, is no longer a small boy; he is to be considered as an adult person who like the Apostle Paul has put away childish things. I have little doubt, if he were invited to select a house in Lloyd Street, that in defiance of the younger members of his family, he would see that this shunting yard was as far away from him as possible." [5]

---

[5] *Forshaw* v. *Turner* [1957] LVC/520/1956, 1 at 3.

IV

Corpus Juris

Chaos and Old Night

SIMPLICITY has never been the dominant feature of fiscal legislation. "No other branch of the law touches human activities at so many points. It can never be made simple, but we can try to avoid making it needlessly complex."[1] "Elaborate machinery, designed to bring about a perfect equilibrium between benefit and burden, may at times defeat its aim through its own elaboration."[2] Yet "Taxes cannot be escaped 'by anticipatory arrangements and contracts however skilfully devised . . . by which the fruits are attributed to a different tree from that on which they grew.'"[3] Equally, "Solicitude for the revenues is a plausible but treacherous basis upon which to decide a particular tax case."[4] An argument based on analogies may be brushed aside. "This is simply to take the name of a well understood concept and assign that name as a label to something which in ordinary understanding never fell within such concept. By this process any exaction can be tortured into something else and then justified under an assumed name."[5] Even so, "Difficulties in applying the test of reason do not justify abandonment of reason,"[6] not least when "Looking backward it is easy to see that the line between the taxable and the immune has been drawn by an unsteady hand."[7]

---

[1] *Dobson* v. *Commissioner of Internal Revenue*, 320 U.S. 489 at 494 (1943), *per* Jackson J.

[2] *Stewart Dry Goods Co.* v. *Lewis*, 294 U.S. 550 at 576 (1935), *per* Cardozo J., dissenting.

[3] *Griffiths* v. *Commissioner of Internal Revenue*, 308 U.S. 355 at 358 (1939), *per* Frankfurter J., citing *Lucas* v. *Earl*, 281 U.S. 111 at 115 (1930), *per* Holmes J.

[4] *Arrowsmith* v. *Commissioner of Internal Revenue*, 344 U.S. 6 at 11 (1952), *per* Jackson J., dissenting.

[5] *Wisconsin* v. *J. C. Penney Co.*, 311 U.S. 435 at 449 (1940), *per* Roberts J., dissenting.

[6] *Capitol Greyhound Lines* v. *Brice*, 339 U.S. 542 at 556 (1950), *per* Frankfurter J.

[7] *United States* v. *County of Allegheny*, 322 U.S. 174 at 176 (1944), *per* Jackson J.

During the argument of one tax case [8] Viscount Simonds observed " The subject is excessively complicated. Going home yesterday I kept asking myself: who said ' chaos and old night ' and in reference to what? " [9] The answer lies in Milton's *Paradise Lost* [10]:

> " Sonorous metal blowing martial sounds:
> At which the universal host up sent
> A shout that tore hell's concave, and beyond
> Frighted the reign of Chaos and old Night."

Some years earlier South African thoughts had turned to the same passage in a quite different context. " The general maintenance of law and order is of infinitely greater importance than mere rights of particular individuals to recover possession of their property. If it becomes an established practice for the Court to fail to enforce a spoliation order because it was made to appear that in the ultimate result the rightful owner of the property in dispute would be injured in his enjoyment of that property, we should very soon find that the slender paradise our toil has gained for us of an ordered community had been lost and the dreadful ' reign of chaos and old night ' would be upon us." [11]

Lord Sumner expressed his views about income tax statutes with accustomed clarity. " It is a most wholesome rule that in taxing the subject the Crown must show that clear powers to tax were given by the Legislature. Applied to income tax, however, this is an ironical proposition. Most of the operative clauses are unintelligible to those who have to pay the taxes and in any case derive such clarity as they possess from the judges, who have interpreted them. After the puzzle has been solved no doubt the answer seems clear and the solution is arrived at as a matter of construction. The question is always what is the meaning of the words of the statute? If they have none there is no need to

8 *Inland Revenue Commissioners* v. *Wood Brothers (Birkenhead) Ltd.* [1959] A.C. 487.
9 S.C. [1958] *The Times* Nov. 5.
10 Book I, lines 540–543.
11 *Greyling* v. *Estate Pretorius*, 1947 (3) S.A. 514 at 517, *per* Price J.

invoke the proposition, that the meaning must be clear." [12]
Even so, the argument of a revenue case must at times appear
curious to the beholder. Consider what to the uninitiated must
seem the inspired inconsequence of one section of an argument
in 1956 on rule 7 of the 9th Schedule to the Income Tax Act,
1952, in a case concerning the deduction of the expenses of a
trip to Australia by a business man and his wife.

> "*His Lordship.*—I suppose the word ' horse ' in the rule
> does not include an aeroplane?
> *Counsel.*—No, I think not.
> *His Lordship.*—It ought to, it is much the same thing.
> *Counsel.*—I think that it was put in for the relief of
> archdeacons." [13]

Judicial views on tax avoidance have not been constant.
" Any one may so arrange his affairs that his taxes shall be as
low as possible; he is not bound to choose that pattern which
will best pay the Treasury; there is not even a patriotic duty to
increase one's taxes." [14] This is so even though " It costs something to be governed." [15] " No man in this country is under
the smallest obligation, moral or other, so to arrange his legal
relations to his business or to his property as to enable the Inland
Revenue to put the largest possible shovel into his stores. The
Inland Revenue is not slow—and quite rightly—to take every
advantage which is open to it under the taxing statutes for the
purpose of depleting the taxpayer's pocket. And the taxpayer
is, in like manner, entitled to be astute to prevent, so far as he
honestly can, the depletion of his means by the Revenue." [16]
Even so, " The fact that the incidences of income taxation may
have been taken into account by arranging matters one way
rather than another so long as the way chosen was the way the

---

[12] *Brown* v. *National Provident Institution* [1921] 2 A.C. 222 at 257.
[13] *Maclean* v. *Trembath* [1956] 1 W.L.R. 437, as reported [1956] *The Times*
March 16: *per* Roxburgh J. and Heyworth Talbot Q.C.
[14] *Helvering* v. *Gregory*, 69 F. 2d 809 at 810 (1934), *per* Learned Hand J.
[15] *Merrick* v. *N. W. Halsey & Co.*, 242 U.S. 568 at 587 (1917), *per* McKenna J.
[16] *Ayrshire Pullman Motor Services* v. *I.R.C.* (1929) 14 T.C. 745 at 763, *per*
Lord Clyde.

law allows, does not make a transaction something else than it truly is." [17]

Nevertheless, "There are few greater stimuli to human ingenuity than the prospect of avoiding fiscal liability. Experience shows that under this stimulus human ingenuity outreaches Parliamentary prescience." [18] Accordingly, it has been said that "For years a battle of manoeuvre has been waged between the legislature and those who are minded to throw the burden of taxation off their own shoulders on to those of their fellow subjects. In that battle the legislature has often been worsted by the skill, determination and resourcefulness of its opponents of whom the present appellant has not been the least successful. It would not shock us in the least to find that the legislature has determined to put an end to the struggle by imposing the severest of penalties. It scarcely lies in the mouth of the taxpayer who plays with fire to complain of burnt fingers." [19]

This is not territory abounding in the flawless. "Perfect equality and perfect uniformity of taxation as regards individuals or corporations, or the different classes of property subject to taxation, is a dream unrealized. It may be admitted that the system which most nearly attains this is the best." [20] "Systems of taxation are not framed, nor is it possible to frame them, with perfect distribution of benefit and burden. Their authors must be satisfied with a rough and ready form of justice. This is true in special measure while the workings of a novel method are untested by a rich experience. There must be advance by trial and error." [1] "Eccentricities of incidence are common, and perhaps inevitable, in every system of taxation. The future would have to be scanned with microscopical powers of vision to foresee and forestall every possible diversity." [2] Yet there are

[17] *Commissioner of Internal Revenue* v. *Wodehouse*, 337 U.S. 369 at 410 (1949), *per* Frankfurter J., dissenting.
[18] *Commissioners of Customs and Excise* v. *Top Ten Promotions Ltd.* [1969] 3 All E.R. 39 at 69, *per* Diplock L.J.
[19] *Lord Howard de Walden* v. *Inland Revenue Commissioners* [1942] 1 K.B. 389 at 397, *per* Lord Greene M.R.
[20] *Taylor* v. *Secor*, 92 U.S. 575 at 612 (1875), *per* Miller J.
[1] *Louis K. Liggett Co.* v. *Lee*, 288 U.S. 517 at 586 (1933), *per* Cardozo J., dissenting.
[2] *Binney* v. *Long*, 299 U.S. 280 at 299 (1936), *per* Cardozo J., dissenting.

limits. " Systems of taxation need not achieve the ideal. But the fact that the Constitution does not demand pure reason and is satisfied by practical reason does not justify unreason." [3] " Might does not make right even in taxation." [4] So, too, " gross inequalities may not be ignored for the sake of ease of collection." [5]

In deciding whether for sur-tax purposes a dividend on ordinary shares declared " without deduction of income tax " must be grossed up, MacKinnon L.J. began his judgment in characteristic style. " There is only one thing about this case of which I am certain—namely, that it presents perhaps the most difficult problem I have ever attempted to solve. That difficulty results from three factors: first, the extraordinary obscurity under the Income Tax Acts of the relative positions of a company and its shareholders as to the payment of income tax; secondly, the increase of that obscurity resulting from the introduction of super-tax or sur-tax; and, thirdly, the difficulty of ascertaining with certainty the effect of the case that is said to be most relevant—namely, the decision of the House of Lords in *Neumann's* case.[6]

" The most illuminating explanation of the historical origin of the first-mentioned obscurity I find in the utterance of Lord Phillimore in *Bradbury* v. *English Sewing Cotton Co. Ltd.*[7] It was read by Lord Tomlin in *Neumann's* case,[8] and I need not read it again. But though that may give the reason for the obscurity, it does not dissipate it, still less does it excuse it. In fact a company is a persona distinct from its shareholders, and they are not even quasi partners. In the attempt to grope their way through the region of make-believe thus created various acute minds have been led into error. For instance, Swinfen Eady L.J. said: ' where the duty is paid by a company in respect

[3] *Capitol Greyhound Lines* v. *Brice*, 339 U.S. 542 at 552 (1950), *per* Frankfurter J., dissenting.

[4] *International Harvester Co.* v. *Wisconsin Department of Taxation*, 322 U.S. 435 at 450 (1944), *per* Jackson J., dissenting.

[5] *Stewart Dry Goods Co.* v. *Lewis*, 294 U.S. 550 at 560 (1935), *per* Roberts J.

[6] *Neumann* v. *Inland Revenue Commissioners* [1934] A.C. 215.

[7] [1923] A.C. 744 at 769.

[8] [1934] A.C. 215 at 223.

of the gains and profits of its business it pays the income tax as
agent for its shareholders': *Brooke* v. *Commissioners of Inland
Revenue*.[9]   And Scrutton L.J. (in the same case) said [10]: 'I am
quite clear that a company in paying income tax at the source at
any rate pays as agent of the shareholders.'   But Viscount Cave
(*Inland Revenue Commissioners* v. *Blott* [11]) says: 'Plainly a
company paying income tax on its profits does not pay it as agent
for its shareholders.'   And as the noble Viscount was delivering
his opinion in the House of Lords, I must take it that Swinfen
Eady L.J. and Scrutton L.J. were wrong.   Entertaining, as I do,
a lively expectation that I may be held to be wrong in this, or in
any judgment, about income tax, I comfort myself in anticipation
by the thought that I err in such distinguished company." [12]   In
due course the case went to the House of Lords; and in the event
MacKinnon L.J. proved sounder in prophecy than in law.[13]

Arguments as well as judgments may yield to the pressures
of the subject.   In one case it was decided that a building society
was liable to income tax under Schedule D on weekly payments
of interest on the loans which they made.   The opening shot in
the judgment of Lord Esher M.R. was the sentence "I think I
ought to express my admiration and wonder that so much argument has been used in this case, excellent argument, beautifully
put, but nothing to do with the case at all." [14]   After referring
to the facts of the case, he turned to the "most elaborate argument" of the appellant building society, represented by Dicey
Q.C. and Lord Robert Cecil, an argument, he said, "which I
cannot help thinking, notwithstanding what Lord Robert Cecil
has said to-day, was an unveiled sarcasm from beginning to end
upon the decision of this Court, in a case [15] which has already
been tried, a decision come to by myself, and not only by me;

9 [1918] 1 K.B. 257 at 267.
10 *Ibid.*, at p. 270.
11 [1921] 2 A.C. 171 at 201.
12 *Commissioners of Inland Revenue* v. *Cull* [1938] 2 K.B. 109 at 137.
13 *Cull* v. *Commissioners of Inland Revenue* [1940] A.C. 51.
14 *Leeds Permanent Benefit Building Society* v. *Mallandaine* (1897) 3 T.C. 577 at
590.   The report of the judgment in [1897] 2 Q.B. 402 at 408 is much
curtailed.
15 *Clerical, Medical and General Life Assurance Society* v. *Carter* (1889) 22
Q.B.D. 444; 2 T.C. 437.

that decision approved of and backed by Lord Justice Fry, and approved of and backed by Lord Justice Bowen, which put an interpretation and a rule of interpretation upon this section of Schedule D. But, says Lord Robert Cecil, and I think also his leader, over and over again, ' Yes, we are *bound* by that decision,' which he says in a tone indicating, ' We think it absolutely wrong, but we are *bound* by it; but we are only bound by it if the payment is said to be an annual payment, or is said not to be an annual payment,' whichever they please, and therefore, they adopt this astute mode of, what?—of setting aside the judgment of the Court by taking a distinction between the facts of that case and this case which is wholly immaterial. That is an ordinary artifice of argument; but is this Court, upon a difference of fact which seems to be wholly immaterial, to set aside the grounds of that decision by this Court? The grounds of that decision were the interpretation of this section; and those who say that decision is wrong have their remedy. Let them go to the House of Lords; and, if the House of Lords differs from this case, why, then we must take the same sarcastic view of their decision as Lord Robert Cecil does of ours—we may say, of this decision, ' Yes, we are *bound* by it, because it is a decision of the House of Lords,' meaning thereby, when we do speak in that way, that we think that the House of Lords is absolutely wrong; but they have got autocratic power to do what they think right and proper without appeal." [16]

One case concerned the liability of a professional cricketer to income tax on collections made by him from the spectators of Lancashire League cricket in respect of his meritorious performances. Harman J., who held him not liable,[17] began his judgment by saying: " This case has been an unconscionable time a-trying. I have listened with a patience which, I am afraid, has worn more thin as the hours succeeded one another, to a very nice exercise in dialectic by both Counsel who have addressed me; and what is the subject matter on which they have spent so much forensic skill? £20.

[16] *Leeds Permanent Benefit Building Society* v. *Mallandaine, supra,* at p. 591.
[17] Reversed by the Court of Appeal: [1955] Ch. 284, *infra.*

" The Crown comes here by leading Counsel to assure to itself the right to strike out from [18] the Income Tax return of a professional cricketer a sum of between £40 and £50, which he picked up in the year in the cricket season of 1951 while serving as professional with the East Lancashire Cricket Club in the Lancashire League.

" I seem to have observed lately, though I hope I am mistaken, a tendency on the part of the Crown to spend time catching the financial sprat while the mackerel swims free in the ocean; it is easy enough to make these demands and often difficult enough to decide whether the demands are right, but I cannot help thinking it would be more profitable to the general body of the taxpayers if those more elusive gentry were investigated who, to the wrath of many law-abiding citizens, appear to pay less tax than they ought. It is said that this is a test case, but I do not think the test is a very large one. There were, as I understand it, around 16 professionals playing in the Lancashire League. Those 16 occasionally get a collection on a Saturday afternoon. The taxation of such trifles will hardly pay the legal expenses of a case of this sort." [19]

The difficulty, however, was that nearly fifty years earlier the House of Lords had held [20] that in normal circumstances the Easter offerings to the clergy were subject to income tax in their hands. In the Court of Appeal the cricketer thus lost the judgment in his favour, though Evershed M.R. was moved to say of the decision of the House of Lords that " With the income tax at the present rate, it might perhaps appear startling that those who on a particular Sunday—and that one of the most significant in the Christian Year—contribute to the collection in their church, should be rendering unto Caesar nearly half their contributions." [1]

Startling consequences are, of course, no monopoly of the fiscal world. Yet it is there that those consequences often appear in a simple and dramatic form. Thus in one case in 1825 the

[18] *Sic*; *quaere* whether " strike out from " ought not to be " require to be included in."
[19] *Moorhouse* v. *Dooland* (1954) 36 T.C. 1 at 7.
[20] In *Blakiston* v. *Cooper* [1909] A.C. 104.
[1] *Moorhouse* v. *Dooland* [1955] Ch. 284 at 299.

plaintiff claimed an account, and the defendant's answer did not set out the account. " The Defendant swore, that his Reason for not setting out the Account, was, that it was so voluminous, that the Stamps to the Schedule would alone cost £29,000." [2] In consequence, the court ordered the defendant to deposit his books of account in the Master's Office. This was, indeed, but an early stage in a case destined to proceed (if that be the right word) in the Master's Office for some twenty-five years.[3]

Illegality poses a number of tax problems. Money which an employee has embezzled from his employer has been held by the Supreme Court of the United States not to be taxable income of the employee: for he is legally liable to repay the money, and despite the liability to tax of many classes of unlawful gains,[4] " moral turpitude is not a touchstone of taxability." [5] Again, during the years of Prohibition, a bootlegger contended that the Fifth Amendment, which is directed against compulsion to self-crimination, entitled him to refrain from making an income tax return; and in the Circuit Court of Appeals he succeeded. But the Supreme Court would have none of it. " It would be an extreme if not extravagant application of the Fifth Amendment to say that it authorized a man to refuse to state the amount of his income because it had been made in crime. . . . It is urged that if a return were made the defendant would be entitled to deduct illegal expenses such as bribery. This by no means follows, but it will be time enough to consider the question when a taxpayer has the temerity to raise it." [6]

In Canada, the question whether a prostitute's professional earnings are subject to income tax has been raised and decided. The lady appealed against assessments for four successive years for $2,495.56, $4,366.02, $7,916.05 and $8,825.67 respectively. What was questioned was not the exactitude of the assessments (down to the last precise cent), but the principle: could the State

[2] *Roe* v. *Gudgeon* (1815) G.Coop. 304; and see *Rowe* v. *Gudgeon* (1811) 1 V. & B. 331n.; (1813) 1 V. & B. 331. See also *post*, p. 283.
[3] W. H. Bennet, *Select Biographical Sketches* (1867) p. 113.
[4] See *Commissioner of Internal Revenue* v. *Wilcox*, 327 U.S. 404 at 411 (1946), *per* Burton J., dissenting.
[5] *Ibid.*, at p. 408, *per* Murphy J.
[6] *United States* v. *Sullivan*, 274 U.S. 259 at 263, 264 (1927), *per* Holmes J.

soil its hands with the fruits of an avocation that was *malum in
se?* The answer was Yes, it could and it would; the source
mattered not.[7]

The consequences of this decision were predictable. In 1964
the Exchequer Court of Canada was called upon to determine
which of the expenses of running a " call girl business " in
Vancouver were deductible from the gross income for the purposes of income tax.[8] In 1960 the activities of the respondent,
who was the sole proprietor of the business, " came under the
surveillance of dedicated and efficient members of the morality
squad of the Vancouver police who, after secret and careful preparation, arrested the respondent at her home on the evening of
November 10, 1960, and seized a voluminous amount of documents." [9] The respondent and seven call girls were all convicted
and sentenced to imprisonment; and in addition certain tax
calculations and assessments were made. The respondent
admitted the figures of gross income, but objected to the dis-
allowance of certain expenses. In evidence, she said that she
had " expressed the view to the officers of the Taxation Division
that it was incongruous that the government should seek to live
on the avails of prostitution ' [10]; but it was held to be abundantly
clear that earnings from illicit businesses were subject to tax.

The business was highly organised. A telephone switch-
board was staffed by two or sometimes three girls " who worked
in shifts from 11.00 a.m. to 7.00 a.m." [11]; there was a system of
recording how long each girl was engaged on each assignation
(the rate being $25 an hour); and there were arrangements for
sending assistance to any girl who seemed to be in difficulties.
The girls accounted for 50 per cent. of their fees to the respondent, who bore the loss on all dishonoured cheques, and discharged all legal expenses in defending any girl who was
arrested. For 1960, the gross income was assessed at nearly
$81,000, and the expenses at over $59,000, leaving a net revenue

[7] *No. 275* v. *Minister of National Revenue* (1955) 13 *Tax Appeal Board Cases*
279.
[8] *Minister of National Revenue* v. *Eldridge* [1965] 1 Ex.C.R. 758 (Cattenach J.).
[9] *Ibid.*, at p. 760.
[10] *Ibid.*, at p. 766.
[11] *Ibid.*, at p. 763. Doubtless the shifts were temporal rather than sartorial.

of over $21,000; but the respondent claimed that further expenses of some $22,000 ought to have been allowed, thus producing a net loss of exactly $336.33. The position in 1959 was similar, though a little less bleak; an assessed net profit of over $24,000 ought really to have been a mere $4,500, she said.

In the result, the respondent established some $8,000 out of the $22,000 further expenses for 1960, but only some $3,000 out of $20,000 for 1959. The claim for the remainder failed, in the main not because the items were inadmissible as deductions but because the respondent had failed to prove that the payments had in fact been made. There were various claims for the rent of apartments and other places of business; for $1,000 a year said to have been paid to an employee of the telephone company for revealing whether the business telephone was being tapped; for protection fees ($9,000 in 1959 and $7,500 in 1960) paid to law enforcement authorities whom the respondent not surprisingly declined to identify; for liquor given to officials of the civic administration ($2,600 in 1959 and $2,000 in 1960); for counsel's fees for defending two of the call girls ($1,925: these payments were allowed); for $1,000 paid in 1959 under " an arrangement with certain men possessed of physical strength and some guile, which they exercised when set to extricate a girl from difficulty " [12] (of which only $100 was held to have been proved); for $6,400 paid to an agent for providing bail bonds when the respondent and the girls were arrested ($1,000 was disallowed as having been paid for the respondent herself); and for $500 paid for purchasing the entire issue of a periodical called *Flash*, containing a story which the respondent (wrongly, as the court held) considered scurrilous and detrimental to her business. No difficulty arose about the expenses of providing the entire company of girls for the entertainment of a client's guests on a weekend yachting cruise on one occasion, and for a " Penthouse party " on another. Once establish the principle of taxing the profits of sinful enterprises, and there follows the unedifying spectacle of the court being obliged to investigate in detail not only the wages of sin but also the extent to which the expenses

[12] *Ibid.*, at p. 773.

of being sinful may legitimately be claimed in making net the gross. Yet is it better that, as in England, immoral earnings should in effect be tax free?

No doubt it is a far leap from brothels to sea walls; but all is grist for the tax-gatherer. In one case it was held that the income tax allowance for making or repairing sea walls [13] applied only to expenditure for the preservation of land in its existing state and did not extend to an outlay in reclaiming land. In his judgment Lord Esher M.R. considered a number of possibilities. " Supposing that the land had been agricultural land, and by reason of the shifting of the River Ribble, which is always shifting (the River Ribble is worse than a woman, it is always shifting), the water threatened to come in upon the agricultural land, why, then you would make a wall to protect that land. But here you did not make the wall to protect the land, you made it to alter the land as it was into some other land." [14] It was also Lord Esher (then merely Brett L.J.) who, when confronted with the question whether certain buildings containing a court house and police station were liable for income tax, coined what is now one of the best-known phrases in the law of rating. " In my opinion, these buildings considered as land are land which cannot, under any circumstances that we have a right to consider, have any annual value whatsoever; they are struck with sterility by statute." [15]

In the United States, there is " a system of taxation by confession. That a people so numerous, scattered and individualistic annually assesses itself with a tax liability, often in highly burdensome amounts, is a reassuring sign of the stability and vitality of our system of self-government. What surprised me in once trying to help administer these laws was not to discover examples of recalcitrance, fraud or self-serving mistakes in reporting, but to discover that such derelictions were so few." [16] It was in the Supreme Court that Marshall C.J. once said " The

[13] Income Tax Act, 1853, s. 37. See now Income and Corporation Taxes Act, 1970, s. 76.
[14] *Hesketh* v. *Bray* (1888) 2 T.C. 380 at 383.
[15] *Coomber* v. *Justices of Berks* (1882) 52 L.J.Q.B. 81 at 89 (reported in variant form, 10 Q.B.D. 267 at 282); affirmed, 9 App.Cas. 91.
[16] *United States* v. *Kahriger*, 345 U.S. 22 at 36 (1953), *per* Jackson J.

power to tax involves the power to destroy." [17]   But over a century later Holmes J. made a significant qualification: " The power to tax is not the power to destroy while this Court sits " [18]; and, added Frankfurter J. fifteen years later, " The power to tax is the power to destroy only in the sense that those who have power can misuse it." [19]

It was in the United States that certain fiscal advantages flowed from having a multiplicity of partners in a business. One result was that lawyers were sometimes called upon to draft a partnership agreement with the name of a new partner left blank " awaiting his expected birth so that sex and name could then be supplied." [20]   In one case the partners were husband and wife and their four children, aged seven, five and two years, and three months, respectively. Part of the evidence given by the wife at the hearing read as follows—

" Q. No, do you participate in the management of the business of the LaSalle Livestock Company?
A. Well, I have been producing partners.
Q. Beg pardon.
A. I have been too busy producing partners, so far." [1]

Lawyers in the United States also enjoy the pleasures of operating a complex system of taxation within a multitude of diverse jurisdictions. When Mr. Edward Green died in 1936, he left a net estate of a little over 36 million dollars. Nearly half of this became payable to the United States for death taxes. In addition, the States of Texas, Florida, New York and Massachusetts each claimed that he had died domiciled in that State and so was liable to the death taxes of that State, amounting very approximately to five million dollars in each State. On this footing the total liability exceeded the net estate by some one-and-a-half million dollars. The United States Supreme

[17] *M'Culloch* v. *The State of Maryland*, 17 U.S. 316 at 431 (1819).
[18] *Panhandle Oil Co.* v. *Mississippi ex rel. Knox*, 277 U.S. 218 at 223 (1928), dissenting.
[19] *Murdock* v. *Pennsylvania (City of Jeannette)*, 319 U.S. 105 at 137 (1943), in a dissent.
[20] R. E. Paul, 65 Yale L.J. 483 at 521 (1956), citing Surrey and Warren, *Federal Income Taxation*, p. 846 (1954 ed.).
[1] *Ibid.*, citing *Redd* v. *Commissioner*, 5 CCH Tax Ct.Mem. 528 (1946).

Corpus Juris

Court accepted jurisdiction, and held that the deceased had died domiciled in Massachusetts, and that Texas, Florida and New York had no claim.[2] Except in cases such as these, the "full faith and credit" clause of the Constitution[3] seems to preclude any federal intervention where two or more States each levy death taxes on the inconsistent footings that the deceased died domiciled in that State.[4] If, say, Texas had made no claim against Mr. Green's estate, all save some three-and-a-half million dollars would have vanished in death taxes; but the Texan last straw, instead of breaking the camel's back, was not only *felo de se* but also lifted the burdens that Florida and New York had sought to impose, and thereby transmuted a deficit of one-and-a-half million dollars into a credit of some thirteen-and-a-half million dollars. Suppose Texas had faltered in making its claim: would it have been the fiduciary duty of Mr. Green's executors to revive the flagging Texan spirits, giving aid and encouragement? Might it not have paid Florida and New York to offer Texas a share of the booty (if they lawfully could) for abstaining from boarding the overloaded craft? No doubt there is an answer; but so far it seems to lie *in gremio legis*.[5]

[2] *Texas* v. *Florida*, 306 U.S. 398 (1939).
[3] Article IV, s. 1.
[4] See *Worcester County Trust Co.* v. *Riley*, 302 U.S. 292 (1937); *Riley* v. *New York Trust Co.*, 315 U.S. 343 (1942); R. H. Jackson J., *The Supreme Court in the American System of Government* (1955) p. 42.
[5] "In the bosom of the law."

Save Honour

" The commercial world bases its transactions, not upon the hypothesis of fraud, but upon the hypothesis of honesty." [1] " We are not called upon to act in business as if every man with whom we come into relation is a thief, and therefore men's actions are not to be judged by a standard of unbelief in professional honesty." [2] When it was suggested by one judge that a banker ought to investigate the validity of each indorsement of a cheque or other bill, Lord Macnaghten said " That is hardly a practical suggestion. A banker so very careful to avoid risk would soon have no risk to avoid." [3] But there are limits. " Experience is not sufficiently uniform to raise a presumption that one who has the means of paying a debt will actually pay it." [4]

The tales in the reports are unending. A label which described a mixture that contained no product of the grape as " Compound Ess Grape " (meaning " Compound Essence of Grape ") was not unexpectedly held to contravene a Food and Drugs Act: for " the statute enjoins truth; this label exhales deceit." [5] Again, there was a time when the Koke Company of America began to sell a drink called " Koke," and also used the name " Dope " for its product; and in due course the Coca-Cola Co. obtained an injunction in the District Court against the use of each name. On appeal, this was reversed, but then there was a further appeal to the Supreme Court of the United States.

The defendant contended that the plaintiff's product, both in its trade mark and in its advertisements, falsely represented that it contained cocaine, so that the court ought not to aid the plaintiff. " Of course a man is not to be protected in the use of a device the very purpose and effect of which is to swindle the

[1] *Easton* v. *London Joint Stock Bank* (1886) 34 Ch.D. 95 at 115, *per* Bowen L.J.
[2] *Marsh* v. *Joseph* [1897] 1 Ch. 213 at 246, *per* Lord Russell of Killowen C.J.
[3] *Governors and Company of the Bank of England* v. *Vagliano Brothers* [1891] A.C. 107 at 157.
[4] *Atwood* v. *Scott*, 99 Mass. 177 at 178 (1868), *per* Chapman C.J.
[5] *United States* v. *Schider*, 246 U.S. 519 at 522 (1918), *per* McReynolds J.

public. But the defects of a plaintiff do not offer a very broad ground for allowing another to swindle him. The defence relied on here should be scrutinized with a critical eye. The main point is this: Before 1900 the beginning of the good will was more or less helped by the presence of cocaine, a drug that, like alcohol or caffein or opium, may be described as a deadly poison or as a valuable item of the pharmacopoea according to the rhetorical purposes in view. The amount seems to have been very small, but it may have been enough to begin a bad habit and after the Food and Drug Act of June 30, 1906, c. 3915, 34 Stat. 768, if not earlier, long before this suit was brought, it was eliminated from the plaintiff's compound. Coca leaves still are used, to be sure, but after they have been subjected to a drastic process that removes from them every characteristic substance except a little tannin and still less chlorophyl. The cola nut, at best, on its side furnishes but a very small portion of the caffein, which is now the only element that has appreciable effect. That comes mainly from other sources. It is argued that the continued use of the name imports a representation that has ceased to be true and that the representation is reinforced by a picture of coca leaves and cola nuts upon the label and by advertisements, which however were many years before this suit was brought, that the drink is an ' ideal nerve tonic and stimulant,' &c., and that thus the very thing sought to be protected is used as a fraud.

" The argument does not satisfy us. We are dealing here with a popular drink not with a medicine, and although what has been said might suggest that its attraction lay in producing the expectation of a toxic effect the facts point to a different conclusion. . . . The coca leaves and whatever of cola nut is employed may be used to justify the continuance of the name or they may affect the flavor as the plaintiff contends, but before this suit was brought the plaintiff had advertised to the public that it must not expect and would not find cocaine, and had eliminated everything tending to suggest cocaine effects except the name and and the picture of the leaves and nuts, which probably conveyed little or nothing to most who saw it. It appears to us that it would be going too far to deny the plaintiff relief against a palpable fraud because possibly here and there an ignorant person might call for the drink with the hope for incipient cocaine intoxication. . . .

" The decree of the District Court restrains the defendant from using the word Dope. The plaintiff illustrated in a very striking way the fact that the word is one of the most featureless known even to the language of those who are incapable of discriminating speech. In some places it would be used to call for Coca-Cola. It equally would have been used to call for anything else having about it a faint aureole of poison." [6] And so the injunction was restored as to " Koke " and refused as to " Dope."

Other countries, other products. Early in the century a company selling " Bile Beans " sought in Scotland to enjoin another trader from selling as " Bile Beans " pills not of the company's manufacture; and well the company must have repented of its litigious venture. The Lord Justice-Clerk,[7] in dismissing the company's appeal, said " The evidence in this case discloses the history of a gigantic and too successful fraud. The two complainers who ask for an interdict do so to protect a business which they have brought to enormous proportions by a course of lying which has been persisted in for years. The scheme they formed was to delude the public into the belief that a valuable discovery had been made of a medical remedy hitherto known only to certain savage tribes in a distant part of the world but known to them for ages, and that the medicine had been prepared by the aid of ' the implements of modern scientific research,' and that ' the best laboratories and most modern plant ' had been requisitioned for compounding this wonderful Australian vegetable substance. The place of the discovery, the mode of the discovery, the discovery itself, the instruments of research, the laboratories, were all deliberate inventions, without any foundation in fact.

" The story was that a certain Charles Forde, who was declared to be a skilled scientist, had, while in Australia, noted the fact that the aborigines were markedly free from certain

[6] *Coca-Cola Co.* v. *Koke Co. of America*, 254 U.S. 143 at 145–147 (1920), *per* Holmes J.
[7] Sir J. H. A. Macdonald.

271

bodily ailments, and that by patient research and exhaustive investigation he had ascertained that this immunity was obtained by the use of a natural vegetable substance whose properties for cure of such ailments were extraordinary, and that as the result of his research this wonderful remedy was now given to the world. All this was in every particular undiluted falsehood. There was no such person as Charles Forde, no eminent scientist had been engaged in researches, no one had gone to Australia and learned of a time-proved native cure. The truth was that the complainers had formed a scheme to palm off upon the public a medicine obtained from drug manufacturers in America as being the embodiment of the imaginary Australian discovery by the eminent scientist Charles Forde. Accordingly, having got their supplies from the American drug dealer they proceeded to create a public demand by flooding this country and other countries with advertisements in the press, and by placards, leaflets, and pamphlets, in which the lying tale was repeated, often embellished with pictorial representations of the healthy savage and with pictures of the imaginary scientist duly bearded and begoggled, having the precious root pointed out to him by the Australian native.

" It was of importance in exploiting a fraud of this kind to get a catching name, and the only trace of discovery in the whole proceedings was that the complainer Fulford thought out the alliterative name of Bile Beans for Biliousness. . . . This name for which the complainers desire to have protection was the name chosen to designate the article about which all those lying statements were put forward in order to make a trade by inducing the public to buy the article as being what the complainers said it was, the article being one to which the description given and the historical statements made in regard to it were wholly inapplicable." [8] In the words of Lord Stormonth-Darling, " What the Lord Ordinary [9] well calls the ' foundation fiction ' of the discovery by an eminent scientist of a vegetable substance growing in Australia which had long ago enabled the natives of that

[8] *Bile Bean Manufacturing Co.* v. *Davidson* (1906) 8 F. 1181 at 1196, 1197.
[9] Lord Ardwell.

country to defy disease, and had at last been reproduced in the most convenient medicinal form as ' bile beans '—this flagrant piece of invention was no casual lapse into hyperbolical language, but was circulated systematically from the very inception of the trade, and plainly formed the basis on which the whole super-structure rested." [10]

The Lord Justice-Clerk also pointed out that " These state-ments were not of the mere puffing order, not of the ' never failing,' the ' incomparable,' the ' unique,' or the ' worth a guinea a box ' order, but were statements of alleged facts, carefully elaborated and intended to be accepted as facts, from which the public might draw a sound inference that the article sold would effect to the buyers what it had done for ages to another race in another part of the world. The purpose was not to catch those who listen to mere assertion about a thing, but to convince them that they were buying a drug which incontestable facts had demonstrated to be a valuable remedy. I agree with the Lord Ordinary in holding that the complainers, being engaged in per-petrating a deliberate fraud upon the public in describing and selling an article as being what it is not, cannot be listened to when they apply to a Court of justice for protection. It is their own case as brought out in the evidence which stamps their whole business with falsity. In bringing forward their case they were compelled to disclose, what otherwise might never have been known, and was not known to the respondent, that the business they sought to protect was tainted with fraudulent mis-representation. . . . No man is entitled to obtain the aid of the law to protect him in carrying on a fraudulent trade." [11]

In England, a Mr. Lewis made a secret profit out of forming a company called the Jubilee Cotton Mills Ltd., but lost much of what he made to an associate, Mr. Ernest Terah Hooley. When the liquidator sought to make Mr. Lewis account for the secret profit, he resisted. One argument on his behalf, said Lord Sumner, was that any shares in the company which came to him " bore so strongly the dubious imprint of Mr. Hooley's fingers,

[10] *Bile Bean Manufacturing Co.* v. *Davidson, supra*, at p. 1200.
[11] *Ibid.*, at pp. 1197, 1198.

that the resulting profit really was not fit to be transferred to the Jubilee Cotton Mills. I think this rather overlooks the object of the rule as to an agent's secret profits, which I take it is to check these breaches of duty by making them not worth while. No money could be more tainted than a bribe paid or promised to an agent to induce him to betray his master, yet both briber and bribee have to hand it over; after all, non olet." [12] On this and other grounds his defence failed. On the facts of the case, Mr. Lewis had still actually " got the profits of his promotion, sadly diminished, it is true. He did not cheat anybody; he was cheated himself. He is not exposed to any claims. Fortunately for himself his opponents have been otherwise dealt with. No contracts of his, tainted or not, have to be adopted or put in suit by the liquidator. Mr. Lewis simply wants to keep what he still has left and cannot quite see how to manage it. He accordingly fails to lay a foundation for these interesting arguments. He has been acquitted of all fraud and no one now charges him with any. By common consent he was Mr. Hooley's victim, not his accomplice, and, if the result of this is to deprive him of a possible opportunity of keeping his money at the cost of his reputation, he must console himself by reflecting that the price of a good name is far above rubies, and that he is not the first person who has had to cry ' all is lost save honour! ' " [13]

A somewhat different type of transaction ultimately confronted Scrutton L.J., delivering the third judgment in the Court of Appeal in 1916. He said that he desired, " in view of the importance to the public of the subject-matter of this case, to express my opinion in my own words. The only thing that has made me hesitate as to whether I should do so is that I am doubtful whether I can express my judgment in language of sufficiently judicial moderation in view of the facts of this case. Any judge who has heard criminal business in the city of London knows that one of the great evils of London at present is the system by which money-lenders lend money to clerks who have small salaries in offices in London, and, under the terror of telling

---

[12] *Official Receiver and Liquidator of Jubilee Cotton Mills Ltd.* v. *Lewis* [1924] A.C. 958 at 977 (" It does not stink ").
[13] *Ibid.*, at p. 979, *per* Lord Sumner.

their employers that they have lent such money, drive clerks to crime and inflict any amount of evil on their families. When sitting as a judge of the King's Bench Division in what is called their Saturday jurisdiction, when gentlemen bearing royal and noble names pass before one as plaintiffs lending money at very high rates of interest, I have seen a good deal of the ways of money-lenders, but it had not entered into my wildest imagination that any of them could have concocted a document of the nature of that which we have before us in this case, and I am glad that at last the Court has an opportunity of pronouncing an opinion upon it—to which from my experience of money-lenders I do not suppose they will pay any attention whatever.

" The case arises in this way : There is a Mr. Bunyan who is a clerk at a small salary in a London office; his salary is under £3 a week. He was in monetary difficulties; he was owing money to three money-lenders and to a solicitor. His only other debts were under £5 to two tradesmen. Mr. Horwood, the plaintiff, who describes himself as a builder, but who appears to be a registered money-lender, lent him money undertaking to pay off or compound with his creditors, and he lent him a sum of £42, which included £4 to himself, some £7 or £8 expenses of the loan, some £20 to pay off the money-lenders, and some £5 or £6 to pay off what I may call the legitimate debts. His loan was repayable by instalments of £2 a month including £30 for interest, but the whole sum to become payable immediately default was made in any instalment or any breach of the covenants to which I am about to refer; and he took as security the document that we have to consider. The document bound the debtor never to change his residence without the consent of the money-lender; it bound him never to change his employment without the consent of the money-lender; it bound him not to consent to a reduction of his salary without the consent of the money-lender; it bound him not to part with any of his property without the consent of the money-lender; it bound him to incur no obligations on credit without the consent of the money-lender, and to incur no obligation, legal or moral, without the consent of the money-lender, and it appears to me that it is not using overstrained or poetical language to say that it made this unfortunate man the slave of the money-lender." [14] The contract was accordingly held void. It was Lord Evershed M.R. who said of another contract "This contract is so one-sided that I am astonished to find it written on both sides of the paper." [15] Diplock J., too, once referred to a clause in a contract as being " an attempt, which only the size of the print in which it is set out prevents one calling blatant, to evade the provisions of section 8 (2) and (3) of the Hire-Purchase Act, 1938." [16]

Commercial documents cover a vast range. As the Bench has often pointed out, many a policy of marine insurance is " a very strange instrument." [17] "It is wonderful, considering how much property is at stake upon instruments of this description, that they should be drawn up with so much laxity as they are, and that those who are interested should not apply to some man whose habits of life and professional skill will enable him to adapt the words of the policy to the intention professed by the parties. In construing these instruments we must always look for what was the intention of the parties, without confining ourselves to a strict grammatical construction; for it is impossible in many instances so to construe them without departing widely from the object intended." [18] In one such case, neither a fine verbal distinction nor the citation of certain decisions on the Workmen's Compensation Acts received an enthusiastic welcome from Lord Sumner. "Of course perils of the sea are not the same as perils on the sea, but in law epigrams only dazzle, and as for decisions on the Workmen's Compensation Act, they shed even on that Act an illumination which is sometimes dim. In marine insurance we shall do better with the light of reason." [19]

In one case the issue was whether the shipowners were entitled to recover on a policy of marine insurance in respect of their ship *Arnus*, or whether it had been scuttled with their

14 *Horwood* v. *Millar's Timber & Trading Co. Ltd.* [1917] 1 K.B. 305 at 316.
15 *Per* Birkett L.J. in the Foreword to Stanley Jackson, *Laughter at Law* (1961) p. 10.
16 *Lowe* v. *Lombank Ltd.* [1960] 1 W.L.R. 196 at 205.
17 *Le Cheminant* v. *Pearson* (1812) 4 Taunt. 367 at 380, *per* Mansfield C.J.
18 *Marsden* v. *Reid* (1803) 3 East 572 at 578, *per* Lawrence J.
19 *P. Samuel and Co. Ltd.* v. *Dumas* [1924] A.C. 431 at 464.

privity. Bailhache J. found for the owners, but the Court of Appeal reversed this decision, and the owners appealed to the House of Lords. There, the Earl of Birkenhead regarded the case as " a particularly clear one." He referred to the judgment at first instance, and said " The second officer of the vessel was one Felipi Ybarra, of whom the learned Judge observes: ' He gave his evidence on commission, and repeated it here, and I was impressed with his demeanour and his frankness.' This impression was somewhat surprising, having regard to the fact that Felipi Ybarra gave no evidence before the learned Judge at all, and enjoyed therefore small opportunity of exhibiting either his demeanour or his frankness." [20]

After referring to certain of the facts, Lord Birkenhead observed that the plaintiff company which owned the ship " carried on its affairs in a pleasant family atmosphere. Its managing director was Juan de Longaray. He, his two brothers, and his ten step-children held the bulk of the 4,800 shares of 500 pesetas each issued by the company. On the night when the Arnus commenced her last voyage of all the only assets of the company were the ship and the sum of about £400. And there were outstanding liabilities in respect of loans amounting to 936,986 pesetas. The company was insolvent; there was not the slightest prospect of paying its creditors; if such indeed was its purpose. The intimate family atmosphere which was so striking a feature of the company is not altogether lost when we pass to consider the vessel. She was commanded by Thomas Enciendo. The captain was in a position somewhat singular in that he had no shares in the company. The first mate was Jose Ybarra. The second was Felipe Ybarra. Both these men were nephews and also step-sons of Longaray, the managing director. The chief engineer was one Gomeza, who held 80 shares in the company. Each of the Ybarras was the owner of 72. The enterprise had all the elements of co-adventureship.

" The voyage, and the loss of the ship which followed, presented remarkable incidents. The course from Vivero to Rotter-

---

[20] *Compania Martiartu* v. *Royal Exchange Assurance Corporation* (1924) 40 T.L.R. 669 at 670.

dam would, in normal circumstances, be laid by a competent navigator so as to pass clear of the dangers of Ushant. A course, in fact, was set which, if prolonged, would have taken the vessel ashore inside Armen Rock; a course altogether unexplained; out of the track of ships passing from Finisterre to Ushant; but presenting the advantage to anyone who had by good fortune foreseen the casualty, that it would bring the vessel nearer the fishing fleet south of Penmarch. This fleet, in fact, by a happy coincidence, picked up the crew when in their boats.

"On the night of April 27, in fine weather; with a smooth sea; little or no wind blowing; the vessel sank in deep water. The vessel did not actually founder for five hours after the crew had prudently taken to their boats. No attempt was made to attract attention or secure assistance by wireless or by rockets. To complete a singular chapter of maritime misfortune, we are assured that all the ship's logs and papers perished in an attempt which failed to launch the first boat. No evidence whatever was offered at the hearing of any casualty to which the sinking of the ship could be attributed except the influx of sea water. The second mate indeed says that he saw some wreckage. But his evidence is valueless because he evidently had not formed the view that the Arnus was struck by it. Other evidence there was none. I find myself, as I have already indicated, in complete agreement with all the Judges who have reached the conclusion that the vessel was scuttled. Mr. Justice Bailhache alone has taken a different view." The irresistible inference, he said, was that the owners were accomplices in the fraudulent destruction of the vessel.[1]

Lord Sumner pointed out that " Ships are not cast away out of lightness of heart or sheer animal spirits. There must be some strong motive at work and this is usually the hope of gain. In the present case there was no operative motive to lead the engineer and captain to sink the ship on their own account. The engineer, it is true, had 80 shares in the appellant company, but he is not shown to have had any knowledge of the state of the company's finances and insurances, such as would be requisite,

---

[1] *Ibid.*, at pp. 670, 671.

if he is to be taken to have had an eye to improving the value of his shares. The captain was not a shareholder at all. Both lost their effects and their employment, and both risked their lives while at sea and their liberty, I hope, when they got ashore. It is idle to suppose that they—strangers to one another as they were, and one of them quite recently unemployed—would have cast the ship away except at the instigation of others interested, since they had no motive of their own, and in the company we find a full interest, and an overwhelming motive. In their case and in theirs alone there was a golden prize in the case of complete success and complete insolvency if the ship was not got rid of on this very voyage. There was further full opportunity for arranging the plot with all the advantage given by the relation of employer and employee. Nothing was easier than to pass the necessary word before the ship left Bilbao, and it seems to me a matter of just and inevitable inference from the circumstantial evidence, of which the whole case is full, that the word was, in fact, passed by someone charged with the management of the company's affairs.

" We were told that the principal shareholders were rich and respectable men. Don Jesus de la Roca had a jute mill; Don Luis Leguizamon was brother to a Spanish senator; Mr. Longaray had been his college friend; and Bilbao thought highly of them all. I do not know if the proposition intended really was that rich and respectable men do not commit crimes, even for money, but that mariners and seafaring men do so and for nothing at all, but, at any rate, my experience does not bear it out. It is not necessary to name particular persons as the culprits, and as for generalities I am sure the loss of the ship, and of the action too, will bite deeper than any censure. I will only say that I think the decision of the Court of Appeal was right." [2]

On land, too, insurance policies have their temptations. In one case, two partners in a tailors' business insured their stock in trade against burglary. A burglary occurred, and the insurance company contested the claim on the ground that there had in fact been no stock in trade and no burglary. The arbitrator

[2] *Ibid.*, at p. 672.

279

rejected this defence, but in the course of the hearing it emerged that one of the partners had previously been refused a burglary policy by another insurance office. The insurance company then contested the claim on this ground; for in applying for the policy a proposal form had been filled in, and in answer to a question whether any company had refused to accept or renew " your burglary policy," nothing had been said about the refusal. This raised the question whether " your " was singular or plural: for while one partner had been refused a policy, both partners had not. When the case ultimately reached the House of Lords, Viscount Dunedin referred thus to the scene when the proposal was made: "On the one hand Mr. Cohen, agent for the insurance company, keen, as he was quite entitled and bound to be, to get business for the insurance company, and, on the other hand, this wretched little ladies' tailor of whom the arbitrator tells us that he could neither read or write and could only sign his name, and whose natural and best language was Yiddish and not English—surely an impar congressus. . . ." [3] Lord Dunedin was highly critical of the insurance company, but on the ground that the question had made it plain that the company regarded the point as material, and that as the contract was one *uberrimae fidei* the partners were bound to disclose the previous refusal,[4] he came to the conclusion, " with unfeigned regret," [5] that the claim failed. Lord Wrenbury added that he thought that the company's attitude was " mean and contemptible." [6]

Sometimes insurance is linked with alcohol. In 1881, a Scottish engineer who soon afterwards became Provost of the town of Johnstone, took out a life insurance policy. He answered two of the questions in the proposal form as follows " Are you temperate in your habits? Temperate "; and " Have you always been strictly so? Yes." Eight months later he was dead, with the primary cause of death certified as chronic hepatitis. The Scottish courts held that the insurers were liable on

---

[3] *Glicksman* v. *Lancashire and General Assurance Co. Ltd.* [1927] A.C. 139 at 142 (" An unequal confrontation ").
[4] *Ibid.*, at p. 144 (" of the utmost good faith ").
[5] *Ibid.*
[6] *Ibid.*

the policy; but the House of Lords reversed the decision. Lord FitzGerald, indeed, was moved to verse. " ' Temperate in habits' is a sentence to be interpreted, and though not to be taken in the Pythagorean sense of ' total abstinence,' yet seems to import abstemiousness, or at least moderation—

> ' The rule of " not too much,"
> By temperance taught.' "

After referring to the intemperate habits displayed by the deceased at meetings of the town council, and his election as Provost " in the hope that the responsibilities of office might produce reformation of habit," Lord FitzGerald observed that the cause of death was " confirmation strongly of the assured having fallen into that fatal habit which produces

> '. . . . all the kinds
> Of maladies that lead to death's grim cave
> Wrought by intemperance.' " [7]

The Registration of Business Names Act, 1916, has accomplished much in the world of business; but it has its difficulties. The Act requires all persons carrying on business otherwise than under their true surnames to register under the Act " within fourteen days after the firm or person commences business "; and similarly if any person carrying on business has changed his name.[8] Where, however, registration is required " in consequence of a change of name," this provision applies " as if for references to the date of the commencement of the business there were substituted references to the date of such change." [9] These provisions cannot easily be applied literally in the case of at least some changes of name. Even when aided by a deed poll, most changes of name are effected only by repute, and a new reputation cannot be acquired at a stroke. Further, there are difficulties in cases of past changes of name. If Smith changed his name to Brown in 1930, and begins to trade in 1958, how can he register within fourteen days of his change of name in 1930? If

---

[7] *Thomson* v. *Weems* (1884) 9 App.Cas. 671 at 697, 698.
[8] ss. 1, 5.
[9] s. 5.

he trades under the name of Brown, registration is required because although he trades under his new (and true) name, he has changed his name. If on the other hand he trades under the name of Smith, registration is required because he is not trading under his true name, though but for the change of name he would be, and so no registration would have been requisite; it is thus " in consequence of a change of name " that registration is required.

Commerce is ever increasingly the world of the corporation; and this is " a creature of the legal imagination." [10] " But it leads nowhere to call a corporation a fiction. If it is a fiction it is a fiction created by law with intent that it should be acted on as if true." [11] " The existence of a corporation is a fiction, but the very meaning of that fiction is that the liability of its members shall be determined as if the fiction were the truth." [12]

In discovering the intention of a corporation, many problems arise; for with no mind of its own, the corporation may have many servants, both high and low, and the state of mind of any of them may have to be imputed to the corporation.[13] In one action for rectification, Evershed M.R. was inclined to place less emphasis than counsel " upon the distinction between the Olympians at the board table and the more terrestrial bodies in other parts of the premises." [14] Further, " Companies, no doubt, are not conspicuous for generosity. Corporations, however easily they assimilate the more predatory human qualities, do not as easily acquire the higher attributes; and gratitude is not a feeling which we generally associate with joint stock activity." [15]

Some of the incidentals of commerce are unexpected. Butler, the famous conveyancer, was once instructed to prepare a deed of

[10] *State Tax Commission of Utah* v. *Aldrich*, 316 U.S. 174 at 186 (1942), *per* Jackson J., dissenting.
[11] *Klein* v. *Board of Tax Supervisors of Jefferson County, Kentucky*, 282 U.S. 19 at 24 (1930), *per* Holmes J.
[12] *E. Remington & Sons* v. *Samana Bay Co.*, 140 Mass. 494 at 501 (1886), *per* Holmes J.
[13] See *H. L. Bolton (Engineering) Ltd.* v. *T. J. Graham & Sons Ltd.* [1957] 1 Q.B. 159.
[14] *George Cohen, Sons & Co. Ltd.* v. *Docks and Inland Waterways Executive* (1950) 84 Ll.L.R. 97 at 112.
[15] *Commissioner for Inland Revenue* v. *Lunnon*, 1924 A.D. 94 at 96, *per* Innes C.J.

partnership between ten landowners who were engaging in a mining enterprise. He was told to include a provision that if any one or more of the partners advanced money to any other or others of them, the money lent should constitute a charge upon the share or respective shares of the borrower or respective borrowers. At that time any mortgage for an indefinite sum was liable to duty of £25,[16] and on this ground Butler advised his clients against inserting the proposed provision, because the stamp duty would be £90,720,000. For the property would have been subjected to " as many possible mortgages as there can be combinations of the number 10," and " $25 \times 2 \times 3 \times 4 \times 5 \times 6 \times 7 \times 8 \times 9 \times 10 = 90,720,000$." [17] A mathematical friend questions the arithmetic of this, and suggests that the true answer is $£25(3^{10} - 2^{11} + 1)$, which comes to a little under £1,500,000. Even so, Butler could well consider that he had earned whatever fee was charged for his advice.

Money, like all else, has become increasingly complex in the law. Modern conditions have brought about a situation in which a sovereign has three values. First, it has a face value of £1; secondly, the intrinsic value of the gold contained in it has a fluctuating value which in 1953 and 1954 varied from a little under £3 to considerably more than £3. Thirdly, as a market commodity a sovereign has an even higher value, uncertain in amount, based mainly on an overseas demand (particularly in the Middle East) for coins of an assured gold content and fineness. Thus at Lady Day, 1955, 1,900 sovereigns had a face value of £1,900, a value as gold of £5,610 6s. 1d., and a value as gold coins of £6,412 10s. 0d.

Accordingly, where a lease made in 1938 provided for the payment of rent at a rate of £1,900 a year " either in gold sterling or in Bank of England notes to the equivalent value," many questions arose when in 1953 the parties were at issue as to the precise amount payable; and the courts obligingly provided at least one judge to support each view.[18] Lord Goddard C.J. went the whole way with the landlords, and held that they were

[16] Stamp Act, 1815, s. 2, Sched., Pt. I.
[17] Charles Butler, *Reminiscences* (4th ed. 1824) vol. 1, p. 61; and see *ante*, p. 263.
[18] *Treseder-Griffin* v. *Co-operative Insurance Society Ltd.* [1956] 2 Q.B. 127.

entitled to payment on the third basis, that of the value of the gold coins. In the Court of Appeal Denning and Morris L.JJ. went the whole way with the tenants, and held that the landlords were entitled only to a sum of £1,900, the face value of the sovereigns. But Harman J. dissented, holding that the value of the gold content of 1,900 sovereigns was the amount recoverable. In rejecting Lord Goddard's view, he observed that " it would indeed be a bizarre result that the liability of an English lessee under a lease of English land should be measured by the cupidity of the unknown ruler of an oasis near the Persian Gulf." [19]

[19] *Ibid.*, at p. 163.

Nebuchadnezzar's Tree

THE law of property, so painfully evolved in England over the centuries, has not always met unqualified adulation. "It has been said that the law of land in countries under the Common Law of England is a ' rubbish-heap which has been accumulating for hundreds of years, and . . . is . . . based upon feudal doctrines which no one (except professors in law schools) understands '— and rather with the implication that even the professors do not thoroughly understand them or all understand them the same way." [1] There have even been accusations of tautology amongst the faithful. "If a man would, according to law, give to another an orange, instead of saying:—' I give you that orange,' which one should think would be what is called in legal phraseology ' an absolute conveyance of all right and title therein,' the phrase would run thus:—' I give you all and singular, my estate and interest, right, title, claim and advantage of and in that orange, with all its rind, skin, juice, pulp and pips, and all right and advantage therein, with full power to bite, cut, suck, and otherwise eat the same, or give the same away as fully and effectually as I the said A.B. am now entitled to bite, cut, suck, or otherwise eat the same orange, or give the same away, with or without its rind, skin, juice, pulp, and pips, anything hereinbefore, or hereinafter, or in any other deed, or deeds, instrument or instruments of what nature or kind soever, to the contrary in any wise, notwithstanding.' " [2] Even title deeds, those most venerated of documents, have been described by Lord Westbury as being "difficult to read, disgusting to touch, and impossible to understand." [3]

Feudalism had its full share of formalism. When a tenant made homage to his lord, "he shall be ungirt, and his head un-

---

[1] *Miller* v. *Tipling* (1918) 43 O.L.R. 88 at 97, *per* Riddell J. (not indicating the source of the quotation).
[2] A. Symonds, *Mechanics of Law-Making* (1835) p. 75.
[3] J. Willock, *Legal Facetiae* (1887) p. 420. See *Wroth* v. *Tyler* [1973] 2 W.L.R. 405 at 426.

covered, and his lord shall sit, and the tenant shall kneele before him on both his knees, and hold his hands joyntly together betweene the hands of his lord, and shall say thus: I become your man (Jeo deveigne vostre home) from this day forward of life and limbe, and of earthly worship, and unto you shall be true and faithfull, and beare to you faith for the tenements that I claime to hold of you, saving the faith that I owe unto our soveraigne lord the king; and then the lord so sitting shall kisse him." [4] Yet in feudal days the proprieties were scrupulously observed. " If a woman sole shall doe homage, she shal not say, I become your woman; for it is not fitting that a woman should say, that she will become a woman to any man, but to her husband, when she is married." [5]

One illuminating story [6] that appears from the Year Books concerns succession to land by the heir. Not infrequently in the middle ages the eldest son had been born before his parents married; sometimes he was allowed to succeed his father without objection,[7] but often he was not. Questions of the illegitimacy of living persons [8] were exclusively within the province of the ecclesiastical courts, so that as soon as the issue was raised in an action in the common law courts concerning the land, the common law courts were bound to send it for determination by the ecclesiastical courts, and to accept and apply the decision of those courts.

The trouble was that Church and State differed upon the rule of law to apply. By Canon law the eldest son was legitimated by the marriage, and this was the rule that, with modifications, Parliament was to enact in 1926 [9]; but when at Merton in 1235 the bishops had proposed that this should become the law of the land, all the earls and barons had answered with one voice that

[4] Litt. 85.
[5] Litt. 87.
[6] This is a shortened version of the account given by Dr. W. C. Bolland in *A Manual of Year Book Studies* (1925) pp. 89, 90, and in *Chief Justice Sir William Bereford* (1924) pp. 20–23.
[7] If he did, and held the land until his death, even the common law treated him as legitimated *quoad* the land: see F. E. Farrer (1917) 33 L.Q.R. 135; (1918) 34 L.Q.R. 27; and see C. Sweet (1918) 34 L.Q.R. 402.
[8] See (1917) 33 L.Q.R. 135.
[9] Legitimacy Act, 1926.

"*Nolunt leges Anglie mutare.*" [10]   Yet as the common law courts were bound to accept the certificates of the ecclesiastical courts on matters of illegitimacy, the result was that the King's judges were continually being forced to give judgments holding to be the lawful heir a son who by common law was a mere bastard. Not for the first time had procedure controlled substance.

How could the legal profession escape? The solution, when it came, was simplicity itself. Let the plaintiff utter no word of illegitimacy in his pleadings. Instead, let him plead quite simply that the defendant was born before the marriage of his parents. That was a simple question of fact, eminently suitable for determination by a jury, and overtly raising no issue for reference to the ecclesiastical courts. Once the jury had determined the fact, the court applied the law: not the canon law, but the common law that excluded the bastard eigné and held the mulier puisne to be the true heir. In short, the issue of general bastardy in the ecclesiastical courts was replaced by an issue of special bastardy before a jury.[11] The remedy for an unwelcome state of procedure controlling substance is often itself procedural.

Judgments on property law today have lost the touch of the picturesque that they once had. In commenting on the efficacy of a statute of 1489 [12] in making a fine a final determination of the rights of the various parties to the land concerned, Catline C.J. " compared the fine upon this Act to Janus, who, he said, was Noah, but the Romans occasionally called him Janus, and used to paint him with two faces, one looking backwards, in respect that he had seen the former world which was lost by the Flood, and the other looking forwards, in respect that he begun a new world commencing at the Flood, and proceeding from thence forwards, for which reason they call him Janus *bifrons*. And also he carried a key in his hand, signifying, by that key,

---

[10] Statute of Merton, 1235, c. 9 (" They were unwilling to change the laws of England ").

[11] See Pollock and Maitland, *History of English Law* (2nd ed. 1898) vol. 1, pp. 127, 128. (" Eigné ": elder. " Mulier puisne ": legitimate younger.)

[12] Statute of Fines, 1489 (4 Hen. 7, c. 24).

his power to renew the new world by his generation. So here this Act creates, as it were, a flood, by which all former rights before the fine shall be drowned by non-claim, for non-claim is the flood, and the fine begets a new generation, which is the new right, for the fine makes a new right, and is the beginning of a new world, which proceeds from the time of the fine downwards." [13]

In Ireland, even statute was not always a sure remedy. In one case, the Landed Estates Court had conducted a sale of land, and had duly executed a conveyance to the purchaser. Through some mistake of an official of the court, however, the conveyance included certain other land, the property of X, and the question was whether the Landed Estates Court could make an order requiring the purchaser to reconvey to X the land that had been X's. The Court of Appeal in Chancery held that this could not be done. In concurring with O'Hagan L.C., Christian L.J. expressed himself with emphasis. "The Landed Estates Court is the immediate successor of the Incumbered Estates Commission. The Incumbered Estates Act was passed at an abnormal time, with certain objects, political and social, which need not here be dwelt on. Towards those objects, the first and indispensable necessity was this—to sweep from the land of Ireland, at one stroke, that *incubus* of complicated title and incumbrance which had been a terror or a snare to intending purchasers, and by which a large part of the island was practically withdrawn from the land market.

"With this object a special (originally a temporary) tribunal was constituted, with powers hitherto unknown to the law, and especially shocking to the prepossessions of the British jurist. It was to be a great manufactory of brand-new titles. The grant of the Commissioners was so to work that, by a sort of conveyancing magnetism, it would draw out, not merely from the owner whose estate was under sale, or from whatever other persons might intervene as parties in the proceeding, but from the absent, the helpless, the infant, the married woman, the mentally imbecile, nay even the unborn, every particle of estate and

---

[13] *Stowel* v. *Lord Zouch* (1569) 1 Plowd. 353 at 369.

interest, legal or equitable, present or future, known or unknown, patent or latent, in the land expressed to be conveyed, and would concentrate the whole in the purchaser, freed from everything that the conveyance itself did not save. He was told that he would go forth with a title regenerated, purified from antecedents, and which itself should be the starting point for future derivation. And, to dispel all misgiving as to the impregnability of his position, there was added that wholly *unique* provision in the 49th section, till then without a parallel, I believe, in our law, by which, if there was anything that could be done or consented to by any human being, by which wrong could be turned into right, all Courts were enjoined to presume conclusively that such act had been done, or that such consent had been given.

"How this prodigious measure was received in this country, when it was brought forward twenty years ago, many of us are old enough to remember. Revolution,—confiscation,—a new Cromwellian settlement.—*experimentum in corpore vili* [14]— insult, which no Government would dare to offer to any other part of the empire; nor even to this, if men of weight or authority were in its high places:—these are the things which were thought and freely spoken at the time. Lord Brougham, no timid legislator in legal change, opposed the bill by reason of this very aspect of it—its menace to unguarded rights. But the bill became law. The Commission held its way. It was well and ably administered, as the political engine it was meant to be; not, however, without much havoc among incumbrancers and owners. How slow even the Judges of the day were to realize the portentous efficacy attached to the conveyances, is shown by their divisions in *O'Donnell* v. *Ryan*,[15] and *Errington* v. *Rorke*.[16] In 1859 the Parliamentary Title was made a permanent institution. A Court of higher *status* was constituted, and to it was confided the same extraordinary conveyancing potency which had belonged to the Commissioners of Incumbered Estates.

"To apply to cases of individual grievance, wrought in the working of such an engine as I have sketched, sentiments and

[14] "An experiment on a worthless body."
[15] (1854) 4 Ir.C.L.R. 44, *semble*.
[16] (1859) 7 H.L.C. 617.

language which might have been appropriate if confiscation had not been legalized, and to do so for the sake of setting up a jurisdiction for the redress of such grievances, though the distinctive policy of the measure required that, if unhappily permitted to occur, they should be absolutely irremediable, is simply to blind one's self alike to the legislation and to the history of the period. The present case brings out in strong relief the features of what I have ventured to designate as *legalized confiscation*." [17]

Statute is not the only source of unorthodox conveyancing. One of the more unusual dispositions of land took place on September 30, 1929, when the City of Oxford,[18] acting by commissioners, conveyed to an ancient tree the 1,256 square feet of land in which it stood, together with a house built on the land.[19] The tree, a large white oak believed to be over 200 years old, thus owns itself, if the conveyance be valid; and on this hypothesis many engaging questions arise. One fears, however, that in England the courts would unromantically hold such a deed to be a nullity. " If one covenant to stand seised to the use of Salisbury Plain, for the life of I.S. and after the remainder to A: it is a plain [20] case, that he in the remainder shall take presently." [1]

Trees have given rise to other difficulties. Holt C.J. once held that " if A plants a tree upon the extremest limits of his land, and the tree growing extend its root into the land of B next adjoining, A and B are tenants in common of the tree." [2] An earlier case where " les rootes prist nourishment in le terre de A & auxi de B " was decided similarly.[3] Yet between these two decisions lay another, in which a different view was taken. The action was for trespass *quare clausum fregit*, and the defendant " justifie pur ceo, que fuit un grand arbor quel cresce inter le close del' plaintiff & del' defendant, & que part del' roots de cest

---

17 *Re Tottenham's Estate* (1869) I.R. 3 Eq. 528 at 547. See Incumbered Estates Act, 1849; Landed Estates Court Act, 1858.
18 Newton County, State of Georgia, U.S.A.
19 *The Atlanta Journal* for November 20, 1960, printed a copy of the conveyance and a photograph of the grantee.
20 " Clear " would have done.
1 *Lord Paget's Case* (1589) 1 Leon. 194 at 195, *per* Manwood C.B.
2 *Waterman* v. *Soper* (1698) 1 Ld.Raym. 737.
3 *Anon.* (1622) 2 Roll.Rep. 255.

arbor extend into the close del' defendant, & que le arbor fuit nourished per le soile, & que le plaintiff succide le arbor, and carryed it away into his own close, & ceo sawed into boards, & le defendant entered & prist ascun del' boards, & carried eux away. . . ."[4] Here " it was considered that if a tree grows in A's close, though the roots grow in B's, yet the body of the tree being in A's soil, the tree belongs to him "[5]; and this view later prevailed.[6] The cases are perhaps reconcilable on the basis that the tree is owned by him on whose land the trunk stands, irrespective of any straying roots, and that it is only if the trunk stands athwart the boundary line that there is a tenancy in common.[7] The trunk is thus all, and the roots and their sources of nourishment mere red herrings.

Land has also proved a touchstone in defamation. Over three centuries ago, the words " Thou art a thief, and has stollen my dung " were held actionable.[8] This was so despite an argument that " dung " might mean " dung spread or scattered on the ground, which is parcel of the freehold, and then no felony may be committed of it," and not merely dung in a heap, which is a chattel and so the subject of larceny; for the initial words showed the sense. Even without them, Rolle J. held, the remaining words would have been actionable, for " dung in common parlance is understood of dung in a heap."[9] This authority might have helped in a later case in Ireland, where there was much argument whether a dung heap was real or personal property. On one side, an admirable argument was submitted to the court, demonstrating that the dung was realty. On the other side there was merely a farmer, appearing in person. " I'm puzzled indeed by all these strange words. But the lawyer says, fair play to him, that cows is personal property, and the hay they eat is personal property, and I ask your Honour, as one man to another, how, except for miracles, *personal property* can go on eating *personal* property and excreting *real property*."[10]

---

[4] *Masters* v. *Pollie* (1620) 2 Roll.Rep. 141.
[5] *Holder* v. *Coates* (1827) M. & M. 112 at 113, *per* Littledale J.
[6] *Ibid.*   [7] See *Lemmon* v. *Webb* [1894] 3 Ch. 1 at 20.
[8] *Yearworth* v. *Pierce* (1647) Aleyn 31; *sub nom. Carver* v. *Pierce* (1647) Sty. 66, 73.   [9] *Ibid.*, Aleyn at p. 32.
[10] Sir Edward Parry, *My Own Way* (1932) p. 250 (with minor revisions).

The transition to equity is, of course, by means of uses. The importance of uses, the predecessors of trusts, became so great that Periam C.B., speaking at the end of the sixteenth century, said in one case that " These uses have extended themselves into many branches, and are to be resembled to Nebuchadnezzar's tree [11]; for in this tree the fowls of the air build their nests, and the nobles of this realm erect and establish their houses, and under this tree lie *infinita pecora campi*,[12] and great part of the copyholders and farmers of the land for shelter and safety; and he said, if this tree should be felled or subverted, it would make a great print and impression in the land. And therefore it was convenient to repress the mischief after by Parliament, and not to have any retrospect to cases before." [13]

Today, equity has a popularity in some courts that is perhaps not altogether deserved. As Harman L.J. once said, " Equitable principles are, I think, perhaps rather too often bandied about in common law courts as though the Chancellor still had only the length of his own foot to measure when coming to a conclusion.[14] Since the time of Lord Eldon anyhow the system of equity for good or evil has been a very precise one, and equitable jurisdiction is exercised only on well-known principles. There are some who would have it otherwise, and I think Lord Denning is one of them. He, it will be remembered, invented an equity called the equity of the deserted wife.[15] That distressful female's condition has really not been improved at all now that this so-called equity has been analysed.

" Similarly I rather deprecate the attempt to urge the court on what are called equitable principles to dissolve contracts which are thought to be harsh, or which have turned out to be disadvantageous to one of the parties. It is pointed out in one of the cases cited to us yesterday (and Lord Nottingham's observation in *Maynard* v. *Moseley* [16] is still true) that: ' the Chancery

---

11 See Daniel iv, 10–12.
12 " Countless beasts of the field."
13 *Chudleigh's Case* (1595) 1 Co.Rep. 113b at 134b.
14 For the Chancellor's foot, see 1 Misc. 139, 140.
15 Subsequently held to be non-existent: *National Provincial Bank Ltd.* v. *Ainsworth* [1965] A.C. 1175.
16 (1676) 3 Swans. 651 at 655.

mends no man's bargain,' and I do not therefore see my way to call in aid equity to mend what may be an unfortunate situation and one which, if it calls for remedy, calls for aid by the legislature rather than by the justiciary."[17] On appeal, Lord Radcliffe observed that "'Unconscionable' must not be taken to be a panacea for adjusting any contract between competent persons when it shows a rough edge to one side or the other, and equity lawyers are, I notice, sometimes both surprised and discomfited by the plenitude of jurisdiction, and the imprecision of rules that are attributed to 'equity' by their more enthusiastic colleagues."[18]

One of the judicial comments in modern times that has attained a wide currency is that uttered by Harman J. about equity and childbearing.[19] Of this, Sir Raymond Evershed M.R. in 1953 wrote in an article in the *Sydney Law Review* that the aphorism "was quoted in the Press but I am unable (as is the learned Judge) to recall its context. Probably it was spoken during the argument on an interlocutory application. It is perhaps pertinent to this paper to note that the Judge doubts its originality, recalling some similar utterance by Lord Mansfield."[20] Some research shows that it was probably emitted in a case in 1951 concerning the power of the court to apportion, as between tenant for life and remainderman, the money involved on a sale or purchase of stock cum dividend or ex dividend.[1] Counsel was arguing that there existed no general equitable jurisdiction to apportion in such cases, whereat Harman J. observed "Equity is not to be presumed to be of an age past childbearing."[2] Lord Mansfield's contribution, however, still remains obscure. At least he could not claim the credit for the occasion a dozen years later when the House of Lords and a stroke of printer's genius transformed the dictum into a state-

[17] *Campbell Discount Co. Ltd.* v. *Bridge* [1961] 2 W.L.R. 596 at 605; cp. the report in [1961] 1 Q.B. 445 at 459. See also *post*, p. 333.
[18] *Bridge* v. *Campbell Discount Co. Ltd.* [1962] A.C. 600 at 626.
[19] See 1 Misc. 142.
[20] (1953) 1 Sydney L.R. 1, n. 1.
[1] *Re Maclaren's Settlement Trusts* [1951] 2 All E.R. 414.
[2] I am indebted to many members of the Bar, and ultimately to those engaged in this case, for suffering my inquiries with patience and an appearance of interest.

ment that equity was not presumed to be of an "age past childbeating." [3]

Even the claim of equity is not undisputed: the rival is the common law itself. In one appeal Fletcher Moulton L.J. objected that counsel's argument was supported by no precedent. Counsel's reply was that "the common law is the mother of precedents." "Yes, Mr. Blank," came the reply, "but she is a mother who is now past the age of child-bearing." "With your Lordship's assistance," counsel promptly responded, "I shall hope to prove the contrary." [4]

The influence of equity is great. "Who can doubt that courts of equity in enforcing the great principle that a trustee shall not profit by his trust nor even place himself in a position where his private interest may collide with his fiduciary duty, have raised the level of business honor, and kept awake a conscience that might otherwise have slumbered?" [5] Again, "Equity has its distinctive standards of fidelity and honor, higher at times than the standards of the market place." [6] "There are canons of the Court of equity which have their foundation, not in the actual commission of fraud, but in that hallowed orison, 'lead us not into temptation.'" [7] "A constructive trust is the formula through which the conscience of equity finds expression." [8]

True, "Equity follows the law, but not slavishly nor always." [9] Fortunately, too, "Equity does not demand that its suitors shall have led blameless lives." [10] Even so, "Extravagant liberality and immoderate folly do not of themselves provide a

3 *Simpson's Motor Sales (London) Ltd.* v. *Hendon Corporation* [1963] *The Times* May 7; cp. S.C. as reported [1964] A.C. 1088 at 1127.
4 H. Fletcher Moulton, *The Life of Lord Moulton* (1922) p. 69. Private information suggests that Vaughan Williams and Farwell L.JJ. were the other members of the court, and Leslie Scott K.C. (later Scott L.J.) the counsel. If this is right, it would date the occurrence between 1909 and 1912.
5 Cardozo J., *The Growth of the Law* (1924) p. 96.
6 *Buffum* v. *Peter Barceloux Co.*, 289 U.S. 227 at 237 (1933), *per* Cardozo J.
7 *Wormley* v. *Wormley*, 21 U.S. 421 at 463 (1823), *per* Johnson J.
8 *Beatty* v. *Guggenheim Exploration Co.*, 225 N.Y. 380 at 386 (1919), *per* Cardozo J.
9 *Graf* v. *Hope Building Corporation*, 254 N.Y. 1 at 9 (1930), *per* Cardozo C.J., dissenting.
10 *Loughran* v. *Loughran*, 292 U.S. 216 at 229 (1934), *per* Brandeis J.

passport to equitable relief." [11] Thus, if a man voluntarily
settles property without reserving any power of revocation, equity
will not supply one; for " this court will not loose the fetters he
hath put upon himself, but he must lie down under his own
folly." [12] Yet as was said last century equity " never does a vain
thing, or enforces a void or impossible contract. Men may
divide the moon by imaginary lines, but equity will not enforce
their contract." [13]

Charitable trusts have their own problems. In one case a
charitable corporation established for " the reception, maintenance and employment of penitent prostitutes " succeeded in an
action for possession of a public house on the grounds that the
lease which the corporation had granted to the lessee's predecessor in title some eighty-five years earlier was, for technical
reasons, void. At the end of his judgment, Fry J. observed " It
does appear to me that this is a very hard case upon the defendants, and I should be very glad if the plaintiffs should be able to
recollect that charity may be shewn to publicans as well as to
sinners." [14] In due course the Court of Appeal, by a judicious
use of the Real Property Limitation Act, 1833, was able to give
practical effect to the judge's adjuration [15]; and the House of
Lords agreed.[16] But a line has to be drawn somewhere, as in
the case of a testator who set up a trust for the purchase of
" reasonable food and drink " for distribution among twenty
communicants of a specified church. Harman J. held that this
was not a charitable bequest, for there was nothing to confine
the gift to the relief of poverty, and he was " not prepared to
hold that the provision of plum pudding was for the advancement
of religion." [17]

[11] *Tufton* v. *Sperni* [1952] 2 T.L.R. 516 at 519, *per* Evershed M.R.
[12] *Villers* v. *Beaumont* (1682) 1 Vern. 100 at 101, *per* North L.K.
[13] *Hall* v. *Vernon*, 34 S.E. 764 at 765 (1899), *per* Dent P.
[14] *Governors of Magdalen Hospital* v. *Knotts* (1877) 8 Ch.D. 709 at 720.
[15] *Ibid.*
[16] *President & Governors of the Magdalen Hospital* v. *Knotts* (1879) 4 App.Cas. 324.
[17] *Re Geere's Will Trusts (No. 1)* [1954] *The Times* March 20.

Gnawn All To Pieces

IN times past many believed that there could be no perjury and no moral sin if the evidence given was literally true, even though in substance it was false; and such beliefs die hard. Even in nineteenth-century Ireland, it seems to have been thought that if a man died intestate or leaving an unsatisfactory will, all might be saved if a new will could be made for him, and his signature or mark affixed to it by a pen held for him in his dead hand, provided a live fly were first placed in his mouth; for then all concerned could safely swear that when he signed the will, " There was life in him." [1] But Ireland was not alone in such practices, although the live fly seems to have been a Hibernian improvement. In one seventeenth-century English case judgment was given in the following terms " You are convicted of forgeing a deed, by putting a dead mans hand unto it, therefore the Court gives this judgement against you, that you are fined at a hundred pound, and shall stand in the pillory two hours before the hall dore, with a paper on your head showing the nature of your offence." [2] The report adds " Memorandum the party cut off a dead mans hand, and put a pen, and a seal in it, and so signed, and sealed, and delivered the deed with the dead hand, and swore that he saw the deed sealed and delivered." [3]

The statutory requirement that a will should be attested and subscribed by the witnesses " in the presence " of the testator [4] is plainly capable of giving rise to nice questions on the meaning of " presence." In one case in 1781,[5] a lady went to her attorney's office to execute her will. " Being asthmatical, and the office very hot, she retired to her carriage to execute the will, the witnesses attending her: after having seen the execution,

---

[1] See, e.g., Croake James, *Curiosities of Law and Lawyers* (1882) p. 458.
[2] *Custodes and Howell Gwin* (1652) Sty. 362 at 363, *per* Rolle C.J.
[3] *Ibid.* See also *Custodes* v. *Howell Gwinn* (1652) Sty. 336 (perjury).
[4] Statute of Frauds, 1677, s. 5; see now Wills Act, 1837, s. 9.
[5] *Casson* v. *Dade* (1781) 1 Bro.C.C. 99; Dick. 586.

they returned into the office to attest it, and the carriage was accidentally put back to the windows of the office, through which, it was sworn by a person in the carriage, the testatrix might see what passed." Lord Thurlow L.C. held that this was a valid execution of the will; the witnesses in the office were, it seems, " in the presence " of the testatrix in her carriage.

Such a doctrine is susceptible of much refinement. If the testator lies in one room and the witnesses sign in an adjoining room connected by a door, the will is bad if the witnesses sign at a table which is so situated that it is impossible for the testator to have seen them sign.[6] Accordingly, evidence as to the exact position of the table is of great importance,[7] and so may be evidence whether the testator could have seen the execution [8] " by inclining his body and advancing his head." [9] If the will is signed behind his back at a time when he was incapable of turning himself, and drawn curtains [10] would have prevented him from seeing the witnesses, the will is bad.[11] It is also important to ascertain whether the testator knew that the witnesses were there; for there can be no " presence " unless " each is aware of the other's presence." [12] Even the sound of breathing is no substitute for vision.[13] Lord Ellenborough C.J. once observed that he was old enough to remember the case of the testatrix in her coach, and that he afterwards went to view the office through the windows of which the testatrix might have seen what passed.[14] There seems to be no English case on the use of mirrors, though in one there was a broken window in the line of vision.[15] Lord Ellenborough spoke of the rule as

---

[6] *In b. Colman* (1842) 3 Curt. 118.
[7] See *Winchilsea* v. *Wauchope* (1829) 3 Russ. 441; and see *Norton* v. *Bazett* (1856) Dea. & Sw. 259.
[8] See *In b. Trimnell* (1865) 11 Jur.N.S. 248; *In b. Piercy* (1845) 1 Rob.Ecc. 278 (blind testatrix: the test is whether, if she had had sight, she could have seen the witnesses).
[9] *Doe* d. *Wright* v. *Manifold* (1813) 1 M. & S. 294 (see at p. 295).
[10] See *Davy* v. *Smith* (1693) 3 Salk. 395.
[11] *Tribe* v. *Tribe* (1849) 1 Rob.Ecc. 775; and see *Carter* v. *Seaton* (1901) 85 L.T. 76.
[12] *In b. Killick* (1864) 3 Sw. & Tr. 578 at 580, *per* Sir James Wilde; and see *Jenner* v. *Ffinch* (1879) 5 P.D. 106; *Brown* v. *Skirrow* [1902] P. 3; *In b. Chalcraft* [1948] P. 222.   [13] See *In b. Ellis* (1840) 2 Curt. 395.
[14] *Doe* d. *Wright* v. *Manifold*, *supra*, at p. 296.
[15] *Shires* v. *Glascock* (1687) 2 Salk. 688.

requiring that "the witnesses should be actually within the reach of the organs of sight"[16]; but if vision through glass suffices, reflection by glass should be enough.

Few physical difficulties proved insurmountable. In Ireland a man suffering from progressive paralysis wanted to change his will at a time when he could no longer speak. He was able to move nothing save some muscles of his face, though his brain was unaffected and his intellect clear. His solicitor solved the difficulty by arranging for the testator to shut his eyes for Yes and to keep them open for No, and then asking a series of questions. In this way instructions for a new will were given, and finally a pen was held in the testator's hand for the making of his mark on the will. In due course Barton J. granted probate of the will.[17] Where the witnesses to a will could not write, there was the question how they could satisfy the statutory requirement[18] that they "shall attest and shall subscribe" the will. The solution adopted was for some third party to write each of their names on the will and for each of the witnesses to hold the pen at the top while his name was being thus written; and the will was held valid.[19]

In a neighbouring field, few counsel would feel bold enough even to contend that a document executed on stamped paper was necessarily an instrument under seal. Yet the authority of a Master of the Rolls can be prayed in aid of such an argument. A lady had a power of appointment exercisable (*inter alia*) by her will "to be by her signed, sealed[20] and published" in the presence of two credible witnesses. She signed a will on stamped paper, believing this to be material, but did not even purport to seal it. Arden M.R. held this to be a good execution of the power,[1] saying "I think the stamp equivalent to a seal."[2]

Maurice Healy recounts the story of a well-to-do Irishman who made his money in America, and returned to Ireland to die.

---

16 *Doe* d. *Wright* v. *Manifold, supra,* at p. 296.
17 *Ryan* v. *Ryan* (1903) 4 New Ir.Jur.Rep. 164.
18 Wills Act, 1837, s. 9.
19 *Lewis* v. *Lewis* (1861) 2 Sw. & Tr. 153; and see *Fulton* v. *Kee* [1961] N.I. 1.
20 *Quaere*, however, whether this word did in fact appear in the power: see Sugden, *Powers* (8th ed. 1861) p. 231n.
1 See now Wills Act, 1837, s. 10.
2 *Sprange* v. *Barnard* (1789) 2 Bro.C.C. 585 at 587.

He had quarrelled with his own people, and lived with a small farmer and his wife, who cared for him well. The wife's one thought was to get his money; she feared that a solicitor would persuade him to make a will leaving all his money to his family. When he lay on his death bed, the priest, finding that he had made no will, turned the wife out of the room, and helped the dying man to make his will; a servant girl was called in as the second witness. As soon as he had gone, the wife searched everywhere for the will. At last she found it; everything was left to her, her husband and the survivor of them. " There it stood, witnessed by the priest and the girl; but she felt unsafe. She took pen and ink and wrote in her own name as a third witness; and thereby signed away the inheritance of herself and her husband to the relatives the testator had declined to benefit." [3] A footnote adds " Perhaps I should explain for non-legal readers' benefit that neither a witness nor the spouse of a witness can receive anything under the will he or she attests." [4]

With the law stated in the footnote one can agree; not so with its application to the facts stated. If after a will has been duly executed by the testator and the requisite two witnesses another person signs it not with the intention of attesting it but for some other reason, *e.g.*, because of a belief that it would otherwise not be valid, or to show concurrence with its terms, probate will be granted with the omission of the superfluous signature, and any gift to the person who affixed it will be valid.[5] If in the Irish case the wife meekly submitted to the proposition that she had " signed away the inheritance of herself and her husband," one can only regard the case as one of an unhappy combination of an atypical unlitigiousness with an unexpected deficiency of competent legal advice.

There is no rule that a will must be made on paper or some similar substance. The best-authenticated substitute was a hen's egg from which the contents had been removed. The testator, James Barnes, was a pilot on the Manchester Ship Canal, and

[3] M. Healy, *The Old Munster Circuit* (1939) pp. 182, 183.
[4] *Ibid.*, at p. 183.
[5] *In b. Sharman* (1869) L.R. 1 P. & D. 661; *In b. Smith* (1889) 15 P.D. 2; *Kitcat* v. *King* [1930] P. 266; and see now Wills Act 1968, s. 1.

he had written in indelible ink on the outside of the shell
" 17-1925-Mag. Everything i possess. J.B." His widow's
christian name was Margaret, and the testator always called her
" Mag"; and the eggshell had been found in a very dusty
recess on top of a wardrobe in his bedroom. Lord Merrivale P.
refused to grant probate of the eggshell on the ground that he
was not satisfied that the testator, who had made earlier and
more orthodox wills, had intended the writing on the eggshell
to be a testamentary disposition.[6] If it had read " To Mag . . . ,"
the word " to " might have made " a considerable difference ";
but there was no " to " there.[7] Lord Merrivale's observation
" It is a fragile thing. It is here "[8] was true in more senses
than one.

Other substances seem to have been used. A step-ladder
appears to have been admitted to probate in Los Angeles. On
one rung were the words " December 2nd 1933. I love her.
Give all to Mrs. Gotts. She is my good spirit."[9] And
Somerset House is reputed to have " the will of a groom which
he chalked on a stable door."[10] Probate has been granted to
the will of a Californian business man made on his hospital
nurse's petticoat[11]; and in England a seventy-five-word will
scratched by a naval stoker on his brass identity disk is said to
have been proved.[12] At the other extreme, a Mrs. Frederica
Cook is reputed to have made a valid will 95,940 words long,
contained in four large gilt-edged volumes.[13] Even if none of
these instances is authentic, there seems to be nothing to make
them impossible.

One more recent case is beyond doubt. A Canadian farmer
who for over nine hours lay by himself, trapped by a wheel of the
tractor which he had been driving, scratched with his knife on
the fender the words " In case I die in this mess, I leave all to

---

[6] *In b. Barnes* (1926) 136 L.T. 380; 43 T.L.R. 71. The egg shell was proffered
as being the privileged will of a mariner at sea and so as requiring no witness.
[7] S.C., 43 T.L.R. 71 at 72.
[8] S.C., 43 T.L.R. 71.
[9] (1934) 53 *Law Notes* 67. [10] *Ibid. Sed quaere.*
[11] J. M. Gest (1934) 8 Temp.L.Q. 297 at 302 gives the details.
[12] G. Rentoul, *Sometimes I Think* (1940) p. 142; E. Million (1958) 11
Vanderbilt L.R. 737 at 739, citing (1923) 29 *Case & Com.* No. 1, p. 28.
[13] G. Rentoul, *supra*, at p. 142.

the wife. Cecil Geo. Harris." Within forty-eight hours he was dead. The Surrogate Court in Saskatchewan granted Letters of Administration with the Will Annexed in respect of the portion of the fender on which this writing appeared, as being a valid holograph will.[14] It seems a little too enthusiastic to require the relevant portion of the fender to be cut off and filed, instead of accepting a photographic copy; what if a dying thief had written his will on the back of a Rubens that he had been stealing? But a court cannot be too careful.

The most remarkable will of all is admittedly fictional. In a Victorian novel,[15] a short will (" I leave my property to Eustace Meeson ") was tattooed on the back of a young lady, together with the necessary signatures; and after a probate action (*Meeson* v. *Addison*) she was duly admitted to probate. The susceptibilities of the day were happily not shocked by any anatomical discussion whether the signatures to the will satisfied the statutory requirement of appearing " at the foot or end thereof." [16] At the hearing the will gave evidence of due execution; and although she was engaged to the sole beneficiary, she was not married to him, and so no question arose whether, *qua* will, she had been revoked or invalidated by marriage to a beneficiary.[17]

Will forms have their uses and abuses. " The applicant is the surviving spouse of a marriage in community of property between himself and his late wife, who died on 15th April, last year. On 28th December, 1925, the applicant and his late wife executed a mutual will, and it is this will which I now have to interpret. The will is a peculiar document written into a printed form, one of those forms which are usually sold for sixpence. There are printed skeleton clauses with blank spaces for filling in names and other particulars. At the top of the form is a symbolic picture showing a house standing in grounds, an angel hovers over the entrance-gate to the grounds, brandishing a sword in the face of a wolf which is endeavouring to force an entrance. The symbolism of the picture appears to be that the

[14] W. M. Elliott (1948) 26 Can.B.R. 1242.
[15] H. Rider Haggard, *Mr. Meeson's Will* (1894).
[16] Wills Act, 1837, s. 9.
[17] Would the Wills Act, 1837, s. 15 (gift to the spouse of a witness) or s. 18 (marriage of the testator) support *a fortiori* arguments?

angel represents the vendor of the wills and the wolf stands for the legal profession, and if any words were printed below the picture they would probably be, ' Invest your sixpences and save your guineas, and so load the dice in favour of the angel so that he can keep the wolf from the door.' The testator spent his sixpence, brought this form and completed it, but, unhappily, in so doing vastly improved the odds in favour of the wolf, since the will now has to be interpreted by the Court at a cost certainly exceeding twenty times what it would have cost to have had a proper will drawn. I do not, however, have to resolve the issue between the angel and the wolf, but the issue I have to determine is that between the surviving spouse and the *curator-ad-litem*, who represents the minor children. . . ." [18]

Infancy has always been troublesome. Before 1970 it was ancient law that an infant was deemed to attain full age at the first moment of the day preceding the twenty-first anniversary of his birth. This was so no matter the hour at which his birth occurred; for this purpose English law ignored fractions of a day. If the birth occurred just before midnight on January 1, 1940, the child was accordingly deemed to be of full age at the first moment of December 31, 1960,[19] even though this was nearly forty-eight hours before he had lived for twenty-one complete years. Consequently as soon as December 31, 1960, began the former infant could make a valid will.[20] At the same moment he would become entitled to a gift made to him conditionally upon attaining the age of twenty-one years,[1] although if the gift had been to him " upon the day he attains his twenty-first year," he could have claimed it a year earlier.[2]

This rule, however, was neither universal nor pellucid. Thus

---

[18] *Ex p. Van Niekerk*, 1947 W.L.D. unrep.: see [1951] *The Commercial Law Reporter* 314 (not naming the judge).

[19] See, *e.g.*, *Nichols* v. *Ramsel* (1677) 2 Mod. 280 at 281; and see generally *Prowse* v. *McIntyre* (1961) 111 C.L.R. 264.

[20] *Herbert* v. *Turball* (1663) 1 Keb. 589; *Howard's Case* (1699) 2 Salk. 625; *Fitzhugh* v. *Dennington* (1704) 2 Ld.Raym. 1094 at 1096.

[1] *Toder* v. *Sansam* (1775) 1 Bro.P.C. 468; *Re Shurey* [1918] 1 Ch. 263 (age of 25 years).

[2] *Grant* v. *Grant* (1840) 4 Y. & C.Ex. 256 (twenty-fifth year).

for certain limited purposes Parliament [3] gave effect to the understandable preference of the populace in England and the judiciary in Scotland for birthdays instead of birthday eves. And what of leap years? If X was born on February 29, 1936 (whether early in the morning or late at night), he was of full age at the first moment of February 28, 1957. But consider Y, born a day later, on March 1, 1936: did he attain full age at the same moment? If X was born early on February 29, and Y late on March 1, X might have been born nearly forty-eight hours earlier than Y, and yet on this footing he might in law have attained full age *eo instanti* with him. If there was a gift to the first of a class of beneficiaries to attain full age, and X and Y were both members of the class, Y's chances might be as good as X's, despite X's start.

What, too, of international differences in time? Thus Hong Kong time is eight hours in advance of English time. When it was 12.01 a.m. on February 28, 1957, in Hong Kong, it was still 4.01 p.m. on February 27, 1957, in England. If Y was born in England on March 1, 1936, would he have attained full age earlier (and so beaten the less enterprising X in the testamentary stakes) if he had gone to Hong Kong? And if he had died at 1 a.m. on February 28, 1957, in Hong Kong, had he attained full age even though he died seven hours before February 28 began in England? [4]

On January 1, 1970, however, great changes were made. Leap years and international differences still remained capable of posing their problems; but birthdays have now come into their own in law as well as in popular belief. In addition to altering the age of majority from twenty-one years to eighteen, [5] statute has now provided that after 1969 the time at which a person attains a particular age expressed in years should be the commencement of the relevant anniversary of the date of his birth. [6] A child born on December 31, 1960, will accordingly be eighteen years old at the first moment of December 31, 1978,

[3] By the National Insurance Act, 1946, s. 78 (4) (*c*).
[4] See (1957) 73 L.Q.R. 462 at 463, based on *R.* v. *Logan* [1957] 2 Q.B. 589.
[5] Family Law Reform Act, 1969, s. 1 (1).
[6] *Ibid.*, s. 9 (1).

instead of a day earlier. One consequence of this change is that
January 1, 1970, became a unique day; for it was the only day
under English law upon which nobody attained any given age.
Thus a child born on January 1, 1969, attained one year of age
on December 31, 1969, for the old law was still in force then,
whereas a child born on January 2, 1969, attained one year of age
on January 2, 1970, since the new law applied.[7] The one day
upon which neither he nor anybody else could attain the age of
one year, or any other age, was January 1, 1970.

In one Irish case a daughter who had just attained full age
signed a joint promissory note for £1,550 in favour of a bank
to whom her mother was indebted. The daughter had no
independent advice, and it was held that she was not liable to
the bank on the note. Barton J. said " It is quite true that
young persons (male or female) upon coming of age obtain
capacity to sign notes and to execute mortgages, and that they
may render themselves liable by so doing. But it is not correct
to suppose that, as soon as the clock has struck the hour of
technical legal emancipation, the young person is discharged
from all protection of the law. The law recognises that a young
person, living with or under the influence of a parent, is likely to
remain for some time under parental dominion, and is at an
impressionable age, when gratitude, affection, and respect for a
parent are fresh and strong, while knowledge and experience of
the stress and struggle and varied obligations of human life
have yet to be acquired. The law protects young persons under
such circumstances and at such age, not by curtailing their
capacity to deal with others, but by binding the consciences of
those who deal with them." [8]

Forgery, of course, invalidates all. *Cresswell* v. *Jackson*, or
the *Matlock Will Case*, concerned an attempt to set up three
codicils to a will. If they were genuine, they would virtually
have disinherited a relation of the testator by carrying the bulk
of an estate of some £50,000 to an employee of the testator and
certain other persons. Sir John Romilly M.R. directed an issue to
be tried, and in 1859 a jury under Erle C.J. declared the codicils

[7] *Ibid.*, ss. 9 (2), 28 (3); S.I. 1969 No. 1140.
[8] *M'Mackin* v. *Hibernian Bank* [1905] 1 I.R. 296 at 304.

valid. Romilly M.R. was not satisfied, and in 1860 a jury under
Pollock C.B. held the codicils invalid.[9]   Romilly M.R. refused
a new trial, and the Court of Appeal in Chancery was equally
divided (*pro*, Turner L.J.; *con.*, Knight Bruce L.J.); but by a
majority the House of Lords ordered a new trial. This took
place before Cockburn C.J. in 1864 and again the codicils were
rejected.[10]

The codicils had all been found in odd circumstances by the
person who received the main benefit under them. Thus one
was in a penny memorandum book, and another (which Knight-
Bruce L.J. had styled " the hay-loft codicil ") was in a pickle jar
in a hole in the wall under the window-cill of an out-house; and
two of them had been witnessed by one Job Knowles, a quarry
owner. Serjeant Hayes (later Hayes J.) attacked the codicils in
a fine satirical vein. " What," said Serjeant Hayes, " will the
jury say, when I tell them that I will prove that an iron vice,
weighing sixty pounds was, in the testator's life, screwed over
the window-board, under which the hole containing the pickle-
jar and the third codicil were found, so that the testator, two
months before his death, with an abscess in his back, (which he
described in one of his letters, as five inches long, three inches
broad, and one and a half deep,) must have gone up to the loft,
unscrewed the vice, lifted it up, made the hole in the wall, and
deposited the jar with the twenty sovereigns and the codicil,
then covered it up, and screwed the vice over it again; and all
this—to prevent any one from finding it! The hole in the
wall! Why, imagination could hardly go beyond it! No more
codicils had been found, and one blessing of these Chancery
proceedings had been, that they had stopped the finding of
codicils. But for them, a *fourth* codicil must have been found.
It must have come! The second and third had each been found
after nine months—the usual period of gestation—but perhaps,
as there was so little of the property then left to be disposed of,
this might have been only a seven months' codicil! It was
certainly difficult to conceive where it could have been found.
One could hardly imagine a more obscure place for secreting a

[9] *Cresswell* v. *Jackson* (1860) 2 F. & F. 24.
[10] *Cresswell* v. *Jackson* (1864) 4 F. & F. 1.

codicil. Perhaps, however, in *Job Knowles's* quarry, whilst his men were blasting the rock—with gun-powder, of course—in some fissure, the person chiefly interested in these findings might have seen an ante-diluvian toad sitting on something, and said, ' Bless me! what is that? ' Why, what could it be?—but a codicil! " [11]

After the verdict of the jury and the mordant words of Serjeant Hayes, it might be thought that the end had come. But Victorian tenacity must not be under-rated; and in due time there appeared a fourth codicil which, if genuine, would have established the other three. The battle was resumed, but by then Romilly M.R. had had enough. Without even calling on Serjeant Hayes, he rejected the newcomer,[12] and so, no doubt, restored to the serjeant's antediluvian toad its accustomed means of support.

Another cause of disaster is mental incapacity. One testator left half his residuary estate to the Bishop of Bath and Wells to be applied towards the reconversion of the inhabitants of Wookey. Less than four months later he was certified insane, and when he died a nephew of his applied to the court to have probate revoked on the ground that the testator was insane when he made the will. Davies J. agreed that the will was an odd will, but said that people were entitled to make odd wills; and he held that on the facts the executors had discharged the burden of proof of establishing the will. He refused the nephew costs out of the estate, saying that although he had some sympathy for him, and realised that he felt that he should have had some of his uncle's money, " the action was not merely a damp squib, it was a squib which had no powder in it at all ": for there was no evidence whatever of the testator's incapacity other than the nephew's belief in it.[13] As has been said pointedly in Scotland, " Just as a mad person cannot make any will, so a sane person cannot make a mad will." [14] Yet for some it does

[11] *Hayesiana* (1892) p. xi, *per* Wills J.; and see R. Walton, *Random Recollections of the Midland Circuit* (1869) pp. 216–219.
[12] *Hayesiana* (1892) p. x.
[13] *In b. Elgar* [1955] *The Times* Oct. 26.
[14] *MacKintosh's Judicial Factor* v. *Lord Advocate*, 1935 S.C. 406 at 411, *per* Lord President Clyde.

not seem to be for the want of trying; nor is the margin of failure always great.

One may also have to reckon with public policy. A Canadian silk, one Charles Millar, died in 1926 leaving a will made some five years earlier. He prefaced his benefactions by reciting that " this will is necessarily uncommon and capricious because I have no dependents or near relations and no duty rests upon me to leave any property at my death and what I do leave is proof of my folly in gathering and retaining more than I required in my lifetime." [15] After a number of orthodox legacies and " a number of gifts which may well be described in the language of Mr. Millar as uncommon and capricious," [16] the testator gave his residue to his executors and trustees in trust to convert it into money, invest it until the expiration of nine years from his death, and then " at the expiration of ten years from my death to give it and its accumulations to the mother who has since my death given birth in Toronto to the greatest number of children as shown by the registrations under the Vital Statistics Act. If one or more mothers have equal highest number of registrations under the said Act to divide the said moneys and accumulations equally between them." [17]

At the end of the ten years, remote next-of-kin of the testator attacked the will on the ground that it was contrary to public policy, in that it tended to induce mothers to have offspring in rapid succession, and further that, not being confined to legitimate children, it would encourage illegitimate births. This latter point was doomed to failure by reason of the well-established rule of construction which prima facie confines " children " to " legitimate children " [18]; but there was a stout argument on the point of public policy. The next-of-kin sought to introduce evidence " as to the effect of the clause:

(a) upon the mothers who are claiming and upon their children, from a medical and economic point of view;

(b) the tendency to illegitimacy;

---

[15] *Re Millar* [1936] O.R. 554 at 556.
[16] *Ibid.*, at p. 556, *per* Middleton J.A.
[17] *Ibid.*, at pp. 556, 557. For the Act, see now R.S.O. 1970, c. 483.
[18] In England, see now Family Law Reform Act, 1969, s. 15.

(c) the high mortality rate among the children of the mothers who are claimants;

(d) the moral and physical effect on mothers and children;

(e) the injury and detriment to the welfare of the community;

(f) the disgusting and revolting nature of the competition among the mothers to obtain the benefit of this bequest." [19]

This, however, was rejected as being evidence as to opinion on the subject of public policy rather than fact. No doubt the same would apply to the possibility that towards the end of the ten years well-placed mothers would realise that prematurity might mean victory.

In the event, Middleton J.A. held that the will was valid. "I know no ground of public policy which recognizes the undesirability of having children at too frequent intervals. It may well be that there are many distinguished physicians and others who believe this to be the case, but public policy as such lags far behind the opinions of scientists and sociologists. Public policy is not what a Judge thinks is best for the community. It is something far more than that. It is that which for many years has been recognized as for the public weal and the common law, and the principle must be found to be embedded in the authorities. No Judge has a right to declare that which he does not himself believe in to be against public policy simply because it is against his opinion and his idea of that which is for the welfare of the community." [20]

The learned judge ended with a few words on Mr. Millar and the next-of-kin. "I should like to say a word concerning Mr. Millar. He rightly described his will as necessarily uncommon and capricious and his estate as proof of his folly in 'gathering and retaining more than I required in my lifetime.' He evidently regarded his remote relatives as having no claim upon him, for he states that 'I have no dependents or near relations and no duty rests upon me to leave any property at my death.' I would regard the clause in question as prompted

[19] *Re Millar, supra,* at p. 558.
[20] *Ibid.,* at p. 565.

rather by sympathy for the mothers of large families, who are often extremely poor people, not unmingled with a grim sense of humour. As to the effect of such a gift, the testator's attitude seems to me rather like the throwing of a handful of coins for the pleasure of seeing children scramble for it. The argument by the next-of-kin purports to be based on high motives of public policy and not upon mere greed, but the next-of-kin have waited until all the harm possible has been done, instead of prosecuting their claim immediately after Mr. Millar's death, when the evils, which it is said result from the tendency detrimental to public policy set forth, might have been prevented." [1]

An appeal was carried to the Court of Appeal,[2] and thence to the Supreme Court,[3] but without success. In Canada, at all events, a testamentary parturition Derby is one of the established rights of citizenship; with the novelist [4] and playwright,[5] one may lawfully say " Ripeness is all."

Once validly made, a will may survive much. In the seventeenth century, a testator gave his will to the scrivener to keep. Four years later the testator died, and a fortnight after his death " this writing was found in the scrivener's study; gnawn all to pieces with rats, yet he with help of the pieces, and of his memory and other witnesses, caused it to be proved in the Ecclesiastical Court." However, the question then arose in the King's Bench whether the will was effective to dispose of land, since a stranger could not decipher the devise by joining the pieces together. " Whereupon the Court directed the jury, that if they found that the will was gnawn before the death of the devisor, then 'twas for the plaintiff; if after, for the defendant; and the jury found for the defendant in favour of the will." [6] On the other hand, in 1973 a judge was able to fit together some forty fragments of a will which the testatrix had torn in pieces while of unsound mind. There were no gaps in the jigsaw,

---

[1] *Ibid.*, at p. 567.
[2] [1937] O.R. 382.
[3] [1938] S.C.R. 1.
[4] Eric Linklater's *Ripeness is All* was published in 1935, after Mr. Millar's death but before the litigation.
[5] *King Lear*, Act 5, Sc. 2, line 11.
[6] *Etheringham* v. *Etheringham* (1646) Aleyn 2.

and so probate was granted to the fragments as constituting a complete and perfect will; the document had been destroyed, but the will had not been revoked.[7]   To avoid others having to do what had already been done judicially, the order of the court recited that an intact copy of the will which the judge had compared with the reassembled fragments was a true copy of the will [8]; *Nemo debet bis vexari pro eadem causa.*[9]

---

[7] *In b. Aynsley* [1973] *Daily Telegraph* Feb. 6.
[8] *Ex rel.* the judge (Megarry J.).
[9] " Nobody ought to be troubled twice for the same cause."

King Solomon in Georgia

THE *Duchess of Kingston's Case* [1] is well known in history, biography and law; but with a small change in the facts, it might have been even more memorable. The lady had first married a man who had later succeeded to the Earldom of Bristol, and then in his lifetime she had married the Duke of Kingston. On any footing she was thus a peeress, and could be tried for bigamy only by the House of Lords; and, as is well known, in due course she was tried and convicted. The position would have been otherwise, however, had her first husband remained a commoner; for then, if she had been tried by the House of Lords, she must necessarily have escaped conviction. If the first marriage had not been established, she would have been a peeress over whom the House would have had jurisdiction, but, *ex hypothesi*, she could be no bigamist. On the other hand, if the first marriage had been duly established, she could be no peeress and so the House could have had no jurisdiction. [2]

Sometimes there were other problems of jurisdiction. " Sir M. Hale mentions, [3] without remark, a great scandal occasioned by the law of abduction, arising from the necessity, in his time, of proving an actual marriage, or actual defilement, viz., ' That if a woman be taken forcibly in the County of Middlesex, and married in the County of Surrey, the fact is indictable in neither county.' [4] So, because the force and defilement were in different counties, in the year 1804, two prisoners, a clergyman and his brother, were acquitted. They had forcibly taken away in a chaise Mrs. Lee, from her house in London, and one of them defiled her at Oxford; but, before entering Oxfordshire, she took a steel necklace with a camphor bag attached to it from her

---

[1] (1776) 20 St.Tr. 355.
[2] See 7 Camp.L.CC. 137.
[3] See Hale, *Pleas of the Crown* (1800 ed.) vol. 1, p. 660, citing *Fulwood's Case* (1637) Cro.Car. 482, 484, 488, 492.
[4] " For the taking without the marriage, nor the marriage without the taking, make not felony ": *Hale, supra.*

neck, (which camphor she explained to be a sedative against sensual desire) and threw it out of the window of the chaise, saying, ' That was my charm against pleasure, I have now no occasion for it! ' " A footnote adds a valuable suggestion for defending counsel in cases of this nature. " Previous to the trial of this case, the counsel for the prisoner, at his request, attended him in prison, when he told them that he had only one suggestion to make, leaving his defence, in other respects, entirely to them; he suggested that in such a cause, he had most to fear from passionless, pale, and Cassius-looking jurymen, and therefore he wished them to challenge every juryman who had not a red face." [5]

It is sometimes difficult to draw the line in this type of offence. " If a man wooing a girl should tentatively and with due decorum test his prospects by a ventured kiss or embrace, such action on his part might actually be against the woman's will in the sense that she has given no previous consent to it, express or implied, and be, therefore, an assault, but I can scarcely conceive of a charge being brought in such a case or, if brought, that any punishment would be meted out in respect of it." [6] This is perhaps in the same gallery as a bad case of indecent assault that once came before Maule J. The accused had found the girl in his orchard picking apples. At his trial he defended himself, and in due course cross-examined the girl.

Q. " I caught you picking apples from my trees, didn't I? "

A. " Yes, you did, Sir."

Q. " That was not the first time I caught you picking my apples, was it? "

A. " No, Sir."

Q. " When I caught you there before, I told you what I would do to you if I caught you again, didn't I? "

A. " Yes, you did, Sir."

Q. " And that was what I did to you, wasn't it? "

A. " Yes, it was, Sir."

[5] A. Amos, *The Ruins of Time Exemplified in Sir Matthew Hale's History of the Pleas of the Crown* (1856) p. 162.

[6] *R. v. M.*, 1947 (4) S.A. 489 at 492, *per* Milne J.

At this, the judge stopped the case. He told the jury that the girl had clearly gone to the orchard knowing what would happen, so that she was a consenting party. He then spoke to the accused before ordering his discharge. "Now, my man, I want to give you a serious caution. Don't you go on threatening girls you find in your orchard that you will do this sort of thing to them; for if you do you will soon have no apples at all." [7]

La donna è mobile. In one case of alleged rape, the act was admitted, and the main issue was that of consent. There seems to have been a previous history between the parties of sexual acts short of full intercourse, and on this occasion it was said that the man had, without consent, exceeded the permissible. However, the woman's account of the event was "an extremely improbable one," which "suggests a contortionist's feat." [8] Nor did her subsequent tears impress the court. "One knows from the cases that even spouses may reproach each other with sexual acts, fully acquiesced in, which might lead to pregnancy. It is to be supposed that in illicit intercourse such reproaches are more frequent. Tears after the event are not necessarily indications of absence of consent. They may be tears of remorse or apprehension. Gretchen's famous lament is no pointer to her having been ravished by Faust." [9] On the other hand, the man's account had its surprises. He alleged that "on the day in question he was passing the kitchen to get some water at the windmill when the complainant called him. She asked him for some tobacco and said she wanted to show him her buttocks." [10] Understandably, the appeal succeeded.

Such spheres of human activity may seem remote from the Almighty and Equity alike: but not so. In 1718 a man was tried and convicted before Probyn J. of an offence against one Jane Mills. The indictment charged, *inter alia*, that the accused "diabolice, felonice & contra Ordinem Naturae in . . . Ano ipsius Janae Mills adtunc & ibidem carnaliter cognovit, Peccatumque illud sodomiticum, detestabile & abominabile, anglice vocat'

[7] See D. Walker-Smith and E. Clarke, *Life of Sir Edward Clarke* (1939) p. 34.
[8] *R. v. M.*, 1953 (4) S.A. 393 at 395, *per* van den Heever J.A.
[9] *Ibid.*, at p. 397, *per* van den Heever J.A.
[10] *Ibid.*, at p. 396, *per* van den Heever J.A.

buggery, inter Christianos non nominandum . . . commisit & perpetravit." [11]   The accused was convicted, but the judge reprieved him for the judges to consider whether in law it was possible for this offence to be committed with a girl.   Most of the judges had little difficulty in saying that it was, but two or three held out against this view.   " It being so horrid and great a crime, and that no colour should be given to such an offence, Justice Fortescue A.[12] wrote to the Earl of Macclesfield, then Chancellor of Great Britain, concerning this matter; and his answer was by way of letter, that he wondered at the variety of opinions; that he had not the least hesitation . . ." [13]   Not only did he consider the majority to be plainly right, but he seems also to have thought the case of a girl to be theologically *a fortiori*.   " The unnatural abuse of a woman, seems worse than either that of a man or a beast; for it seems a more direct affront to the Author of Nature, and a more insolent expression of contempt of His wisdom, condemning the provision made by Him, and defying both it and Him." [14]

There are, of course, those who are not merely willing but also anxious.   In 1960 a woman was convicted of soliciting men for the purposes of prostitution.   She had conducted her operations from behind the closed windows of a house abutting on the street, and she appealed against her conviction (unsuccessfully) on the ground that she had not solicited " in a street " within the meaning of the Act.[15]   The case stated by the magistrate described her *modus operandi* with some elegance.   " The defendant's method of soliciting the men was (i) to attract their attention to her by tapping on the window pane with some metal object as they passed in the street in front of her and (ii) having so attracted their attention, to invite them in for a price which she indicated by extending three fingers of her hand and indicating the correct door of the premises.   On one occasion the price so indicated by the defendant was agreed and the man entered

[11] *R.* v. *Wiseman* (1718) Fort. 91.
[12] Fortescue Aland J. (later Lord Fortescue), the reporter.
[13] *R.* v. *Wiseman*, *supra*, at p. 92.
[14] *Ibid.*, at p. 93.
[15] Street Offences Act, 1959, s. 1 (1).

the premises, leaving some 15 minutes later. On another occasion, the price so indicated by the defendant was not agreed by
the man concerned who, in his turn, made a counter-proposal as
to price by extending two fingers of his hand. That counter-
proposal was not accepted by the defendant and that man walked
away." [16]

By the common law of Scotland, "all shamelessly indecent
conduct is criminal," even if the parties concerned are adults.[17]
Thus a man was held to be rightfully convicted of using "lewd,
indecent, and libidinous practices" towards another man by
seizing his hand and placing it upon the accused's private parts.[18]
The defendants who escaped in some English cases [19] would not,
it seems, have gone free in Scotland. Yet whatever advantages
the Scottish rule may have, there are grave disadvantages in such
wide and general prohibitions. The Canadian Criminal Code
provided that "every one who commits an act of gross indecency
with another person" was guilty of an offence.[20] This took the
place of an earlier provision which, as in England,[1] was confined
to any *male* person who committed an act of gross indecency
with another *male* person,[2] so that the broadening of the provision seemed marked. In England, any sexual act between
males involving the use of the genital organs is regarded as an
act of gross indecency, even if there is no physical contact [3]; and
heterosexual handling of the genitalia has also been judicially
described as an act of gross indecency.[4]

What, then, was the position in Canada, at all events in
theory? Was not any sexual conduct between male and female
criminal, so that simple fornication and marital intercourse were
alike proscribed? Or was there a concealed exception for
"normal intercourse" (whatever that may be), with criminal

[16] *Smith* v. *Hughes* [1960] 1 W.L.R. 830 at 831, *per* Mr. Graham Rogers.
[17] *M'Laughlan* v. *Boyd*, 1934 J.C. 19.
[18] *Ibid.*
[19] See, *e.g.*, *Fairclough* v. *Whipp* [1951] 2 T.L.R. 909; *Director of Public
Prosecutions* v. *Rogers* [1953] 1 W.L.R. 1017; contrast *Beal* v. *Kelley* [1951]
2 T.L.R. 865. See now Indecency with Children Act, 1960.
[20] Statutes of Canada 1953–54, c. 51, s. 149.
[1] Criminal Law Amendment Act, 1885, s. 11.
[2] Revised Statutes of 1927, c. 36, s. 206.
[3] See, *e.g.*, *R.* v. *Hornby* [1946] 2 All E.R. 487.
[4] See, *e.g.*, *R.* v. *Turner* [1944] K.B. 463 at 465.

sanctions for those who experimented or were over-enthusiastic?
When a word as indefinite as " gross " was coupled with a word
as subjective and emotional in its content as " indecency," there
could be little of that precision which is so desirable in criminal
law. However, in the end there was amending legislation in
order to meet criticisms such as these, made soon after the Code
was enacted.[5] In 1968, the operation of the provision was
excluded where the act was committed in private between man
and wife, or between " any two persons, each of whom is twenty-
one years or more of age," provided in each case both consented
to the act.[6] " Until 1968 such conduct was considered criminal
and punishable " [7]; and on this footing the preceding fifteen years
must have been permeated by an incalculable number of un-
punished sexual offences. The amendment represents a striking
swing of the pendulum. From a total prohibition of all " gross
indecency," no matter where or by whom, the rigours of the law
swept past the old proscription of gross indecency between males
to a state of affairs in which there is immunity for all acts,
whether heterosexual or homosexual, provided they occur in
private between consenting spouses or adults.

In England, neither adultery nor fornication has, *per se*,
been a criminal offence since Oliver Cromwell's time, when an
Act of May 10, 1650,[8] made adultery with a married woman (and
incest also) felony without benefit of clergy, and made fornication punishable by three months' imprisonment. With certain
qualifications, the Act applied to men and women alike. The
drafting of these qualifications led to the somewhat odd conclusion that a man indulging in intercourse with a married woman
whom he believed to be single was guilty of no offence, though
it was felony in the woman; while if the woman had a husband
who had been continually beyond the seas for three years, or was
reputed to be dead, she was guilty of no offence, although it
seems to have been felony in the man. Like the other statutes
of the Interregnum, the Act lapsed with the Restoration; and not

[5] See, *e.g.*, (1955) 71 L.Q.R. 463.
[6] See s. 149A, added by 1968–69, c. 38, s. 7. Ss. 149 and 149A later became
ss. 157 and 158 in R.S.C. 1970, c. 34.
[7] *M*. v. *M*. (1972) 24 D.L.R. (3d) 114 at 126, *per* Nicholson J.
[8] Firth and Rait, *Acts & Ordinances of the Interregnum* (1911) vol. 2, p. 387.

until incest was made a crime by the Punishment of Incest Act, 1908, did any of the offences created by the Act of 1650 again become criminal.

Whether there were any convictions under the Act of 1650 seems doubtful.[9] The generally accepted view is that for at least three centuries adultery and incest were cognisable only in the Ecclesiastical Courts. In these courts, said Blackstone, the law " treated the offence of incontinence, nay even adultery itself, with a great degree of tenderness and lenity; owing perhaps to the constrained celibacy of its first compilers." [10] Yet there are records of a series of indictments for these offences in the reigns of Elizabeth I, James I, Charles I and James II,[11] and in at least one case a sentence is recorded, namely, that the male adulterer should be carted.[12] Coke, indeed, says that " in ancient times adultery and fornication were punished by fine and imprisonment, and were inquirable in turnes and leets by the name of Letherwite." He then cites Domesday Book, and adds " But now these offences belong to the ecclesiasticall court." [13] Yet a proposition established in the King's Bench in 1696 is that " Fine on indictment for lying with another's wife prevents an action." The entire report reads : " The defendant appeared to be fined upon an indictment for seducing and lying with another man's wife. Northy moved to charge him with an action, but the Court would not suffer that now he comes to submit to a fine." [14]

If one turns to modern times and the other side of the Atlantic, it may be observed that as recently as 1951 in the then forty-eight States of the U.S.A. and the District of Columbia, adultery was criminal in forty-four jurisdictions, in all save five of which there was liability to imprisonment : only in Arkansas, Louisiana, Nevada, New Mexico and Tennessee was it no offence. Fornication was similarly criminal in twenty-nine jurisdictions, though in seven of these only a fine might be imposed;

---

[9] 7 C. & P. 200n. states " We are not aware of any convictions upon these enactments."
[10] See 4 Bl.Comm. 65.
[11] A. Cleveland (1913) 29 L.Q.R. 57.
[12] *Ibid.*, at pp. 57, 59, 60 (where the uncertainty of the offence for which Anne Gilbey was convicted is noted). For carting, see 1 Misc. 185.
[13] 3 Co.Inst. 206.
[14] *R.* v. *Johnson* (1696) Comb. 377.

and in fifteen it was no crime. This last category included California and New York, where adultery might (but usually did not) lead to gaol.[15]

In Georgia in 1910 it was held that a statute which made punishable " any person who shall be guilty of open lewdness, or any notorious act of public indecency, tending to debauch the morals " had been infringed by two men who took a bull to a cow in heat in a pasture adjoining a highway on which there was a woman and several children. On appeal, it was contended that, according to this view, " the patriarch Jacob standing at the public watering place and holding the striped rods before Laban's bulls, rams, and he-goats when they leaped, in order that the young might be marked with stripes, would have been guilty of public indecency." On this, the court observed " Perhaps so. But, as able counsel for the state has replied, it will not do to measure modern morals according to the standards of ancient and Biblical times. King Solomon with his thousand wives would not be tolerated in Georgia; and King David, he the man after God's own heart, could hardly justify his whole life according to the provisions of the Penal Code of this state." [16]

Over a decade later in Missouri, a prisoner was accused of having carnal knowledge of a girl under the age of fifteen years. The girl, who was in a reform school, repeatedly refused to answer questions in cross-examination, and thereupon (in the absence of the jury) there was a remarkable colloquy between the trial judge, both counsel, the girl's mother and the sheriff. The judge suggested that the sheriff or the mother should give the girl " a good licking "; the mother said that she would try to get the girl to answer questions; one counsel suggested bread and water in jail, and the other supported the suggestion of whipping; the judge then asked the sheriff to whip the girl; the sheriff demurred, but suggested putting her in the dungeon; the appellants' counsel advised tying her up by her thumbs; and finally the sheriff suggested putting her in jail with " a crazy man " that

[15] See I. Drummond, *The Sex Paradox* (1953) pp. 356–359, where the law is stated as at August 29, 1951 (see p. 345).
[16] *Redd* v. *State*, 67 S.E. 709 at 711 (1910), *per* Powell J.

he had in there. At this point the girl said she would answer questions; and she duly named such a variety of other young men of the neighbourhood who had enjoyed her favours that the appellate court observed that the " wretched girl was young in years but old in sin and shame." [17]

In the same State in the following year, there was a case [18] in which a married girl who seems to have been just under sixteen years old had arrived with her husband at Chillicothe one morning. Her husband at once proceeded to hold discussions with a number of men, and during the day and following night several men visited the girl's room for immoral purposes, including the defendant who later was to appeal. " She, herself, testified that she received no fewer than nine men, among them negroes and the appellant. The next morning she and her husband appeared at the police station and informed against the defendant, the defense claims because she failed to get money which was promised her." [19] On these facts the defendant was convicted of statutory rape, and sentenced to *twenty years* in the State penitentiary. Mercifully, on appeal the judgment was reversed on account of the wrongful admission of evidence.

In North Carolina, a negro was convicted of assault and battery with intent to commit a rape because when he saw a white woman he called after her to stop several times, and ran after her, fleeing when he came in sight of a house. The majority of the North Carolina Supreme Court held the conviction to be right. Speaking for the majority, Pearson C.J. said " I see a chicken-cock drop his wings and take after a hen: my experience and observation assure me that his purpose is sexual intercourse; no other evidence is needed. Whether the cock supposes that the hen is running by female instinct to increase the estimate of her favor and excite passion, or whether the cock intends to carry his purpose by force and against her will, is a question about which there may be some doubt: as, for instance, if she is a sitting hen and ' makes fight,' not merely amorous resistance . . .

[17] *State* v. *Snow*, 252 S.W. 629 at 632 (1923), *per* Commissioner Higbee.
[18] *State* v. *Shobe*, 268 S.W. 81 (1924).
[19] *Ibid.*, at p. 82, *per* White J. See also *People* v. *Sheffield*, 98 Pac. 67 (1908).

Upon this case of the cock and the hen, can any one seriously insist that a jury has no right to call to their assistance their own experience and observation of the nature of animals and of male and female *instincts*? Again: I see a dog in hot pursuit of a rabbit; my experience and observation assure me the intent of the dog is to kill the rabbit; no doubt about it; and yet, according to the argument of the prisoner's counsel, there is no evidence of the intent." [20]

Rodman J., however, dissented. " The argument is, that because from certain actions of certain brute animals a certain intent would be inferred, a like intent must be inferred against the prisoner from like acts. It seems to me that the illustrations are not in point, even if that method of reasoning be allowable at all. The chicken-cock in the case supposed has no intent of violence. He expects acquiescence, and knows he could not succeed without it; and besides, he is dealing with his lawful wife. But the method of reasoning is misleading and objectionable on principle. It assumes that the prisoner is a brute, or so like a brute that it is safe to reason from the one to the other; that he is governed by brutish and, in his case, vicious passions unrestrained by reason or a moral sense. This assumption is unreasonable and unjust." [1]

American authorities are not always justly appreciated in England. In the famous (or infamous) case where starving seamen, cast away at sea, had killed and eaten one of their number, it was held that no defence of necessity availed them against a charge of murder. In delivering the judgment of the court, Lord Coleridge C.J. adverted to an American case [2] " in which it was decided, correctly indeed, that sailors had no right to throw passengers overboard to save themselves, but on the somewhat strange ground that the proper mode of determining who was to be sacrificed was to vote upon the subject by ballot." This, he said, could hardly " be an authority satisfactory to a court in this country." [3]

---

[20] *State* v. *Neely*, 74 N.C. 425 at 427 (1876).
[1] *Ibid.*, at p. 429.
[2] *U.S.* v. *Holmes*, 1 Wallace Jr. 1; 26 Fed.Cas. 360 (1842).
[3] *R.* v. *Dudley and Stephens* (1884) 14 Q.B.D. 273 at 285.

This comment, indeed, appears to display a complete misunderstanding of the case in question. What was there discussed was determining the issue not by secret voting but by the impartial drawing of lots, which is a somewhat different matter. True, in a suitable context " ballot " may indeed mean the drawing of lots[4]; but Lord Coleridge's express reference to " vote " excludes such a construction.

In his summing-up, Baldwin J. had asked a rhetorical question as to what mode of selection was to be employed in such cases, and had said that there was " one condition of extremity for which all writers have prescribed the same rule. When the ship is in no danger of sinking, but all sustenance is exhausted, and a sacrifice of one person is necessary to appease the hunger of others, the selection is by lot. This mode is resorted to as the fairest mode; and, in some sort, as an appeal to God for selection of the victim. . . . For ourselves, we can conceive of no mode so consonant both to humanity and to justice." If there was time to cast lots, " then, as we have said, sortition should be adopted. In no other than this or some like way, are those having equal rights, put upon an equal footing. When the selection has been made by lots, the victim yields of course to his fate; or, if he resists, force may be employed to coerce submission."[5]

English criminal procedure today differs greatly from that in times past and in other countries. Majority verdicts have recently been introduced, under certain strict limitations[6]; but in Scotland such verdicts, without the limitations, have long existed. There, the jury is fifteen in number; and Not Proven is a possible verdict. In one case in 1957 these factors combined oddly. The foreman of a jury announced a verdict of Guilty by a Majority on both the charges before the court. After some discussion on procedural matters but before the verdict had been recorded, the defending advocate asked if he might be told what the majority was; and the foreman then said " Six for guilty,

---

[4] See, *e.g.*, *Eyre* v. *Milton Proprietary Ltd.* [1936] Ch. 244.
[5] *U.S.* v. *Holmes, supra*, 1 Wallace Jr. at pp. 25–27; 26 Fed.Cas. at p. 367.
[6] Criminal Justice Act, 1967, s. 13.

five for not guilty and four for not proven, on each charge." At this, the Sheriff intimated that he did not consider this to be a verdict of guilty, and, on the prosecution making no objection, he directed that a verdict of Not Guilty should be entered.[7] This result may have been due to the lack of popularity for Not Proven as a verdict; for Not Proven seems to have been the only verdict for which there could be said to be at least a theoretical majority. Each vote for Not Guilty must have been *a fortiori* a vote for Not Proven; but the converse is not true. This decision not only demonstrates the circumstances in which five out of a Scottish fifteen may effectively be the majority and six the minority, but also invites speculation: what, for instance, should the verdict have been if the votes had been seven, two and six, respectively?

The more technical the law, the more likely it is to be defeated by technicalities. In 1823 Thomas Halloway enjoyed a modest triumph at Hereford Assizes. He was charged with stealing a brass furnace in the county of Hereford. The evidence showed that he stole the furnace in the county of Radnor, broke it, and then brought the fragments into the county of Hereford. Hullock B. directed an acquittal. "Though a prisoner may be indicted for a larceny in any county, into which he takes stolen property, the present indictment must fail, as he never had the 'brass furnace' in Herefordshire . . . : he merely had there certain pieces of brass."[8] Halloway was then indicted for stealing "two turkies." The evidence showed that two dead turkeys had been stolen from a larder. Hullock B. ruled that "this indictment could not be supported; for 'two turkies' must be taken to mean live turkies. It ought to have been for stealing two dead turkies."[9]

The reporter appends a note to this case in which he refers to "the well-known cases of a man, indicted for stealing a pair of stockings, being acquitted, because the stockings were proved to be odd ones; or of the person acquitted of stealing a duck,

[7] *Lord Advocate* v. *Nicholson*, 1958 S.L.T.(Sh.Ct.) 17.
[8] R. v. *Halloway* (1823) 1 C. & P. 127.
[9] R. v. *Halloway* (1823) 1 C. & P. 128 at 129.

because in proof it turned out to be a drake. . . . Perhaps the most curious distinction between living and dead is, that the stealing the skin of a dog, like stealing any other skin from the furrier, is a larceny; whereas stealing the living dog, which is the skin and something more, is no larceny; dogs being considered in law of a base nature, and not subject to larceny." [10] The reference to odd stockings carries one to Lord Eldon's pairs of gloves. " When I was Solicitor or Attorney General we had this ingenious case of smuggling proved. A person at Dover smuggled 3,000 pairs of French gloves. He sent all the right-hand gloves to London. They were seized and sold. Nobody would buy right-hand gloves, who had not the left-hand gloves. The smuggler therefore bought them for a trifle. Having purchased the right-hand gloves, he then sent the 3,000 left-hand gloves to London. They were also seized, sold, and of course bought by him for a price next to nothing. Thus he became possessed of them, though contraband, according to law, and, as a smuggler would say, in an honest way." [11]

Whiteside C.J. once referred to the rule against mentioning previous convictions to a jury even in cases where there is an increased penalty for second and subsequent offences. He said that it was " most necessary, for securing a fair trial to the prisoner, that this course should be followed. I recollect myself a case of the kind, in which I was concerned at the bar, where the jury were a long time finding a verdict upon the subsequent felony, and when at length they brought in a verdict of guilty, and they were then charged to inquire as to the previous conviction, the foreman said if they had heard of that before it would have saved a world of trouble." [12] It was during argument in a criminal appeal that Lord Russell of Killowen C.J. once said " I remember a case in which a very innocent remark of my own elicited the fact of a previous conviction. A prisoner was addressing the jury very effectively, as I thought, on his own behalf. But he spoke in a low voice, and, not hearing some part

[10] 1 C. & P. 127n.
[11] Twiss, *Eldon*, vol. 1, p. 205; *Lord Eldon's Anecdote Book* (1960) p. 52.
[12] *R.* v. *Fox* (1866) 15 W.R. 106 at 108.

of his observations, I said ' What did you say? What was your last sentence? '—' Six months, my Lord,' he replied." [13]

One summing-up by O'Grady C.B. was pithy. A boy was charged with stealing some trousers. The evidence was clear, though the boy was given an excellent character. " Gentlemen," said the Chief Baron to the jury, " the prisoner was an honest boy, but he stole the breeches." [14] And that was all. It was Lord Campbell who recounted that he once heard a judge at Stafford, in sentencing a prisoner to death for forging a pound note, exhort him to prepare for another world, and add " And I trust that, through the merits and mediation of Our Blessed Redeemer, you may there experience that mercy which a due regard to the credit of the paper currency of the country forbids you to hope for here." [15] To this account Lord Campbell provides a fitting pendant by setting out the words of an unnamed Scottish judge who told the prisoner that as the verdict was only " Not proven," and not " Not guilty," he left the court with the mark of suspicion on him; and, added the judge, " you will do well to remember that you remain under the eyes of an all-searching Providence, and of that active officer Captain Brown of the Edinburgh Police Establishment." [16]

Lord Cockburn himself heard Lord Eskgrove,[17] with his odd ideas and odd diction, sentence a tailor to death for murder. The tailor had stabbed a soldier, and with some particularity the judge expatiated on the gravity of the prisoner's conduct. " Not only did you murder him, whereby he was berea-ved of his life, but you did thrust, or push, or pierce, or project, or propell, the le-thall weapon through the belly-band of his regimen-tal breeches, which were his Majes-ty's! " [18] Over a century and a half later Lord Eskgrove would have found a spiritual cousin of his on the bench at the Old Bailey. Two men had committed mutually indecent assaults under Waterloo Bridge; and in sen-

13 *R.* v. *Gardner* (1898) 15 T.L.R. 26 at 27 (omitted from [1899] 1 Q.B. 150).
14 J. R. Flanagan, *The Irish Bar* (1879) p. 192.
15 2 Camp.C.JJ. 444 (the italics in the original have been suppressed).
16 *Ibid.*
17 Later Lord Justice-Clerk, 1782–1804.
18 Henry Cockburn, *Memorials of His Time* (1856: 1909 ed.) p. 112.

tencing them the judge said, in tones of some emotional indignation, " You two committed this *beastly* crime—and under one of
London's *loveliest* bridges." [19]   In preventive criminology the
judge's words were equally well chosen.   To a labourer who
pleaded that alcohol was always the cause of his downfall, the
judge said " You are not to touch alcohol ever again: not even
a *teeny, weeny* sherry before dinner." [20]

[19] See 1957 S.L.T.News. 143, *per* Judge Maude Q.C.
[20] Eric Stockdale, *The Court and the Offender* (1967) p. 34.

Tiger Days Excepted

THE range of subjects upon which men make contracts is almost infinite. In 1861, in *Rogers* v. *Havergal*,[1] the plaintiff recovered judgment for £2 10s. for twenty sermons sold and delivered. He was a retired clergyman, and the defendant was Vicar of Cople in Bedfordshire. The court was informed that " sermons fetched all prices—some as high as £5 5s. A Bishop's charge or an Archdeacon's address would fetch the latter price." A sermon before the Lord Mayor of London would cost from £3 3s. to £5 5s. Three years later, in *Rogers* v. *Walcot*,[2] the defendant was Rector of Ribbesford, and the sum successfully claimed was £42 14s. 6d. for 326 sermons, including " harvest sermons at 2s. 6d. each, others at 5s. each, and one for a special occasion at a guinea." Indeed, " Illegality apart, a man may make himself answerable in damages for the happening or not happening of what event he likes." [3] Thus " a man may, if he chooses, covenant that it shall rain tomorrow." [4]

Sometimes the question is whether there is any contract at all. A " gentleman's agreement " is said to have been defined by Vaisey J. as " an agreement which is not an agreement, made between two persons, neither of whom is a gentleman, whereby each expects the other to be strictly bound without himself being bound at all." [5] And Hallett J. once observed that " a gentleman's agreement usually ends in each party calling the other no gentleman." [6] Again, the question has been asked whether the giving up of a grievance, real or imagined, will amount to

---

[1] G. Pitt-Lewis, *Commissioner Kerr* (1903) p. 193.
[2] *Ibid.*, at p. 194.
[3] *Beasley* v. *Texas & Pacific Railway Co.*, 191 U.S. 492 at 497 (1903), *per* Holmes J.
[4] *Canham* v. *Barry* (1855) 15 C.B. 597 at 619, *per* Maule J.
[5] Reputedly (i) an unreported interlocutory observation in *Bloom* v. *Kinder* [1958] T.R. 91; 38 T.C. 77; 37 A.T.C. 158; and (ii) a statement in a lecture at the University of Edinburgh (see D. Hughes Parry, *The Sanctity of Contracts in English Law* (1959) p. 27).
[6] *Scene Estate Ltd.* v. *Amos* [1956] Dec. 3, unrep., *ex rel.* R.E.M. (on appeal [1957] 2 Q.B. 205).

valuable consideration that will support a contract. *White* v. *Bluett* [7] demonstrates that the answer must sometimes, at all events, be No. A son gave a promissory note to his father, and in due course his father's executors sued him for payment. It was urged by way of defence that the father had agreed to discharge the son from all liability on the note in return for the son agreeing to cease for ever from complaining that the father had not given him as much money or as many advantages as the other children.

Parke B. really disposed of this contention by a single question to counsel for the defence during the argument: " Is an agreement by a father, in consideration that his son will not bore him, a binding contract? " [8] The judgment of Pollock C.B. was emphatic. The defence, he said, " is clearly bad. By the argument a principle is pressed to an absurdity, as a bubble is blown until it bursts. Looking at the words merely, there is some foundation for the argument, and, following the words only, the conclusion may be arrived at." But, he said, after referring to the facts, if the defence was good " the following would be a binding promise: A man might complain that another person used the public highway more than he ought to do, and that other might say, do not complain, and I will give you five pounds. It is ridiculous to suppose that such promises could be binding. . . . In reality, there was no consideration whatever. The son had no right to complain, for the father might make what distribution of his property he liked; and the son's abstaining from doing what he had no right to do can be no consideration." [9]

Attempts to escape liability, too, are sometimes of engaging simplicity. Twisden J. once recounted " que il remember tiel nice case, quil fuit que Sr. William Fish fuit oblige per obligation pur pay tiel jour in Grays-Inn-Hall fifty pounds (sans dire de argent) et pur ceo sur le jour quant les gent'homes fueront al supper il vient & tender fifty pounds weight de stone, & adjudge nul tender." [10] Some three centuries later another attempt

[7] (1853) 23 L.J.Ex. 36.
[8] *Ibid.*, at p. 37.
[9] *Ibid.*   [10] *Hooker* v. *Swaine* (1663) 1 Sid. 151.

persuaded the court into metaphor. " Although Fry did not
dispute his signature to the judgment note, he testified that he
was unaware that the paper he signed was a judgment note. . . .
This is rather thin ice on which to skate to the shores of non-
liability. . . . The whole business structure of America would
become a shambles if signers in serious transactions were to be
allowed to repudiate their obligations on the basis that they did
not know what they were signing. The ever-constant possibility
of such a disavowal would turn into water the adhesive mortar
of legal responsibility holding together the bricks of every con-
tractual wall; such an accepted possibility would wreck every
business dealing at the slightest touch of the repudiator." [11]

Simple facts sometimes engender nice problems. In Cork, on
a summer's evening in 1900, a Mrs. Wallis sent her grand-
daughter, a Miss Donovan, to Russells, the fishmongers, for two
crabs. " Miss Donovan asked for ' two nice fresh crabs which
Mrs. Wallis wanted for her tea.' " The manager of Russells
" said that ' they had no live crabs in stock, but that he had
boiled crabs.' He ' took up two nice crabs ': he was asked
' Were they nice and fresh? ' He said, ' Yes.' He selected
two, and he ' put away ' one which Miss Donovan said ' looked
better,' because he ' knew by the weight and feel of the crabs
that the ones he selected were better.' Miss Donovan paid 6d.
for them, and took them home." [12] The two ladies ate the crab
that evening, and both became seriously ill in the night; indeed,
Miss Donovan nearly died. Mrs. Wallis sued Russells for
damages for breach of warranty, and relied on the Sale of Goods
Act, 1893, s. 14 (1), which provides that, on the sale of goods
within the course of the seller's business, " if the buyer, expressly
or by implication, makes known to the seller the particular purpose for which the goods are required, so as to show that the
buyer relies upon the seller's skill or judgment," there is an
implied condition that the goods are reasonably fit for that
purpose.

The case was tried by Lord O'Brien C.J. and a jury; and it

11 *General Refrigerator and Store Fixture Co.* v. *Fry*, 141 A. 2d 836 at 838
(1958), *per* Musmanno J.
12 *Wallis* v. *Russell* [1902] 2 I.R. 585 at 607, *per* FitzGibbon L.J.

went on appeal to the King's Bench Division and the Court of
Appeal.[13] The debate ranged wide. FitzGibbon L.J., indeed,
began with the Year Books.[14] Yet as Holmes L.J. observed,
" A young lawyer might think it was a case for applying the rule
of caveat emptor; but with more experience he would know that
a Latin maxim goes but a short way towards solving legal
difficulties." [15] In the end, all concurred in holding that the
plaintiff's claim was well founded, though the damages, a
mere £150, were modest. Such actions were uncommon in
these days, but " Mrs. Wallis happened to be the mother of one
of the most original and courageous solicitors in Cork, who at a
later date distinguished himself by having his office premises
and their gardens situated in the main street of the town of
Midleton, declared to be a holding that was partly agricultural
or pastoral, and thus entitled to the benefit of the Irish Land Acts.
To a mind of such daring an action about a diseased crab would
be a trifle." [16] Today, when under the tutelage of the Parliament
of the United Kingdom the Court of Appeal has established that
a public house in Shropshire entitled " The Live and Let Live
Inn " was part of an agricultural holding within the Agricultural
Holdings Act, 1948,[17] the daring seems less remarkable.

The course of the trial, as revealed by the law reports, may be
supplemented by an account from another source. Miss Donovan
was giving evidence before Lord O'Brien C.J., known universally
to the Bar by his christian name which, by his lisp, had become
" Pether." " ' I am a companion to Mrs. Wallis,' she said. ' I
went out to buy her some little tasty thing that she might fancy
for her tea; and I suddenly thought of a crab. I knew that
Russell's had cooked crabs; so I went in there, and asked the
shopman for a nice cooked crab, telling him I wanted it for Mrs.
Wallis's supper, so as to make known to him the purpose for
which it was to be used.' Pether pricked up his ears. ' You
thaid that? ' he asked. ' Yes, my Lord.' ' In thothe very

13 *Wallis* v. *Russell* [1902] 2 I.R. 585.
14 *Ibid.*, at p. 611.
15 *Ibid.*, at p. 630; and see *ante*, p. 158.
16 M. Healy, *The Old Munster Circuit* (1939) p. 209.
17 *Dunn* v. *Fidoe* [1950] 2 All E.R. 685.

wordth?' 'Yes, my Lord.' Pether reflected a moment.
'Remarkable the thtrideth education ith taking,' he commented.
'Go on.' The young lady took up her tale. 'Well, then, when
I had told him that, he looked at the crabs, and he selected one
and gave it to me. So I, relying on his skill and judgment, took
it—' 'Thtop, thtop!' cried Pether. 'You uthed thothe wordth
also?' 'Yes, my Lord.' 'Where were you educated?' 'At
the Ursuline Convent, Blackrock, my Lord.' 'And thinth when
have the Urthuline Thithters included Thection Fourteen of the
Thale of Goodth Act in their curriculum?' 'I don't know, my
Lord; I did not get beyond domestic economy.' 'Ah-h! That'th
where it ith; they teach you to buy food?' 'Yes, my Lord.'
'And they tell you, "Never buy anything without telling the
shopman what it ith for, tho that you can thay you have relied
on his thkill and judgment"?' 'Yes, my Lord.' 'What
admirable nunth!' said Pether." [18]

Illegality often reaches far, though it is not all-embracing.
"A person does not become an outlaw and lose all rights by
doing an illegal act." [19] In one eighteenth-century case a man
agreed to sell a quantity of counterfeit halfpennies, and gave
them to a carrier to deliver to the purchaser. The carrier was to
collect the purchase price from the purchaser, retaining only a
commission; but when he had received the money, he refused to
pay it to the vendor, and claimed that as the original contract
was illegal the court would not compel him to pay over the fruits
of the contract. This contention failed, however, for the carrier
was no party to the illegal contract, and could not take advantage
of its illegality to retain money delivered to him for the vendor's
use. [20] To modern eyes perhaps the most remarkable feature
of the case is that even in those days it should have been thought
commercially profitable to counterfeit halfpennies.

In one leading case, [1] however, a bond for £700 was given as

[18] M. Healy, *supra*, p. 210; and for a variant, see A. M. Sullivan, *The Last
Serjeant* (1952) p. 117. Deviations from the report (as to the number of
crabs, the words used, and the like) are no doubt to be deplored: but the
substratum remains.
[19] *National Bank & Loan Co.* v. *Petrie*, 189 U.S. 423 at 425 (1903), *per*
Holmes J.
[20] *Farmer* v. *Russell* (1798) 1 B. & P. 296.
[1] *Collins* v. *Blantern* (1767) 2 Wils.K.B. 341.

part of an arrangement to stifle a prosecution for perjury, and when an action was brought for the money, the question was whether illegality was a good defence, and whether the defendant could plead it; for no trace of it appeared on the face of the bond. The Court of King's Bench had no doubt about the answer. Wilmot C.J. said that " the manner of the transaction was to gild over and conceal the truth; and whenever Courts of Law see such attempts made to conceal such wicked deeds, they will brush away the cobweb varnish, and shew the transactions in their true light. . . . This is a contract to tempt a man to transgress the law, to do that which is injurious to the community: it is void by the common law; and the reason why the common law says such contracts are void, is for the public good. You shall not stipulate for iniquity. All writers upon our law agree in this, no polluted hand shall touch the pure fountains of justice. Whoever is a party to an unlawful contract, if he hath once paid the money stipulated to be paid in pursuance thereof, he shall not have the help of a Court to fetch it back again, you shall not have a right of action when you come into a Court of Justice in this unclean manner to recover it back. Procul O! procul este profani." [2]

The argument that the plea of illegality could be advanced in equity but not in a court of law received short shrift. " I answer, we are upon a mere point of common law, which must have been a question of law, long before Courts of Equity exercised that jurisdiction which we now see them exercise; a jurisdiction which never would have swelled to that enormous bulk we now see, if the Judges of the Courts of Common Law had been anciently as liberal as they have been in later times: to send the defendant in this case into a Court of Equity, is to say there never was any remedy at law against such a wicked contract as this is: we all know when the equity part of the Court of Chancery began. I should have been extremely sorry if this case had been without remedy at common law, est boni judicis ampliare jurisdictionem [3]; and I say, est boni judicis ampliare

<hr>

[2] " Begone, begone, ye godless ones " : *Aeneid* iv. 258.
[3] " A good judge extends his jurisdiction."

justitiam [4]; therefore, whenever such cases as this come before
a Court of Law, it is for the public good that the common law
should reach them and give relief. I have always thought that
formerly there was too confined a way of thinking in the Judges
of the Common Law Courts, and that Courts of Equity have
risen by the Judges not properly applying the principles of the
common law, but being too narrowly governed by the old cases
and maxims, which have too much prevented the public from
having the benefit of the common law." [5]

Wilmot C.J. then turned to the argument that the illegality
could not be pleaded as a defence. " If this wicked contract is
not pleadable, it will be good at law, be sanctified thereby, and
have the same legal operation as a good and an honest contract,
which seems to me most unreasonable and unrighteous, and
therefore, unless I am chained down by law to reject this plea, I
will admit it, and let justice take place. What strange absurdity
would it be for the law to say that this contract is wicked and
void, and in the same breath for the law to say, you shall not be
permitted to plead the facts which clearly shew it to be wicked
and void. I am not for stirring a single pebble of the common
law, and without altering the least tittle thereof, I think it is
competent, and reaches the case before us." [6] The Chief Justice
also referred to the contention that whereas a contract made void
by statute was totally void, a contract void at common law might
be void as to part and good as to the rest. " It is said, the statute
is like a tyrant, when he comes he makes all void, but the
common law is like a nursing father, makes only void that part
where the fault is, and preserves the rest." [7] But this, he said,
" proves nothing in the present case " [8]; and so the action failed.

Suretyship gives rise to many problems. "Almost all who
sign as surety have occasion to remember the proverb of Solo-

---

[4] " A good judge increases justice." " Justitiam " and not " jurisdictionem "
is the " true text ": *R.* v. *Philips* (1757) 1 Burr. 292 at 304, *per* Lord
Mansfield C.J. The note at (1968) 84 L.Q.R. 170 (H. W. R. Wade) does
not cite the use of this phrase by Wilmot C.J.

[5] *Collins* v. *Blantern, supra,* at pp. 349, 350.

[6] *Ibid.,* at p. 351.

[7] *Ibid.,* at p. 351: see *Maleverer* v. *Redshaw* (1671) 1 Mod. 35, *per* Twisden J.,
citing Hobart C.J., cited in *Pickering* v. *Ilfracombe Ry.* (1868) L.R. 3 C.P.
235 at 250, *per* Willes J.   [8] *Collins* v. *Blantern, supra,* at p. 351.

mon: ' He that is surety for a stranger shall smart for it, and
he that hateth suretyship is sure.'' [9]   But they are nevertheless
held liable upon their contracts, otherwise there could be no
smarting, and the proverb would fail." [10]   Yet " It would be as
difficult for me to conceive of a surety's liability continuing
after the principal obligation was discharged, as of a shadow's
remaining after the substance was removed." [11]

The frustration of contracts by supervening impossibility is
not the simplest part of this branch of English law.   One theory
upon which frustration has been based is that there is to be
implied in the contract a term excusing performance if it
becomes impossible.   This theory has had its Scottish critics,
one of whom, Lord Sands, ventured an illustrative example.
" A tiger has escaped from a travelling menagerie.   The milkgirl
fails to deliver the milk.   Possibly the milkman may be exonera-
ted from any breach of contract; but, even so, it would seem
hardly reasonable to base that exoneration on the ground that
' tiger days excepted ' must be held as if written into the milk
contract." [12]   Nor have the English cases on the subject exerted
an unqualified appeal to the South African courts.   " If the
Courts are to interfere on grounds of equity alone in commercial
bargains, where does the process end?   Some of the dicta seem
to suggest that we have here the thin end of a wedge whose
exact shape and full dimensions remain undefined.   A few more
taps, maybe, and the granite concept of sanctity of contract will
be shattered." [13]

Taylor v. *Caldwell* [14] has long been one of the leading cases
upon frustration.   Taylor and Lewis agreed with Caldwell and
Bishop to provide a series of concerts and entertainments at the
Surrey Gardens and Music Hall, Newington.   The agreement
provided in some detail for the forms of entertainment and
concluded with a provision that Taylor and Lewis would " find

[9] Proverbs xii, 15.
[10] *Mayo* v. *Hutchinson*, 57 Maine 546 at 547 (1870), *per* Appleton C.J.
[11] *Farmers and Mechanics' Bank of Michigan* v. *Kingsley*, 2 Doug.(Mich.) 379
at 403 (1846), *per* Ransom C.J.
[12] *James Scott & Sons Ltd.* v. *Del Sel*, 1922 S.C. 592 at 597, cited in *Davis
Contractors Ltd.* v. *Fareham U.D.C.* [1956] A.C. 696 at 720, *per* Lord Reid.
[13] *Techni-Pak Sales (Pty.) Ltd.* v. *Hall*, 1968 (3) S.A. 231 at 238, *per* Colman J.;
and see *ante*, p. 292.   [14] (1863) 3 B. & S. 826.

and provide, at their own sole cost, all the necessary artistes for the said concerts, including Mr. Sims Reeves, God's will permitting." After Taylor and Lewis had incurred some preparatory expenses on advertisements and other matters, the music hall was accidentally burnt down, and so the festivities could not take place. Taylor and Lewis claimed damages for breach of contract, but the Court of Queen's Bench held that the contract had been frustrated, and further performance had been excused.

Counsel for the defendants relied strongly on the words " God's will permitting," which, he said, overrode the whole agreement [15]; but the court relied on the common law and the civil law rather than Divine intervention. The reason for the insertion of these words (which must have provoked the curiosity of generations of law students) seems to have been limited and personal rather than general and overriding. For Pollock once wrote of his parents paying homage to Handel's *Messiah*, " more especially when Sims Reeves was the tenor and actually sang, as to which there was a constant element of doubt until the last moment. He preserved his voice for an extraordinary length of time by nursing it with extreme care and strictly refusing to force it when it was not in perfect condition." [16] In this context, " God's will permitting " might with some justice have been construed as meaning " Sims Reeves being willing."

From frustration to breach is no great step. There are many authorities on the extent to which a person will be liable for the consequences which flow from his breach of a contract. Willes J. once said " Cases of this kind have always been found to be very difficult to deal with, beginning with a case said to have been decided about two centuries and a half ago, where a man going to be married to an heiress, his horse having cast a shoe on the journey, employed a blacksmith to replace it, who did the work so unskilfully that the horse was lamed, and, the rider not arriving in time, the lady married another; and the blacksmith was held liable for the loss of the marriage. The question is a very serious one; and we should inevitably fall into a similar absurdity unless we applied the rules of common sense to restrict

---

[15] *Ibid.*, at p. 831.   [16] Sir Frederick Pollock, *For My Grandson* (1933) p. 113.

the extent of liability for the breach of a contract of this sort." [17]
Similarly with tort. " The argument in the old fable in which
the loss of a kingdom is traced back to an originating and ultimate cause in the loss of a single nail from a horse's shoe does
not commend itself to me as adaptable to this case." [18]

If a covenant is broken, the plaintiff " is, at all events, entitled
to nominal damages." However, although "everybody will
admit that there is some vexation in finding that the contract is
not performed," yet "the law allows nothing for that. It is
one of the evils of life, and every one must bear his own share
of them." [19] Indeed, "Nominal damages are a mere peg on
which to hang costs. . . . Nominal damages, in fact, mean a
sum of money that may be spoken of, but that has no existence
in point of quantity: and I think that a man may very well pay
£50 in satisfaction and discharge of a debt of £50 and the
nominal damages due for its detention." [20] Yet this view is not
universal. " The Latin proverb, *qui cito dat bis dat*, — he who
gives quickly gives twice, — has its counterpart in a maxim
equally sound, — *qui serius solvit, minus solvit*, — he who pays
too late, pays less." [1]

There is temptation in the easy phrase of Holmes J. that one
may commit a contract, just as one may commit a tort: in each
case one thereby exposes oneself to liability to another, though
there is the difference that the former creates a liability nisi, while
the latter creates a liability absolute. [2] Yet as Holmes himself
said in one judgment, " People when contracting contemplate
performance, not breach." [3] " A person contemplates the performance and not the breach of his contract; he does not enter
into a kind of second contract to pay damages." [4] " Any party

[17] *British Columbia and Vancouver's Island Spar, Lumber and Saw-Mill Co.
Ltd.* v. *Nettleship* (1868) L.R. 3 C.P. 499 at 508. See also *Everard* v.
Hopkins (1615) 2 Bulstr. 332.
[18] *Norris* v. *W. Moss & Sons Ltd.* [1954] 1 W.L.R. 346 at 351, *per* Vaisey J.
[19] *Hamlin* v. *Great Northern Railway Co.* (1856) 26 L.J.Ex. 20 at 22, 23, *per*
Pollock C.B.
[20] *Beaumont* v. *Greathead* (1846) 2 C.B. 494 at 499, *per* Maule J.
[1] *Louisiana* v. *New Orleans*, 102 U.S. 203 at 207 (1880), *per* Field J.
[2] 1 *Holmes-Pollock Letters* 177; 2 *ibid.* 200.
[3] *Globe Refining Co.* v. *Landa Cotton Oil Co.*, 190 U.S. 540 at 543 (1903).
[4] *Hydraulic Engineering Co. Ltd.* v. *McHaffie, Goslett & Co.* (1878) 4 Q.B.D.
670 at 674, *per* Bramwell L.J.

to a contract can break it if he chooses; but in point of law he is not entitled to break it even on offering to pay damages. If he wants to entitle himself to do that he must stipulate for an option to that effect." [5]

In one case damages were claimed in New York for breach of contract in failing to make available the capital necessary for the construction and operation of a garbage plant in Miami. The jury awarded $560,000.00, but the judge held that there must be a new trial. Much turned on the quantity and quality of saleable humus that the plant would have produced, but the evidence on this point had been inconclusive. " The evidence is clear that the operation of a similar plant in Cannes, France, results in reducing the garbage there dealt with to a so-called humus which is valuable and salable as a fertilizer or soil enricher or soil conditioner." But the real question was " whether or not there is a reasonable basis for a finding as to the amount of humus the operation of the Miami plant would produce; and, if so, what amount has reasonable support in the evidence. There is some opinion evidence that city garbage is much the same the world over, with some slight difference that in this country such garbage will produce more humus than French garbage because Americans are more wasteful than French people in the amount and kind of food they throw away. There is also opinion evidence that garbage varies greatly and that in the absence of data as to the nature of Miami's garbage it is impossible to tell how much humus the operation of Miami's plant would produce. There is here no evidence as to the actual nature of Miami's garbage. . . ." [6] On appeal, it was held that the defendant was entitled to judgment, and that no new trial should be held.[7] The courts thus escaped any inquiry into the comparative opulence of the garbage of Miami, Florida, and Cannes, France.

[5] *South Wales Miners' Federation* v. *Glamorgan Coal Co. Ltd.* [1905] A.C. 239 at 253, *per* Lord Lindley. Contrast the views of Holmes J., and Buckland's answer (not citing the quotations above): (1944) 8 Camb.L.J. 247 *et seq.*; W. W. Buckland, *Some Reflections on Jurisprudence* (1945) p. 97 *et seq.*
[6] *Biothermal Process Corp.* v. *Cohu & Co.*, 119 N.Y.S. 2d 158 at 168 (1953), *per* Walter J.
[7] S.C., 126 N.Y.S. 2d 1 (1953); 124 N.E. 2d 323 (1954).

A Bursen-Bellied Hound

THE profession has not been uniformly successful in proceedings for defamation. All three branches figured in some seventeenth-century cases. " One said, That my Lord Chief Baron cannot hear of one ear colloquio praehabito [1] of his administration of Justice; And it was adjudged actionable. Otherwise it had been if they had no discourse of his Justice." [2] So also with the Bar. " Si home dit al un Utterbarrester, ' Thou art no Lawyer, thou canst not make a Lease, thou hast that degree without desert, they are Fools that come to thee for Law,' Action gist." [3] But alas for the attorneys! For if it were said of an attorney that he had made false writings, " No action will lie, for it is no scandal to him in his profession, for it doth not appertaine to an Attorney, to make writings, no more then it appertaines to an Appothecary to give Physick, and so it is no scandal to him in his profession." [4] There is perhaps some pre-echo here of Lord Sumner's words in an action for slander brought three centuries later. He observed that according to one report " The plaintiff was an ordinary doctor at Hull, and so did not belong to that class of medical practitioners, which the appellant's counsel postulated but never defined, for whose professional wellbeing a reputation at least for continence was said not to be a general requisite." [5]

In 1593 the words " Sir Christopher Hilliard is a blood-sucker, and sucketh blood " were held by the Court of Queen's Bench not to be actionable, even though Sir Christopher was " a justice of the peace, and one of the council in the north "; the words " cannot be any slander, for it cannot be intended what blood he sucketh." [6] Two years later, the point was resolved in the same sense by a majority of all the judges of England, though

---

[1] Freely, " thereby speaking."
[2] *Alleston* v. *Moor* (1631) Het. 167.
[3] *Bankes* v. *Allen* (1615) 1 Roll.Abr. 54.
[4] *Auditor Curles Case* (1622) Winch 39 at 40, *per* Hobart C.J., referring to *Eliot* v. *Brown* (1620), unreported.
[5] *Jones* v. *Jones* [1916] 2 A.C. 481 at 496.
[6] *Hilliard* v. *Constable* (1593) Cro.Eliz. 306.

the words seem to have been slightly varied: "He is a blood-sucker, and sucketh others blood." [7] (Indeed, another report varies it still further: "He is a blood-sucker and thirsteth after blood." [8]) At some stage (it is not clear which) the Queen's Bench had found itself equally divided on the point. Gawdy and Fenner JJ. held that "it is usual when a justice of peace pursues offenders, and does his office, to call him ' blood-sucker '; and it is not any slander unto him, and may be taken in some good sense in executing his office, and not *in malam partem*,[9] that he is a blood-sucker in seeking murder or otherwise." Popham C.J. and Clench J., on the other hand, held that the expression should be "construed according to the common intendment of the word, which is always *in malam partem*; and to suck blood is to take blood unjustly from a person." But this view did not prevail with the majority, and "blood-sucker" obtained its clearance.

One eighteenth-century *cause célèbre* lay in Scotland. "The Society of Procurators practising in the commissary and inferior courts at Edinburgh, obtained a charter from the crown, erecting them into a corporation, under the name of ' The Society of Solicitors before the Commissary, Sheriff, and City Courts of Edinburgh.' This grant was notified in the London Gazette; and an advertisement to the same purpose appeared likewise in the Edinburgh newspapers; in which, however, instead of the word *Solicitors*, as above, the appellation *Solicitors at Law* was used; and in addition to the article contained in the Gazette, it was said, That the Society, by their charter, were invested with ' the sole and exclusive right of pleading and conducting suits before those Courts, the Honourable Faculty of Advocates excepted.'

"Soon after, the following paragraph, apparently drawn up in allusion to these variations, was inserted in a paper called *The Edinburgh Gazette*, published by Thomas Robertson. ' A correspondent informs us, that he hears the Worshipful Society of *Chaldeans, Cadies* [errand boys], or *Running-Stationers*, of this

---

[7] *Hilliard* v. *Constable* (1595) Cro.Eliz. 433.
[8] *Hilliard* v. *Constable* (1595) Moo.K.B. 418.
[9] " In bad part.'

city, are resolved, in imitation, and encouraged by the singular
success of their brethren of an *equally respectable* Society, to
apply for a Charter of their Privileges, particularly of the sole
privilege of PROCURING, in the most extensive sense of the word,
exclusive of chairmen, porters, penny-post men, and all other
inferior ranks; their brethren the R-Y-L S-L-RS, *alias* P-C-RS, *before
the inferior* courts of this city, always excepted.—Should the
Worshipful Society be successful, they are farther resolved not
to be *puffed up* thereby, but to demean themselves with more
equanimity and decency than their *R-y-l*, *learned*, and *very
modest* brethren, above mentioned, have done upon their late
dignification and exaltation.' The Solicitors, thinking themselves injured by the innuendoes conveyed in this paragraph,
instituted an action against Robertson; and, in their libel, concluded for very high damages,[10] both in behalf of the Society,
and of themselves as individuals." [11]

Lord Hailes held that the action lay, but " in regard that no
special damages are proved, and that no great damages could
have ensued from a publication meriting rather scorn than complaint," [12] awarded only £5 damages, with £15 costs. The
defendant appealed, and after some difference of opinion the
majority held that " no sufficient *animus injuriandi* [13] was
proved," so that the action failed.[14] Lord Alva said " Societies
ought not to give themselves trouble about such idle pieces of
buffoonery," and Lord Monboddo observed that " the society
was under no necessity of having the joke recorded in our
books." Lord Braxfield, too, apparently thought that the damages awarded to the plaintiffs would be injury added to insult:
" it would injure them to award such small damages as £5 to be
divided into nineteen shares."

The Lord President (Lord Dundas), on the other hand, said
" I think that it is below a man to bring such an action as this;

[10] " £2000 and upwards ": see *Solicitors at Law* v. *Robertson* (1781) 2 Hailes
Dec. 882, *per* Lord Braxfield.
[11] *The Preses and Society of Solicitors before the Commissary, Sheriff and City
Courts of Edinburgh* v. *Robertson* (1781) 9 Fac.Col. 4.
[12] *Ibid.*, at p. 5.
[13] " Intention of injuring."
[14] *Solicitors at Law* v. *Robertson, supra.*

but, when brought, it must be tried by the rules of law." Lord Gardenstone looked at England: "No society ought to be injured; and when I consider this advertisement, I cannot help thinking that there is something illiberal in it, like what prevails in our neighbouring country." [15] Lord Hailes leaves no doubt as to his view of the reversal of his decision, for he appends an N.B. to his report of the divergent views of the judges. "This question was determined by the vote of Lord A—,[16] who, from infirmity, was not able to form a judgment. The *ratio decidendi* was invented by the President, after the vote was put and carried against his opinion. Had a preliminary question been put, as to the *animus injuriandi*, the Court would have voted in the affirmative; but the manifest absurdity of the prosecution, felt and acknowledged by the Ordinary, diverted the attention of the Judges from considering the abstract proposition fairly laid down in the Ordinary's interlocutor." [17]

The plaintiffs thereupon obtained a rehearing, and James Boswell was retained for the defendant. He obtained the following argument from Dr. Johnson. "All injury is either of the person, the fortune, or the fame. Now, it is a certain thing, it is proverbially known, that *a jest breaks no bones*. They have never gained half-a-crown less in the whole profession since this mischievous paragraph has appeared: and, as to their reputation, What is their reputation but an instrument of getting money? If, therefore, they have lost no money, the question upon reputation may be answered by a very old position, *De minimis non curat Praetor.*

"Whether there was, or was not, an *animus injuriandi*, is not worth inquiring, if no *injuria* can be proved. But the truth is, there was no *animus injuriandi*. It was only an *animus irritandi*, which, happening to be exercised upon a *genus irritabile*,[18] produced unexpected violence of resentment. Their irritability arose only from an opinion of their own importance, and their delight in their new exaltation. What might have been borne

[15] *Ibid.*
[16] Probably Lord Auchinleck, James Boswell's father.
[17] *Solicitors at Law* v. *Robertson, supra.*
[18] " Intention of irritating "; and " an irritable breed."

by a *Procurator* could not be borne by a *Solicitor*. Your Lordships well know, that *honores mutant mores*.[19] Titles and dignities play strongly upon the fancy. As a mad-man is apt to think himself grown suddenly great; so he that grows suddenly great is apt to borrow a little from the mad-man. To co-operate with their resentment would be to promote their phrenzy; nor is it possible to guess to what they might proceed, if to the new title of Solicitor, should be added the elation of victory and triumph.

"We consider your Lordships as the protectors of our rights, and the guardians of our virtues; but believe it not included in your high office, that you should flatter our vices, or solace our vanity: and, as vanity only dictates this prosecution, it is humbly hoped your Lordships will dismiss it.

"If every attempt, however light or ludicrous, to lessen another's reputation, is to be punished by a judicial sentence, what punishment can be sufficiently severe for him who attempts to diminish the reputation of the Supreme Court of Justice, by reclaiming upon a cause already determined, without any change in the state of the question? Does it not imply hopes that the judges will change their opinion? Is not uncertainty and inconstancy in the highest degree disreputable to a Court? Does it not suppose, that the former judgement was temerarious or negligent? Does it not lessen the confidence of the publick? Will it not be said, that *jus est aut incognitum, aut vagum*? [20] and will not the consequence be drawn, *misera est servitus*? [1] Will not the rules of action be obscure? Will not he who knows himself wrong to-day, hope that the Courts of Justice will think him right tomorrow? Surely, my Lords, these are attempts of dangerous tendency, which the Solicitors, as men versed in the law, should have foreseen and avoided. It was natural for an ignorant printer to appeal from the Lord Ordinary; but from lawyers, the descendents of lawyers, who have practised for three hundred years, and have now raised themselves to a higher denomination, it might be expected, that they should know the

---

[19] " Honours change manners."
[20] " The law is either unknown or unsettled."
[1] " Slavery is wretched."

reverence due to a judicial determination; and, having been once dismissed, should sit down in silence." [2]

Presumably Boswell duly argued on these lines. However, in his words, " I am ashamed to mention, that the Court, by a plurality of voices, without having a single additional circumstance before them, reversed their own judgement, made a serious matter of this dull and foolish joke, and adjudged Mr. Robertson to pay to the Society five pounds (sterling money) and costs of suit.[3] The decision will seem strange to English lawyers." [4]

In the seventeenth century, one result of the flood of litigation on defamation was to make the English courts somewhat robust in their approach to the subject. Thus " of a justice of peace, that he is a logger-headed and a slouch-headed bursen-bellied hound, is no cause of indictment before justices of the peace in their sessions; partly for want of jurisdiction, partly because the words are not actionable." [5]   Again, " *He is a great rogue, and deserves to be hanged as well as Gale, who was condemned for stealing at Newgate Sessions. Et ex ulteriori malitia,[6] He bid J.S. steal what goods he could, and he would receive them.* Adjudged that the action does not lie. For as to the first words, the defendant only expressed his opinion, and perhaps he did not think that Gale deserved hanging. Yelv. case of *Heake* against *Moulton*.[7]   And as for the last words, it was only ill counsel, but no act was done, therefore not like the case of *Lewkner and Crichley*,[8] Cr.Car. 140." [9]   Nor was the discouragement for plaintiffs confined to the prospects of defeat. Holt C.J. once said that " he remembered another case very lately, where a fellow brought an action for saying of him, that he was a highway-man; and it appearing upon evidence that he was so, he was taken in Court, committed to prison, and convicted and hang'd the next

[2] Boswell's *Johnson*, vol. 2, p. 491.
[3] *The Preses and Society of Solicitors before the Commissary, Sheriff and City Courts of Edinburgh* v. *Robertson, supra*, p. 6; and see Mor.Dict. 13,935.
[4] Boswell's *Johnson, supra*, at p. 492.
[5] *Anon.* (1663) 1 Keb. 629.
[6] " And from further malice."
[7] *Heake* v. *Moulton* (1606) Yelv. 90 (" Thou are a common barretor, and deservest to be hanged " : held, no action lay).
[8] *Lewknor* v. *Cruchley* (1628) Cro.Car. 140 (charge of assault with intent to rob).
[9] *Bush* v. *Smith* (1681) T.Jo. 157.

sessions of gaol-delivery. So that people ought to be well advised
before they bring such actions." [10] To which Darnell, of
counsel, added that he " remembered the like fate which befel
a client of his." [11]

One manifestation, perhaps, of the discouraging attitude of
the courts was the *Earl of Northampton's Case*.[12] This might
be described as a charter of liberties for the explicit gossip. For
there it was laid down in 1612 that " if J.S. publish that he hath
heard J.N. say, that J.G. was a traitor or thief; in an action on
the case, if the truth be such, he may justify. But if J.S. publish
that he hath heard generally without a certain author, that J.G.
was a traitor or thief, there an action *sur le case* lieth against J.S.
for this, that he hath not given to the party grieved any cause of
action against any, but against himself who published the words,
although that in truth he might hear them; for otherwise this
might tend to a great slander of an innocent; for if one who hath
laesam phantasiam,[13] or who is a drunkard, or of no estimation,
speak scandalous words, if it should be lawful for a man of credit
to report them generally, that he had heard scandalous words,
without mentioning of his author, that would give greater colour
and probability that the words were true in respect of the credit
of the reporter, than if the author himself should be mentioned,
for the reputation and good name of every man is dear and
precious to him." In other words, a man might repeat any
slander with impunity provided he correctly named the person
who uttered it to him. This doctrine still held the field as late
as 1796 [14]; but in 1821 the accuracy of the report was doubted and
the width of the doctrine questioned,[15] and eight years later the
rule was for all practical purposes reversed.[16] To this one may
add that " a man cannot justify a libel by proving that he has
contracted to libel." [17]

Men sometimes seem to have been much preoccupied with

[10] *Johnson* v. *Browning* (1704) Holt K.B. 3 at 4.
[11] S.C., 6 Mod. 216 at 217.
[12] (1612) 12 Co.Rep. 132 at 134.
[13] " A warped imagination."
[14] *Davis* v. *Lewis* (1796) 7 T.R. 17.
[15] *Lewis* v. *Walter* (1821) 4 B. & Ald. 605 at 614.
[16] *M'Pherson* v. *Daniels* (1829) 10 B. & C. 263.
[17] *Weston* v. *Barnicoat*, 56 N.E. 619 at 620 (1900), *per* Holmes C.J.

marriage. In one action on the case for words, for loss of marriage, " The Plaintiffe lays in his Declaration, that there was a speech of Marriage between him and one Susan Watts, and likely to take effect. To which Susan the Defendant did utter these words of the Plaintiffe, (S) My Wife is a Whore, and I will prove it, for she was nought with Will. Selly, the Plaintiffe, and if I had had a Candle, I had taken them together doing the deed; and that by reason of these words, he lost his Marriage; a verdict for the Plaintiffe, and dammages moved in Arrest, that the words not Actionable, being spoken of a man.

" Coke chief Justice. Justice Clenches Grandchilde was to marry with such a man, to whom one said, of her, that she had had two Bastards, one by one Watts, and another by, &c. By which words she lost her Husband; she brought her Action, and recovered 200 Marks, and it is all one, if the words be spoken of a man, as of a woman, laying a speech of Marriage, and the loss of his Wife, it being all one, in the same degree and equipage to lose a Husband, or to lose a Wife, and so by the Rule of the Court, Judgement was given for the Plaintiffe." [18]

Again, one Southold, " of good name and fame," was once " in communication to be married to such a woman, with whom he should have had such a portion." One Daunston, " to scandilize him, and to hinder and deprive him of his marriage," spoke these words: " Southold hath been in bed with Dorchester's wife," so that he lost his marriage. In the ensuing action for words, counsel for the defendant argued that the words were not actionable, " for it may be, he was in bed with her when he was a child, she being his nurse, or it may be that her husband was in bed betwixt them." But Jones and Croke JJ. would have none of this subtlety: " such foreign intendments as have been alledged shall not be taken, but it shall be adjudged *ex effectu dicendi*,[19] which is here to hinder him of his marriage." [20] Yet some distinctions were accepted. Thus Twisden J. once said: " I remember *a shoemaker* brought an action against a man for say-

[18] *Selly* v. *Facy* (1615) 3 Bulstr. 48.
[19] " From the effect of what was said."
[20] *Southold* v. *Daunston* (1632) Cro.Car. 269.

ing that he was *a cobler*; and though a cobler be a trade of itself,
yet it was held that the action lay, in Glyn's [1] time." [2]

If on the analogy of " fuss " [3] it is permissible to use
" bother " as a polite cloak for the abominable, it is possible to
relate here that when Webling, speaking of Snell, said " I know
what I am, and I know what Snell is, I never bothered a mare,"
his defence to an action of slander was that he had not charged
Snell with bothery. Yet " *Curia contra*, It is by implication a
charge of bothery upon the plaintiff, by which the by-standers
satis intellexerunt, and gave judgment for the plaintiff." [4] In
the words of another report of the same case, " The words were
actionable, or else there might be sly ways to defame any man
and evade an action." [5] A third report shows that the court
found that this, " albeit no grammatical affirmation," was nevertheless " a sufficient scandal, being found with such intention,
and being such in the judgment of the hearers, the ironical speaking will not excuse." [6] Some years earlier there had been an
even clearer example of this type of slander by indirection.
When A said to B " One of us is perjured," B replied " It is not
I," whereupon A smartly rejoined " I am sure it is not I." The
result of this sparkling and surprisingly grammatical repartee was
that B sued A for defamation, and recovered, " car les subsequent
Parols monstront apparantment que il luy intend." [7]

Until statute [8] declared the law to be otherwise, the rule was
held to be that it was for the court, and not the jury, to determine
whether or not any words were defamatory. Lord Mansfield
C.J. once set out a verse by Pultney that had been current after
the prosecution of the printer and publisher of *The Craftsman*
for libel in 1731,[9] when Sir Philip Yorke (afterwards Lord
Hardwicke L.C.) was Attorney-General:

[1] John Glynne, C.J.Upper Bench, 1655–60.
[2] *Redman* v *Pyne* (1669) 1 Mod. 19.
[3] See 1 Misc. 203. This passage was written over ten years ago; today it may
need no polite cloak. But perhaps a period charm justifies its retention.
[4] *Snell* v. *Webling* (1675) 2 Lev. 150 (*cf. White* v. *Brough* (1616) 1 Roll.R.
286).
[5] *Snell* v. *Webling* (1675) 1 Ventr. 276.
[6] S.C., 3 Keb. 546.
[7] *Coe* v. *Chambers* (1600) 1 Roll.Abr. 75.
[8] Fox's Libel Act, 1792.   [9] R. v. *Francklin* (1731) 17 St.Tr. 625.

> " For Sir Philip well knows
> His innuendos
> Will serve him no longer
> In verse or in prose;
> For twelve honest men have decided the cause,
> Who are judges of fact, though not judges of laws." [10]

Lord Mansfield added that " To be free is to live under a government by law. The liberty of the press consists in printing without any previous licence, subject to the consequences of law. The licentiousness of the press is Pandora's Box, the source of every evil. Miserable is the condition of individuals, dangerous is the condition of the State, if there is no certain law, or, which is the same thing, no certain administration of law, to protect individuals, or to guard the State. Jealousy of leaving the law to the Court, as in other cases, so in the case of libels, is now, in the present state of things, puerile rant and declamation. The Judges are totally independent of the ministers, that may happen to be, and of the King himself. Their temptation is rather to the popularity of the day. But I agree with the observation cited by Mr. Cowper from Mr. Justice Forster, ' that a popular Judge is an odious and pernicious character.' " [11]

Two great names at the turn of the century were Sir Archibald Levin Smith M.R. and Arthur Lionel Smith, Master of Balliol College, Oxford. It was MacKinnon L.J. who pressed them into service in 1939 to illustrate a distinction in the law of libel. " If a newspaper printed the sentence : ' A. L. Smith, a London man, was fined for drunkenness at Bow Street,' and a man of that name alleged these words to be defamatory of him, I think the judge ought not to let his case go to the jury. But if, forty years ago, a man exhibited a poster at the gate of Balliol, or outside the Law Courts, bearing the words : ' A. L. Smith fined for drunkenness,' either of two distinguished people, if they cared to sue, should have had their cases left to the jury. The words published to the audiences—undergraduates of Balliol, or

[10] *R.* v. *Shipley* (1784) 4 Doug.K.B. 73 at 168; and see *Broome* v. *Agar* (1928) 138 L.T. 698 at 699.
[11] *R.* v. *Shipley, supra,* at p. 170.

lawyers leaving the Courts—would have a special meaning." [12] No special meaning in Oxford was needed for one seventeenth-century case, however. " Ralph Bradwell Principal de Saint Mary Hall in Oxford libell in le Court del Vicechancellour la versus un Master de Art, & commoner de mesme Hall, pur ceo que il appel luy Red-Nose, Mamsey-Nose, Copper-Nose Knave, Rascal, & base Fellow, & auter words non dissonant, & ad damnum. Et Judgment fuit done pur le principal, & processe issue versus le delinquent de Judicio sistendo, & indicanda solvendo." [13]

Newspapers and other periodicals have their troubles, of course; and sometimes these are *inter se* and not *ab extra*. Towards the end of the eighteenth century a newspaper called *The Oracle* launched an attack on a rival, the *True Briton*, describing it as " the most vulgar, ignorant, and scurrilous journal ever published in Great Britain." This, agreed Lord Kenyon C.J., was not defamatory. However, it was a different matter when the attack continued with the words " that the first proprietors abandoned it; and that it is the lowest now in circulation "; for these words affected the sale and the advertising profits, and so were actionable. [14]

Over a century later an American periodical intituled *Hooey* published a drawing which depicted two standard rose trees in a garden bed, closely intertwined, each tree bearing a rose which bent towards the other rose as though kissing. On the left a gardener was talking to a rather stout lady, while in the background there was a large house. The caption was " I guess we shouldn't have planted the Duchess of Marlborough and the Rev. H. Robertson Page in the same bed." The Duchess of Marlborough sued the English distributors of this issue of the periodical for libel. The case came before Lord Hewart C.J., sitting with a special jury; and he took a very serious view of the case. The drawing " would be utterly fatuous if it were not indecent." Not surprisingly, the case was then settled on payment of a sum to the plaintiff. [15]

[12] *Newstead* v. *London Express Newspaper Ltd.* [1940] 1 K.B. 377 at 391.
[13] *Ralph Bradwells Case* (1627) Litt.R. 9 (" to compel him to stand trial and pay what might be adjudged "). [14] *Heriot* v. *Stuart* (1796) 1 Esp. 437.
[15] *Marlborough* v. *Gorringe's Travel & News Agency Ltd.* [1935] *The Times* Jan. 31, Feb. 1.

In Iowa, an action for libel was brought in 1901 by one of the three Cherry sisters in respect of a newspaper critic's appreciation of their performance on the vaudeville stage.[16] The notice recounted that " Effie is an old jade of 50 summers, Jessie a frisky filly of 40, and Addie, the flower of the family, a capering monstrosity of 35. Their long skinny arms, equipped with talons at the extremities, swung mechanically, and anon waived [17] frantically at the suffering audience. The mouths of their rancid features opened like caverns, and sounds like the wailings of damned souls issued therefrom. They pranced around the stage with a motion that suggested a cross between the danse du ventre and fox trot,—strange creatures with painted faces and hideous mien. Effie is spavined, Addie is stringhalt, and Jessie, the only one who showed her stockings, has legs with calves as classic in their outlines as the curves of a broom handle." [18] The trial judge directed a verdict for the defendants on the ground of privilege, and so the plaintiff appealed. After examining the evidence, and considering the fact that the trial court " had the plaintiff [19] before it and saw her repeat some of the performances given by her on the stage " (it is not recorded whether the court became as restive as had the audience in which the critic had sat), the Supreme Court of Iowa dismissed the appeal. " If there ever was a case justifying ridicule and sarcasm,—aye, even gross exaggeration,—it is the one now before us. According to the record, the performance given by the plaintiff and the company of which she was a member was not only childish, but ridiculous in the extreme. A dramatic critic should be allowed considerable license in such a case." [20]

South Africa has made its contributions. In 1878, a minister of the Dutch Reformed Church made statements which in effect charged a young unmarried woman with having given birth to at least one illegitimate child, the result of incestuous intercourse, and with having also been guilty of infanticide or concealment

---

[16] *Cherry* v. *Des Moines Leader*, 86 N.W. 323 (1901).
[17] *Sic.*
[18] *Cherry* v. *Des Moines Leader*, *supra*, at p. 323.
[19] Either Effie or Jessie: the report is not clear.
[20] *Cherry* v. *Des Moines Leader*, *supra*, at p. 325, *per* Deemer J.

of birth; and in consequence she had been arrested. While under arrest, a medical examination showed the charge to be altogether unfounded: and a successful action for defamation was brought against the minister in the Supreme Court of the Cape of Good Hope. As Fitzpatrick J. observed, " the flower of female honour and female chastity is a delicate plant, and you ought to hesitate long before you breathe harshly upon it. I think the defendant was precipitate—very precipitate—in coming to the conclusion he did on the slender evidence before him, that this young woman was guilty." [1]

Dwyer J. was emphatic. He said [2] that " as to the reasonable and probable cause attempted to be set up, I do not believe I ever heard anything so frivolous in my life. I do believe if these gentlemen had gone to London when crinoline was in fashion, they would have found nearly the whole population in the family way, and the next morning, when they got up, they would have found that they had all been delivered, and then come back and informed the Kerkraad how very prevalent was the crime of infanticide in England; because really there is very little more evidence as to reasonable and probable cause in this case than the fact that this unfortunate woman wore a dress one day which made her appear very large, and on another, that she appeared thin and slender. . . . The defendant showed a great want of charity when he got into the box and swore that he still believed the plaintiff was guilty. I can only exclaim with Thomas Hood—

Alas for the rarity of Christian charity! " [3]

More recently, the contributors were two railway foremen. During the last war, the plaintiff, one Marruchi, sued Harris, the defendant, in South Africa for calling him a " Maccaroni Bastard," and saying that " he should have been in an internment camp long ago." It was, however, " freely admitted that the

---

[1] *Dippenaar* v. *Hauman* (1878) 8 Buch. 135 at 145.
[2] *Ibid.*, at p. 146.
[3] Alas! for the rarity
Of Christian charity
Under the sun!
    The Bridge of Sighs.

litigants and their circle habitually use strong language, spiced with salacious terms subolent of the sewer." After one dispute, " threats of violence were exchanged interspersed [4] with the usual pleasantries. Harris called Marruchi a sanguinary Dago and told him to get out in language in which a word signifying the sexual act was substituted for a verb of motion. Marruchi retorted with equal lack of restraint and exactitude, adding that Harris was an epithetised bastard, no white man, but bred between a bastard and a yellow belly. This exchange of civilities is important since plaintiff sought to use it . . . to prove the defamatory nature of the word ' bastard.' " The evidence made it clear, however, " that in the Railway workshops the word ' bastard ' is frequently used as a term of endearment." In the result, the plaintiff got nothing for the " bastard," but £80 for his alleged internability.[5]

Another case raised the question whether it was defamatory of a woman to describe her as " a cheap South Hills cow," and a " bloody bitch," or " old bitch." This was not easy. " Certain characteristics are by common consent associated with certain animals. It would not be difficult, for instance, to prove that if a certain person was referred to as a donkey or an ass, the innuendo was that he was stupid. If a person was referred to as a mule, it would be easy to prove that what was meant was that he was obstinately stupid. The characteristics suggested are often associated with the animals named. Nevertheless, there would have to be some evidence to prove how the words would have been understood.

" A cow has no particular characteristic which would tend to make such a word applied to a person defamatory. After all, a cow is a harmless, docile and useful animal. If a woman is called a cow it is necessary to prove that the word would have been understood in a defamatory sense. The word bitch is a somewhat less pleasant appellation than the word cow; but what is a bitch? It is a female dog. When a woman is referred to as a bitch it may mean that she is an unladylike, coarse and ill-

---

[4] " Interposed " in the original.
[5] *Marruchi* v. *Harris*, 1943 O.P.D. 15 at 18, 19, *per* van den Heever J.

mannered person—and it may have some sexual connotation—
but all this must be proved in a proper legal way according to
the rules of evidence, for to say of a woman that she is a bitch
in its primary sense is mere meaningless abuse.

" One thing that cannot be done is to ask a witness who heard
the words what he understood them to mean, for this is totally
irrelevant. If such evidence were allowed, it would result in a
gilbertian situation, for, owing to some personal idiosyncrasy, a
particular hearer of the words may assign to them an altogether
unusual meaning, which is entirely different from how the words
are usually understood, and a person who had made a perfectly
innocent remark would find himself liable to pay damages for
defamation. It is necessary to show how the words would be
ordinarily understood in the circumstances and in the place and
context in which they were spoken by the ordinary person.

" There is no evidence in this case to prove how the words
complained of would have been understood. To go to a
dictionary to find the meaning of the words is to introduce an
unreal and fictitious element into the enquiry, for it is not the
learned bookish meaning that the words must be given, but the
meaning they convey to the man in the street. The ordinary
man does not carry about with him a pocket dictionary which
he consults to see whether or not he has been defamed. The
exchange of epithet is usually much too rapid for any such dis-
traction. The *Oxford Dictionary*, which has been quoted, gives
the meaning of the word cow when applied to a person as it is
understood in certain parts of educated England; but what has
this to do with how the word is usually understood in the suburb
of South Hills, Johannesburg? Nothing whatever. In some
grades of society Smith may say: ' Mrs. Jones is a pleasant old
cow: I rather like her,' or ' She is a decent old cow.' These
remarks in a different grade of society would be regarded as
uncouth and coarse, but hardly as defamatory. Everything
depends on the context, the tone, the circumstances, the setting
and the locality. The words cannot be regarded *in abstracto*." [6]

---

[6] *Wood, N.O.* v. *Branson*, 1952 (3) S.A. 369 at 371, *per* Price J. I have
divided this passage into paragraphs. The claim failed.

Corpus Juris

In Quebec, a pleasant exchange of insults once formed the subject of an action. A lady sued for damages because a man had " publiquement traitée de ' putain,' dans l'église grecque orthodoxe, à l'issue de l'office divin. Le défendeur plaide compensation d'injures, la demanderesse l'aurait accusé d'être un ' parjure,' un ' bandit ' et un homme ' déshonoré '; il soutient qu'il ne lui a dit que: ' Get out of here, porni,' ce qui en grec n'a d'autre signification que celle ' d'inconduite dans l'occasion en question.' La demanderesse répondit que ' porni,' en grec, veut dire ' putain.' "[7] This was adjudged a fair exchange, leaving no balance in cash due either way.[8] In England, six centuries earlier, a " meretrix " for a " latro " had been held to leave a balance of a shilling due to the man.[9] He would indeed be confident who could say which had the better value for money.

The subject is unending; yet with that, this book must end. As an adieu, perhaps Coke's words are the most apt, as, indeed, so many of his words have been over the centuries. " And for a farewell to our jurisprudent, I wish unto him the gladsome light of jurisprudence, the loveliness of temperance, the stabilitie of fortitude, and the soliditie of justice." [10]

---

[7] " Whore."
[8] *Vousounara* v. *Kautsoginapoulos* (1918) 53 Quebec C.S. 383.
[9] *Bolay* v. *Bindbere* (1321) *The Court Baron* (S.S. vol. IV) 133 (" harlot " and " robber ").
[10] Co.Litt. 395a (last sentence of the book).

Table of Cases

Table of Cases

Table of Statutes

2. OTHER STATUTES

Table of Statutes

Index

Index

aeroplane, horse much the same as, 257

affidavit by informing and believing clerks, 47, 48

Afrikaans, judgment in, 167

age,
equity not past,
child-bearing, of, 293
child-beating, of, 294
female, male incompetence in judging, 244
full,
date nobody attained, 304
judging whether woman of, 244
Hong Kong, earlier attainment in, 303
protection not lost on, 304
leap-years, effect on, 303

agent for shareholders, company, 260

agreement, gentleman's, 326

agricultural holding, public-house as, 329

air, English, too pure for slaves, 198

Aland J., Fortescue. *See* Fortescue, Lord.

Alderson B., sarcasm on Lord Brougham, 12

Alexander C.B. as Deputy Speaker of House of Lords, 58

Alexandra Palace, purchase of, 33

alibi,
anonymous, geographically, 86
clock, outworn, 86
Kerry, 86
Tipperary, 86

aliboy, 86

All Ravished With Gladness, 70–83, Henry IV, 78

Allen J., *Against Quarrelling* in New York, 249

Allsop J., contempt by justifying contempt, 81

also and likewise, 167

Alva, Lord, and idle buffoonery, 339

Alverstone C.J., Lord, George V's marriage, 96

ambidexter, 49

ambidextrous—
sheriff, 20
solicitor, 49

ambiguities,
in statute, 179, 180
unanimity, despite, 180

American throws egg in Chancery, 71

amours, secret, 214

anarchy without liberty or order, 193

anchors of the republique, laws, 117

Anderson C.J.'s judgment according to reason, 149

angel, angels,
dice loaded in favour of, 302
honest man finds twenty, 238, 239
swearing—
sea, on, 84
shore, on, 84
will forms, place on, 301, 302
witness no, 84
wolf and the, 301, 302

anger, rivulets of, 169

angry,
neat but wrong, 4
very, and very wrong, 3

animal spirits, ship not cast away from, 278

animus injuriandi, 340

animus irritandi, 340

annuity retrospectively void, 171

antediluvian toad on codicil, 306

antick the law, old father, 77

any more judges?, 94

appeal,
brooding spirit of the law, to, 148
equal division on, 57, 62, 64, 65, 145–147
God, to, for selection of victim, 321
ground abandoned below, on, 64
half of judges decide, 58
reasons, dismissed without, 64
sentence carried out, after, 175
void decision, from, 15, 16

Appeal, Court of,
concurrence agrees with most, 145
full, infrequency of, 61
reluctant and suspicious, 164

apples,
danger of losing all, 313
sexual consent from picking, 312, 313

Apostle Paul putting away shunting yard, 251

Appleton C.J., a surety's smarting, 333

Arabin, Serjeant, linguistic inglory, 27

arbitrator,
evidence of counsel as, 93
ideot acts as, 238

archdeacon, price of address for, 326

Arches, Dean of the, declares Royal marriage void, 172

Arden M.R.,
stamp equivalent to seal, 298
Vernon, views on, 130

Index

battel, cuntey cuntey preferred to, 163
Baugh J., secret charities as index of character, 243
Bayley J.,
  Modern Reports, views on, 119
  nisi prius, thoughts at, 131
beacon of—
  injustice, 155
  justice, 156
bearer bonds burned before solicitors, 48
bears growl and fight, 249
beauteous in their confusion, 131
Beavan's Reports. *See* reports.
bed, disordered, 160
bedfellow uncovered to show sex, 97
begetting a child—
  at 84 improbable, 230
  at 95 a congeries of improbabilities, 231
beggar—
  feeds on smells, 239
  pays with sound of coin, 239
begoggled and bearded imaginary scientist, 272
beliefs,
  no punishment for, 201
  sincere but unreasonable, 243
believing clerk. *See* informing clerk.
Bell J., eyes of Argus, 213, 214
belly, inspection of, 228
belly-band of regimental breeches, 324
Bench, 3-21
beneficiary,
  marriage of will to, 301
  signs away inheritance, 299
beneficium principis debet esse mansurum, 110
benefit of clergy, 316
Bentham on no traitorous bedfellow, 97
bequest, pauper's munificent, 194
Berryer, M., dinner for, 36
Best J. and C.J.,
  plaintiff and defendant, man cannot be both, 19
  slavery a local law, 198, 199
Bethell S.-G., Sir Richard. *See* Westbury L.C., Lord.
biblical times and modern morals, 318
bigamist,
  George V no, 96
  Kingston, Duchess of, as, 311
Bile Beans, fraud with, 271, 272
bill of exceptions dies with judge, 56
Bill of Rights a suicide pact, 193
  See also Statutes.

Bills,
  royal assent to, 100
  royal veto of, 100
binding over for life, 75
Bingham, Peregrine,
  serjeant, not a, 28
  tempest, reports furious, 28
Birkenhead L.C., Lord,
  maritime misfortunes, 277, 278
  thirty-nine at a blow, 30
Birkett J. and L.J.,
  agreed with result, 145
  contract one-sided, 276
birth, supposititious, writ to prevent, 228
birthdays better than birthday eves, 303
bishop,
  night clubs, asks about, 167
  sermons, charge for writing for, 326
bitch, woman called old or bloody, 350, 351
bite cut suck and eat, power to, 285
black cap not coif, 24
Black J. and C.J. (Penn.),
  death's doing, judgment, 142
  dissent, powerful, 141-143
  rank, sinks in, 140
  sacred duty, judge's, 141
Black J. (U.S. Supreme Court),
  beliefs, no punishment for, 201
  truth needs no disguise, 98
Blackburn J. and Lord,
  Campbell's Reports, views on, 131, 132
  Espinasse's Reports, views on, 118
  Lewin's Reports, views on, 129
  Reports in Chancery, views on, 119
blacksmith liable for loss of marriage, 334
Blackstone J., child more than ordinarily legitimate, 225
Blackstone's Reports. *See* reports.
blatant, size of print stops being, 276
Bleckley J. and C.J.,
  authorities wrong, court right, 137
  hearth, equity's children sit round ancestral, 235
  interest rascal not reprobate, 90
  villainy on veracity, effect of, 89, 90
blockheads, parcel of, 120
blood, thirsting after, 338
blood-sucker, 337, 338
Bolingbroke beds with no traitor, 97
Bolland B., Lord Raymond's Reports, views on, 125, 126
bonds, burning before solicitors, 48

372

*boni judicis ampliare jurisdictionem,
est*, 331
boni judicis ampliare justitiam, est, 331
bookes disregarded if without reason,
149
bookseller's trover against school mistress for dirty book, 242, 243
bore father, promise not to, 327
bosom, boundless, 154
bosom of the law, 268
Boswell, James,
bad cause, supporting, 34
Johnson, argument obtained from
Dr., 340–342
rehearing, loses, 342
bother a polite cloak for abominable,
345
bothery, charge of, 345
bottles, nest feathered with, 152
bouncers a deductible expense for call
girl business, 265
Bourbons, of the blood of, 103
Bovill C.J. upholds own decision, 62
Bowen L.J.,
herrings, three red, 139
indulgence, abusing, 250
brace of mandami, 153
Bramwell B. and L.J.,
rights of man, determining, 35
second contract to pay damages, 335
Brandeis J.,
blameless lives of suitors, 294
casus omissus and judicial legislation,
181
err twice, no need to, 136
freedom of speech, 202, 203
grievances, position to redress, 206
precedent no inexorable demand, 138
wire-tapping, evidence by, 207
brass identity disk, will on, 300
Braxfield, Lord, damages an injury,
339
Bray J. differs from Lush J., 146
bread, seeing side buttered on, 154
breeches,
regimental, pierced, 324
stolen by honest boy, 324
breeding new principles, 136
Brennan J., good dissent deserves
another, 68
Brett L.J. and M.R. *See* Esher M.R.,
Lord.
Brewer J., large returns alluring, 243
bribe *non olet*, 274
bribery, deducting cost of, 263
brickbat thrown at judge, 70

bride,
abandoned, must be, 194
ring pulled off by, 212
bridges, London's loveliest, 325
Bridgman L.K., Sir Orlando, committal by, 73
brief,
diligence, seen by no proper, 83
other side's,
photographed, 83
taken, 82, 83
privileged indefinitely, 83
bristling with irregularities, 248
broken heart, death of,
infant litigant, 5
solicitor, 51
brooding spirit of the law, 148
broom handle, classic curves of, 348
Brother, judges call serjeants, 26
Brougham L.C., Lord,
assault, sued for, 13
brother's decision affirmed by, 143
client's interest, all subordinate to,
36
decision—
fact not law, 144
without reasons in absence, 66
Devon, creates Earl of, 103
dispatch, price of, 11
equitable novelty to be shown to, 234
Incumbered Estates Bill, opposes, 289
irrepressible, 64
peerage, law of, 105
Queen, annuity claimed for, 102
Vernon's Reports, views on, 130
Brougham, Master,
affirmed by brother, 143
contempt to, 79, 80
favourite brother, Lord Brougham's,
143
reversed by brother, 144
Bruce J. *See* Gainsford Bruce Q.C.
bubble blown until it bursts, 327
Buckley, Mr., disappointed at photograph, 244
buffoonery, idle piece of, 339
buggery,
mare, with, 345
unmentionable among Christians,
314
woman, with, affront, 314
buildings struck with sterility, 266
bull,
cow in heat, taken to, 318
judge may be, 169
superior degree, of, 169

Index

Buller J.,
  Atkyns' Reports, views on, 120
  Dyer's Reports, marginal notes in, 70
  Modern Reports, views on, 119
  Noy's Reports, views on, 120
bulls, Laban's, 318
Bunbury's Reports. See reports.
burned, prisoner not staying to be, 181
Burnet J., Keble's Reports, views on, 121
burnt fingers, complaining of, 258
Burrough J., Modern Reports, views on, 120
Burrow, Sir James, as a reporter, 127
Bursen-Bellied Hound, A, 337–352,
  justice of the peace called, 342
Burton J.,
  all over the place, 68
  tax on unlawful gains, 263
burying progenitors of new principles, 136
business honor, standards of, 294
business names, registration of, 281, 282
businessmen not assumed to be thieves, 269
buttered on, side bread, 154
buttocks,
  bare, waggling at spectators, 208
  woman's desire to show, 313
Byles J. asks nice question, 219
Byron's Julia as fitting precedent, 137

Cadies, Society of, 338
Cadmus, Soldiers Of, 117–133,
  reports, wandring and masterless, 117
Caesar, clergy render half to, 262
Cairns L.J. and L.C., Lord,
  dilemma,
    pinned to one horn of, 153
    pinning to one before hearing, 153
  judgment given though brother dead, 57
calf,
  Bastard called, 229
  bulleth my cow, whoso, 229
call girl business, deductible expenses, 264
Calvert, Dr., evidence of impotence, 215
calves as classic as broom handle, 348
Cambridge don's new seeds, 244
camel of injustice in straining for gnats, 156

Campbell C.J. and L.C., Lord,
  Act empowering the impossible, 108
  black cap, idée fixe on, 24
  Brougham rallied by, 103
  coif, idée fixe on, 24
  drawer marked " Bad Law," 132
  Eldon cross-examined by, 13
  Eldon, particular delight of, 8
  George IV, verdict on, 101
  House of Lords order repealed for, 105
  improper instructions to litigant, 90
  judgment read after death, 57
  litigant as own advocate, 90
  moralises, 16
  nisi prius reports, 131
  peers' lives unpublishable, 105
  " person " modern slang, 166
  Royal Mandate, procures, 26, 27
  serjeants' audience assailed by, 26, 27
  Sovereign as witness, 96
  uncritical repetition by, 51
  warning to prisoner, hears, 324
Campbell A.-G., Sir John. See Campbell C.J. and L.C., Lord.
Campbell's Reports. See reports.
camphor sedating sensual desire, 312
Canada,
  four sexes in, 184
  gross indecency in, 315, 316
  ripeness is all in, 309
candle, if, would have taken them, 344
cannibalism by starving sailors, 320
canon law in legitimacy, 286
Canterbury, Archbishop of,
  deodand, horse as a, 19
  judge in own cause, 19
Cantilupe, Lord, 240
Cardozo J.,
  benefit and burden, equilibrium of, 255
  constable has blundered, 199
  criminal goes free, 199
  dissent and majority, 147
  equity,
    business honor, 294
    conscience of, expression, 294
    law followed not slavishly, 294
  extravagantly improbable, 225
  fields, duty to take to, 200
  identity of words and meaning, 151
  incompetence, test of, 243
  indubitably false, 225
  statute revised by construing, 181
  tax systems, trial and error in, 258
carnal knowledge in Missouri, 318

374

Carr J., cases like Swiss troops, 137
Carr, Sir Cecil, statute book beyond all, 170
Carr, William, finding lawyers' patron saint, 41, 42
Carrington & Payne's Reports. *See* reports.
Carter's Reports. *See* reports.
Casberd within Bar and out, 23
case stated,
  commissioners, by one of two, 55
  justices, by two of three, 55, 56
Cases in Chancery. *See* reports.
Cassius-looking jurymen, 312
casta et sola, actuary estimates, 232
casus omissus, 181, 183
cat jumps, sitting on fence to see way, 154
catachrestic use of *causa causans*, 159
cates and sweet sauces, smell of, 238
Catline C.J., fine with two faces, 287, 288
causa causans,
  death, in at, 158
  epithets for, 157, 158
  Latin deprecated, 158
  marching on, 159
  varieties of, 157
causa sine qua non, 158, 159
cause causes, 157, 158
cavalier, old, got off easier, 18
caveat emptor, 329
cave, death's grim, 281
Cave J., ingenuity of counsel, 139
Cave, Viscount, holds Court of Appeal wrong, 260
Cavendish J., judging woman's age, 244
Cecil, Lord Robert, unveiled sarcasm, 260
celibacy, constrained, of Act's compilers, 317
censors,
  shielded better than censored, 201
  teacher's shoulder, looking over, 205
certainty mother of repose, 135, 235
Chaldeans, Society of, 338
chance, law a game of, 134
Chancellor's foot, more to measure than, 292
Chancery Bar, talent of, 32
Chancery Court, Hot Spring(s), 185, 189
Chaos And Old Night, 255–268,
  reign of, 256
Chapman C.J., presumption of paying debt, 269

character, secret charities index to, 243
charitable trusts. *See* trusts, charitable.
charity,
  acts of, found no rights, 250
  publicans and sinners, to, 295
  rarity of Christian, 349
  secret, 243
Charles I,
  lawyer, inability to become, 33, 34
  logic, lack of, 101
Charles II, wigs come into fashion with, 24
Charles J. finds doctor unbiased, 17
Charlotte, Princess, reluctance to wed Prince of Orange, 234
chart, law not a, 134
Charter, Royal, 338, 339
charter of liberty for explicit gossips, 343
chastity,
  continuance of, estimating, 232
  flower of female, delicate, 349
  marriage, condition precedent to, 214
Chelmsford, gaols at, 174, 175
Cherry sisters defamed, 348
Chief Baron of the Exchequer,
  commoner, mere, 58
  ear, hears with only one, 337
  serjeant, always a, 25
chief courts, three, 10
chien est un vermin, 249
child,
  begetting at 95...231
  cloathes of, serve grown man, 112
  discretion of judge, left to, 240
  father dying to avoid supporting, 232, 233
  fathers, electing between two, 225
  human, whether, 239
  petticoats, under mother's at her wedding, 209
  See also father; infant.
child-bearing, equity not past, 293
child-beating, equity not past, 294
children,
  angry passions rise, 249
  custody of, 233
  equity, of, trusts as, 235
  tearing out each other's eyes, 249
chivalry, muted, 244
chlorophyl, little left, 270
choate,
  lien doctrine, 161
  saga of, 160, 161
  status, 161
  verb, as, 161

Index

choateness, requirements of, 161
choater, choatest, 161
choatitude, 161
chord not melodious, 157
Christian L.J. and legalised confiscation, 288–290
Christian charity, rarity of, 349
Christ's Hospital, riot at, 242
church, coercion by, 219
church bells, sound of, 210
churl, covetous, 238
churlish, people forced to be, 250
circumstances, old principles applied to new, 136
citizens,
    thinking, wrong better than not, 201
    unpopular, protected by law, 204
City of London Court, 220
civil law, doctor highest degree in, 23
civilised man, mark of,
    confidence, 202
    doubt, 201
Clanrickard(e), Earl of, marriage, 106
Clarence, Duke of, 77
Clark J., words and mathematical symbols, 151, 152
Clarke Q.C., Sir Edward, as witness, 92
Clarkson J., potter's hand trembling, 148
classroom, fear stalks, 205
Clavering, Sir Thomas, promotes Dog Act, 175
clear and present danger, 204, 206, 207
Cleland J., keeping wolf from backyard, 232
Clench J.'s grandchild, 344
clergy rendering half to Caesar, 262
clergyman, scholar beats, 242
Clerk, John (Lord Eldin),
    also not likewise, 167
    apology doubling insult, 167
clerk,
    believing, 47, 48
    informing, 47
clerks driven to crime, 275
cliff, falling over edge of, 138
Clifton, Lord, promise to convey land, 94
cloak for malevolent, 194
cloaths, child's, not fitting grown man, 112
clock,
    crazy, 98
    strikes—
        hour of legal emancipation, 304
        thirteen, 98

Clyde, Lord (1863–1944),
    mad will and sane testator, 306
    moral obligations to Revenue, 257
Clyde, Lord (1898–   ), law of jungle, 250
cobbler, calling shoemaker, 344, 345
Coca-Cola, 269–271
cocaine in Coca-Cola, 269–271
cock using force on lawful wife, 319, 320
Cockburn C.J.,
    advocate a warrior not assassin, 36
    serjeants called to front row, 23
Cockburn, Lord, hears Lord Eskgrove, 324
codicil,
    gestation, period of, 305
    hay-loft, 305
    memorandum book, penny, 305
    toad and pickles, with, 305, 306
    See also Wills, will.
cohate not yet exported, 161
coif, serjeants', 24
Coke C.J.,
    adulterous widow's dower, 219
    jurisprudent, farewell to, 352
    law nothing but reason, 111, 187
    novelty, establishing, 150
    prisoner fleeing burning prison, 180
cola-nut, 270
Coleridge C.J., Lord, lot and ballot, 320, 321
Coleridge J., getting good laws by enforcing bad, 165
Coleridge, Lord, first peer at Bar, 31
college porch called Jumbo, 165
Collier J., Sir Robert,
    industrious, 26
    serjeant not joining Serjeants' Inn, 26
    sworn in after resigning, 26
Collingwood J.'s judgment read when ill, 54
Colman J., sanctity of contract, 335
Colombine, fraudulent settlement by, 240, 241
Comberbach's Reports. See reports.
comfortable society, marriage for, 215
Commandment to bear false witness, 86
Commerce, 269–284
commercial,
    halfpennies, to counterfeit, 330
    hypothesis of honesty, 269
Commission of Delegates, 213
Commissioners on Uniform Laws called on, 188
committal. See Contempt.

376

Index

convenient even if heavens fall, 18
convent teaches Sale of Goods Act, 330
conveyance,
　orange, of, 285
　tree to itself, of, 290
conveyancing,
　magnetism, by, 288
　orange, of, 285
　tautology in, 285
　technicalities of, 13
　unorthodox, 290
　wife,
　　bargain and sale of, 219
　　voluntary conveyance of, 218
　　See also titles.
convictions, mentioning previous, 323
cook,
　crafty, demands payment for smell, 238
　refusal to marry because, 220
　sound of coin, paid by, 238
copper-nose knave, 347
copula, marriage by promise subsequente, 209, 210
copyright, thought-control, 201
corantoes, 100
corporation,
　fiction to be acted on, 282
　gratitude, feeling, 282
　imagination, creature of legal, 282
　liability, member, 282
　mind, state of, 282
　predatory human qualities of, 282
Corpus Juris, 255–352
correspondence, progenitive, 183
corrupt, cloak for, 194
Cosgrave, Robert, flings egg, 71
costermongers, obscure law for, 179
Cottenham L.C., Lord,
　attorney, crazy, commits, 13
　barrister, commits, 80
　Brougham, argues with Lord, 144
　decision, affirms own, 64
　Dickens' Reports, views on, 124
　differentiates, 124
　killed by case, 13
　records, court, to be searched, 124
　resigns, 15
　Royal Mandate, legality of, 27
　shareholding, undisclosed, 14–16
counsel,
　advocate not agent, 38
　blows, hard not foul, 39
　bread and water suggested by, 318
　crick in neck of, 92
　difficulty, position of utmost, 37
　dissimulation by, 34

counsel—cont.
　duty of, 33–41
　evidence by, 90–93
　gag, order to, 75
　harsh terms, propriety of using, 40
　honour, experience and learning, man of, 38
　indecorous and improper manner of, 39
　Johnson's views on, Dr., 34–36
　justice, ministers of, 38
　mercenary, not a, 37
　noise and gesticulation by, 40
　opulence of, 32, 33
　prosecuting, burden on, 38
　tears, undue excitement from, 40
　thief robber and cheat, called, 37
　thumbs, tying up by, suggested by, 318
　weep, duty to, 41
　whipping suggested by, 318
　See also advocate; attorney; Bar; lawyer; serjeants.
counsel's row,
　junior,
　　evidence from, 93
　　female litigant retreats to, 73
　　silks in, 33
　Q.C.s',
　　evidence from, 92, 93
　　full, 33
counterfeit halfpennies profitable, 330
counterpane a smooth cover, 160
county, wrong, in indictment, 311, 322
county court,
　defendant residing in, 184
　precedence of judge of, 22
　witnesses out of court, 87
court,
　abstract point, no opinion on, 170
　Chancery, Hot Spring(s), 185, 189
　cobweb varnish, brushing away, 33
　defamation, robust approach to, 342
　flag or fail, will not, 186
　land, manufacturing new titles to, 288
　performance, sees plaintiffs', 348
　prone, almost, 70
　sin, investigate wages of, 265
　tears, unimpressed by, 313
　unclean manner, coming to, in, 331
　vices, no duty to flatter, 341
　See also county court; Court of Arches; House of Lords; judge, judges.
Court of Arches, 213
Court of England much altered, 100

378

Index

death,
  as in, so in life, 58
  doings of, one of, 141
  grim case of, maladies leading to,
    281
  life and, mingling, 58
  113, at, improbability of, 230
  paramount claims of, 53
  taxes on, $5m., 267
  See also judge, judges.
debitum petendi, 213
debt, payment not presumed, 269
deceit, label exhales, 269
deed poll, name changed by, 281
Deemer J., critic's dramatic license, 348
defamation,
  defence if author named, 343
  gallows, leads plaintiff to, 342
  marriage, leads to loss of, 344
  minister, by, 348, 349
  newspaper, of, by another, 347
  robust approach to, 342
  value for money, 352
  See also libel; slander.
defects, having qualities of, 243
defilement and force in two counties,
  311
deformed brat, reports no, 118
Delina Delaney, 154
denial of justice, complete, 65
Denman C.J., Lord (Sir Thomas,
  A.-G.),
  argument defective, 103
  Espinasse's Reports, views on, 118,
    119
  statute, construing by altering, 178
  youth of reporter immaterial, 126
Denning M.R., Lord,
  blinded by dust, not, 140
  cliff, edge of, not fall over, 138
  deserted wife's equity, 292
  illegitimate child a descendant, 137
  invitation falling on unreceptive soil,
    139
  legislation function, usurpation of,
    183
  statutory interpretation, 182, 183
Dent P., dividing moon, 295
deodand, archbishop's horse a, 19
Derby, testamentary parturition, 309
descendant, illegitimate excluded, 137
deserted wife's equity, 292
desire, sensual, sedative against, 312
desires not in unsubdued provocation,
  215
De Ventre Inspiciendo, 225-235,
  writ of, 228

Devil, The, 151-169,
  patron saint of lawyers, 41
  words are the, 152
Devon, Earl of,
  creation, 104, 105
  peerage claim, 103, 104
Devonshire, Dukes of, 105
dialectic, nice exercise in, 261
Dickens' Reports. *See* reports.
dicta, spawn of careless, 147
dictionaries,
  baffled judge, last resort of, 151
  defamed, consulting to see if, 350
  fortress, making out of, 151
  persuasive not controlling, 151
Dictionary, Oxford, cow in South
  Africa, 351
difficult to read, title deeds, 285
difficulted, legitimacy of, 162
difficulty, needless verbosity mother of,
  151
dilemma, horns of, hear and pin, 153
Dilhorne, Viscount, Lord Donovan's
  opinion, 57
Diplock J. and L.J.,
  breeding new principles, 136
  burying progenitors, 136
  dissent, refusal to read, 148
  fiscal liability, avoiding, 258
  illegitimate child no descendant, 137
  maze, common law a, 113
  print prevents blatant evasion, 276
diplomacy,
  delicate and elusive, 113
  explicitness, founders on, 113
disconnexion, rich, 51
discord triumphs, 157
discretion, absolute, ends liberty, 194
discursive view, enlarged and, 10
disguise, truth needs no, 98
disgusting to touch, title deeds, 285
disk, identity, will on, 300
dissent,
  another deserved by one good, 68
  brooding spirit, appeal to, 148
  disagrees, because judge, 188
  eulogy of, 149
  failure, confession of, 149
  majority, 69, 189
  right of, 149
  stock of descent, 148
  unanimous, 66-69
dissenter,
  answered back, 149
  gladiator against lions, 147
  irresponsible, position, 147

dissimulation by counsel, 34
distinctions too numerous and refined,
Lord Eldon's, 11
distinguished with zest, 54
distressful female, unhelped by equity,
292
dividend, cum or ex, 293
divisible divorce, 212
Divisional Court,
audience by solicitors, 47
judgment, junior withdraws, 145–
147
divorce,
decree illegal and collusive, 223
divisible, 212
estopped from questioning, 211
spouses half bound, half free, 212
See also adultery; husband; Marriage;
nullity; wife.
doctor,
civil law, of, highest degree, 23
continence of, not requisite, 337
Dodd J., solicitor's inactivity, 46
Doe J. and C.J.,
precedent,
doing without, 149
respect for, 138
' does it work? ' John Bull asks, 113
dog,
Act, obscurities in, 175, 176
bark and bite, delight to, 249
disdain, gesture of, 249
larceny of, dead not alive, 323
Newfoundland, settled, 240
rabbit, hot pursuit of, 320
stealing, penalty for, 175, 176
vermin, condemned as, 249
dogma, deadening, not free enquiry,
205
Dolan J., artificial virginity, 214, 215
Dolben J.,
own cause, judging in, 19
Siderfin's Reports, fit to burn, 128
dom. proc., in. See House of Lords.
Domesday Book, 317
domicile, taxes for multiple, 267
don,
Cambridge, and new seeds, 244
Oxford, vengeance on footnotes, 244
donna è mobile, la, 313
Donovan, Lord, speech after death, 57
Dooley, Mr., discovers unanimous dissent, 66–69
door, stable, will on, 300
" Dope,"
cocaine, whether contains, 269

" Dope "—*cont.*
drink called, 269, 271
poison, faint aureole of, 271
dormio, non omnibus, 123
Douglas J.,
expertise becoming monster, 193, 194
fear stalks the classroom, 205
sexes not fungible, 247
dower if wife sold, 218, 219
drake no duck, 323
dramatic critic, license allowed to, 348
drawer for bad law, 132
drawing lots to be victim, 321
dream, unrealised, 258
drink, water not, 164
driving under influence of water, 164
drollery in self-service, 21
dubious litigation, heavy seas of, 156
duchess and clergy planted in same
bed, 347
duck no drake, 323
Dundas, Lord, action below man, 339,
340
Dunedin, Viscount,
impar congressus, 280
unfeigned regret, 280
dung,
heaped or scattered, 291
larceny of, 291
realty or personalty, whether, 291
dust, counsel raising the, 140
Dutch Reformed Church, minister of,
348
Dwyer J., rarity of Christian charity,
349
Dyer C.J., peace, laws ordained for,
135
Dyer's Reports. *See* reports.
dying, injunction against, 233

ear,
man cannot hear by another's, 196
promise to, broken, 194
ears, setting neighbours by, 42
East Anglia, lawless lawyers of, 44
eat orange, power to, 285
ecclesiastical courts, 317
economists protect slave trade, 199
Edinburgh Police Establishment, 324
education of wards of court, 233
Edward IV,
children bastardised, 110
troth-plight, 110
Edwards, Mr., cheerfulness breaks in
on philosophy, 45
effective cause, 157

Index

egg,
  American throws in Chancery, 71
  Bacon and, 70
  contemptuous, 71
  hen, comes from, 71
  testamentary disposition on, 300
  thrown with much force, 72
  will written on, 299, 300
Egypt, grasshoppers of, 44
Egyptian, old-fashioned, marries, 217
eigné, bastard, 287
ejectment in Pennsylvania,
  precedent no protection, 141, 142
  repeated trials, 140–143
ejusdem generis rule, 160
elaboration self-defeating, 255
Eldin, Lord. *See* Clerk, John.
Eldon L.C., Lord,
  angry, very, and very wrong, 3
  answer silences Thurlow, 172
  argument before, 4
  Barnardiston's Reports, views on, 122, 123
  begs solicitor for indulgence, 5
  certainty better than speculation, 135
  change, mischief of continual, 135
  Chelmsford Gaol, rebuilding, 174
  chief courts, reference to three, 10
  counsel, lack of confidence in, 6
  cunctative, has somewhat of, 5, 6
  Dickens' Reports, view on, 124
  dilatory in decision, 6
  disrespectful to King's Bench, 10
  dissents from own motion, 66
  distinctions numerous and refined, 11
  doubts and delays, proverbial, 4
  enlarged and discursive view, 10
  Equity Cases Abridged, views on, 128
  forgets argument, 5
  gaol, Chelmsford, absurdity of, 174, 175
  gloves, 3,000 pairs of, 323
  guinea brief, 3
  indulgence, begs for, 5
  King's Bench and Common Pleas, obtains different opinions from, 8
  landed owner, saves, 6
  lease, setting aside on ground not pleaded, 8
  Moseley's Reports, accuracy of, 125
  qualities of, 10
  Scottish appeals, unwilling to hear, 60
  solicitor's letter to, remarkable, 4
  subpoenaed in 83rd year, 13
  tardy justice preferred, 11

Eldon L.C., Lord—*cont.*
  Thurlow, silences, 172
  Vernon's Reports, views on, 130
  wiser upon advice, 6
  Woolsack, 25 years on, 3
Eliot J., infamous condemnation of dogs, 249
Elizabeth I. *See* Queen Elizabeth I.
ell of cloath, ideot cannot measure, 163
Ellenborough C.J., Lord,
  decisions uniformly right, 132
  testator's organs of sight, 297, 298
  views place where will signed, 297
Ellesmere L.C., Lord, every precedent has a commencement, 150
elopement at 75 with young woman, 231
eloquence sets fire to reason, 206
elusive and delicate expressions of diplomacy, 113
Elyot, Sir Thomas, Prince Hal's contempt, 77, 78
emancipation, clock strikes hour of, 304
embezzlement not taxable, 263
embrangled with cases, covenant, 139
Emperors of the East, same blood as, 103
encroachment, feminine, ever-increasing, 246
English Bar. *See* Bar.
English law,
  accused, judge counsel for, 39
  God, is law of, 111
    founded on revealed law of, 198
  human humours, unpolluted by, 111
  nature, is law of, 198
  pure primitive reason, 111
Englishman's hovel his castle, 200
enlarged and discursive view, 10
enrichment, unjust, 160
Ephraimite at Gileadite's sword point, 200
epigrams only dazzle, 276
equal division,
  appeal fails if, 57, 62, 64, 65
  Court of Common Pleas, 62
  Divisional Court, 145–147
  Exchequer Chamber, 62
  law lords, of, 57, 64, 65
equanimity, serene, born of courage, 188
equilibrium, perfect, 255
equitable principles bandied about, 292
equitable relief, folly no passport to, 294, 295

Index

gremio legis, in, 268
Gretchen's famous lament, 313
Grey, Lord, counts fat lord as ten, 106
grievance, giving up, no consideration, 326, 327
Grimm, gibe by Louis XVI, 12
Grimstone M.R., Sir Harbottle,
    attachment for familiarity, orders, 73
    £100 to kill, offer of, 74
groom, lord and, 100
gross indecency,
    Canada, in, 315
    England, in, 315
grossement enceinte, widow, 226
guaranties, legal, of civil liberties, 202
Guildhall Banquet, 23
guinea brief, 3

habeas corpus,
    Act due to very fat lord, 106
    attorney, frees, 15
    Cromwell defies, 197
    war bride, for, 194
Hailes, Lord,
    publication merits scorn, 339
    ratio decidendi, names inventor, 340
Hailsham L.C., Lord, bows to storm, 171
Hailsham of St. Marylebone L.C., Lord, makes 46 silks, 31
Hal, Prince. *See* Prince Hal.
Hale, C.J., Sir Matthew,
    abduction, law a scandal, 311
    laws to change with times, 111, 112
haleluiah, 42
halfpennies, counterfeit, 330
Hallett J.,
    gentleman's agreement, no, 326
    theology, exercise in comparative, 85
Halsbury L.C., Earl of,
    advocate's duty to client, 36
    concurs silently, 64
    improbable stories true, 36
    language imperfect instrument, 152
    legislature, reflection on, 176
    logical,
        law not always, 113
        public policy less, 113
    rides roughshod over brethren, 62
hammering, noisy, a contempt, 82
Hampton Court plot, the, 248
hand,
    dead man's, signs will, 296
    polluted, 331
hanged, not, for not burning, 181

Hannen, J.O., P. and Lord,
    duty not to let wife fall, 217
    King testifying unseemly, 94
    solicitor's duty to client, 49
harbor of objective revelation, 154
Hardwicke, C.J. and L.C., Lord (Sir Philip Yorke A.-G.),
    Barnardiston's Reports, views on, 122, 123
    certainty mother of remorse, 135
    Comberbach's Reports incorrect, 126
    Fitzgibbon's Reports no authority, 119
    innuendos in verse or prose, 346
    Keble a good register, 121
    Levinz a careless reporter, 125
    Reports in Chancery no authority, 119
    Reports *t.* Finch, views on, 128, 129
    Vernon's Reports imperfect, 130
    verse about, 345, 346
    wife, directs prosecution for assigning, 219
Harlan J. half right, 69
"harlot" for "robber," balance of 1s., 352
Harman J. and L.J.,
    acrimony, no tea sign of, 248, 249
    bargains, equity mending, 292, 293
    Beavan, late, in last ditch, 124
    bristling with irregularities, 248
    financial sprats and mackerel, 262
    irrefragable, 164
    nursery poem, recites, 249
    paternity of posthumous child, 227
    patience wears thin, 261, 262
    plum pudding and religion, 295
    prefers upright posture, 70
    rent,
        cupidity of oasis ruler fixes, 284
        meal or malt, in, 247
    harmonium, keeping, in room, 216
Hatherley L.C., Lord (Page Wood V.-C.),
    mind unchanged, 65
    status changed, 65
Havvards come pretty dear, 68
Hawkins J., serjeants' dress, 23
Hayes, Serjeant and J.,
    children's poem, cites, 249
    codicils, attacks, 305, 306
    widow's claim, opposes, 219
hayloft codicil, 305
headlights of reality, 156
heads, how many, so many wits, 225

Index

Healy K.C., Maurice,
  bright reply, 46
  crab, diseased, only trifle, 329
  inheritance, signing away, 299
hear other side, time to, 11
hearsay in affidavits, 47
Heath J.,
  acts of charity found no rights, 250
  policy of law, 250
heavens fall, let the, for convenience,
  18
heavy seas of dubious litigation, 156
heels, laid by the, 18
Heever, van den, J. and J.A.,
  exchange of civilities, 350
  fossil, law a, 244, 245
  tears, unimpressed by, 313
Hegham B., gross insult to, 79
he-goats, Laban's leaping, 318
heir,
  born before parents' marriage, 286,
    287
  true, mulier puisne not bastard
    eigné, 287
Hell, constable named, 236
hell hound, counsel calls defendant, 40
hen,
  amorous resistance by, no, 319
  egg,
    comes from, 71
    will written on, 299, 300
  runs to excite passion, 319
  sitting, makes fight, 319
Henn Collins J., nullity of marriage to
  Old Egyptian, 218
Henry IV, 77–79
Henry V, 77–79
heresy dignified as reform, 130
Herring C.J., moment of marriage, 212
herrings, three red, 139
Herschell, Lord,
  roughshod over, ridden, 62
  speech after death, 57
heterodoxy dignified as reform, 136
Hewart C.J., Lord,
  clause worst ever to appear, 171
  drawing fatuous if not indecent, 347
Higbe, Commissioner, girl old in sin,
  319
High Court, solicitors' audience in, 47
highest degree,
  civil law, of, 23
  common law, of, 23
high-speed main track of jurisprudence, 156
highway of logic, argument misses, 113

highwayman hanged for suing in
  slander, 342
Hill J., judgment read after retiring,
  54
hills, steadfast as the, 142
hinder part, mayor told to kiss, 208
Hindus swear in Scottish form, 85
Hobart C.J.,
  appothecary gives physick, 337
  attorney makes false writings, 337
Hobart's Reports deformed without
  correction, 130
Hodson, Lord, not allowed to swear,
  93
holes, rabbit, of irrelevancy, 155
Holmes J. (S.A.),
  judgment in loser's language, 168
  question John Bull asks, 113
  sheriff serving self, 20, 21
Holmes J. (U.S.),
  civilised man, mark of, 201
  contempt no better if true, 81
  contract, committing a, 335
  corporation, existence of, a fiction,
    282
  damages, liability in, 326
  dead pull, a month's, 5
  free speech, 204–206
    limits of, 205, 206
  fruits, attributing to different tree,
    255
  generalise, to, is to omit, 169
  ideas,
    encysted in phrases, 151
    hard, not often, 152
  illegal—
    act, effect of, 330
    expenses, taxpayer deducts, 263
  impact, day's, 5
  judgments, reserved, 5
  Koke, not Dope, enjoins, 271
  libel unjustified by contract, 343
  memory spreads floor of light, 244
  men and women, 19th Amendment,
    247
  outlaw, not becoming, 330
  Quakers have done their share, 199
  qualities of man, 243
  split writ, caught with a, 67, 68
  tax, power to, 267
  wife's celebrated answer, 248
  words are the devil, 152
  writ, sooner caught with split, 68
Holmes L.J. (Ir.),
  Latin solves little, 329
  young lawyer thinks, 329

Index

jigsaw puzzle,
  judge solves, 309
  will torn into, 309
John Bull asks if it works, 113
John, King, rights of succession, 229
Johnson, Dr.,
  attorney, speaking ill of behind
    back, 45
  bookish man needs lawyers, 45
  Boswell, writes argument for, 340
  counsel, duty of, 34–36
  dissimulation, affecting warmth no,
    34
  jest breaks no bones, 340
  lawyers know life practically, 45
  moralist, a, 34
  Scottish solicitors, argument against
    340
  tumbling on hands, 35
  women, power given to, 247
Johnson J.,
  hallowed orison of equity, 294
  joint stock activity, gratitude not
    associated with, 282
  language, half doubts in life, 151
  " lead us not into temptation," 294
joke, dull and foolish, serious, 342
Jones, J., subtlety rejected by, 344
judge, judges,
  Act, help House of Lords with, 172
  answer peers' questions, 172
  attendance adds to costs, 64
  blockheads, parcel of, 120
  bull, arguable he is, 169
  cause, in own, 16, 18, 19
  common law, too confined in
    thought, 332
  Commons, two carry Bill to, 173
  counsel for accused, 39
  counsel's tears, not asked to check,
    41
  Cromwell,
    severely reprehended by, 197
    subservience to commands of, 198
  dead, whether draft judgment final,
    54
  death,
    instructions for draft judgment, 54
    unsealed bill of exceptions, 56
  Deputy Speakers, appointed, 58
  dissent,
    majority, 69, 189
    unanimous, 67
  dissenter,
    individuality, can express, 148
    irresponsible, 147
    technique of, 149

judge, judges—*cont.*
  doubled numbers reserve against
    disaster, 56
  equal division of,
    appeal fails, 57, 62, 65
    junior judge withdraws, 145–147
    rehearing with another, 64
  evanescent irritation, show of, 75
  evidence,
    giving, 17, 93, 94
    ruling on own, 17
  expediency, disdain to bend to, 199
  fact, of, not of laws, 346
  function to interpret not amend,
    181–183
  girl, suggests good licking for, 318
  good,
    jurisdiction, extends his, 331
    justice, extends, 332
  gravity of, marvellous, 78
  guess parliament's intention, 181
  half right, all, all right none, 69
  hands, do not simply fold, 182
  heart, tuned piano in, 157
  impartiality as own, 16–19
  insured, 56, 57
  intention, legislature's, giving force
    and life to, 182
  iron out creases, 182
  irritation, evanescent, allowed, 75
  libel of, contempt to justify, 81
  lies to, telling, 34
  lost sleep, 187
  minority view *obiter* and *per in-
    curiam* becomes *ratio decidendi*,
    189
  modicum of quick temper allowed,
    75
  own cause, in, 16–19
  popular, odious and pernicious, 346
  public feeling, too apt to be moved
    by, 202
  quit, not often enough, 69
  resignation, judgment after, 26, 54
  right, stand on high ground of
    natural, 199
  sacred duty of, 141
  serjeants, mode of addressing, 26
  seven prevail over eight, 61
  side-room, give reasons in, 59
  silently concur, 64
  slavery, condemn, 198, 199
  speculation, better to avoid, 135
  speechless in judgment, vigorous in
    discussion, 59

judge, judges—*cont.*
  spokesman,
    dreams of unworthy brood of
      scions, 147
    vivid words, heightened phrase,
      avoids, 147
    statute, interpret not amend, 181–
      183
    summoned to assist law lords, 62, 63
    tellin' on each other, 69
    tinkering at the law, 141
    upright, would have been slain, 70
    Wales, going circuit in, 169
    witness, as, 17, 93, 94
    See also court; House of Lords;
      justices of the peace.
judgment,
  advocacy preferred to lawyer's, 36
  antedated, 56
  concurring, agrees with most, 145
  death's doings, one of, 142
  dissenting,
    confession of failure to convince
      colleagues, 149
    parent stock of motley progeny,
      148
    potter's hand trembling at wheel,
      148
    refusal to read, call of table, 148
  language,
    loser, of, in, 168
    winner, of, in, if Welsh, 168
  negligent, 341
  reserved,
    consideration, decided on great, 5
    note to registrar, given by, 12
    post, given by, 55
  rival petitions each affirmed, 12
  sermons sold and delivered, for
    price of, 326
  temerarious, 341
  tempest, furious, greets, 28
  withdrawing, 145–147
judicial—
  genius, 87
  gobbley-dook, 68
Judicial Process, 53–69
jungle, law of, and common sense,
  250
junior counsel's row. *See* counsel's
  row.
jurisprudence,
  fickle uncertain and vicious, 142
  gladsome light of, 352
  high-speed main track of, 156
  mathematical, apotheosis of, 99
jurisprudent, farewell to, 352

jury,
  forsworn before tribunal of con-
    science, 196
  immunity from punishment, 196
  passions and peculiarities of, 40
jurymen,
  passionless pale and Cassius-looking,
    312
  redfaced, challenge if not, 312
  unduly excited by counsel's tears, 40
jus est aut incognitum aut vagum, 341
jus petendi, 213
jus vagum aut incertum, 141
just and generous rule, 160
justice,
  administration of, stabbed in vitals,
    153
  baffled by falsehood or chicane, 88
  beacon of, beams ignored, 156
  daughter of law, 235
  piano of, tuned in judge's heart, 157
  pure fountains of, 331
  scales of, shaken by hands that
    hold, 141
  soliditie of, 352
  tardy, better than swift injustice, 11
justices of the peace, 55, 56,
  " bloodsucker," no slander to call,
    338
  come and go but justice endures, 56
  See also judge, judges.

Karminski J. and L.J.,
  evidence, gives, 94
  rises without biting, 139
  swear, prefers not to, 94
Karslake, Sir John, refuses to practise,
  32
Kay L.J.,
  freehold no easement, 107
  mathematics, turns to, 107
K.C. *See* Queen's Counsel.
Keble's Reports. *See* reports.
Kekewich J.,
  inactivity prudent or rash, 243
  solicitor, commits, 82
Kelyng C.J.,
  arbitrary committal, 198
  Magna Carta, Cromwell's answer,
    198
Kennedy L.J.,
  life insured, 56
  post mortem judgment, 56
Kenyon M.R. and C.J., Lord,
  Barnardiston bad reporter, 123
  Burrow's Reports, views on, 127

Index

Kenyon M.R. and C.J., Lord—*cont.*
  Equity Cases Abridged, authority of, 128
  Hobart's Reports excellent, 131
  Keble,
    feeble and bad reporter, 120
    reprimand for citing, 121
    views on, mellower, 121
  latet anguis in herbâ, 153
  Latin, frailty of, 152, 153
  mandami, no brace of, 153
  mantle of, 154
  metaphor,
    mixed, 152
    multi-, 153, 154
  modus in rebus, 153
  newspaper attacks another, 347
  Raymond, Lord, comments on youth of, 125
  reporter, plays the law, 127
  solicitor suspended without hearing, 50
  ventre inspiciendo, de, 229
  Vernon's Reports, views on, 130
  Winch's Reports, questions parentage of, 118
  witnesses, weigh not number, 99
  words actionable if sales affected, 347
Kerkraad told infanticide prevalent, 349
Kerry alibi, 86
Kindersley V.-C., absolute nonsense in statute, 170
King. *See* Sovereign.
King's Bench Saturday jurisdiction, 275
King's College porch called Jumbo, 165
King's Proctor intervenes, no, 52
King's Serjeants. *See* serjeants.
King Solomon In Georgia, 311–325
  thousand wives not tolerated, 318
kingdom lost from lost nail, 335
Kinnear, Lord, sad brevity of, 63
kiss,
  arse, M.R. told to, 73
  assault, whether, 312
  come and, Mayor told to, 208
  lady's hand, by knight, 209
kitchin maid, lady and, 100
Knight Bruce V.-C. and L.J.,
  attorney, rough and harsh language for, 50
  exuberance of sympathy, no, 49
  hayloft codicil, 305
  informing and believing clerks, 47
  overrules demurrer, 109

knights,
  inspection in presence of, 228
  kissing lady's hand, 209
Koke, drink called, 269

Laban's bulls rams and he-goats leap, 318
label exhales deceit, 269
labourer forbidden teeny weeny sherry, 325
ladder, step-, admitted to probate, 300
lady,
  elopes with husband's servant, 219
  kitchin maid, and, 100
  livery,
    grantee footman, if, lies in, 220
    lying in grant or in, 219
laesam phantasiam, 343
laid by the heels, 18
lamp of abstract meditation, 156
land-marks of the law sacred, 135
Langdale M.R., Lord,
  attendance adds to costs, 64
  confidence reposed in counsel, 38
Langton J. appraises witness, 54
Language, 151–169,
  Arabin, Serjeant, glory or inglory, 27
  defects of, half doubts arise, 151
  French, 163
  gold-mine, law reports, 162
  instrument, imperfect, 152
  judgment in loser's, 168
  Latin, 157–160
  Old Bailey, 166
  oratio obliqua, 169
  Parliament's choice of, 166
  pictures not mathematics, 152
  precision, law French, 163
  Scottish—
    delicacy, 161
    weight, 161
  Welsh, 168, 169
  See also words.
lapsus calami, 160
larceny. *See* theft.
lasciviousness, protection against, 214
last—
  Q.C. of Ireland, 29
  serjeant, 29
late, pay, pay less, 335
late Beavan, 124
latet anguis in herbâ, 153
Latin maxim solves little, 329
Latinity,
  falling behind in, 158
  threadbare mantle of, 159

latro for *meretrix*, 1s. balance, 352
Lattimore J.,
  church bells, sound of, 210
  common law marriage in Texas, 210
law, laws,
  anchors of the Republique, 117
  bad,
    inconvenience fully felt, 165
    spirit of, acting fully up to, 165
  bosom of, answer lies in, 268
  bushes of, beaten, 155
  Canadian, proscribed marital inter-
    course, 315
  changes with society, 112
  English. *See* English law.
  judge-made, 141
    saved by absence of ' s ', 187
  jungle of, 250
  justice daughter of, 235
  land, of, rubbish heap, 285
  married, telling if, 212
  new, with new lords, 142
  old father antick, 77
  old principles and new circum-
    stances, 136
  peace and concord, 135
  Pennsylvanian, short-lived principles
    of, 142
  permanent and correct, 136
  prodigious numbers of, better none
    than, 187
  public policy less logical than, 113
  Scottish, shamelessly indecent con-
    duct criminal, 315
  ship without ballast, 117
  single-track spur track of, 156
  unknown or unsettled, 341
  women, gives little power to, 247
  wonderful, obviously too, 187
  See also common law.
law clerks worked to bone, 187
Law Courts poster defaming judge,
  346, 347
law French a language of precision,
  163
law lord by prescription, 33. *See also*
  House of Lords.
law reporter. *See* reporter.
law reports. *See* Reports.
lawfully and irremediably asunder, 51
Lawrence Q.C. and J. (1902–67),
  agenda, tea on, 249
  tea not served, 249
Lawrence J. (1751–1824),
  grammar, no strict, 276
  laxity of commercial documents, 276

lawyer,
  advocacy of, preferred to judgment,
    36
  bookish man, needed by, 45
  client not keeper of professional
    conscience, 37
  duty to court large not obsequious, 75
  evidence—
    against client's interests, 91
    for client, 90
  fees on both sides, taking, 42
  gag, threatened with, 75
  lawless, of East Anglia, 44
  usurping province of jury and
    judge, 35
  witness, as, 90–93
  See also advocate; attorney; counsel;
    Solicitors.
lazie recklesse manner of judge, 70
Lea, Sir Henry, King's evidence
  against, 95
Leach V.-C. and M.R., Sir John,
  Deputy Speaker of House of Lords,
    58, 60
  hear other side, time to, 11
  private explanation by, 60
  speech, made a, 4
  swift injustice of, 11
leap-years, effect on age, 303
Learned Hand J.,
  dictionary no fortress, 151
  interpretation, purpose and meaning,
    182
  patriotic duty, no, 257
  sympathetic and imaginative dis-
    covery, 151
Leather-head, Dr., argues, 212
Lee C.J., Holt's Reports, views on,
  119
legal imagination, corporations creatures of, 282
legal responsibility, adhesive mortar
  of, 328
legal rights pressed to extreme, 250
legislature,
  male, predominantly, 246
  reflection on, 176
  See also parliament.
legitimacy, superfluity of, 225
Leicester, Earl of, certifies Queen's
  words, 95
lemon,
  oranges and/or, 52
  sour, 52
letchers and whores. *See* whores and
  letchers.

Index

lethal weapon pierces royal breeches, 324

letherwite, adultery and fornication, 317

letters learned, troubles not done, 179

letters of administration with the will annexed of tractor fender granted, 300, 301

letters parent, 183

Levinz's Reports. *See* reports.

Lewin's Reports. *See* reports.

libel, 337–352
  contract to, no justification, 343
  George V bigamist, a, 96
  kissing, two roses, 347
  See also defamation; slander.

liberties, charter of, for explicit gossip, 343

Liberty, 193–208,
  absolute discretion end of, 194
  civil, legal guaranties give little, 202
  courage, secret of, 203
  ends and means, 203
  eternal vigilance condition for, 193
  happiness, secret of, 203
  insidious encroachment on, 207
  invasion by evil-minded rulers, 207
  jury, large part played by, 196
  liberties with, no, 205
  limits to claims of, 195
  nice people, not very, 193
  protection against beneficent, 207
  restrictions on, whether constitutional, 206
  safeguards forged in controversies, 193
  secret of happiness, 203
  thought, of, soon shrivels, 201
  valued as end and means, 203
  vanished, saddest epitaph for, 193
  See also freedom.

licentiousness of press, 346

lien, choatitude of, 161

life,
  death and, mingling, 58
  so in, as in death, 58
  unbearable if all rights pressed, 250

Lifford, Lord, presides, 167

Light C.J., Lord, crazy clock strikes thirteen, 98

likewise and also, 167

Lincoln's Inn, informing clerk in, 47

Lindley J. and Lord,
  last English serjeant, 28
  option to break contract, 336

line drawn by unsteady hand, 255

lion,
  growl and fight, 249
  shutting door after, 154

liquor,
  sharp line between sexes, 247
  widow's damages against store selling, 222

literalness strangles meaning, 151

litigant in person says Act unconstitutional, 109

litigation, heavy seas of dubious, 156

little of law, little of everything, 12

Littledale J., ninth Mod. worse than tenth, 119

live fly validates will, 296

Lloyd's Evening Post intermeddles, 106

Lockwood Q.C., Sir Frank,
  counsel, calls, 92
  Queen's Proctor, for, 92

logger-headed hound, 342

logic,
  highway of, argument misses, 113
  interred in deep grave, 157
  Pennsylvania, dead in, 156
  retreat from, 157
  Thermopylae of, 157

logical,
  dilemma, 16
  public policy less than law, 113

logically insupportable but works well, 113

Lolme, de,
  anticipated by Earl of Pembroke, 107
  parliament making woman man, 107

London's loveliest bridges, 325

Lopes L.J. *See* Ludlow, Lord.

lord, very fat, counts for ten, 106

lord and groome, no distinction, 100

Lord Chancellor,
  deputy, 58, 59
  England, of, 16
  four in one case, 13
  Great Britain, of, 16
  hearing, request to attend, 143
  motion, votes against own, 66
  Punch, most frequently in, 12

Lord Chief Baron. *See* Chief Baron of the Exchequer.

Lord Keeper. *See* Lord Chancellor.

Loreburn L.C., Earl,
  appeal dismissed without reasons, 64
  result manifestly deplorable, 63, 64

loser,
  judgment in language of, 168
  why, wants to know, 168

loss of husband or wife all one, 344

396

lot, selection of victim by, 321
Loughborough L.C., Lord,
Cases in Chancery, views on, 130
courage, not enough, 66
Vernon's Reports, usual inaccuracy
of, 130
Louis XVI's gibe at Abbé Maury, 12
loveliness of temperance, 352
' Lres ' in bill, 45
lucus a non lucendo, 160
Ludlow, Lord (Lopes L.J.),
dies before writing judgment, 56
junior judge to withdraw judgment,
146
Lush J. withdraws judgment, 146, 147
Lushington, Dr., Modern Reports
unreliable, 119
Lyndhurst C.B. and L.C., Lord,
Barnardiston, wags scribble in note
book, 123
Deputy Speakers, defends, 60
Gibbs C.J. and year books, 139
Lord Chancellor not liable as judge,
13

Maccaroni bastard, 349
Macclesfield L.C., Earl of (Lord Parker
L.C.),
affront to Author of Nature, 314
hesitation, no, 314
law settled more important than
how, 135
McAdam J., basis of marriage, 214
Macdonald, Sir J. H. A., Lord Justice-
Clerk,
bile beans, 271–273
complainers stamp business with
falsity, 273
McDonald C.J., insufficient evidence,
223
McHaney J. implies missing words, 189
Mackay, Lord,
individual linguistic style, 161, 162
parallelity between two inquiries,
162
simplification, great, 162
McKenna J., cost of being governed,
257
mackerel free but sprat caught, 262
MacKinnon L.J.,
certain of only one thing, 259
errs in distinguished company, 260
problem, most difficult, 259
prophecy than law, sounder in, 260
McLean J. no passive candidate for
presidency, 149

McMahon M.R.,
horse-whipping in porch, 82
insults in Master's office, 82
Macmillan, Lord, curious logical
dilemma, 16
Macnaghten J.,
quorum, case not stated by, 55
Yes, no difficulty in saying, 55
Macnaghten, Lord,
bankers so very careful, 269
concurs silently, 64
risk to avoid, no, 269
McReynolds J.,
interjections by court, 181
lawmakers thinking long enough,
181
magistrate,
electors of, affection and simplicitie,
239
wealth and authoritie exceed wit,
239
Magna Charta,
Magna ——A, 198
Magna F——, 197
mail,
carrier of, arrested for murder, 181
sheriff charged for obstructing, 181
maintenance, proper,
frees the mind, 232
wolf, keeps from pattering, 232
majority,
Arkansas, one out of six, 189
Scottish, five out of fifteen, 322
malam partem, in, 338
" male,"
females, drives out, 105
potent for peerages, 105
malevolent, cloak for, 194
Malins V.-C.,
egg thrown at, 70
insulted anyone, never, 71
mamsey-nose copper-nose knave, 347
man, men,
civilized,
enquiring mind mark of, 202
principles, doubts own first, 201
creature without shape of, 239
defects of qualities forgiveable, 243
famous, married young, 248
feared witches and burned women,
203
forty, over,
desires subdued, 215
placid gratifications for, 215
free, must be reasoning, 201
grandfather, own, 235

Index

man, men—*cont.*
  how many, so many minds, 225
  influence imponderable, 247
  island on sea of life reserved for, 245
  qualities of, 243
    defects of his, 243
  rich and respectable, no crime if, 279
  self-made, hasn't made much, 243
  sidewalk underfoot, knowing, 243
  temperate, dies of chronic hepatitis, 280
  twelve honest, judges of fact, 346
  wife,
    basely slays, 220
    liability for torts of, 221
    unity with, will of God, 221
  will, broken, recovery from, 243
  woman,
    interplay of influence, 247
    not, save by statute, 107
  See also human; husband; widow; wife; woman.
Manchester Ship Canal, pilot on, 299
mandami, brace of, 153
Manisty J.,
  absurd for authority, nothing too, 139
  doubt, none but for authorities, 139
Manitoba,
  banns in, 183
  religious observance in, 184
  strait-laced volume, 184
  worship in, 183
manners fit (or not) for pig, 167
Manners L.C., Lord,
  Barnardiston, mild words for, 122
  Equity Cases Abridged, views on, 128
manoeuvre, battle of, 258
manor, lord of, 13
Mansfield C.J., Lord (William Murray),
  assignment of female singer immoral, 219
  Barnardiston, 122, 123
    Reports, forbids citation of, 123
  Blackstone's Reports inaccurate, 125
  Bunbury's Reports never meant to be published, 121, 122
  child-bearing, obscure contribution, 293
  Comberbach's Report, judgment only sensible part, 126, 127
  conscience, attempts to force, 201
  judge, good, increases jurisdiction, 332
  judge, good, increases justice, 332

Mansfield C.J., Lord (William Murray) —*cont.*
  judging impartially in own cause, 19
  Keble a bad reporter, 120
  liberty of press, 346
  metaphors apt to mislead, 152
  Moseley's Reports, views on, 125
  patents of precedence, 22
  Raymond too young to report, 125
  reporters, two bad, 131
  verse, sets out, 345, 346
  words, disputes arise from, 151
Mansfield C.J., Sir James,
  Act, cannot understand, 45
  Atkyns' Reports extremely inaccurate, 120
  Campbell reports Lord Ellenborough if right, 132
  marine policy strange instrument, 276
  manuscripts a monument to posterity, 129
Manwood C.B.,
  pun, shocking, 290
  Salisbury Plain, seised to use of, 290
mare, bothering, 345
marine insurance policy strange instrument, 276
maritime misfortune, chapter of, 278
market-place, standards of, 294
Marriage, 209–224,
  agreements defining rights, 216–218
  chastity as condition precedent to, 214
  comfortable society, only for, 215
  common law,
    church bells, sound of, 210
    cloak, polite verbal, 210
    Texas, respectable ancestry in, 210
  concubinage, degraded to mere, 221
  condition precedent, chastity no, 214
  desperate device of, 240
  Egyptian, old-fashioned, to, 217
  loss of, blacksmith liable for, 334
  moment of, 212
  placid gratifications of, 215
  promise *subsequente copula*, by, 209
  proposal under cross-examination, 209
  saves woman from shaming friends, 216
  Scottish law of, 209, 210
  second,
    reasons for prompt, 226
    widow grossement enceinte, to, 226

Marriage—*cont.*
settlement,
desperate device of, 240
fraudulent and void, 240, 241
toothbrush and Newfoundland dog, includes, 240
shot-gun, 225
slander deprives of, 344
tanquam soror, taking woman, 215
virginity as condition precedent to, 214
See also adultery; divorce; husband; wife.
Marryat, Serjeant, brace of mandami, 153
Marshall C.J.,
constitution approaches immortality, 112
power to tax, power to destroy, 266, 267
Martin B., water not drink, 164
Martin J., moment of marriage, 212
Mason, Simon, *ambidexter*, 49
Master,
indecency in court, 80
office of, case in for 25 years, 263
punctuality, want of, 80
Master in Lunacy, precedence, 22
Master of Rolls,
commoner, mere, 58
" kiss my arse," 73
masterly inactivity may be—
prudence, 243
rashness, desperate, 243
mathematical—
rules, words disdain, 152
symbols, words not, 152
matrimonial strife, slaying wife in, 220
Maude Q.C., Judge,
beastly crime under lovely bridge, 325
teeny weeny sherry before dinner, 325
Maugham J. strikes out Public Trustee, 19
Maule J.,
apples endangered by indecency, 313
covenant for rain, 326
nominal damages peg for costs, 335
" person " means private parts, 166
water not drink, 164
Maury, Abbé, Louis XVI's gibe at, 12
Maynard committed by Cromwell, 197
mayor,
hinder part of body,
come and kiss, invitation to, 208
turns towards, 208

maze not motorway, common law, 113
Meadowbank, Lord, also not likewise, 168
meal or malt, rent in, 247, 248
meat,
ice-cream not, 165
water not, 164
meddlesome, cloak for, 194
meditation, lamp of abstract, 156
Megarry Q.C. and J.,
concurrence makes majority, contends, 145
dust, raises wrong kind of, 140
jig-saw puzzle, solves, 309, 310
life insured, 57
Melmoth edits Vernon's Reports, 130
melodious chord, not very, 157
Member of Parliament,
barrister M.P.'s privilege from committal, 80
patent of precedence saves seat, 22
Memoirs of a Woman of Pleasure, 242
memory spreads floor of light, 244
men. *See* man, men.
menagerie, tiger escapes from, 333
mends no man's bargain, Chancery, 292
Merchant of Venice in Court of Appeal, 138
mercy, paper currency forbids, 324
meretrix for *latro* leaves 1s. balance, 352
Merriman, Lord, speech after death, 57
Merrivale P., Lord,
fragile will, 300
judgment of Hill J., reads, 54
mess?, how could judges get in such a, 68
metaphors, 152–157,
mislead, apt to, 152
mixed, weakness for, 152
multi-, 153
See also Musmannodicts.
Metingham C.J., boled kyn calf myn, 229
Mexican administration immortal, 142
Miami's garbage, nature of, 336
Middle Temple invites serjeants to return, 29
Middleton J. upholds capricious will, 307–309
midstream of indecision, 156
might does not make right, 259
milk, tiger days excepted for, 333
Miller J., tax uniformity unrealised dream, 258

Index

Milne J., tentative ventured kiss, 312
miner of 112 working, 231
minister shows no charity, 348, 349
mink, geese may stand up to, 200
minority *obiter per incuriam* prevails, 189
minstrels. *See* whores and letchers.
Minton J., choate lien, 160
miracle multiplied, 230
mirage of speculation, 155
mire, Lord Brougham's face in, 12
mischief of changing continually, 135
misera est servitus, 341
misinformed, cloak for, 194
Modern Reports. *See* reports.
modesty in woman, jewel equal to setting, 214
modus in rebus, 153
modus operandi of prostitute, 314
Molony L.J. and C.J., 55
Monboddo, Lord,
    Darwin, anticipates, 209
    joke, no need to record, 339
Moncrieff, Lord,
    conscience, appeal to, 89
    oath, reference to, 89
money, three values of, 283
moneylenders,
    evil, great, of London, 274–276
    royal and noble names, bearing, 275
    slave of, borrower made, 276
monstrosity, capering, 348
monument, reports a, 129
moon, dividing by imaginary lines, 295
moralist, law hurting finer feelings of, 34
morality squad, dedicated members of, 264
morals, modern, not Biblical, 318
mortar of legal responsibility,
    adhesive, is, 328
    water, turned to, 328
mortgage to be stamped £90,720,000, 283
Moseley's Reports. *See* reports.
Mother Of Repose, The, 134–150,
    certainty the, 135
mothers,
    competition, disgusting and revolting, among, 308
    gift to most fecund, 307
motion, sexual act for verb of, 350
motions, going through the, 20
motley progeny from parent stock, 148
motorway, common law maze not, 113

Moulton, Lord (Fletcher Moulton L.J.),
    common law fecund, 294
    silenced absentee, 61
mule brought to bed, 230
mulier puisne, heir, 287
murder,
    father beating son's assailant, 242
    starving seaman, by, 320
Murphy J.,
    law's finest hour, 204
    touchstone of taxability, 263
Murray, Lord, draft judgment, whether final view, 54
Murray, William. *See* Mansfield C.J., Lord.
Musmanno J.,
    dissent, does not, 328
    metaphors. *See* Musmannodicts.
Musmannodicts, 113, 154–157, 169, 328

name, good, far above rubies, 274
names, business, registration, 281, 282
Napier L.C., Sir Joseph, idiom in truth, 98, 99
National Canine Defence League meets, 248
natural right, judges stand on high ground of, 199
Neaves, Lord, verses on law of marriage, 209
Nebuchadnezzar's Tree, 285–295,
    uses resemble, 292
necklace, steel,
    camphor bag attached, 311
    sensual desire, sedative against, 312
nefas, per, upholding client's interests, 36
neighbourly, dangers of being, 250
neighbours,
    bad or good, depends on fences, 249
    Church and State, 250
    false witness for, giving, 86
    set together by ears, 42
neminem oportet esse sapientiorem legibus, 111
nemo bis vexari pro eadem causa, 310
nemo nascitur artifex, 111
nemo tenetur ad impossibile, 213
nest, feathering with master's bottles, 152
Nevada divorce, 211
new lords, new laws, 141
Newfoundland dog settled, 240
newspaper, ignorant and scurrilous, 347
Nicholl, Sir John, marriage of elderly man, 215

400

Reports—*cont.*

Benloe and Dalison's, preface doubts Winch, 118

Blackstone's inaccurate, 125

Bunbury's compiled by postman, 121, 122

Campbell's,
Ellenborough's decisions always right, 132
high authority, 131–133

Carter's unknown to judge, 128

Cases in Chancery, doubtful authority, 128

Coke's high authority, 119

Comberbach's,
accuracy of, 127
Holt made to say what he could not, 127
incorrect, 126, 127

Dickens' practical but inaccurate, 124

Dyer's marginal notes good authority, 70

Equity Cases Abridged not first authority, 128

Espinasse's,
accuracy, want of, 118, 119
apology, cited with, 119
fatherless, 117

Fitzgibbon's no authority, 119

Gouldborough's no spurious deformed Brat, 118

Hobart's,
beauteous in their confusion, 131
deformed, 130

Holt's King's Bench no authority, 119

Keble's, conflicting views on, 120, 121

legitimacy of, 117

Levinz's careless, 125

linguistic goldmine, 162

Modern,
scambling, 120
volume 8 miserably bad, 119
volume 9 worse than 10, 119

monument, a, 129

Moseley's, opinions differ, 125

Noy's bad authority, 120

Popham's no authority, 120

posthumous, disallowed, 117

Raymond's criticised for reporter's youth, 125

Reports in Chancery no authority, 119

Reports—*cont.*

Reports *t.* Finch no authority, 128, 129

" Shiboleth " pronounced " Siboleth," 117

Shower's disallowed as authority, 127

" Siboleth " for " Shiboleth," 117

Siderfin's fit to be burned, 128

squadron, flying, of thin, 118

Taunton's, apocryphal authority, 129

Vernon's, 129, 130,
cases usually inaccurate, 130
manuscripts monument to posterity, 129
wandring and masterless like soldiers of Cadmus, 117

Wentworth's *Pleader* very vicious, 129

Winch's, cases decided after his death, 118

repose, certainty mother of, 135

repression,
emergency, justified only by, 204
fear, bred by, 203
hate breeds, 203

repudiator, wrecked at touch of, 328

resceit, 149

respect, lawyers owe court large not obsequious, 75

responsibility, rudder of, 155

revelation, harbor of objective, 154

revolutionary spark,
kindles fire, 205
sweeping and destructive conflagration, 206

rhetoric, use by counsel, 40

Ribble, River, worse than woman, 266

Richard III, Act of, burned, 110

Richards C.B., Thurlow praises Scott, 3

Richardson C.J.,
hat, loses only, 70
slaine if upright judge, 70

Richmond, doctrine of unjust in, 160

Rickhill J., cow bulled calf mine, 229

Ridley J. refuses costs for pleading Gaming Acts, 176

right,
great, a little wrong to do, 138
legal, trodden down may bee but never out, 195

right to be let alone, 207

ringing of bells if man of 84 begat child, 230

ripeness is all, 309

Index

Ritchie J., division of spoils, 223
river of conjecture, 154
River Ribble worse than woman, 266
rivulets of anger, 169
" robber " is. worse than " harlot,"
352
Roberts J.,
exactions tortured and justified, 255
inequalities and ease, 259
law game of chance, 134
robots, students trained as, 205
robots, students trained as, 205
Rodman J.,
animals, inferences from, 320
brute, unjust to assume prisoner, 320
Rogers, Graham,
fingers show price, 314, 315
prostitute, *modus operandi* of, 314,
315
Rogers, Samuel,
Brougham more than six in one, 12
post-chaise, overcrowded, 12
Rolle J. and C.J.,
deed sealed with dead hand, 296
dung commonly in heap, 291
Roman Bath, partners immersed in, 52
Romilly M.R., Sir John,
codicils, too many, 304–306
new trials, ordering, 304, 305
vintages, later, not dependable, 124
Romilly, Sir Samuel, tardy justice
beter than swift injustice, 11
roof-tree, family, trusts at home under,
235
Ros, Amanda M'Kittrick,
author, 154
Kenyon's mantle pauses at tomb of,
154
Rose, Sir George, hear other side, 11
Roxburgh J.,
" Jumbo," college porch called, 165
language pictures not mathematics, 152
Royal Charter, 338, 339
Royal Mandate,
audience, ends serjeants' exclusive, 26
ineffective, 27, 28
precedence, confers, 27
royal marriages, 172
rubbish, paying for, as price of freedom, 195
rubbish-heap, law of land is, 285
Rubens, will on back of stolen, 301
rubies, good name far above, 274
rudder of responsibility, 155
rule,
anything, for, found in Barnes, 129
backside, wiping with, 74

rung out of Inn of call, serjeant, 26
Running-Stationers, Society of, 338
Russell Q.C. and L.J.,
dust, raises wrong kind of, 140
Portia man, is, 137, 138
Russell of Killowen C.J., Lord,
innocent question, 323, 324
unbelief in professional honesty, no,
269
Rutledge J.,
lawyers duty of respect to court, 75
lien becomes choate, 160
will, man broken in, 243
Ryder C.J., Holt's Reports, views on,
119

Sachs J., proliferation of umbrellas, 50
sacrifice,
ballot to decide, 320
hunger appeased by, 321
lots drawn to decide, 321
sagacity, lack of, not incompetence,
243
sailor,
cannibalism by starving, 320, 321
passengers, throwing overboard, 320
saint, patron, of lawyers, 41
St. Clement Danes,
children of, 52
Rector of, 51
St. Evona,
advocat non larron, 42
blindfold choice of lawyers' patron,
41
Divell, seizes, 41
St. Leonards L.C., Lord, House of
Lords not bound by own decision,
144
St. Mary Hall, Oxford, 347
St. Paul's, judges' service at, 23
St. Peter, advocate in heaven, only
One, 42
salacious terms subolent of sewer, 350
sale of wife,
adulterer, to, 219
cook, common, to, 220
Salisbury Plain, seised to use of, 290
salus populi suprema lex esto, 112
sanctity of contract granite concept, 333
Sanders C.J., action not taken seriously,
223
Sands, Lord,
Ephraimite's complaint, 200
finger-prints, forcibly taking, 190, 200
knight kneeling no marriage, 209
Scottish mind and marriages *subsequente copula*, 210

408

Sands, Lord—*cont.*
 tiger days excepted for milk, 333
 wedlock, fiction child born after, 210
Sandford J., incitement to revolution,
 205, 206
sanguinary Dago, 350
sarcasm, unveiled, 260
Sargant, L.J., defendant twice over
 wrong, 20
satis intellexerunt, 345
Saturday jurisdiction, King's Bench,
 275
savage, healthy, pictures of, 272
Save Honour, 69–284,
 all is lost, 274
Sayer, Serjeant, attorney and client
 one, 48
Scala di Seta, La, 31
scales of justice shaken by hands holding them, 141
scambling reports, 120
schedule to be stamped £29,000…263
scholar,
 beaten to death by father of another,
 242
 master, second, assaults, 242
schools, liberty in, 204, 205
schoolmistress confiscates dirty book,
 242
scientist, imaginary, bearded and
 begoggled, 272
Scott, John. *See* Eldon L.C., Lord.
Scott K.C. and L.J., Leslie,
 common law fecund, 294
 judicial assistance, seeks, 294
Scott, Sir William,
 comfortable society, marriage for,
 215
 gratifications, more placid, 215
 passions subdued, 215
Scottish majority five out of fifteen, 322
Scottish marriage lore, 209, 210
Scottish oath for Hindus, 85
Scottish silk, 31
scoundrel, counsel calls defendant, 40
scrivener's study, gnawn will in, 309
Scroggs, Serjeant and C.J., Sir William
 (1623–83),
 battery, sued for, 24
 plea of serjeanty denied, 24
Scroggs, Sir William (1652–95),
 battery, sued for, 24
 treat, gives, 24
Scrutton L.J.,
 company shareholders' agent, 260
 cross-examination, effect on evidence,
 98

Scrutton L.J.—*cont.*
 distinguished with zest, words, 54
 faith, good, not enough, 243
 honest but unreasonable, 243
 judicial moderation, difficulty in,
 274
 money-lending, evil system of, 274–
 276
 parliament can make 2+2=5, 107
 precedent not to be followed, 53
sea,
 heavy, of dubious litigation, 156
 perils of, not same as on, 276
 presumption, of, boundless bosom of,
 154
 safety and truth, of, 155, 156
 starving seamen cast away at, 320
sea walls,
 cost of, 266
 tax-gatherer, grist for, 266
seal, stamp equivalent to, 298
search,
 arbitrary government, weapon of,
 200
 character not changed by success, 201
second calling,
 Irish practice, 45
 last trumpet, at, 46
secondary road of complete irrelevancy,
 113
secret charities key to character, 243
secret voting for victim, 320
security, crimes in name of, 194
Selborne L.C., Lord,
 life unbearable if, 250
 seven trials in one case, 250
Selden,
 Charles I, logic of, 101
 boisterous dances in time of, 100,
 101
 terpsichorean picture of court, 100
self-made man hasn't made much, 243
selfish voluptuary, George IV, 101
Semanticity, 117–189
Senatus Consultum Velleianum, 244,
 245
sentence,
 girl under 16, 20 years for not paying, 319
 last, 324
 sound for smell, 238
serjeants, 22–30,
 appointment of, 23
 audience, exclusive rights of, 23
 assailed, 26, 27
 lost, 28

Index

Wilmot J. and C.J.,
  chained down by law, 332
  common law like nursing father, 332
  godless ones, begone, 331
  jurisdiction, judge increases, 331
  justice, judge increases, 331, 332
  Modern Reports, views on, 119
Wilson, Serjeant, edits Bunbury, 121
Winch's Reports. *See* reports.
Winchester scholar beats master, 242
Windeyer J.,
  begging the question, 159
  catachrestic, 159
  causa causans, 159
window, soliciting from, 314, 315
wings, chicken-cock drops his, 319
Winn L.J.,
  lucus a non lucendo, 160
  " quasi " not conducive to clarity,
    159
winner content to know result, 168
wire-tapping, evidence obtained by, 207
Wisest Thing Under Heaven, The,
    100–113,
  time is, 112
wishy-washiness, demands of, 188
witches, men feared, 203
witness,
  after-state of rewards and punish-
    ments, no belief in, 85
  aliboy, 86
  angel, no, 84
  crazy clock, 13th chime of, 98
  demeanour impressive though absent,
    277
  false, Commandment to bear, 86
  frank though absent, 277
  good clear alert and very fair, 54
  judge as, 93, 94
  lawyer as, 90–93
  none as all felons, 172
  opponent called by litigant, 87
  out of court,
    kept, 87
    sent, 87
  prisoner as, 97
  six left by subtraction, 99
  Sovereign as, 94–97
  spelling book as good as Bible, thinks,
    85
  weighed not numbered, 99
  And see Evidence; oath; testimony.
wives, thousand not tolerated, 318
wolf and angel, issue between, 301, 302

woman,
  abuse of, unnatural,
    affront to Author of Nature, 314
    divine provision condemned, 314
  age;
    full, court will not judge, 244
    male incompetence, 244
  bobbed hair, 246
  casta et sola, duration, 232
  deflowered, need for Argus, 213
  fecklessness, innate, 245
  grandmother, own, 235
  homage, doing, 286
  incapacity a fossil, 245
  influence imponderable, 247
  island impregnable to, 246
  law gives little power to, 247
  man,
    interplay of influence, 247
    not, save by statute, 107
  modesty indicates jewel, 214
  nature gives much power to, 247
  30, of, wish to appear 18...244
  tresses, long, 246
  wrestling in public forbidden, 245,
    246
  And see husband; man; widow; wife.
Woman of Pleasure, Memoirs of a, 242
Woodward J.,
  saves State from era of discord, 222
  unity of spouses a fiction, 221
Wookey, reconverting inhabitants of,
    306
words,
  abstracto, in, cannot be regarded,
    351
  devil, are the, 152
  disputes, most arise from, 151
  gender, one includes all, 184
  individuality, grow an, 165
  long, 160
  pictures not mathematics, 152
  will, 95, 940, words in, 300
  See also Language.
working, miner, at age of 112...231
world, whirling, of awesome pheno-
    mena, 155
worth a guinea a box, 273
worthless body, experiment on, 289
wrangling, continuous, 75
Wrenbury, Lord,
  company's attitude mean and con-
    temptible, 280
  law lord by prescription, 33
wrestling by women forbidden, 245,
    246